Living Gluten-Free

FOR DUMMIES®

A Wiley Brand

2ND EDITION

by Hilary Du Cane, Sue Baic, Nigel Denby
and Danna Korn

Foreword by Norma McGough, Coeliac UK

7/13

Living Gluten-Free For Dummies,® 2nd Edition

Published by:
John Wiley & Sons, Ltd
The Atrium
Southern Gate
Chichester
West Sussex
PO19 8SQ
England

www.wiley.com

For general information on our other products and services, please contact our Customer Care Department within the U.S. at 877-762-2974, outside the U.S. at (001) 317-572-3993, or fax 317-572-4002.

For technical support, please visit www.wiley.com/techsupport.

A catalogue record for this book is available from the British Library.

ISBN: 978-1-118-53099-3 (pbk) ISBN: 978-1-118-53096-2 (ebk)

ISBN: 978-1-118-53098-6 (ebk) ISBN: 978-1-118-53097-9 (ebk)

Printed in Great Britain by TJ International Ltd, Padstow, Cornwall

MIX
Paper from
responsible sources
FSC® C013056

Contents at a Glance

Recipes at a Glance

Sweet Treats.. *302*

Table of Contents

Foreword

• •

During the last decade we have seen real advances in living gluten-free. Today, you can travel all over the world and find gluten-free bread or pasta in supermarkets or you can even be served them in restaurants. Ten years ago you would never be able to imagine walking into a high street pizza chain and be able to order off the menu. In fact, someone with coeliac disease couldn't tell whether a can of beans or a carton of soup contained gluten or not! Now we have legislation that enables identification of all packaged foods containing gluten and a legal framework covering the use of the term 'gluten-free'.

Although we have seen improvements in food labelling, and developments in the variety and quality of foods available both in retail and catering, there are still challenges to meet.

Coeliac UK is the national charity for people with coeliac disease and dermatitis herpetiformis. Our mission is to improve the lives of people with coeliac disease through support, campaigning and research. We support those people who are on a gluten-free diet by providing a range of information booklets, diet and health advice, support networks and electronic services. Our campaigns focus on raising awareness about diagnosis, improving the care of people with coeliac disease, improving choice in restaurants, working with catering staff in hospitals and schools, and improving access to gluten-free foods.

Essential funding allows Coeliac UK to support research into the nature of coeliac disease, potential cures and research that improves our understanding of living with the disease. Ongoing projects include identifying the genes most likely to cause coeliac disease, benchmarking current diagnosis rates and understanding more about osteoporosis in coeliac disease.

To find out more about what Coeliac UK can do to help you, to learn how you can get involved and for information on how to become a Member, visit www.coeliac.org.uk or call the Helpline on 0845 305 2060.

Living Gluten-Free For Dummies, 2nd Edition, is an excellent introduction to help you understand more about coeliac disease, gluten sensitivity and the gluten-free diet. It can be daunting when you are first diagnosed with a condition like coeliac disease, and changing your whole diet and lifestyle can seem like a huge task. This book helps to put your mind at rest with explanations of what you can and can't eat, and how to cope with a diagnosis, as well as practical hints and tips for living gluten-free.

Norma McGough, *Registered Dietitian, Coeliac UK*

Introduction

• •

*N*ot so many years ago, the gluten-free lifestyle was reserved for a small cluster of people who were forced to settle for foods that often looked like cardboard but didn't taste as good.

Today, with improved diagnostic tools and with many people simply choosing to give up gluten, the gluten-free lifestyle is far more common. Attractive and palatable gluten-free products abound (and they're a far cry from the only foods that used to be available), food labelling is far less ambiguous, and people no longer look at you as if you have four heads when you ask for a burger without the bun.

Being gluten-free isn't about being on a diet. It's about living a lifestyle. Whether you've been gluten-free for decades, or are only considering the idea, or you're reeling from being diagnosed with a condition that demands a gluten-free diet, this book is packed with information that can help in every aspect of your life, from the obvious – your health and how you shop, cook and eat – to more subtle facets like finances, socialising and eating with friends and family.

We have no supplements to sell you and no gluten-free food products that we endorse. Between us, we have a wealth of personal experience to offer, from living gluten-free ourselves and caring for a loved one who lives gluten-free to working professionally with many people to help them make the transition to a gluten-free lifestyle.

This book is the reference you need to help you with living – and loving – a gluten-free lifestyle.

About This Book

Living Gluten-Free For Dummies, 2nd Edition, like all *For Dummies* books, is divided up so that you don't have to read it all at once or from front to back if you don't want to. You can read it sideways and standing on your head if you like; all you do is find a section you're interested in and dip in. We suggest you peruse the Table of Contents and see whether any particular chapter or subject appeals and start there. Or you can flip through the book and see whether any of the headings catch your eye.

If you're new to the gluten-free lifestyle and have plenty of questions, you're probably best off starting at Chapter 1 and working your way through Part I first. After that, you may want to skip to Chapter 7, your quick-start guide to . . . well, making a quick start – that is, getting your gluten-free lifestyle up and running with the minimum of fuss.

If you've been gluten-free for years, you may want to take a look at Chapter 4. You may be surprised at some of the foods that are allowed on the gluten-free diet that used to be considered no-nos. This chapter can open a lot of cupboard doors that you once thought were closed! And Chapter 5 gives you an update on what you'll be seeing on food labels and menus and hearing from waiters and chefs about the presence or absence of gluten in your food.

Whether you're new to cooking gluten-free or do it all the time or only occasionally, you're sure to find inspiration and ideas in Part IV, where seven chapters of recipes offer really scrumptious gluten-free foods. They're all dishes that would normally contain gluten, and even include those tricky ones you probably thought were off the gluten-free menu: home-made pizza, breads and fresh pasta. And if you're wondering where on earth you're going to get hold of the ingredients you need to pull off these recipes, rest assured: everything we use is easily available either in the shops or online.

Conventions Used in This Book

To keep the book consistent and easy to follow, here are some of the basic ground rules and conventions we use:

- ✔ In printing this book, the publisher may have needed to break some web addresses across two lines of text. If that happened, you can be certain that we haven't put in any extra characters (such as hyphens) to indicate the break. So when using one of these web addresses, just type in exactly what you see in this book, pretending the line break doesn't exist. If you're reading this as an e-book, simply click on the link to go directly to the particular website we mention.

- ✔ We use **bold** font to indicate the action part of numbered steps, and *italics* when we introduce and define a new word.

- ✔ Go to www.dummies.com/cheatsheet/livingglutenfreeuk for the online cheat sheet created especially for this book, and www.dummies.com/extras/livingglutenfreeuk for free articles and a bonus Part of Tens chapter.

Here are some conventions for the ingredients we use in recipes:

✔ If an ingredient appears in a recipe, we mean it to be gluten-free. For instance, we don't specify 'gluten-free vanilla', because all vanilla is gluten-free. But soy sauce usually has gluten in it, so you need to use a gluten-free one such as tamari, even if we haven't pointed that out to you. Food manufacturers change their formulations all the time, so keep an eye on their labels to see what's new on the market that you can eat and which foods that used to be gluten-free suddenly aren't. While we've been putting the finishing touches to the book, for instance, the leading brand of baking powder has become gluten-free (yay!), but the leading brand of tacos has gone the other way (sigh!).

✔ Baking with gluten-free flours works best if you use a mixture of them. Chapter 9 goes into detail about what to mix with what. All our recipes spell out which ones we use, in what proportion.

✔ You can use milk substitutes in place of milk in most recipes.

✔ Eggs are large and free-range.

✔ Butter and margarine are interchangeable, although if we've suggested butter, we mean the unsalted kind, so if you replace it with margarine (which you can't get unsalted), you may need to cut down on any other ingredients which are salty, and of course any added salt.

Feel free to tinker with the recipes. If you don't have an ingredient that a recipe calls for, don't worry: make a substitution. You may find your swap is a huge improvement. And that goes for your old gluten-containing recipes too. We give you all the techniques and substitute ingredients you need to make anything gluten-free – even bread and cakes – along with almost 100 gluten-free recipes.

What You're Not to Read

You won't get in trouble if you *do* read everything, but if you're a skimmer, you can skip some parts and not miss anything important. In other words, we won't be testing you on the following:

✔ **Anything that has a Technical Stuff icon:** The Technical Stuff icon represents information that's interesting but not crucial to your understanding of the subject.

✔ **Sidebars:** These are the stories and snippets of information in shaded boxes scattered throughout the chapters. Just like the Technical Stuff, you may find the information interesting, but you won't miss anything crucial if you skip them.

✓ **Recipes:** Unless you're actually using them to cook or to decide what to make for dinner, recipes aren't the best late-night reading material. Feel free to skip them until you're ready to whip up some gluten-free goodies. But do have a look through the recipe chapters even if you're not a keen cook. You'll be surprised at the range of dishes you can make and the general information about ingredients and methods.

Foolish Assumptions

You spent your hard-earned dosh on this book, and that means either you want to learn more about the gluten-free lifestyle or you're related to us. Because our family members have already heard far more about gluten than any human should have to endure (sorry, everyone), we've written this book with you in mind – and we've taken the liberty of making a few assumptions about you. One or more of the following is likely to apply to you:

✓ You're considering going gluten-free and will use this book to determine whether to take the plunge.

✓ You love or take care of someone who's going, has gone or should go gluten-free, and you want to learn about the lifestyle so you can be supportive.

✓ You're new to the diet and are looking for the 'manual' that can tell you how to live a gluten-free lifestyle.

✓ You've been gluten-free for years and noticed you're meeting more and more people like yourself these days. You want to find out why and get the latest information about dietary guidelines, state-of-the-art research and new labelling laws.

✓ You're a professional who has gluten-free clients, pupils, charges, guests, attendees, participants, customers or patients – people of all ages and with all kinds of professional association to you. You want to find out more about the gluten-free lifestyle, the medical conditions that benefit from it and how to get your contribution to the lives of those you work with just right.

At the same time, you can make a few assumptions about us and what we tell you in this book:

✓ We generally know what we're talking about. As a card-carrying coeliac, diagnosed like most people these days in adulthood, Hilary lives the gluten-free life herself. Danna, our American co-author, raised her son on a gluten-free diet from when he was a young baby. As registered dietitians in the UK, Hilary, Sue and Nigel have worked for many years with patients who have coeliac disease or other gluten intolerances, seeing them through the transition from eating gluten every day to enjoyably avoiding it while still eating well and healthily. We all have the experience to help you too.

✔ The book is endorsed by Coeliac UK, the charity that supports everyone with an interest in living gluten-free or in helping someone else to do so. Coeliac UK sits squarely at the interface of the medical profession, international researchers in the field, the food and catering industries, the National Health Service (NHS) and thousands of people just like you. Not only are those at Coeliac UK experts in the subject, but they're also great at getting their knowledge across in terms you can understand, apply in real life and really relate to.

✔ This book is intended to supplement but not replace medical advice from your healthcare team and the processes they use to diagnose and manage gluten-related disorders. Always consult your healthcare team for clarification if you're unclear about anything we say – don't forget, their advice is tailored to you individually, whereas our content is more general. Medical follow-up and monitoring is vital to staying in tip-top health on a gluten-free diet.

How This Book Is Organised

Living Gluten-Free For Dummies, 2nd Edition, is organised so that all related material goes together. So that we don't repeat too much information, we sometimes include cross-references to related topics. This book has six parts. Each part has several chapters, and each chapter is divided into sections. In the following sections, we explain how we divide up the parts.

Part 1: Ready, Set, Going Gluten-Free

As the name implies, this part gives you the big picture of living gluten-free.

Chapter 1 is an overview. If you read nothing else in this book, read Chapter 1, because then you'll at least sound like you know what you're talking about.

The rest of this part talks about who may want to consider going gluten-free and why. We describe the full range of gluten-related health disorders, explain the benefits of the gluten-free diet in their treatment and then delve more specifically into coeliac disease – who gets it, why and what it is.

Part II: Digging Deeper into Eating Gluten-Free

This part covers what you can and can't eat on the gluten-free diet, and how to dig a little deeper so you're *sure* the foods you're eating are really safe for you. If you want the inside track on the fabulous range of substitutes for glutenous foods, how to interpret food labels and menus, and how to eat a diet that's not only gluten-free but also good for you, we have it all in Part II.

Part III: Taking the Plunge: How to Go Gluten-Free

Part III takes you to the next level: how to get started right away on your new gluten-free diet and lifestyle.

We begin with a quick-start guide to what to do on day one and in the first week, and then take you smoothly on to the few changes and preparations you need to make at home and everywhere else where food is involved.

Chapter 9 amounts to a manual for cooking gluten-free at home, whether the whole household is kept gluten-free or not. We hope you find this section realistic, practical, upbeat and encouraging.

Part IV: Scrumptious Recipes for Gluten-Free Food

In this part, you can find nearly 100 recipes plus dozens of variations on the basic dishes and lots of practical tips, techniques and suggested ingredients to help you make your favourite dishes gluten-free. We take you right through the day, from breakfast to dinner, and include snacks and tempting baked treats.

You can serve all the dishes to all people, whether they normally eat gluten or not. The dishes don't look like special diet foods that elicit 'Poor you' reactions from gluten guzzlers, and they certainly don't taste that way. In fact, we're often asked for our recipes.

You can make all our recipes with ingredients that are available easily and affordably in the shops or online. You don't need a prescription for anything, which means you can serve the dishes to anyone.

So go ahead: get stewing or baking – or whatever it is you want to do in the kitchen. Whether you're a culinary fledgling or high-flyer, you'll find these recipes simple, delicious, sometimes impressive and always gluten-free.

Part V: Living – and Loving – the Gluten-Free Lifestyle

For some people, the gluten-free lifestyle presents unique social, practical and emotional challenges. In this part, we help you work out ways to deal with some of the issues like eating at social events and when out and about, travelling, as well as talking with friends and loved ones about your new life-style and raising happy, healthy gluten-free kids. We also help you deal with some of the emotional challenges that can come up, so that you can truly learn to love the gluten-free lifestyle.

Part VI: The Part of Tens

What would a *For Dummies* book be without a Part of Tens? Incomplete, that's what, because all *For Dummies* books have one, and this book is no exception. The Part of Tens contains a few short chapters, each with ten tips, questions and answers, factoids and nuggets of information about the gluten-free lifestyle. Take a look at www.dummies.com/extras/livingglutenfreeuk for an extra Part of Tens chapter: 'Ten Good Things About Living Gluten-Free'.

Icons Used in This Book

Some people are more visual than others. That's why icons are helpful. This book uses several icons, and each has a little snippet of information associated with it. Here's what each icon means:

Everyone can use a friendly little reminder. The Remember icon is a quick and easy way to identify some of the more important points that you may want to make a note of throughout the book.

Sometimes we get really into the juicy, technical and scientific stuff to explain a medical, food science or legal point in a bit more detail than you really need in order to grasp the subject. That's why we put this info in its own area, marked by a Technical Stuff icon, so that you can skip it if you want to without missing the gist of what's going on in that section.

These tips can help you live (and love!) the gluten-free lifestyle. They include info to help save you time or cut down on frustration.

If you want a vegetarian recipe, just look for the tomato icons. (We assume you'll use vegetarian cheese with no animal rennet for veggie recipes that call for cheese.)

Text flagged with the Warning icon can keep you out of trouble.

Where to Go from Here

What we suggest you do at this point is curl up in your comfiest chair and dip into the book. Eating out tonight and want to ensure your meal is gluten-free? Head to Chapter 17. Cruising the 'free-from' aisles? Chapter 8's a good place to start. Do you glaze over when you read food labels? Chapter 5 helps you learn what to look out for. Your child has just been diagnosed as sensitive to gluten? Chapter 18 can help. Just want to make a clean, fast start on your gluten-free life? Head to Chapter 7 and go for it. Use the full Table of Contents and Index to find exactly what you need . . . or be our guest and read the whole book!

If you're feeling a little down about going gluten-free, we hope our sincere passion for the gluten-free lifestyle and the healthy benefits that go along with it helps you, along with our positive, practical advice, support and inspiration.

Part I
Ready, Set, Going Gluten-Free

Go to www.dummies.com/extras/livingglutenfreeuk for online bonus content.

In this part . . .

- ✔ Understand the different types of gluten intolerance.
- ✔ Find out all you need to know about coeliac disease.
- ✔ Know the association between dermatitis herpetiformis and coeliac disease.
- ✔ Get familiar with the foods you can enjoy – and know which to avoid.
- ✔ Enjoy the many benefits of living gluten-free, including the immediate positive effect on your body.
- ✔ Go to www.dummies.com/extras/livingglutenfreeuk for online bonus content, including an extra Part of Tens chapter: 'Ten Benefits of Being Gluten-Free'.

Chapter 1

Getting Started: Going Gluten-Free

. . . .

. . . .

You're looking at this book because gluten is a problem for you or some-one close to you. You suspect that eating it brings on troublesome, painful or even embarrassing symptoms. You may not know for sure that it's gluten that does the damage or how something as commonplace as an every-day food could possibly be the culprit. After all, you've been eating it all your life, every day, several times a day, if you're like most people, and it didn't used to be a problem. What could have changed?

Gluten seems to be public enemy number one in some quarters. It gets a bad rap in the media – accused of making people fat, badly behaved and sluggish, stopping top sportsmen performing at their peak, and squeezing other crops out of production, thus reducing agricultural diversity on a worldwide scale. Maybe you just want to give the gluten-free diet a trial run for these reasons.

On the other hand, maybe you've been diagnosed with a disorder that's related to gluten, such as coeliac disease or gluten sensitivity. You didn't spot it, because the symptoms were so subtle or had nothing to do with your digestive system. We now know that about 8 per cent of people in the UK have one or other of these disorders, and that most of them have yet to come forward for diagnosis and treatment. Many are treating themselves, having decided to go gluten-free without any medical support, and many have just cut gluten down but not out.

Alternatively, you may have been living gluten-free for years and want to get up to date with the new gluten-free foods available, find out what all the fuss is about with oats, and extend your repertoire of gluten-free recipes.

How many authors does it take to write a book about living gluten-free?

You may be wondering why this book needs four authors. Discovering that you need to live a gluten-free life can be a big shock for some people. You need to take in a whole load of information, and as you try to get your head around what you can and can't eat, you may start to think that life is never going to be the same again. Living gluten-free has a lot to do with food, and for dietitians food is their raison d'être, so that's why three of your authors are dietitians who have experience of working with gluten-free diets. One of the three, Hilary, is coeliac herself and so lives the gluten-free life for real. Danna has also been on the receiving end of all that information and has applied the recommendations on a daily basis. They've both discovered that living gluten-free becomes a way of life and is pretty easy once you know what to look out for. We think our combined experience is just right to help you make a smooth and easy-as-pie move to a gluten-free life – gluten-free pie, of course!

All the answers are in this book for you. In this first chapter, you find up-to-date facts on these subjects and an introduction to the rest of the book. You can find out what exactly gluten is and what foods contain it. You see why gluten's important in a healthy diet for people who can tolerate it, plus how to avoid it and still eat healthily if you can't tolerate it, and if so, what benefits you can expect from going gluten-free.

What Is Gluten Anyway?

Gluten has a couple of definitions; one is technically correct but not commonly used, and the other is commonly used but not technically correct. We give you more details on both definitions in Chapter 4, but to get you started and for the purposes of most of this book, here's the common definition: *gluten* is a group of proteins found in wheat, rye and barley.

Proteins in the gluten group are what give foods made from gluten-containing cereals their characteristic silky stretchiness, lightness and slight chewiness, particularly baked goods and pasta. If you've ever made fresh pasta from durum wheat, which contains a lot of gluten, and rolled it out using a pasta machine, you'll have felt that silky stretchiness at the first pass through the rollers. And think of the texture of fresh bread: all those bubbles are created when gluten stretches around the gas produced as the yeast ferments. It's the gluten that holds the loaf up as it bakes and cools.

Oats don't contain gluten, but they may be contaminated by the other cereals that do – in the field and during processing or storage. Not only that, but many people with a gluten-related disorder find they can't tolerate oat protein itself for the first few months after they start living gluten-free. A few people remain intolerant of oat protein permanently. So, if you're just starting out on your gluten-free diet, we suggest you get some expert and individual advice about whether you should or shouldn't eat oats for a while.

If you are going to eat oats at any stage in your gluten-free diet, choose the ones that are labelled gluten-free. This means they've been grown and kept well away from any cereals containing gluten and also tested for gluten content and found to have only a minute amount of it, far too little to cause you a problem.

Knowing which foods contain gluten and which ones don't

There's no getting away from it, gluten is a common constituent in the typical British diet. In fact, most people eat it two or three times a day. It's in anything made from wheat, rye or barley including flour milled from these grains, whether white, wholemeal or anything in between. But luckily there's no gluten in a great many other foods, which include things you're sure to be eating every day.

Foods that normally contain gluten and aren't suitable for you

To get the bad news out of the way, here are some of the most common foods and drinks that contain gluten and which you'll need to avoid:

- Batter such as in pancakes, tempura, fried fish and chicken nuggets
- Beer and lager, brewed from barley or wheat
- Biscuits, cakes, pies, pastries, waffles and most other baked goods
- Bread and similar products, such as pitta, crumpets, bagels, muffins, naans, chapatis, buns and wraps
- Crackers and crispbreads
- Many breakfast cereals in flaked, shredded and biscuit forms
- Pasta, cous cous and bulgur wheat
- Pearl barley
- Pizza
- Wheat-based snacks, such as pretzels and cheesy nibbles

Gluten also pops up in some surprising foods like: sausages (as rusk); brown sauce (with rye flour as a thickener); soy sauce (stabilised with wheat flour); oven chips (if coated in batter); stuffing (made from breadcrumbs); gravy, stock cubes and cheese sauce (containing flour); semolina (a grainy wheat flour); liquorice sweets (to stop them sticking together); and mincemeat (on the suet). 'Blimey,' you're thinking, 'this is going to get hard.' No worries. When you're gluten-free, you soon get used to reading labels and digging a little deeper to see what you can and can't eat. (More on that in Chapter 5.)

And just to clear up a common question, if gluten gets into a food as a component of a raw ingredient, it's still present after cooking or other processing. For example, although gluten is affected by the process of making sourdough, it's still there in the finished product and ready to damage your health if you're intolerant of it.

Foods that are naturally gluten-free and suitable for you

Now for the good news – and plenty of it. If the previous section is making you want to snap the book shut and put it back on the bookshelf, stay with us because you really don't have to do without many foods. These are some common foods that are gluten-free by nature: all types of rice, potatoes, sweetcorn or maize, plain meat, plain fish, eggs, cheese, milk, yoghurt (most), all fruits, vegetables, plain salads and pulses (fresh, canned, frozen or dried), plain nuts and peanuts, tea, coffee, cocoa, sugar, butter, margarine, jam, honey, most tomato ketchups, vinegar, salt, spices, seeds, fruit juices, most chocolate (milk, plain and white), plain crisps, wine, spirits, water.

What's more, food manufacturers make delicious gluten-free versions of just about every food imaginable these days, and they really are good to eat. That includes gluten-free versions of everything we list in the previous section as off limits for anyone living gluten-free – well, okay, not the pearl barley, but you can replace that with plenty of other cereals. Even better, you can make a lot of gluten-free foods at home, even if your cooking skills and experience are on the first rung. We show you how with seven chapters of easy-to-follow recipes in Part IV using ingredients you can get hold of either in the shops or online. We talk more about these ingredients, where to buy them and how to use them in Chapters 4 and 9.

You can find lots more information about what you can and can't eat by visiting www.coeliac.org.uk, the website for the UK's only support charity for people who can't tolerate gluten, Coeliac UK. And for our quick-start guide to living gluten-free, head to Chapter 7.

Understanding that wheat-free doesn't mean gluten-free

You may see lots of labels proudly declaring a product to be wheat-free (although some of these products, like spelt and triticale, aren't really wheat-free at all and certainly aren't gluten-free). Wheat-free doesn't necessarily mean the food's gluten-free. It could contain rye or barley, or possibly one of the primitive wheat relatives like emmer, kamut, dinkel or spelt. These days, more and more people believe they can't tolerate wheat, or just feel better without it, so you often see 'wheat-free' trumpeted on the front of the pack, and have to go looking to make sure the food is also gluten-free.

Malt is conventionally made from barley, so is wheat-free but not gluten-free. But then again, malt extract, whisky and malt vinegar all contain so little malt, and the malt contains so little gluten, they can safely be counted as gluten-free.

Food labels have to comply with a new EU regulation that states that the presence of any gluten-containing cereal must be clearly indicated on the packet. The list of ingredients must highlight the name of the cereal that's contributing the gluten, such as wheat, so you need to get into the habit of reading ingredients lists as a matter of course. After December 2014, this rule also applies to food and drink served loose or in restaurants and takeaways, where you'll see 'Contains wheat' or similar declarations prominently displayed and explained to you by the staff. For more details, head to Chapter 5.

Discovering the Ins and Outs of the Gluten-Free Lifestyle

A gluten-free lifestyle isn't just about your diet. Yes, this book talks about food, but being gluten-free involves a lot more than just cutting gluten out of your diet. Following this method can affect many aspects of your life, from how you handle ordering food at restaurants to attending social functions and dealing with emotional challenges.

We believe that the key is to take control of the diet rather than letting the diet take control of you. If your children are gluten-free, you need to help them gain control. Going gluten-free also gives you a chance to discover more about eating well and eating healthily, and about what you're actually putting into your body on a daily basis. If that sounds like a lot of work, relax. In this book we guide you along the path to being gluten-free pleasurably and healthily. Yes, really. Food and cooking will become, or continue to be, a pleasure and the centre of both your home life and social life. And not only can you feel physically better, but you can feel emotionally better too!

You're in good company. The gluten-free population is growing for lots of reasons, but the one that stands out is that when people who are intolerant of gluten give it up, they almost always feel better. This section tells you what the gluten-free diet can do for your body, and whether going gluten-free can help you – as well as the benefits you can enjoy. People today live in a panacea-pursuing, pill-popping, make-me-better-fast society, and if they see the promise of a quick fix, they want it. Changing both your diet and lifestyle isn't quick or easy, but when you need to do so, the benefits of going gluten-free can be fantastic – no surgery or medication required!

If you have a problem with consuming gluten, then following a gluten-free diet is a great idea. If you don't, it isn't. Gluten-free living isn't a quick fix, a fashion accessory or slimming nirvana. It's a therapeutic diet for people with specific conditions.

Eating isn't supposed to hurt

Food is supposed to give you energy and make you feel good, not make you ill. But when you eat things that your body doesn't like for one reason or another, your body has a sometimes not-so-subtle way of telling you to cut it out. Food to which your body objects can cause the following:

- ✔ Depression
- ✔ Fatigue
- ✔ Gastrointestinal distress (wind, bloating, diarrhoea, constipation, vomiting, heartburn and acid reflux)
- ✔ Headaches (including migraines)
- ✔ Inability to concentrate
- ✔ Infertility
- ✔ Joint, bone or muscle pain
- ✔ Weight gain or weight loss

Gluten-related disorders in the news

Research into the range of conditions that need a gluten-free or wheat-free diet is all the rage at the moment, with new findings coming to light in the medical press every month. That's why Coeliac UK now opens its doors and puts out the welcome mat to anyone with an interest in living gluten-free, with or without a definite diagnosis of coeliac disease. We now understand a lot more about the causes and symptoms of coeliac disease, wheat allergy and the new kid on the block, gluten sensitivity, and about the inter-relationships between these conditions. Researchers are also postulating relationships between these disorders and irritable bowel syndrome.

We've known all along that wheat allergy needs a wheat-free diet, and that coeliac disease, dermatitis herpetiformis and gluten ataxia all need to be treated with a gluten-free diet. But now it's becoming best practice to diagnose gluten sensitivity as a condition in its own right and treat it with a gluten-free diet. Previously,

if you went along to your doctor complaining of symptoms similar to those of coeliac disease or wheat allergy, but tested negatively for these and other possible conditions, the doctor would have told you to go back to eating gluten, even though you protested that it seemed to be the cause of the problems. Now you're more likely to be taken through a monitored trial period on a gluten-free diet to confirm the diagnosis of gluten sensitivity, and if the results are positive, advised to avoid gluten in future.

We give you more detail about all these conditions and the tests for them in Chapter 2. We do encourage you to go for a thorough professional investigation of your symptoms and not to self-diagnose and put yourself on a gluten-free diet without any proper medical supervision and follow-up. The problem with self-diagnosis and using unregulated diagnostic tests is that your symptoms may be nothing to do with gluten and may be masked by the diet instead of being treated by it.

The list's impressive, isn't it? The idea that eliminating one thing from your diet – gluten – can overcome so many different conditions is almost hard to believe. Yet, it's true – and changing to gluten-free really makes sense when you realise that if the food you're eating is toxic to your body or stopping you absorbing nutrients, then your body's going to complain in lots of different ways. So no matter how your symptoms manifest an intolerance of gluten, the only thing that's likely to make you feel any better is a gluten-free diet.

For more on the symptoms of gluten-related conditions on the body, and their effects, look at Chapter 2.

Head-to-toe health benefits

The 12th-century physician Maimonides said, 'Man should strive to have his intestines relaxed all the days of his life.' No kidding! When your intestines aren't relaxed – or when they're downright edgy or uptight – they affect all your other parts too. You can compare the situation to when you're in a really good mood and your best friend is grumpy – the atmosphere can make you grumpy too; a cantankerous intestine can be a downer for the entire body.

Doctors once thought that all gluten intolerances showed themselves with obvious intestinal symptoms. But now we accept that the intestine may be virtually normal in some of these disorders, and that other organs and parts of the body are on the receiving end of the damage, including the brain, nerves, muscles, liver and glands. Plus, even an impaired intestine may not produce symptoms that are obviously related, such as tummy aches and diarrhoea, but secondary symptoms resulting from the body not absorbing nutrients from the intestine properly. These symptoms might include anaemia and osteoporosis, or thinning bones.

If gluten is causing this damage, either directly or indirectly, it's acting as a toxin to your tissues. Eliminating it completely from your diet stops the toxicity, so that your tissues can recover from the damage. Whichever tissues have been affected – from your head to your toes – start to heal and you begin to feel better. For many people, the improvement is swift and dramatic, but even if you haven't been aware of any problem or if your symptoms have been too subtle to worry about, you'll still notice the improvement.

Many restricted diets are unhealthy and lacking in essential nutrients, but the gluten-free diet is balanced, complete and healthy. It can bring with it other benefits to your health apart from overcoming the symptoms of gluten intolerance, such as a healthy weight, fewer infections, improved fitness, better sleep and concentration, lower cholesterol, and the ultimate benefit: a longer life. We explain how you can eat healthily and gluten-free in Chapter 6.

So, is wheat good or bad for you?

People are barraged with messages hailing the virtues of wheat – especially in its wholegrain form! Along with other grains and potatoes, it makes the biggest contribution to a healthy, balanced diet in terms of total food intake. Wholegrain, unrefined wheat is a good source of fibre and nutrients, and provides plenty of health benefits. So, those who have no problem eating wheat can and should consume lots of the stuff.

If you're going to live without wholewheat, as in a gluten-free diet, you need to ensure you still get enough fibre and nutrients from other foods, particularly other whole grains besides wheat, rye, barley and, at first, oats. Living gluten-free isn't just about cutting gluten-containing foods out, but also replacing them with healthy sources of all the essential nutrients you once relied on them to provide.

You can do it – easily, affordably and enjoyably. But you need to work at it to some extent, probably eat a more varied diet than you once did, and get to know food and what's in it, so that you can make the choices that are best for you.

Mastering Meals

Living Gluten-Free For Dummies is really about a lifestyle, not a diet. But no matter where that lifestyle takes you – eating in, eating out, social events, choosing, planning, shopping, cooking – being gluten-free all comes down to one thing: food.

If you're a culinary catastrophe and you're afraid that you're going to have to wake up at 4 a.m. to bake gluten-free bread and make fresh pasta, turn off the alarm and go back to sleep. You can find plenty of gluten-free foods available to take the place of all your old favourites, and you don't have to go to obscure speciality shops to buy them. Most are available in your local supermarket, and some are on prescription if you have a diagnosis of coeliac disease. (For more on coeliac disease, go to Chapter 3.)

Whether you're a kitchenphobe or a foodie living a gluten-free lifestyle, modern food shopping offers you an enormous selection of foods and ingredients to choose from.

Planning and preparing

Putting together delicious and healthy gluten-free meals is a lot easier if you plan ahead and keep a reasonable stock of basic foods you like in store. If you find yourself in need of a quick meal and you're without a few basics, you can't just order a takeaway or nip out to the chippie any more. Gluten-free pizza is available, and we give you a recipe for making your own in Chapter 15, but it's not always available as a takeaway. At the time of writing, most Chinese takeaways use soy sauce containing wheat flour, so they're out, and you obviously can't eat anything in gluten-laden batter or bread.

 Give yourself a healthy advantage by planning and preparing meals in advance, especially if your busy schedule means you're eating away from home frequently. If you know you're pressed for time at breakfast or lunch, make your meals the night before.

One of the best things about adopting a new dietary lifestyle is exploring new and sometimes unusual foods. You may never have heard of lots of the gluten-free foods and ingredients, many of which aren't only gluten-free and delicious but are also nutritional powerhouses. With the new perspective on food that the gluten-free lifestyle can offer, you may find yourself inspired to think outside your usual menu plan, exploring unique and nutritious alternatives.

Shopping shrewdly

The healthiest way to enjoy a gluten-free lifestyle is to eat things you can find at any supermarket or farmers' market: meat, fish, seafood, fruits and a variety of fresh vegetables (but resist the temptation to load up your shopping basket with potatoes too often). If you want to add canned, processed and even junk foods to your shopping list, you can still do most of your shopping at a regular supermarket, and you can buy own-label brands.

If you hope to enjoy the delicious gluten-free speciality products that are available these days, you can find them in 'free-from' aisles, ethnic and speciality shops, some health food stores and, of course, online.

Some people worry about the cost of the gluten-free lifestyle, but eating this way doesn't have to be more expensive. We talk about shopping and eating gluten-free affordably in Chapter 8.

Rearranging the kitchen

For the most part, a gluten-free kitchen looks the same as any other kitchen. You don't need to go out and buy special gadgets and tools, and with only a couple of exceptions, which we cover in Chapter 9, you don't need two sets of pots, pans, utensils or storage containers either.

If you're sharing a kitchen where food with gluten is prepared, you need to be aware of some contamination issues so that you don't inadvertently *glutenate* (contaminate with gluten) a perfectly good gluten-free meal. Keeping crumbs out isn't just a matter of hygiene, but can mean the difference between a meal you can eat and one you can't.

Some people find having separate areas in the cupboards and fridge for the gluten-containing products helpful. This idea is especially good if you have gluten-free children in the house, because they can easily see that the gluten zone is a no-go area for them, but that they can eat what they want from everywhere else.

Cooking outside the recipe box

We believe you can make anything gluten-free – yes, even bread. You're not constrained by recipes or the fact that you can't use wheat flour or bread-crumbs. All you need is a little creativity and some basic guidelines for using gluten-free substitutions, which you can find in Chapter 9.

If you're a die-hard recipe fan, never fear: we give you about a hundred recipes in Chapters 10 to 16. Most of them are really simple to follow but leave your guests with the impression that you spent all day in the kitchen (and being thus indebted, they may volunteer to do the dishes).

Getting Excited about the Gluten-Free Lifestyle

Most people who embark on a gluten-free lifestyle do so because of health issues – and that means they have little or no choice in the matter. When people are forced to make changes in their routine, especially changes that affect what they can and can't eat, they're not always quick to see the joy in the adjustments.

If you're a little gloomy about going from being a gluten-glutton to a gluten-free freak, we understand. But prepare yourself to read about the scores of reasons why you can be excited about a gluten-free lifestyle. (For you impatient types like us, feel free to head to www.dummies.com/extras/livingglutenfreeuk for a jump-start on the positive, fluffy side of being gluten-free.)

Adapting your perspective on food

If you've been eating gluten for a long time – say, for most of your life – then giving up familiar foods may seem like a difficult transition at first. Besides the obvious practical challenges of discovering how to ferret out gluten where it may hide, you have to deal with the emotional, physical, social and even financial challenges of going gluten-free.

You have to do only one thing in order to love the gluten-free lifestyle, and that's adjust your perspective on food just a tad. You really don't have to give anything up; you just have to make some modifications. The foods that used to be your favourites can still be your favourites if you want them to be, just in a slightly different form.

Or you may want to take the opportunity to change to a new and super-healthy approach, eating leaner meats, oily fish, fresh fruits and a wider variety of fresh vegetables. Again, you may have to tweak your perspective a bit before the diet feels natural to you, but it is, in fact, natural, nutritious and naturally nutritious. We talk more about this healthy approach in Chapter 6.

Savouring gluten-free flavours

People who are new to the concept of being gluten-free sometimes comment that the diet is boring. When we ask what they're eating, their cuisine routine usually centres on carrots and rice cakes. Who wouldn't be bored with that? That type of diet is appalling, not appealing.

We *love* food. We love the flavour, the feeling of being full and the nutritional value that food provides. Most of all, we love to explore foods we've never tried before – as long as they're gluten-free, of course. We don't encourage you to endure a diet of foods so bland they can double up as cardboard.

A healthy, gluten-free diet doesn't have to be boring or restrictive. If you enjoy bland foods, good for you. But if you think gluten-free has to be flavour-free, you're in for a pleasant surprise.

Getting out and about

You don't have to let the gluten-free lifestyle hold you back from doing anything you want to do. Well, okay, you can't do some things – like devour a stack of gluten-laden doughnuts. But as far as your activities and lifestyle are concerned, you can – and should – get out and about as you always have.

In the majority of cases, eating out isn't as easy as walking into a restaurant and ordering off the menu. But eating at restaurants is definitely possible and getting a lot easier than it was a few years ago; you just need to make some enquiries in advance, make clear what you want and be alert to contamination concerns. More and more restaurants now offer a gluten-free menu, indicate a good selection of gluten-free choices on the main menu or are prepared to make some swaps and changes to their usual dishes to make them gluten-free.

Travelling is a doddle after you master eating at restaurants (and get your head around language considerations if you're travelling abroad). Going to social events just requires a little planning, and holidays may barely faze you – after you get the hang of getting out and about gluten-free-style. Chapter 17 gives you more information on this aspect.

Before you travel, check out www.coeliac.org.uk for some great resources to help translate common gluten-free terms into a variety of different languages.

Bringing up your children to love the lifestyle

When Danna heard that her son Tyler would have to be gluten-free for the rest of his life, she was flooded with a bunch of emotions, most of which weren't very pleasant. At first, she felt burdened and overcome with grief and frustration, and longed for the perfectly healthy little baby she thought she was entitled to. Focusing on what she'd lost and all that she'd have to change in their lives was all too easy. But making adjustments didn't take long, and soon she discovered not just how to live the gluten-free lifestyle – but how to *love* it.

Most importantly, Danna wanted Tyler to love the lifestyle. After all, it was his diet, his life and his future that would be most impacted. Thankfully, Tyler does love the gluten-free lifestyle, and your children can too.

Trying out lots of ideas is key to raising happy, healthy gluten-free children. Some other important tactics include:

✔ Giving them control of their diet from day one

✔ Always having tasty gluten-free treats on hand

✔ Reinforcing the benefits of the gluten-free lifestyle (if you need some crib notes, head to Chapter 21)

✔ Always remembering that they're finding out how to feel about the lifestyle from *you*; promoting an optimistic outlook can instil a positive approach in them

Chapter 18 deals in detail with raising children to love the gluten-free lifestyle, and for even more inspiration and practical advice, visit the www.coeliac.org.uk website.

Children are flexible and resilient. Adopting a new lifestyle is usually harder for the parents than for the child.

Setting realistic expectations

Setting reasonable expectations for what things are going to be like when you adopt a gluten-free lifestyle is important, because you *will* encounter challenges, and you need to prepare to handle them well. Friends, family and loved ones may not understand. They may not accommodate your diet when you hope they will. You may find social events tricky at first, or you may get confused or frustrated and feel like giving up on the diet. You can overcome these trials and come out the other side stronger; being prepared is the best way to get through the transition time.

This book is the resource you need to guide you through – so make your way through it, and bookmark the pages you want to come back to when you need some practical or emotional reminders for how to deal with difficult issues. If you have an optimistic but realistic approach, you'll encounter fewer obstacles along the way.

Chapter 2

Going Gluten-Free: Who's Doing It and Why

So you've given up – or are considering giving up – gluten, or a loved one is doing so. If you're like most people, this is for one of three reasons:

✔ A medical professional has diagnosed you with a gluten-related disorder and advised a gluten-free diet in order to safeguard your health.

✔ You haven't had a diagnosis as such, but you suspect you've identified a bad reaction to eating gluten.

✔ Every celebrity in town says gluten-free is the way to go!

Which group you fall into doesn't matter – your reasoning may be right on all counts (except maybe the last one). You're definitely not alone. Millions of people live gluten-free for a variety of reasons, and some see dramatic improvements in their health. The bottom line is that some people can't tolerate gluten in their diet.

This chapter explains how gluten, a group of proteins found in wheat, rye and barley, can affect your body and in some cases even your behaviour, what tests you can expect when you go for diagnosis, and why eliminating gluten from your diet is essential if you do have a disorder that's related to it.

Mapping Gluten-Related Disorders

Gluten-related disorders, including coeliac disease, gluten sensitivity, wheat allergy and several others, are hot topics among researchers, immunologists and gastroenterologists worldwide, so aren't yet fully mapped out and unanimously agreed by all experts. That's why we gave this section its title. Drawing the map, identifying all the disorders to put on it, and getting to the bottom of how they arise and the relationships between them is still work in progress.

Gluten-related disorders involve one of three quite distinct channels in the body's immune defence system. Each disorder has its own mechanism for damaging health, and different resulting symptoms. The picture is further blurred by the fact that these disorders manifest themselves in a wide array of symptoms, many of which are common in other conditions that have nothing to do with gluten. The severity of symptoms varies, and in some cases the symptoms come and go unexpectedly at different times of life.

Moreover, gluten is not only a ubiquitous presence in most people's daily lives, but also something they can choose to eat or not, unlike, say, an airborne virus that they can't see and can't help breathing in if it happens along. In a way, people taking matters into their own hands and opting to live gluten-free without any specific diagnosis have confounded the experts in their efforts to diagnose and treat these conditions and to map out how they relate to gluten.

As well as allergy, disease and sensitivity, you often see the terms intolerance and hypersensitivity:

✔ In the past, medics used the term *gluten intolerance* to distinguish non-allergic adverse reactions to gluten from coeliac disease. But now the term is frowned upon as too loose a description. It's still in use, though, as an umbrella term for the whole spectrum of gluten-related disorders, and you see it here and there throughout this book in that context.

✔ *Food hypersensitivity* is an umbrella term for any adverse reaction after eating a food or food additive, other than a reaction to food that's infected or contains a toxin like *E. coli* or an aflatoxin. The term food hypersensitivity was coined by the European Academy of Allergy and Clinical Immunology, an organisation not given to snappy names, it seems. That organisation uses the term to encompass food allergy and food intolerance, although it prefers the latter to be called non-allergic food hypersensitivity.

Here are the three main groupings of gluten-related disorders, as at the time of writing.

Wheat allergy

This is an allergic reaction to proteins found in wheat, not in rye and barley. These proteins are globulins, albumins, glutenins and gliadins, and only the gliadins and glutenins are gluten, the component that causes the problem in coeliac disease (see the next section, 'Autoimmune gluten-related disorders'). Wheat allergy may be a reaction to any of the proteins in wheat, but it's often to the albumins.

Generally, the reaction comes on within minutes of exposure to wheat – although it may be delayed for a day or so – and can include a runny nose, breathing difficulties, rash and swollen face and throat. Acute allergic reactions usually start in the mouth, with tingling, itching and a metallic taste. Later on may come vomiting, diarrhoea, tummy ache and a worsening of eczema. These reactions can be very severe, indeed life-threatening, and are very distressing to experience or witness, particularly in a child. Many sufferers are children, but it's not unknown for the onset to be in adulthood.

Exposure to wheat is the problem. As well as the allergic reaction after eating wheat, a reaction can occur after breathing in or touching wheat. A condition called baker's asthma, which has been known about since the time of the Roman Empire, results from repeatedly inhaling fine wheat flour.

A peculiar disorder in this category that's on the rise is *wheat-dependent exercise-induced anaphylaxis*. In this, the allergic reaction doesn't come on straight away after exposure to wheat, but is only triggered by subsequent vigorous exercise.

Autoimmune gluten-related disorders

Autoimmune conditions are not allergies, although they do engage the body's immune system. Normally, the immune system is extremely efficient at distinguishing between its 'friends' and its 'foes' and at defending against the foes, which it recognises as foreign invaders. Its friends are the body's own tissues and harmless substances such as fully digested food. Its foes are harmful substances such as partially digested food, transplanted organs from other people and germs. With *autoimmunity*, the immune system fails to recognise some of its friends, even the body's own healthy tissues, and attacks them as though they were foes. Various tissues around the body can be attacked and damaged as a result.

Gluten-related autoimmune disorders are those in which this attack on the body's own tissues is triggered by gluten, and include coeliac disease, dermatitis herpetiformis and gluten ataxia.

Coeliac disease

This is a relatively common yet significantly under-diagnosed disorder that's triggered in genetically susceptible people when they eat gluten. It's a lifelong condition that you can only treat with a strictly gluten-free diet. Its onset can be at any age, and it has a wide range of non-specific symptoms, classically affecting the small intestine to produce digestive upsets and poor absorption of nutrients. Although it's often these problems in the gut or secondary concerns like iron-deficiency anaemia from the under-absorption that bring people to the doctors for investigation, the effects of coeliac disease aren't confined to the gut by any means. In fact, it's a multisystem disease that can affect almost any organ in the body.

Coeliac UK, an organisation working in the field of all the gluten-related disorders, estimates that around 125,000 people have been diagnosed with coeliac disease in the UK. However, it believes that this figure is just the tip of the iceberg. Estimates are that 1 in 100 people in the UK have coeliac disease, which means that another 500,000 people are, as yet, undiagnosed. These figures include people who don't have a clue that anything is wrong, and others who've been diagnosed with something different. Very often that something is irritable bowel syndrome.

We now know that coeliac disease isn't simply one set of conditions and symptoms, but several. The most up-to-date categorisation of these conditions is as follows:

- **Classic coeliac disease:** If you have classic coeliac disease you have obvious symptoms of damage to your gut, particularly diarrhoea, greasy stools, weight loss and, in children, failure to grow and thrive. If you have both weight loss and anaemia, you're also in this group. All the tests for coeliac disease will be positive, so it's straightforward for your doctors to make a definite diagnosis.

- **Non-classic coeliac disease:** This is like the classic category in that the tests are positive, but here you don't have the classic symptoms of not absorbing your food properly, even though the tests show that the lining of your gut is damaged. You may have other minor intestinal problems such as constipation, tummy aches and wind, plus symptoms affecting other parts of your body, such as anaemia in the absence of weight loss, osteoporosis, headaches, tingling or deadness in your limbs, or mouth ulcers. From the doctors' point of view, this type is trickier to identify, because the symptoms are so common in other illnesses. Nowadays, about half of all coeliac cases fall into this category.

- **Potential coeliac disease:** If you have potential coeliac disease, your blood tests are positive but the lining of your gut is normal and you don't have any noticeable symptoms troubling you. This condition may be the very early stages of either classic or non-classic coeliac disease and may be picked up at a general check-up or blood screening. If you have potential coeliac disease, you'll be advised to go gluten-free and be tested again in future.

✔ **Genetically at risk of coeliac disease:** If you're in this group, you don't have coeliac disease, but you have a coeliac in your immediate family. You have the genetic markers of the disease, but your tests are negative. Other reasons to be categorised into this group if you don't have a coeliac in the family would be that you have type 1 diabetes, thyroiditis or any other condition that makes you more likely to develop coeliac disease in future, such as Down's syndrome. If you're in this group, you don't need to go gluten-free, but you need to be on the look-out for symptoms of coeliac disease and go back for another test if they develop in future.

For more details on coeliac disease, head to Chapter 3.

Dermatitis herpetiformis

This is a manifestation of coeliac disease, rather than a diagnostic category of it. Everyone with this condition is coeliac and has positive blood tests for the disease. Most have a damaged gut lining and symptoms of coeliac disease.

In dermatitis herpetiformis, the problem is an intensely itchy, burning, red rash on the skin, especially on the elbows and forearms, but also liable to erupt anywhere on the body. It's a lot rarer than coeliac disease as a whole, affecting 1 in every 10,000 people in the UK but 1 in 20 people who have the condition in the family.

If you have dermatitis herpetiformis, you need to eat a strictly gluten-free diet permanently. Drugs can treat the skin rashes, but these have nasty side-effects, so your doctor needs to give you the lowest possible dose and monitor you carefully. You may well find that the rashes clear up when you avoid gluten scrupulously, so that the drug treatment isn't necessary. You can read more about dermatitis herpetiformis in Chapter 3.

Gluten ataxia

Ataxia means loss of coordination, and *gluten ataxia* is a result of an autoimmune response to gluten, which damages the part of the brain responsible for balance. It's rare compared with other gluten-related disorders, with less than 4 cases per 100,000 people in the general population. According to Ataxia UK, the British charity that helps people with ataxia, the condition is progressive but normally only slowly, and it arises insidiously, the average age at onset being the early 50s.

What's the difference between wheat allergy, coeliac disease and gluten sensitivity?

To help you to see where you may be on the map of gluten-related disorders, and to increase your confidence in talking to health professionals about your diagnosis and treatment, here's an outline of the differences between the three most common conditions.

Wheat Allergy	Coeliac Disease	Gluten Sensitivity
An allergic reaction to wheat proteins.	An autoimmune reaction to gluten, where the body attacks its own tissues.	Believed to be an immune-mediated condition, but research goes on to pinpoint the exact mechanisms.
You react within minutes of eating wheat.	Some symptoms appear a few hours after eating gluten. Some people being diagnosed today have had the disease for many years.	You react within hours or possibly days of eating gluten.
Affects the skin, respiratory tract and gut.	Multisystem, so can affect different organs in the body.	Multisystem, so can affect different organs in the body.
No complications.	Long-term complications associated with untreated coeliac disease.	No research available yet to identify resulting complications.
May have damaged gut lining.	Always has damaged gut lining.	Rarely has a damaged gut lining, although research continues.
Treated with a wheat-free diet.	Treated with a gluten-free diet only.	Treated with a gluten-free diet only.
May be temporary; can grow out of it.	Permanent.	Unknown. May be temporary.
Diagnosed by a combination of diet history and skin-prick tests.	A clear process for diagnosis, with blood tests for the specific markers for the disease, plus an endoscopy with biopsy (see 'Getting Tested' below).	No precise and specific markers for diagnosis, currently. Diagnosis is based on symptoms and response to a gluten-free diet and a gluten challenge.
Estimates of prevalence vary from less than 1% of the population to up to 9%.	Affects about 1% of the population, although many are as yet undiagnosed.	Believed to affect between 6 and 10% of the population.

If you have gluten ataxia, you have great difficulty keeping your balance when walking, and others may notice your eyes flicking from side to side involuntarily. Although gluten is involved, and gluten ataxia is an autoimmune response like coeliac disease, only about a third of people with gluten ataxia also have a damaged gut lining, and only 10 per cent notice any digestive symptoms. Nevertheless, your neurologist will advise you to go strictly gluten-free as a key part of your treatment.

Gluten sensitivity

The third strand of the gluten-related disorders map is non-coeliac gluten sensitivity. This is the area at the centre of a sea-change among medical professionals. Until recently, doctors tested people complaining of the typical symptoms of coeliac disease or wheat allergy for those conditions and if the tests were negative – no damage to the gut lining and none of the markers in the blood – told the patients to continue to eat gluten. People often reported that the symptoms had cleared up on a gluten-free diet and promptly returned when they started eating gluten again. Now, doctors have identified gluten sensitivity as a separate condition affecting about 6 per cent of the population, far more than the 1 per cent known to have coeliac disease. Gluten sensitivity is an immune reaction to gluten, as opposed to an autoimmune reaction to it or an immediate allergic reaction to wheat.

People with gluten sensitivity have a virtually normal lining in their small intestine, yet many have intestinal symptoms such as bloating, diarrhoea and pain, as well as non-intestinal symptoms such as headache, confusion, tingling and deadness in the limbs, and muscular pain. The key thing is that these symptoms clear up completely when the patient scrupulously avoids gluten, and they return when the patient eats gluten again.

Identifying Symptoms of Gluten Sensitivity and Coeliac Disease

The symptoms that we describe in this section apply to both conditions, but you won't experience all of them. Hundreds of symptoms exist, so we can't list them all. The following sections give some of the more common ones. Notice that the symptoms can affect all parts of the body.

Symptoms are as varied as people themselves. You can talk to a hundred people with these conditions and each will tell you about a different set of symptoms. But ignoring *your* symptoms means you may be one of the many people in the UK who go undiagnosed.

When no symptoms *are* a symptom of coeliac disease

Some undiagnosed coeliacs have no noticeable symptoms whatsoever – they're described as *asymptomatic*. (Truly, though, if they read the list of 250-plus symptoms, we're wondering whether they can honestly say they have *none* of them!) Even though they don't feel any symptoms, gluten is damaging their small intestine in the same way it does in a coeliac who has obvious symptoms, and it can result in the same nutritional deficiencies and associated conditions. These people have it tough, in terms of both diagnosis and treatment. They may get diagnosed because they have a relative who has coeliac disease and they realise that means they should be tested too, or they go along for a routine test such as of blood cholesterol or for a medical, perhaps for a new job or an insurance policy, and it comes to light there.

Going for the gut: Intestinal symptoms

The following are some of the classic symptoms that affect the gut:

- Abdominal pain and distension
- Acid reflux
- Bloating
- Constipation
- Diarrhoea
- Greasy, foul-smelling, floating stools
- Lactose intolerance
- Mouth ulcers
- Nausea
- Vomiting
- Excessive wind

Doing your head in – and other parts

In coeliac disease, many of the non-intestinal symptoms are a result of poor nutrient absorption because of the damaged lining of the small intestine. With gluten sensitivity, these non-intestinal symptoms are more prevalent than the intestinal ones. The non-intestinal symptoms seem to arise directly, because the gut is almost always intact. There are hundreds of possible non-intestinal symptoms, and here are the most common:

✔ Acne

✔ Bruising easily

✔ Clumsiness

✔ Dental enamel deficiencies and irregularities

✔ Depression, irritability, listlessness and low mood

✔ Early-onset osteoporosis

✔ Eczema/psoriasis (skin conditions; not to be confused with dermatitis herpetiformis, which we talk about in Chapter 3)

✔ Fatigue and weakness

✔ 'Fuzzy brain' or an inability to concentrate

✔ Hair loss (alopecia)

✔ Headaches (including migraines)

✔ Infertility

✔ Joint/bone pain

✔ Low blood sugar (hypoglycaemia)

✔ Muscle cramping

✔ Nerve damage (peripheral neuropathy)

✔ Night blindness

✔ Nosebleeds

✔ Respiratory problems

✔ Rosacea (a skin disorder)

✔ Seizures

✔ Swelling and inflammation

✔ Vitamin and/or mineral deficiencies

✔ Weight loss

Research into coeliac disease shows it's likely to have further repercussions for women:

✔ **Birth weight:** A Danish study found that 29 per cent of women with untreated coeliac disease gave birth to unusually small babies, far more than in a non-coeliac control group and a group of coeliac women who were successfully being treated with a gluten-free diet.

✓ **Infertility:** The prevalence of untreated coeliac disease (as a cause of low fertility) in women presenting to fertility clinics is in the range of 2.7 to 3 per cent, significantly higher than that found in the general population (1.06 per cent).

✓ **Disrupted menstruation:** Girls with untreated coeliac disease tend to start having their periods later than others, yet women with untreated coeliac disease tend to go into the menopause earlier and have disrupted menstrual cycles.

✓ **Miscarriage:** Studies have found an increased incidence of miscarriage among patients with untreated coeliac disease.

Spotting symptoms in kids

Children who have coeliac disease tend to have the 'classic' gastrointestinal symptoms of diarrhoea and weight loss. They may also have some of the following symptoms:

✓ Abdominal pain and distension

✓ Delayed onset of puberty

✓ Failure to thrive (in infants and toddlers)

✓ Inability to concentrate

✓ Irritability

✓ Nosebleeds

✓ Short stature or delayed growth

✓ Weak bones or bone pain

Children and adults behaving badly

The theory that eating gluten is a direct cause of behavioural problems in some adults and children is gaining ground in the popular media, although there's no convincing clinical evidence of the relationship as yet. The theory is at full stretch when it links gluten sensitivity or coeliac disease to schizophrenia, attention deficit disorder, autism, clinical depression and bipolar disorder. The trend for gluten-free diets as the answer to many emotional and psychological disorders and illnesses is on the up, but much of the evidence to support the trend is anecdotal – that is, not supported by validated clinical trials, so the gluten-free diet is not currently used to treat these serious conditions. If you're thinking of going gluten-free or putting your child onto a gluten-free diet for these conditions, our advice is to consult a medical team with a broad range of expertise to help you decide.

Watching Out for Misdiagnoses and Missed Diagnoses

Doctors now know that coeliac disease and gluten sensitivity affect far more people than previously thought. For example, the discovery that coeliac disease affects 1 per cent of the UK population makes it one of the most common chronic autoimmune disorders and the most common cause of nutrient mal-absorption in the UK. We don't yet know the true prevalence of gluten sensitivity, because markers for it in blood have not yet been identified, but doctors believe it affects between 6 and 10 per cent of the population at all ages.

We know from comparing these figures with the number of diagnosed cases of the two conditions that they've both been under-diagnosed. This is partly due to people not coming forward for treatment, or presenting themselves for treatment having already given up eating gluten, so that the test results are falsely negative, and finally to doctors mis-reading the signs and misdiagnosing. Common misdiagnoses include:

- ✔ Acid reflux
- ✔ Cancer
- ✔ Chronic fatigue syndrome (CFS) or fibromyalgia
- ✔ Cystic fibrosis (a genetic respiratory disorder)
- ✔ Diabetes
- ✔ Diverticulosis (small pouches in the colon where food gets trapped)
- ✔ Eczema or psoriasis (skin conditions)
- ✔ Food allergies or lactose intolerance
- ✔ Gall bladder disease
- ✔ Crohn's disease and ulcerative colitis
- ✔ Irritable bowel syndrome (IBS) or spastic colon
- ✔ Lupus (an autoimmune disease)
- ✔ Migraines or unexplained headaches
- ✔ Parasites or other infections
- ✔ Psychological issues (hypochondria, depression, anxiety or neurosis)
- ✔ Thyroid disease
- ✔ Unexplained anaemia
- ✔ Unexplained infertility
- ✔ Viral infections (viral gastroenteritis)

So why do doctors miss gluten sensitivity and coeliac disease so often? Well . . .

✓ **Doctors aren't exposed to the conditions enough in medical training.** Time spent at medical school is influential in forming doctors' opinions and future practices. If they don't hear enough about the disorders during their period of training, they're not likely to look for it after they graduate. Plus, gluten sensitivity has only recently been recognised as a condition in its own right, so it wouldn't have been on the curriculum for any but the most recently qualified.

✓ **Doctors see, hear and read a lot more about illnesses that are treated by drugs than those that aren't.** Right now, no drugs are available to treat these conditions, so drug reps aren't strolling into doctors' offices, and drug companies aren't organising conferences and sending out press releases about gluten-related disorders.

✓ **Symptoms are wide-ranging, variable, sometimes absent, usually come on gradually, and they're common to many other complaints.** Symptoms of gluten sensitivity and coeliac disease are often quite varied, affecting many different parts of the body, sometimes all at once. Some people don't seem to have any symptoms, which makes pinpointing a cause difficult.

✓ **Some people have a gluten-related disorder in addition to another illness.** Once a doctor has diagnosed and started treating the other illness, say irritable bowel syndrome, all symptoms are put down to that and not investigated as thoroughly as if the patient had previously been well.

✓ **Doctors may think that patients are exaggerating.** More than one person with coeliac disease or gluten sensitivity has been called neurotic or a hypochondriac because of the many and sometimes dramatic symptoms involved.

✓ **Routine blood tests don't look for coeliac disease and they don't exist for gluten sensitivity.** Full blood counts (FBCs) and routine biochemical tests don't test specifically for coeliac disease. So although a doctor is likely to order FBC and biochemical tests, the results don't offer any hints that a patient may have gluten sensitivity. An astute doctor, though, sees the signs. Anaemia, low potassium, low bicarbonate, low albumin (protein) levels and high liver enzymes are red flags.

✓ **Routine endoscopies and colonoscopies don't detect coeliac disease or gluten sensitivity.** Some people think they've been tested for these conditions because they've had an *endoscopy* or a *colonoscopy*. Both tests involve a camera being inserted into the gut. An endoscopy is done through the mouth and examines the upper part of the gut, and a colonoscopy is done through the anus and examines only the lower end of the gut. But neither examination on its own can detect coeliac disease or gluten sensitivity. (Jump forward to the later section 'Biopsy' for more.)

If you feel sure you've been misdiagnosed, it's worth returning to your doctor for fresh tests, particularly if you think you may have gluten sensitivity, which is uncharted water for most GPs at the moment. It's worth taking new information for the doctor to consider, such as a food and symptom diary which you've kept for at least a week, or perhaps the news that a close family member has been diagnosed with a gluten-related disorder, or the results of tests you've had done for your employer or insurer. If the GP still thinks that no tests or treatment are necessary but you disagree, your next option is to go for the tests privately.

Official medical guidelines in the UK now urge doctors to test for coeliac disease in people who have type 1 diabetes, autoimmune thyroid disease, dermatitis herpetiformis and irritable bowel syndrome. So if you have any one of these conditions, even if you've had it for some time, you can alert the doctor to the need to test you for coeliac disease.

Getting Tested

Testing for coeliac disease or wheat allergy is now a more standard process than it once was, but gluten sensitivity is still new and not such an exact science. Whichever disorder you suspect, the first port of call is your GP, who either orders the tests directly or sends you off to specialists to get them done. Even if your doctor suspects sensitivity, the initial steps for diagnosing it are to eliminate both wheat allergy and coeliac disease.

If you think you have a gluten-related disorder, it's important to get a proper diagnosis as soon as you can and, with the exception of wheat allergy, to continue to eat gluten until you've had the tests. Otherwise, the results will come back negative even if you have one of the conditions and need treatment. Pinning down exactly which condition you have can be tricky, and if you don't go for diagnosis at all and simply go gluten-free willy-nilly, you may mask another disease that needs a different treatment. If the gluten-free diet is right for you, your doctor will let you know and, importantly, follow up with you so that you get the treatment you need, now and in the future.

Blood tests for coeliac disease

A blood test is the first step towards a diagnosis of coeliac disease. You need a test that looks for antibodies that are only in your blood if you have coeliac disease.

The blood test can uncover two types of antibodies:

- **tTGA (tissue transglutaminase antibodies)-IgA (Ig = Immumoglobulin Antibody, A = type A):** This antibody is very specific to coeliac disease, meaning that if you have a positive tTGA, it's very likely that you have coeliac disease. The tTGA blood test is essential as an initial screening test. This test can have a number of different names, including tTGA, tTG or TG-IgA, but they're essentially the same.

- **EMA (endomysial antibodies)-IgA:** This test is also specific to coeliac disease. It's the initial screening test of choice but may be negative in 2 per cent of people with coeliac disease who are IgA-deficient. When you test positive, especially if tTGA is positive too, you're extremely likely to have coeliac disease.

Current research suggests that blood tests that look for both of these antibodies together are highly accurate and specific to coeliac disease, but the possibility of getting a negative result and still having coeliac disease does crop up. So what if you have strong coeliac symptoms but get a negative test result? That's where the biopsy comes into its own.

Neither antibody will show up in your blood test if you haven't been eating gluten in the run-up to the test. You need to eat one meal that contains gluten every day for at least six weeks before your blood sample is taken for the test. For example, you could have wheat-based breakfast cereal every day, or lunch or dinner based on pasta or bread.

Biopsy

Doctors diagnose coeliac disease using blood tests, and if these show a likelihood of the disease, an *endoscopy* and *biopsy* – procedures in which a gastroenterologist investigates your upper gut with a camera and pinches off a minute piece of the gut lining to examine under a microscope. A biopsy is the gold standard for the diagnosis of coeliac disease and also to assess the extent of the damage you have to the lining of your small intestine. (We explain in Chapter 3 what abnormalities the biopsy can show if you're coeliac.)

The whole procedure takes only minutes and you'll be conscious throughout. You can't feel the biopsy, and any damage it does to your gut is negligible. However, swallowing the camera attached to a tube called an endoscope is uncomfortable and can make you gag. You may be offered a sedative or local anaesthetic, and your throat may feel a little sore for a few days afterwards.

Other blood tests the doctor may carry out

Your doctor may also want to run some other blood tests to see whether malabsorption has affected your nutrient status. You may feel like you're having a lot of tests, but they provide important information to help you on the road to recovery. The other blood tests may include:

- ✔ **Haemoglobin (Hb) level:** This test shows the amount of oxygen-carrying pigment in your red blood cells. If the result is lower than normal, you may be suffering from anaemia. This test is often combined with a *serum ferritin* test that shows whether your iron stores have been depleted as a result of anaemia.

- ✔ **Red cell folate:** This substance (made from the B vitamin folic acid) is another important constituent of red blood cells. The level may be lower than normal if you're suffering from malabsorption.

- ✔ **Serum albumin:** The amount of this plasma protein can be low if you've not been absorbing protein properly.

- ✔ **Alkaline phosphatase:** The amount of this enzyme in the sample can be raised if you're suffering from a shortage of vitamin D or calcium through malabsorption.

- ✔ **B12 and vitamin D status:** These two vitamins are often badly absorbed in coeliac disease and are likely to be below the normal range.

Getting tested for wheat allergy

Like all allergies, for wheat allergy you can get a definitive diagnosis from a registered health professional such as your GP, who can arrange skin-prick tests for you. We advise you against having a test done by a laboratory that tests you remotely, or going to an unregistered adviser. You need professional and individual testing followed up with advice about what to do if you're allergic to something. You need to be in a clinical setting when you have the test, in case you have a severe reaction and need emergency treatment on the spot.

An immunologist performs the following tests for wheat and other food allergies. It's important to be tested for allergy to a range of commonly eaten foods, as well as wheat, because multiple allergies are quite common:

- ✔ **Blood tests:** If you have an allergy to wheat or another food, your blood will contain markers known as immunoglobulin type E, which your body will have produced to defend itself against the troublesome food. Doctors can easily identify these markers in your blood sample.

✔ **Open food challenges:** In this test, you take a minute amount of food protein by mouth, and the doctor observes your reaction. A true food allergy can result in a sudden, severe reaction.

✔ **Skin-prick test:** The doctor places a minute amount of food protein on your skin and then pricks the skin. If a small, red, swollen weal occurs, this indicates an allergy to that specific food.

Sensing gluten sensitivity

If you've tested negatively for both wheat allergy and coeliac disease, and other conditions not related to gluten have been ruled out, your doctor may suspect gluten sensitivity. Then your doctor works with you to test your response to a gluten-free diet for about three months, and then a gluten-containing diet for a short while. You need to keep a diary of what you eat and your symptoms throughout this process, and you must be rigorous about sticking to the gluten-free diet in the test period and eating gluten again during the challenge. Doing so is worthwhile in order to arrive at a clear picture of your condition.

Testing Positive: Now What?

The only treatment for a gluten-related disorder is a strictly gluten-free diet from now on, and you've got the ideal book in your hand to help you get started on it right away.

When we talk about going 'gluten-free', we mean going cold turkey and cutting out every scrap of gluten in your diet all at once. This is not a diet to start gradually, for example by changing your usual breakfast but leaving your other meals the same, or by cutting out ordinary bread but sticking with ordinary pasta. Any gluten you eat continues to damage your health, and you have everything to gain by getting on with your new gluten-free diet right away. We give you the low-down on what to eat instead of your old gluten-loaded foods, so that your diet is healthy, balanced, enjoyable, practical and completely free of gluten.

Testing positive for wheat allergy

If you're allergic to wheat, you must avoid it completely – that is, eat a thoroughly wheat-free diet. Many people with wheat allergy choose a gluten-free diet, particularly now that gluten-free food is widely available and much of it is also wheat-free.

Gluten-free food is also free of rye and barley, which you should be able to eat, so in theory you could supplement your gluten-free diet with these two cereals and foods made with them, provided they are labelled 'wheat-free'. The problem is that many foods made with rye and barley also include wheat as a major component or as a contaminant. For example, at least half the flour in a typical rye bread is wheat, and crops of barley are likely to be contaminated with wheat at some stage, either in the fields or during processing. And leading brands of rye crispbreads declare on the labels that the products may contain wheat. You'll struggle to find a wheat-free beer made from pure barley, but in any case why bother when so many gluten-free beers are available which are also wheat-free? Our advice is to go gluten-free and if you do incorporate any products containing rye and barley into your diet, take extreme care when choosing them.

 If you suspect that you may have an anaphylactic response to wheat, consider carrying an epinephrine shot (a drug that stops the anaphylactic response) that you can quickly inject into yourself, in case you accidentally eat any wheat. Anaphylactic shock is an extreme allergic reaction, which is sometimes seen in people who have an allergy to bee stings or nuts.

Testing positive for coeliac disease or gluten sensitivity

In coeliac disease, the gluten-free diet is for life. In gluten sensitivity, you may be able to eat gluten again in future. If you do so, you'll soon see whether you're still sensitive to gluten, and of course if you are, you must stop eating it at once.

Thinking of staying glued to gluten?

If you have coeliac disease, you've already been through so much effort to get diagnosed that we suspect you're not tempted to go back to eating gluten. Whatever symptoms drove you to the doctor in the first place will have cleared up completely during the gluten-free testing phase. The last thing most people with this disorder want is a return of these problems.

However, in our careers, we've identified certain groups of people who continue to eat gluten even though they know it damages their health. If you're in one of these groups, examine what's motivating you to stay glued to gluten even though you know it's harmful:

✔ **You feel that the gluten-free diet is too restrictive and too expensive.** The gluten-free diet is nowhere near as restrictive as it once was. So many people are going gluten-free these days that retailers and restaurateurs are falling over themselves to supply the demand. Most of the food you eat is naturally gluten-free, and you can continue to enjoy it. For the gluten-containing things that you presently eat, loads of alternative foods are available, and if you're coeliac, you can get a lot of the staple food you eat on prescription. Have a look at Chapter 4 for more on the gluten-free diet.

✔ **You like taking risks.** Eating gluten isn't a risk that comes with a reward or one that you can take without consequences. It's not like bungee-jumping, where you get a thrill from taking the risk. You can't control or limit the damage gluten is doing to you. And the longer you go on eating it, the more damage you're doing and the less likely you'll repair it fully when you do eventually go gluten-free.

✔ **You have persuasive friends, relatives and colleagues who refuse to hear anything about cutting out gluten: 'One little bit of cake won't hurt!'** Read the rest of the book and put such people straight. If they really had your best interests in mind, they'd help you to go gluten-free, not hold you back.

✔ **You decide that cheating from time to time is okay.** If you have a gluten-related disorder and you eat any gluten, you're undoubtedly compromising your health, now and for the future. Furthermore, your body is probably being robbed of vital nutrients that it needs to function properly and to stay healthy.

If you've tested positive for coeliac disease and you don't go completely gluten-free, you're almost certainly already deficient in a number of vital nutrients, particularly the vitamins and minerals, and you won't be able to make up the shortfall. Your damaged gut will continue to work against your intake of these nutrients, even if you increase it. You may already be suffering from anaemia and osteoporosis or other bone-depleted conditions. If not, you're highly likely to get them in future if you stay glued to gluten.

Certain conditions are associated with coeliac disease, meaning that someone who has one is more likely to have the other. Doctors aren't always sure which one develops first and whether, as a coeliac, you're more likely to develop one of these conditions if you don't stay gluten-free. But why take that risk? Also, if you do develop, or already have, one of these conditions, its treatment may be impaired if you don't also treat your coeliac disease by staying strictly gluten-free. For example, people with both diabetes and coeliac disease have better-controlled blood sugar when they stay gluten-free compared with when they don't. Conditions associated with coeliac disease include:

✔ Addison's disease (hypoadrenocorticism)

✔ Autoimmune chronic active hepatitis

✔ Cancer of the small bowel

✔ Crohn's disease

✔ Insulin-dependent diabetes mellitus (type 1)

✔ Infertility in women and adverse events in pregnancy

✔ Myasthenia gravis

✔ Raynaud's phenomenon

✔ Scleroderma

✔ Sjögren's syndrome

✔ Systemic lupus erythematosus

✔ Thyroid disease (Graves' disease and Hashimoto's disease)

✔ Ulcerative colitis

Benefiting by going gluten-free

One of the best things about going gluten-free when you have a gluten-related disorder is that you begin to get better the minute you start on the gluten-free diet. Some of your symptoms disappear or become less severe within days; others can take a long time to improve. But rest assured, the healing process will be underway.

Many people who, before they were diagnosed, weren't bothered by their symptoms or didn't notice them are surprised at just how much better they feel in general when they go gluten-free. They tend to report that they didn't realise how bad they felt before. They find that minor complaints such as headaches, which they hadn't connected to gluten in their diet, cease to be a problem.

Some people take a few months before they realise they feel a lot better, and some feel better initially but then take a nosedive a few months into the diet. All these responses are normal in the healing process, but in the long run you can look forward to improved health in ways that you may not even have expected.

Know that you're doing the best you can for your future health and quality of life, and are beginning to absorb all the nutrients you've been lacking if you had a damaged lining to your gut, which may have been the case for many years. Although most, if not all, of the intestinal damage caused by gluten is reversible, some of the prolonged malnutrition and malabsorption issues, such as short stature and weakened bones, may have long-lasting or perhaps permanent effects. That's one of the reasons for catching gluten sensitivity or coeliac disease early – so you can start on the road to recovery.

The gluten-free diet is easy to understand and to adapt to your lifestyle. For the fastest start, we suggest you go to Chapter 7 – our quick-start guide. Take a peek at the online extras at www.dummies.com/extras/livingglutenfreeuk for ten ways to live gluten-free joyfully. We help you to sort out the kitchen in Chapter 9 and, in Part IV, give you almost 100 tempting recipes for morning-noon-and-night gorgeous gluten-free meals.

Chapter 3

Taking a Closer Look at Coeliac Disease

C oeliac disease is a common but much under-diagnosed condition. Contrary to popular belief, it's not an allergy but an autoimmune disease in which the body produces cells and substances that attack its own tissues in response to the presence of gluten in the gut. Coeliac disease is unique in that it can only be treated by diet. If undiagnosed or diagnosed but not treated, it can result in severely compromised health. But the good news is that it's fully treatable with a gluten-free diet.

In this chapter, we explain why more coeliacs seem to be about these days. We outline what your immune system does and what happens in an autoimmune condition like coeliac disease. We get down into the intestines – yuk! – to show you the damage the disease does there, why it impairs your ability to absorb nutrients properly and what effects that has. Changing your diet can help to overcome the nutritional deficiencies you may have, and you'll find all the details you need in this chapter. Finally, we look forward to other potential treatments on the horizon.

If all this sounds a bit alarming to you, take comfort in the fact that you can repair much of this damage, stop the disease doing you any more harm, and get your health, fitness and joie de vivre back on track as simply as by going gluten-free, as long as you do it completely. No cheating – ever.

Exposing One of the Most Common Genetic Diseases of Humankind

Doctors now know that coeliac disease is much more common than previously thought. Indeed, the condition is arguably one of the most common genetic diseases affecting humans. When we first qualified as dietitians, back in the Dark Ages, our lecture notes told us that the prevalence was 1 in 1,000 people and that the initial onset was always in childhood. However, in recent years, since diagnosis has become easier, screening has become more widespread. Large-scale surveys across several countries, such as the European Cluster Project, screened thousands of healthy people and showed that the average prevalence is as high as 1 in 100 (or 1 per cent) of the population.

The present population of the UK is almost 62 million people, so in theory more than 600,000 coeliacs are out there. As yet, though, only 125,000 of them have been diagnosed, and the others are unaware that they have the disease. Many don't find their symptoms troubling and others believe, or have been told, they have some other condition that's causing these symptoms. Whatever the reason, one thing is clear: people diagnosed as typical coeliacs are just the tip of the iceberg. We give you the categories of coeliac disease (classic, non-classic, potential and at risk) in Chapter 2.

Due to the strong genetic component in coeliac disease, the prevalence of coeliac disease goes up to 10 per cent, or one in ten, among people with a coeliac in their immediate family. So, anyone who has a close relative – a parent, child or sibling – who has coeliac disease has a ten times higher risk.

The diagnosis rate has increased massively since the 1970s – ten-fold in some coeliac clinics around the UK – and it's still going up all the time. This is due in part to greater awareness among doctors of the diverse array of typical symptoms and of the likelihood of its initial onset among people in their 40s and 50s. The screening programme, relatives of diagnosed people putting themselves forward for testing, and improved diagnostic techniques all mean that more and more coeliacs are being picked up. But specialists also believe that a real increase in the incidence of the disease is underway. Statistically, it appears that for every child diagnosed, nine adult cases go undetected, and for every adult diagnosed, seven others are still to be recognised.

Coeliac disease is a non-discriminatory condition, found in all races and nationalities. Experts once thought that occurrence was more prevalent in people with Northern European ancestry, but that distinction is diminishing as populations intermingle and diagnosis improves worldwide. Geographically, coeliac disease is becoming a global phenomenon. The area with the highest incidence in the population is the west of Ireland. And numbers of diagnosed cases as a proportion of the population are going up across Europe, North America, India and the Antipodes, and cases are now emerging in China, where once coeliac disease was rare.

Myths and misconceptions

Some of the things that we hear about coeliac disease are simply myths and misconceptions. Here are some of the more common ones:

Myth: Coeliac disease is catching.

Fact: Although coeliac disease runs in families, that's a genetic effect and nothing to do with infection.

Myth: Coeliac disease is rare.

Fact: It's one of the world's most common genetic diseases, affecting about 1 per cent of the population in Europe and North America.

Myth: Coeliac disease is a childhood condition.

Fact: Actually, if you inherit the genes, the symptoms can be triggered at any time in your life – for example, during illness or stress. Diagnosis in childhood is now much less common than in adulthood. Data from the organisation Coeliac UK suggests that most coeliacs are diagnosed in their 40s and 50s, the peak age being around 50, and more over-60s are diagnosed each year than under-16s.

Myth: It's cured by eating a gluten-free diet for a while.

Fact: Coeliac disease is treated, not cured, by a gluten-free diet, and it's a permanent condition, needing a gluten-free diet for life.

Myth: If you only have mild symptoms, you're okay to eat gluten from time to time.

Fact: You can't. If you're coeliac, you must scrupulously and completely avoid eating any gluten. Any scrap of it in your food can damage your health.

Myth: If you're coeliac, you have severe gastro-intestinal problems, like nausea, wind, bloating and diarrhoea.

Fact: Many people with coeliac disease don't have any of these classic gastrointestinal symptoms, or have them only mildly – their symptoms are outside the bowel. Symptoms can range from headaches, chronic tiredness, bone or joint pain, anaemia, persistent mouth ulcers, neurological problems and hair loss, through to fertility problems, including spontaneous miscarriage, and depression. Adults may show signs of weight loss or be overweight. Children with coeliac disease can experience the same symptoms and if left untreated, can suffer from wasting and faltering growth.

Experts struggle to account for this dramatic rise in prevalence of the disease. Some speculate that one cause is the five-fold increase in wheat consumption worldwide, which occurred in the second half of the 20th century, and the lack of diversity in the wheat we consume.

The disease is less common in the Middle and Near East than elsewhere in the world. Gluten-containing grains were first cultivated and eaten in any quantity in this area about 10,000 years ago. The wheat has evolved slowly over the millennia, and the people may have evolved with it to develop biological mechanisms to cope with gluten in their food.

Table 3-1 shows the incidence of coeliac disease compared with the incidence of other diseases.

Table 3-1	Prevalence of Common Diseases in the UK
Disease	*Estimated Number of People Diagnosed in the UK*
Epilepsy	500,000 (National Society for Epilepsy)
Inflammatory bowel diseases (Crohn's disease and ulcerative colitis)	240,000 (British Society of Gastroenterology)
Parkinson's disease	127,000 (Parkinson's Disease Society)
Coeliac disease	125,000 (Coeliac UK)
Multiple sclerosis	100,000 (Multiple Sclerosis Society)
Cystic fibrosis	9,000 (Cystic Fibrosis Trust)

Pinpointing Who Develops Coeliac Disease and Why

Doctors have no way of identifying people who will develop coeliac disease. What we *do* know is that you need at least three things in order to develop it:

- ✔ A genetic predisposition
- ✔ A diet that includes gluten
- ✔ Something to launch the disease into activity

If just one of these factors is missing in your life, you won't become coeliac.

Finding the key genes

No one has yet discovered all the genes specifically involved in developing coeliac disease, so there's no way of testing genes to identify those who'll definitely become coeliac in future. However, researchers have made great strides in genetics in recent years. Now, using genetics alone, it's possible to rule coeliac disease out for some people, but not to rule it in, that is to predict it or diagnose it.

Researchers have identified, largely from studies of twins, two of the key genes involved. These are located on chromosome 6 in the body's cells. Both are forms of the human leukocyte antigen (HLA) genes known to their friends as HLA DQ2 and HLA DQ8. You don't need both to develop coeliac disease – one gene will do – and DQ2 is the one seen in 95 per cent of coeliacs.

Interestingly, about 20 to 30 per cent of the general population have these genes yet don't develop coeliac disease. In other words, if you have the genes, you may or may not develop coeliac disease. But if you don't have either gene, you're very unlikely to develop the disease. Doctors could use this knowledge to help in the diagnostic process they adopt, with the aim of avoiding sending people for endoscopy and biopsy (physical examination of the upper parts of the gut) unnecessarily. Some paediatric gastroenterologists are using genetic testing as an alternative to endoscopy and biopsy in order to exclude coeliac disease where it's one of several possible diagnoses in young children. (Read more about the tests used in the diagnosis in Chapter 2.)

Coeliac disease isn't a single dominant or recessive genetic condition – unlike, for example, cystic fibrosis, colour blindness or haemophilia. It's a complex *multifactorial* or *polygenic disease*, meaning several different types of genes play a part in the full manifestation of the condition, in combination with lifestyle and environmental factors.

Launching coeliac disease

For you to become coeliac, your disease has to be launched or kick-started by some event. After they've been diagnosed and look back over their lives, some people have a pretty clear idea of when their coeliac disease started, because they were relatively healthy and then – boom! – their symptoms appeared out of the blue.

Common events that launch the disease into its active mode include:

- ✔ Car accident or other physical injury
- ✔ Emotional stress – for example, divorce, redundancy, bereavement or other emotional trauma
- ✔ Illness or infection
- ✔ Pregnancy
- ✔ Surgery

Other people have their suspicions about what may have started the disease, but their symptoms have developed so gradually or are so mild they can't be sure. If you're like that, don't worry about it. You can't undo the past or kid yourself that you don't have coeliac disease. The thing to do now is to start treating your condition with a strictly gluten-free diet.

Understanding Coeliac Disease and What It Does to the Body

Coeliac disease is an *autoimmune disease* (a disease in which the immune system attacks healthy tissues in the body) that's activated when a susceptible individual eats gluten. To help you understand exactly what damage is being done, in this section we review just a bit of the basic human anatomy of the gastrointestinal tract.

However, it's not only the gut that's affected. Untreated, the disease can affect many other organs of the body, including the liver, skin, nerves, muscles, thyroid and spleen, and in women, the reproductive system. Because coeliac disease affects the gut, it leads to nutrients being absorbed poorly. It can therefore produce an unusually wide range of manifestations or associated conditions as diverse as diarrhoea from a fast-moving gut, constipation from a slow-moving one, an underactive spleen, abnormal liver function, both over- and underactive thyroid, itchy blisters on the skin, mouth ulcers, arthritis and joint pain, poorly mineralised bone and tooth enamel, infertility in women, recurrent miscarriage, migraine, tummy aches, loss of balance and depression. If that list isn't enough to get you onto a strictly gluten-free diet, the increased risk of tumours of the intestine will. The risk of these tumours begins to reduce as soon as you start the diet, and after five years it's no more than everyone else's.

The immune system is a complex set of organs, cells, molecules and a distribution network similar to veins and arteries, known as lymphatic vessels. It's absolutely essential to good health, because we're constantly exposed to disease-causing organisms like bacteria, viruses and fungi. Sometimes a tiny element of the immune system malfunctions and actually causes disease rather than preventing it. Allergies, such as wheat allergy or hay fever, are the most common form of disease resulting from such a malfunction. An *autoimmune disease*, like coeliac disease or rheumatoid arthritis, is caused by another much more unusual malfunction of the immune system. Normally, the system produces substances and cells that destroy anything foreign detected in the body. But in autoimmune diseases, the system reacts to the body's own tissues as though they were foreign and attacks them, damaging and inflaming the surrounding healthy tissues.

Scientists have identified about 100 autoimmune diseases, including type 1 diabetes, psoriasis, multiple sclerosis and autoimmune thyroid disease. Families may inherit the predisposition to autoimmunity, which can manifest itself differently in different members. If a family has a history of autoimmune disease, getting other members screened for coeliac disease is worthwhile. Doctors believe that people with untreated coeliac disease may be more at risk of developing other autoimmune disorders.

How your small intestine should work

Open your hand and put it flat against your belly button, with your thumb pointing up and your little finger pointing down. Your hand is now covering most of the relatively small space into which your small intestine – up to 4 metres of it – is neatly coiled.

By the time it gets here, your food has already been chewed, swallowed, passed through the stomach and begun to be broken down by enzymes into nutrients that the body needs to absorb to nourish itself. Digestion is largely completed in the small intestine, and most nutrients are absorbed there.

To help it to absorb nutrients, the lining or *mucosa* of the small intestine is made up of a series of folds covered with finger-like projections. The technical name for these small fingers is *villi* (singular: villus). Each villus is covered with smaller projections called *microvilli*. The purpose of the villi and microvilli, shown in Figure 3-1, is to increase the surface area of the intestine so that it's large enough to absorb nutrients into the body effectively.

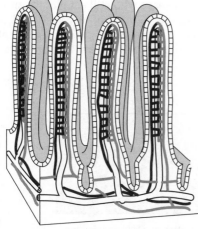

Figure 3-1:
The villi of your small intestine.

How your small intestine works with coeliac disease

Normally, the digestive system breaks down gluten into much smaller molecules or fractions which the body can absorb and use as proteins in building and repairing tissues. The body recognises these molecules as being the same as its own, not as unwanted intruders. But in coeliacs, some of these fractions of gluten are still a tiny bit bigger and more complex than they should be, so they're not the same as the body's own, and the body sees them as intruders – something to mount an immediate defence against.

This defence is mounted by the immune system and involves specialised cells called *T-lymphocytes*, which are on patrol all over the body, and specialised molecules called antibodies, also known as *immunoglobulins* or Igs, which are produced 'to order' by the immune system when it senses intruders, known as *antigens*. Each antibody is specific to just one antigen, and researchers have identified the ones that arise only in coeliac disease. These specific *auto-antibodies*, as they're known, are detectable in diagnostic blood tests.

Anyway, back to your small intestine. The defensive cells and antibodies arrive in the gut lining to overcome the perceived intruders, and the lining becomes something of a battleground. The fight damages the lining itself, making it inflamed and swollen, thus flattening the villi (*villous atrophy*), as shown in Figure 3-2. The lining of the small intestine therefore has a drastically reduced surface area, inadequate for complete absorption of nutrients from food. After nutrients pass through the small intestine and on into the large intestine, they can't be absorbed, and literally go to waste in faeces. That's why you see *malabsorption* (poor nutrient absorption) and nutritional deficiencies in people with coeliac disease who still eat gluten. And because the food is just passing through without being properly absorbed, some of it arrives in the large intestine, where it's fermented, producing symptoms like wind and pain, and where some of the fats and sugars in it produce diarrhoea.

Villi   Villi

Figure 3-2:
Villi flat-
tened in
coeliac
disease.

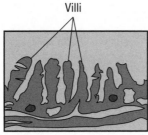
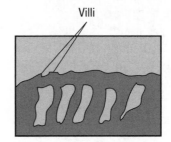

Villi in a healthy intestine   Flattened villi in an intestine
                                        with coeliac disease

When you're on a gluten-free diet, the gut starts to heal immediately. You may feel better within a few weeks, but it can take between six months and two years for the villi to recover fully. The reaction to eating gluten again can range from an immediate triggering of bowel symptoms to no symptoms at all. However, whether or not you notice any symptoms, damage to the bowel will occur.

Reducing the chance of your baby developing coeliac disease

Some coeliac mothers believe that it's best if their baby is never exposed to gluten, and impose a gluten-free diet. This is a mistake. If you're coeliac, your baby has a one in ten chance of the disease, but a nine in ten chance of avoiding it and being able to eat a normal gluten-containing diet. You can only find out whether your baby is coeliac by introducing gluten and watching carefully for any reaction.

New studies show that you may be able to protect your baby from developing coeliac disease later in life, even if you're coeliac yourself as a mother. Research shows that breastfeeding and carefully timing when you first give your baby gluten can protect against coeliac disease. It appears that the best time to introduce small amounts of gluten into your baby's food is at six to seven months of age, ideally while still breastfeeding.

Introducing gluten for the first time before or after your baby is six to seven months old seems to have the opposite effect by increasing your baby's risk of developing the disease – as much as five-fold if introduced in the first three months of life.

Scratching the Surface of Dermatitis Herpetiformis

Dermatitis herpetiformis (or *DH* as we refer to it from now on) is a skin-blistering disease associated with coeliac disease. Although DH was first described as long ago as 1884, researchers didn't make the link between DH and coeliac disease until 1968.

DH is much less common than coeliac disease itself, with a prevalence of about 1 in 10,000, but it also has the tendency to be inherited. It usually first appears in young to middle-aged adults, although it can occur for the first time at any age. The occurrence is slightly more common in men than women; 60 per cent of adult sufferers are male.

The symptoms of DH are mainly external – on the skin – and include:

- ✔ A rash that may occur on the elbows, upper forearms, knees, buttocks and scalp, but can also be on the face, trunk and other areas on the limbs – in fact, almost anywhere. It's usually symmetrical, affecting, for example, both elbows or both knees.
- ✔ Intense itching and often stinging.

- ✔ Persistent raised, red-coloured bumps.
- ✔ Watery blisters on the surface that are easily scratched away and scab over.

Everyone with DH has coeliac disease, but not everyone with coeliac disease has DH. In DH, villous flattening in the small intestine may be minor and not the cause of any symptoms, although most people with DH have some gut inflammation.

To diagnose DH, a dermatologist takes a biopsy of the skin in an unaffected area, under local anaesthetic. The dermatologist is looking for the same specific auto-antibodies as in the tests for coeliac disease. Blood tests can confirm the diagnosis and help your doctor to monitor your progress on a gluten-free diet afterwards. You usually have a small intestinal biopsy as part of the diagnosis.

The cornerstone of the treatment of DH is a strict gluten-free diet, but the diet usually takes some time to become effective. To reduce the rash more quickly, you may need medication such as Dapsone, but if so, your doctor will carefully monitor you for side-effects, which can include a form of anae-mia, nerve damage, depression and headaches. The intense itchiness reduces within a few days, but you may need to stay on the medication for up to two years. If you stop the medication before the gluten-free diet has become effective, the rash may return.

The name for DH comes from *dermatitis*, meaning inflammation of the skin, and *herpetiformis*, because it looks similar to herpes, which involves clusters of lesions. Some people have made the erroneous assumption that DH is caused by the herpes virus, but in fact that has nothing to do with it.

Pumping Iron to Get Over Anaemia

Iron-deficiency anaemia is a common outcome of untreated coeliac disease, so much so that if a doctor can't put anaemia down to other causes, such as very heavy periods, persistent and long-term bleeding or a deficient diet, it's the chief factor to arouse suspicions of coeliac disease in adults. If you have coeliac disease but you're not aware of it, a situation that may persist for many years, you may well have been eating enough iron but not absorb-ing it all. The main part of the gut where iron is absorbed is the upper part of the small intestine, so when the lining there is flattened, the gut doesn't have time to absorb all the available iron before the digested food passes by and on into the large intestine.

People think of iron-deficiency anaemia as causing regular periods to stop, very noticeable fatigue, pallor and obvious bald patches, but the noticeable symptoms may be as mild as a little more hair than usual coming out when you wash and brush your hair. You may still be growing new hair as normal, and the rate of hair loss increases so gradually that you don't really notice it. Another reason why anaemia may not flag up coeliac disease is that it often doesn't come to the attention of a doctor. People self-treat with over-the-counter supplements, or lessen it by taking a daily multi-supplement all the time, and don't explore the cause.

If you're anaemic when you're diagnosed with coeliac disease, you should find that as your gut heals, which starts at once when you completely eradicate gluten from your diet, you begin to absorb iron very efficiently.

Most coeliacs don't need to take iron supplements. In fact, we recommend avoiding supplements, because taking just one mineral in excessive amounts can compromise the absorption of others, and if you've been going short of iron, you're likely to have been short of several others as well.

Your gluten-free diet must be complete with every essential nutrient – balanced and nutritious overall – particularly because the gluten-free flours you'll be eating instead of wheat flour may not be fortified the way wheat flour is. If you eat meat, regularly choose red meats like beef and lamb, which have a much higher iron content than chicken and pork, and eat a wide variety of vegetables, wholegrains, pulses, nuts, seeds and dried fruits. The vitamin C content of citrus fruits, potatoes and other fruits and vegetables helps you absorb iron, but drinking tea with meals has the opposite effect, so leave the tea for enjoying separately at other times.

Maintaining Healthy Bones with Coeliac Disease

Bones are living tissues, and the whole skeleton is replenished about every seven to ten years in adults and more frequently in children. The body contains at least a kilogram of calcium, 99 per cent of it in the bones and teeth. The remainder plays a vital role in almost every cell of the body. So you need a regular dietary supply of calcium, along with vitamin D to help your body absorb it.

What can happen to your bones with coeliac disease

In the UK alone, three million people have *osteoporosis*, a disease which causes a porous, brittle bone structure that's prone to fracture, particularly of the wrists, hips and spine. As many as one in three women and one in five men over the age of 50 suffer from it. Osteoporosis is particularly common in people with coeliac disease, especially those diagnosed later in life, about half of whom already have either osteoporosis or the earlier stage of low bone density at diagnosis. This is due to reduced absorption of calcium and vitamin D in the damaged small intestine. Sometimes this is the only clinical sign of coeliac disease.

The older you are at diagnosis, the more likely you are to have osteoporosis or low bone density, because your bones naturally become less dense as you get older. No cure for osteoporosis has been developed, but studies on people diagnosed with coeliac disease as adults suggest that within about one year on a strict gluten-free diet, the density of their bones improves considerably, and the risk of continued mineral loss with age reduces. For those diagnosed at a young age, osteoporosis is less of a problem provided they stick to their gluten-free diet.

Doctors can usually detect low bone density with a simple and painless scan by means of dual-energy X-ray absorptiometry (DEXA). You can have this scan as soon as you receive a diagnosis of coeliac disease, or as part of the follow-up.

Adopting strategies to help keep your bones strong

Strategies to prevent osteoporosis are especially important in people with coeliac disease. For strong bones, adopt all of the following strategies, as well as sticking rigidly to your gluten-free diet:

- Eat plenty of calcium-rich foods (see the following section)
- Get enough vitamin D (see the later section 'Getting enough, but not too much, vitamin D')
- Take regular physical activity, especially where you bear the weight of your body, as when walking, jogging, dancing or playing tennis
- Avoid smoking, excess alcohol and salt, all of which can inhibit normal bone construction.

For more information, visit www.nos.org.uk, the website of the National Osteoporosis Society, the UK's only charity dedicated to osteoporosis.

Following a diet rich in calcium

The goal is to get 1,000 to 1,500 milligrams of calcium a day. To get this, you need at least four servings of dairy products per day – that is, of milk, cheese and yoghurt. Choose the lower-fat varieties of these foods, which contain as much calcium but fewer calories than the full-fat creamy versions.

When you're first diagnosed, you may notice that dairy products, particularly uncooked milk, upset your stomach. This is due to *lactose intolerance*. Lactose is the sugar in milk. It's digested by the enzyme lactase; this enzyme is secreted in the small intestine, which is very likely to have been damaged by eating gluten. You can get calcium in non-dairy foods such as fortified soy milk or rice milk, tofu, oranges, beans and dried fruits, and now lactose-free cow's milk. However, if you cut out lactose completely and permanently, you won't encourage your gut to start producing lactase normally when it does heal. It's very difficult to get enough calcium from non-dairy foods. So the best advice is to experiment with low-lactose dairy foods like cheese and yoghurt, and include milk in hot drinks and cooked dishes, for example in sauces, puddings, bread and mashed potato. Then, as you find the stomach upsets becoming less troublesome, increase your intake of dairy products gradually to the required four portions a day.

Here are some dietary sources of calcium, each providing approximately 250 milligrams:

- ✔ Cheese: Small chunk (30 grams)
- ✔ Custard or rice pudding: One serving (200 grams)
- ✔ Fish of a type where you can safely eat the bones (such as canned salmon, sardines and pilchards, or whitebait): One small serving (60 grams)
- ✔ Milk: ⅓ pint (200 millilitres)
- ✔ Soya milk fortified with calcium: ⅓ pint (200 millilitres)
- ✔ Soya yoghurt fortified with calcium: One and a half small cartons (200 grams)
- ✔ Tofu (soybean curd): One serving (50 grams)
- ✔ Yoghurt: One small carton (150 grams)

The following foods contain less calcium but can still contribute significantly to your intake. These portions provide 50 milligrams of calcium:

- ✔ Baked beans: One small serving (100 grams)
- ✔ Cottage cheese: 2 tablespoons (60 grams)
- ✔ Dried fig: One (30 grams)

✔ Eggs: Two small to medium eggs (90 grams)

✔ Fortified gluten-free bread: Two slices or one roll (60 grams)

✔ Green vegetables (such as broccoli, kale, watercress, green beans): One serving (100 grams)

✔ Milk and white chocolate: Treat-sized bar (25 grams)

✔ Mixed nuts: Few handfuls (65 grams)

✔ Red kidney beans: One serving (100 grams)

✔ Sesame seeds: 2 teaspoons (10 grams)

✔ Whole orange: One (200 grams)

Ensure an adequate intake of fruit and vegetables. Recent studies show that the alkaline nature of the minerals left after you digest fruit and vegetables helps to maintain the chemical balance in your body and reduce calcium loss from your bones caused by the over-production of acidic urine.

Getting enough, but not too much, vitamin D

Vitamin D helps you absorb and use calcium more efficiently. Sources of vitamin D include egg yolks, oily fish and fortified foods including margarine, milk powder and breakfast cereals.

Vitamin D is also made from the action of sunlight on your skin, but only when you expose naked skin to the sun without sunscreens. You make vitamin D only when the sun is strong enough to cast a shadow that's no taller than you. In the UK, this means only between March and October on sunny days in the daytime, not during early morning or evening. If you can get 10 to 15 minutes a day of these conditions, with your forearms, legs and chest exposed, you can build up enough vitamin D to last you through the winter, but of course that's unlikely unless you work out of doors and the UK has a sunny summer – remember those? – so don't neglect the food sources. You can't overdose on vitamin D from the sun, but avoid sunburn, by not exposing your naked skin for too long, particularly on sensitive spots such as your ears, nose, nape and shoulders.

The Department of Health now recommends taking a daily supplement of 10 micrograms of vitamin D a day if you're pregnant, breastfeeding, over 65 or get very little exposure to the sun, and 8.5 micrograms for babies and young children aged from six months to five years. However, don't exceed these amounts, because vitamin D can build up in your body and cause calcium to damage your kidneys.

If you take any supplements that include vitamin D, be sure to tot up the total amount you're taking (from the information on the label) and ensure you don't exceed 10 micrograms a day.

Following Up After Diagnosis: What to Expect from Your Healthcare Team

Coeliac disease is a lifelong condition, and successful treatment depends on your ability to follow a continuous and strict gluten-free diet. Completely removing gluten from your diet is essential in order to resolve symptoms and reduce the risk of complications, even if you had only mild (or even no) symptoms in the first place.

As a minimum, you should see a healthcare professional (such as your dietitian or doctor) at three months, six months and one year following diagnosis to check that you're sticking to the diet successfully, and to monitor your return to full health. You may undergo further blood antibody tests or another intestinal biopsy. Children and teenagers may need more frequent monitoring to check growth and to encourage them to stick to the diet.

In the longer term, you may benefit from continued, regular follow-up by a healthcare professional to monitor your overall health, weight and nutritional status, and to deal with any difficulties you experience. The policy on long-term follow-up may vary locally, but for the most effective outcome you should have access to a dietitian, specialist gastroenterologist or your GP.

Long-term compliance with the diet can be poor, and unintentional lapses can occur. Coeliacs who didn't have digestive problems before diagnosis are more likely to lapse, perhaps without realising. One study found that about a quarter of patients who believed that they remained strictly gluten-free were actually consuming up to 10 grams of gluten per day.

Continued support from a dietitian once or twice a year is useful in helping to avoid lapses and to keep you up to date with new products and advances. Dietitians can help you to choose a varied and well-balanced diet, with adequate calories (especially from carbohydrate), fibre, calcium, iron and B vitamins, and to ensure that you're obtaining sufficient food on prescription. (You can find more information on prescription foods in Chapter 4.) For this reason, more and more patients receive their follow-ups at specialist dietitian-led clinics. You should be referred to a specialist, probably a gastroenterologist, if you respond poorly to the diet, lose weight, have a change in bowel habits, abdominal pain or abnormal blood test results, or have other symptoms you're worried about.

Looking forward

You may be wondering whether any other treatments for coeliac disease are on the horizon besides a gluten-free diet. The answer is yes, but they're still on the far-distant horizon, being researched and trialled, so aren't likely to arrive in your local pharmacy or surgery just yet, and certainly aren't to be tried at home. Several lines of enquiry are underway:

✔ Treating food with enzymes to pre-digest the gluten before it's eaten and to block the body's inflammatory response to it.

✔ Treating mixtures of wheat and gluten-free flours with the bacteria that ferment sourdough, and taking certain friendly bacteria in food, rather like probiotics, to reduce inflammation.

✔ Taking enzymes by mouth to modify the digestion of small amounts of gluten to make the gluten less harmful.

✔ Taking special peptides by mouth to make the gut lining less porous and therefore more able to withstand small amounts of gluten.

✔ A vaccine to desensitise coeliacs to the fractions of gluten that cause the problem.

✔ The development of drugs to inhibit or block the immune response.

✔ The cultivation of new wheat strains that don't produce the same immune response.

If successful and safe for long-term use, some of these approaches would mean that you'd be able to eat gluten-containing foods again, or at least that you could avoid severe symptoms if you'd eaten a tiny amount of gluten by mistake.

Even if you're coping well with your coeliac disease, attending at least an annual review is a good idea. The review ensures that you remain aware of all the latest developments in the field. Your care can also be tailored to your circumstances as they change – for example, during illness, pregnancy or after the menopause in women. A recent survey showed that current follow-up arrangements can be variable, with 38 per cent of coeliacs receiving no follow-up care. Of those who did, nearly all found the visit had a positive impact and was useful. The preferred method of follow-up was with a dietitian, with a doctor being available if required.

Part II

Digging Deeper into Living Gluten-Free

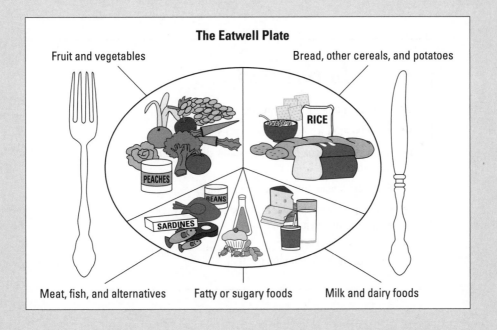

The Eatwell Plate

Fruit and vegetables

Bread, other cereals, and potatoes

RICE

PEACHES

BEANS

SARDINES

Meat, fish, and alternatives   Fatty or sugary foods   Milk and dairy foods

Go to www.dummies.com/extras/livingglutenfreeuk for online bonus content.

In this part . . .

✔ Discover gluten-free grains for everyday use.

✔ Obtain gluten-free products on prescription.

✔ Know what to look for on labels and symbols on food packaging.

✔ Find help online and in your community.

✔ Get to grips with the glycaemic index and glycaemic load to keep your health in check.

✔ Go to `www.dummies.com/extras/livinggluten freeuk` for online bonus content.

Chapter 4

Grasping the Ground Rules of the Gluten-Free Diet

*W*hether you're brand new to the world of gluten-freedom or an old hand who's been gluten-free for years, we hope this chapter tells you things about the gluten-free diet that may surprise you.

The essence of the diet sounds so easy: gluten is in wheat, rye and barley – so just avoid those foods, right? If the diet were that simple, we'd feel happy signing off right now, and this chapter would be finished. Unfortunately, things aren't quite that straightforward, thanks to the complexities of food manufacturing and catering, and the presence of ingredients and additives derived from wheat, rye and barley in foods you wouldn't expect to contain them. Because these grains are so commonplace in the UK (particularly wheat), they often get into other foods being prepared in the same factory or kitchen.

The good news is that the list of things you can eat is a lot longer than the list of things you can't. In fact, most of the food you probably eat already is naturally free from gluten. Yes, you're going to have to say goodbye to gluten-containing pizza, along with your usual bread, biscuits, cakes, pasta, beer and sausages too, but – and we stress this point – only the gluten-loaded brands that you're currently used to. Luckily, you'll find plenty of delicious and healthy alternatives. The range of foods you can eat is getting bigger and bigger every week as manufacturers hurry to launch gluten-free foods and quietly remove gluten from products that don't really need it.

You'll come to know the world of incredible gluten-free foods that can take the place of your old favourites. You'll find them in the shops and online, and many are available to you on prescription if you're diagnosed with coeliac disease. You can enjoy a whole range of naturally gluten-free cereals and starchy ingredients – some of which you may never have heard of before. And you'll probably find yourself exploring a wider variety of foods from around the world, especially from countries where wheat has never been a staple. So, if you think *buckwheat* is a type of wheat or *sorghum* is what you get when you break in a new toothbrush, now's the time to find out more about the wonderful choices available to you on your gluten-free diet.

Don't be discouraged if you find the diet a little confusing at first. For some people, discovering what's allowed and what isn't on a gluten-free diet requires an entirely different mindset, but experience comes with time. Whether you're a 1 or a 10 on the 'I'm-totally-confused-by-this-diet' scale, this chapter is vital reading because it establishes basic gluten-free guidelines. We outline what is and isn't gluten-free and why you sometimes have to question a product. We introduce you to gluten-free alternatives and talk about non-food items that you may or may not need to be concerned about, such as alcoholic drinks, medicines and non-consumable products like play-dough.

When In Doubt, Leave It Out

We can say unequivocally that at some point you're sure to wonder whether a product is gluten-free. You're at a restaurant or party and you have no idea what's in the food, no list of ingredients is provided, and your waiter or host doesn't seem sure. You don't want to make a fuss, and you don't have your handy copy of *Living Gluten-Free For Dummies* nearby, so you may be tempted to make assumptions that can cause problems.

If you're not sure whether something is safe to eat, don't risk it. If you need a reminder of what you're doing to your body when you eat gluten, take a look at Chapter 2, which talks about associated conditions and serious complications that can develop if you have gluten sensitivity or coeliac disease and eat gluten, even from time to time in small amounts.

Even if your symptoms are mild or absent, the damage gluten causes – even tiny amounts of gluten – can be severe. You're a lot better off being safe than sorry, so follow our common-sense rule: when in doubt, leave it out.

Defining Gluten So You Can Avoid It

You need to know what gluten is so you can avoid it. The definition of this term is so convoluted that offering a technically correct definition of gluten is difficult, but we're going to try.

Gluten is a storage protein found in the endosperm – or food supply of a seed – of wheat. Technically, gluten comes from wheat and only wheat. Gluten is what gives wheat flour, especially 'strong' flour, its elastic qualities when you knead dough. This elastic property traps the carbon dioxide gas that's released when yeast ferments or baking powder is activated, allowing bread and cakes to rise. Gluten also gives the chewy texture to foods such as bagels and crumpets.

At some point in our past, someone made the association between wheat (specifically gluten) and coeliac disease. Soon, doctors realised that barley and rye make people with coeliac disease ill too, and the habit of calling the proteins in all three cereals 'gluten' stuck. It's not scientifically correct, but it works in practice. For the purposes of this book, we stick with it too.

Prolamins is the collective name for the group of storage proteins present in a variety of grains, and they're what cause problems for people who can't eat 'gluten'. Technically, gluten is made up of the proteins glutenin and alpha gliadin, a specific type of prolamin in wheat. However, gluten has become a general term for any kind of potentially harmful prolamins. The prolamins that cause damage to people with gluten-related disorders include alpha gliadin (in wheat), secalin (in rye) and hordein (in barley). You find prolamins in other grains too – zein (in maize or corn), avenin (in oats) and orzenin (in rice) – but these prolamins aren't toxic to people with gluten intolerances, probably as a result of the different amounts of amino acids, specifically the proline content.

Wheat-free doesn't mean gluten-free. Something can be wheat-free and still contain, for instance, rye flour, so it's not gluten-free. Some gluten-free foods contain wheat starch but the toxic fraction – the gluten – has been removed right down to a level below an agreed safe standard.

Discovering What Is and Isn't Gluten-Free

The reason the gluten-free diet can seem cumbersome at first is that gluten-containing cereals, particularly wheat and barley, are so common in the Western diet. In fact, wheat is the number one staple food in the UK, and food manufacturers use it in a great many products, either as the major component, as in pasta and bread, or as a minor one, as in battered fish and sauces. The word 'flour' in the UK means wheat flour, in law. Millers don't have to put the word 'wheat' onto the front of the bag but can simply describe the products as 'flour', usually with a description such as 'self-raising', 'strong white' or 'wholemeal'. Additionally, many processed foods can contain ingredients and additives that raise questions.

Luckily, our labelling regulations mean that food packs must include in the ingredients list the name of any cereal that contains gluten. The gluten in these cereals is a problem for so many people throughout Europe that it's one of only a dozen or so allergens that food suppliers must declare if it's in the food. You won't always see the word 'gluten'. It's the cereals that contain it that must be declared and highlighted, according to new laws coming in over the next few years. You'll find that reading labels gets easier then, because the cereal names will be highlighted in the ingredients list. You can find more detail on food labelling in Chapter 5.

Breaking foods down into those that usually have gluten and those that don't isn't too difficult. Bear in mind that the lists we provide in this chapter are only intended to get you started. The *Food and Drink Directory* produced by Coeliac UK is really the bible for anyone following a gluten-free diet. This annually produced booklet is sent to members of the charity each year, or you can simply buy it from them. It lists thousands of foods that don't contain gluten from a range of brands and retailers. Always use an up-to-date version, because manufacturers have an annoying habit of changing the ingredients in their products. If you're thinking that surely things can't change that often, read on. We selected a month at random and found 35 new products that were added to the directory and 15 modified products that were no longer suitable for the gluten-free diet. It pays to check! You can access monthly updates via the Coeliac UK website or receive them via a monthly e-newsletter. You can also source them via the Coeliac UK Helpline, or even via good old Royal Mail (if you send a self-addressed envelope to Coeliac UK). Visit www.coeliac.org.uk for full details.

Where, in this book, we talk about cereals, we don't mean breakfast cereals but the seeds of edible grassy crops like wheat, rye, barley, oats, maize (corn), millet, sorghum and rice. The cereals are all members of the Gramineae family, which has about 9,000 species, very few of which are cultivated for human consumption of the seeds.

Out: Five forbidden grains

We're not starting with the forbidden grains just to be negative – we're starting with them because the list is a lot shorter than the list of those you can eat, let alone that of the huge range of non-cereal foods that are okay for you.

Here are the only grains you need to avoid on a gluten-free diet:

✔ Wheat, which means any *Triticum* species, and includes kamut and spelt

✔ Barley

✔ Oats, unless labelled gluten-free (see the sidebar 'Notes on oats', later in the chapter)

✔ Rye

✔ Triticale (a hybrid of wheat and rye)

You need to double-check any product with the word *wheat* in its name. This includes hydrolysed wheat protein, wheat starch, wheatgerm and so on:

✔ **Wheatgrass**, like all grasses, is gluten-free. (But see the nearby sidebar 'Grasses, sprouted grains and wheat berries' to make sure that you're not dealing with contamination. Hey, we know it's confusing; don't shoot the messenger!)

✔ **Wheat starch** is not normally gluten-free. But, in the UK, a special type called, rather mysteriously, Codex wheat starch is allowed in the manufacture of gluten-free foods. It enables these products to resemble standard foods closely in both texture and taste, making it easier for you to stick to your gluten-free diet. The Codex standard is internationally recognised to mean that the gluten content has been reduced to a trace level so as not to cause problems in the majority of people with gluten intolerance. As far as we know, in the UK, Codex wheat starch is used only in flour mixes and baked goods on prescription. When you see 'wheat starch' in the ingredients list of foods that are not labelled gluten-free, it means the manufacturer isn't using Codex wheat starch or testing for gluten, so such foods are not safe for you to eat.

✔ **Wheat glucose syrup** is safe, because all the gluten has been removed.

Wheat has several names and varieties, and all varieties contain gluten. Beware of aliases such as bulgur (or bulgar), semolina, spelt, durum, kamut, farina, cous cous, emmer, einkorn, dinkel, rusk, poulard, atta, breadcrumbs, pourgouri, club wheat and bran. You'll also find other varieties of wheat in ethnic food shops such as Polish, Vavilova, oriental, macha and several more. These products are often labelled in foreign languages, but they should still carry an English label stating that they're a type of wheat. As usual, our advice is: when in doubt, leave it out.

Spelt is often marketed as a wheat alternative, but it's definitely a type of wheat and not even remotely gluten-free.

Mulling over 'may contain' labels

You often see labels that state either 'May contain gluten' or 'Made in a factory that handles gluten', although less frequently these days. This is intended as a useful warning to consumers, but how are you supposed to judge whether the food actually contains gluten? And you have the worry that they're really telling you this to protect themselves, not you.

In the UK, a code of practice (not a law) encourages manufacturers to conduct a proper and realistic assessment of the risk of gluten being present and only declare that a food may contain it if a risk really exists. Statements about gluten being handled in the factory are frowned upon but still crop up here and there. Our advice is to avoid foods labelled 'May contain gluten' or 'Made in a factory that handles gluten'. For more on labelling, see Chapter 5.

Out: Foods made from gluten-containing grains

Obviously, foods that are made from one of the five gluten-loaded grains contain gluten and therefore aren't suitable on a gluten-free diet. We list the more common ones here, along with a few foods you may not have thought about but that are off the menu for you. We're thinking here of mainstream foods, and luckily, almost all of them have a gluten-free alternative on offer. A huge range of gluten-free foods is in the shops and online, both in the free-from section and in other categories, plus many on prescription. We explore these later in this chapter. Meanwhile, you should assume that the following foods contain gluten unless otherwise identified:

- Bagels
- Barley water
- Batter, pancakes and Yorkshire puddings
- Beer, lager and stout, including Guinness
- Bread and rolls, including white, brown, wholemeal, mixed grain and rye
- Biscuits and cookies
- Breakfast cereals
- Cakes, including sponges, doughnuts, muffins, scones, brownies, buns and other baked goods
- Confectionery (some of it anyway, including liquorice, chocolates and bars with wafers and biscuit pieces)

Crackers and crispbreads

Croissants and Danish pastries

Croutons

Crumpets

Flatbreads, including naan, chapattis, parathas, pittas and poppadoms

Flour, including white, plain, self-raising, wholemeal, barley flour, rye flour

Frozen chips and potato wedges with batter coating

Ice-cream cones and cornets

Imitation seafood sticks (for example, crabsticks)

Marinades and thickened sauces

Mincemeat

Mixes for cakes, breads and pancakes

Muesli and muesli products, such as bars and flapjacks

Made-up English mustard

Oats, oatcakes and oatmeal, unless labelled gluten-free (see the sidebar 'Notes on oats')

Pasta and noodles (dried, fresh and canned)

Pastry (all types, pies and tarts both savoury and sweet, crumbles)

Pizzas and pizza bases

Pretzels, some savoury snacks and dry-roasted nuts

Sauces and sauce mixes, gravy

Sausages and other manufactured meat products, such as rissoles, haggis and faggots

Soft tortillas and wraps

Some soups

Soy sauce

Stock cubes, bouillon, spice mixes and rubs

Stuffing and stuffing mix

Suet

Vending machine hot chocolate, malted milk drinks, coffee essence and coffee substitutes made from barley

Wafers (communion and ice-cream)

Waffles

Grasses, sprouted grains and wheat berries

Grasses such as wheatgrass and barley grass, frequently sold in health-food stores and at juice bars, are gluten-free. The grass hasn't yet formed the gluten-containing seeds that cause problems in people with coeliac disease. Be careful, though, of grasses that are an ingredient in a product. They may be contaminated with cereal seeds, and because you don't know for sure, you can't risk eating them.

Avoid sprouted grains, because the grain is still attached and you don't know how much of the storage gluten has been used for growth and how much remains in the plant. Wheat berries are wheatgrass seeds and they're definitely not safe. Remember the common-sense rule we refer to in this chapter: when in doubt, leave it out.

In: Gluten-free cereals, seeds and starches

You can include a large choice of gluten-free grains and starches in your diet (You can find more about these foods and how to use them in the section 'Exploring Gluten-Free Cereals and Starchy Foods'). Even if you've been gluten-free for years, we're guessing some of these may be new to you:

Amaranth

Arrowroot

Buckwheat (and kasha)

Carob

Chestnut (fresh, flour and puree)

Chickpeas (fresh, dried and tinned, ceci flour, garbanzos)

Chana dal (gram and gram flour, besan, Bengal gram dal)

Coconut (fresh, creamed, dried or desiccated, or as cream, milk or flour)

Cocoyam (elephant's ear plant)

Corn or maize (cornflour, polenta, cornstarch, cornmeal, corn kernels, sweetcorn)

Kuzu root

Lupin (whole, dried, boiled, flour)

Millet (whole and cracked grains, flakes, flour)

Nuts and peanuts (fresh, roasted, flaked, chopped, ground)

Oats (only if pure and labelled gluten-free; see the sidebar 'Notes on oats')

Plantain (fresh, flour)

Potato (fresh, flour, starch, plain crisps)

Psyllium husk

Pulses (peas, beans and lentils, and their flours, starches and dahls)

Quinoa

Rice (dried, brown and white flour, ground rice, flakes, rice bran)

Sago

Sorghum (white sorghum, cholam, juwar, juwari)

Soya (fresh, dried, frozen or tinned, or as bean curd, bran, textured vegetable protein or flour)

Starchy fruits and vegetables (banana, sweet potato, carrots, pumpkin, squash, parsnip, beetroot, broccoli stalks, aubergine, courgette)

Sugar beet fibre

Tapioca (cassava, manioc)

Teff (white and brown, raji)

Yams (fresh, dried and pounded)

Notes on oats

Experts have debated whether to include oats in the gluten-free diet for years, and recently some clear-cut answers have emerged. For most people on a gluten-free diet, oats are a useful additional cereal that's readily available, familiar, popular, versatile and not too expensive. We know that people desperately want to include oats in their gluten-free diet. However, oats contain proteins that are similar to those in gluten in other cereals, and most commercially available oats aren't guaranteed to be pure. They're often contaminated with up to 15 per cent of other cereals that were grown nearby or harvested, stored or milled with the same equipment. These contaminating cereals caused problems for coeliacs, so oats were considered unsuitable.

We now know from clinical trials that around 95 per cent of coeliacs can in fact tolerate oats very well, even eating them daily, as long as the oats are free from other contaminating sources of gluten. Manufacturers can now legally label oats as gluten-free provided they've been tested to ensure they really are. Gluten-free oats are available in the shops and on prescription, and they're used in food products including muesli, flapjacks and oatcakes.

When you're newly diagnosed, we advise avoiding oats altogether until your gut has healed, your blood antibodies have returned to normal and any symptoms have subsided. This could take six months or longer. Then you can introduce gluten-free oats, watch for any symptoms and have your blood tested again to ensure you're not among the small percentage of people who can't tolerate oats. Discussing this subject with informed healthcare professionals is always worthwhile, and they'll help you with the monitoring.

In: Other foods that are naturally gluten-free

Step into any large supermarket and look around. Most of the foods and drinks you see are naturally gluten-free and safe for you to eat. That's as long as they're in their plain and unprocessed forms. So, for example, meat is naturally gluten-free, but most sausages, casseroles and pies aren't, because they have added wheat. You won't see 'gluten-free' on the label of a naturally gluten-free product, and the *Food and Drink Directory* doesn't list such products, because that would make the list too long; but trust us, these foods in their plain, unadulterated forms don't contain gluten:

Baking aids, including bicarbonate of soda, cream of tartar, arrowroot, food colourings, flavouring essences and extracts, glycerine, yeast, xanthan and guar gums (but not all baking powder brands)

Cocoa powder, drinking chocolate

Dairy products, including milk, cheese, yoghurt, buttermilk, cream and milk powder

Eggs

Fats, including butter, margarine, lard, ghee and oils

Fish and seafood

Fruit, juice, pressés, smoothies, fruit drinks, squash (except barley water) and cordials

Herbs

Meat and poultry

Non-cereal seeds (such as sesame, pinenuts, sunflower seeds, linseed, poppy seeds and hemp)

Nuts

Pulses (all the peas, beans and lentils): dried, canned, fresh, frozen, in or out of the pods

Salt, pepper and monosodium glutamate (sea salt, peppercorns)

Spices (including cumin, cinnamon, nutmeg, caraway, coriander, turmeric, mustard seeds, aniseed, paprika, chilli)

Soft drinks (except barley water and shandy)

Sugar, sweeteners, jam, marmalade, honey, golden syrup, treacle, jelly, molasses, gelatine, agar, carrageenan, glucose syrup, pectin

Tea, coffee (fresh or instant), herbal teas

Vegetables, salad crops

Vinegars, including malt vinegar

Yeast extract

Exploring Gluten-Free Cereals And Starchy Foods

When people come to consider cereals beyond wheat and rice, many don't know their amaranth from their arrowroot. Actually, you can find a huge range of gluten-free cereals and starchy foods out there to replace the wheat, rye and barley products you used to eat. Many of these are both delicious and nutritious, and they all have their place in making your diet complete and well balanced and your food as appetising as ever – perhaps even more so. Now's your chance to try some of these alternatives and discover an entirely new world of gluten-free foods.

For years, rumours have spread that some of these alternative foods aren't gluten-free. Although some people may have had reactions to these foods (as they would to nuts, soya or other allergens or foods to which they have sensitivity), it's not a reaction to gluten. But regardless of whether a food contains gluten, if it makes you ill, don't eat it!

Amaranth

Amaranth isn't a true cereal grain at all but a relative of the ornamental flower called cockscomb or plume plant. Loaded with fibre, iron, calcium and other vitamins and minerals, amaranth is also high in essential amino acids and so is an excellent source of protein. Small and bead-like, the seeds of amaranth aren't only good for you but also delicious, with a pleasant peppery and hearty nutty flavour.

Amaranth can be toasted, which gives it extra flavour. You can even 'pop' whole amaranth like popcorn to add crunchiness to homemade bread, salads, soup and muesli. You can also boil the seeds and eat them like porridge, or as a starch with meals. Amaranth flour makes good bread and acts as a thickener for gravies, soups and stews. Sprouted amaranth goes well in salads and sandwiches.

Arrowroot

Arrowroot is a fine white powder similar to cornflour. The translucent paste has no flavour and sets to an almost clear gel. You can use arrowroot as a thickener, although it thickens at a lower temperature than cornflour and its consistency doesn't hold as long after cooking.

Buckwheat

The fact that buckwheat is gluten-free often confuses people; after all, buckwheat has the word 'wheat' right there in the name. But buckwheat isn't even related to wheat; in fact, it's not even a true cereal grain but the seed of a plant in the dock family. High in essential amino acids, which the body doesn't make for itself, buckwheat is closer to being a source of biologically valuable protein than many other plants. It's also high in B vitamins as well as minerals, and a good source of linoleic acid, an essential fatty acid.

Whole buckwheat is naturally dried and has a delicate nutty flavour and unusual pyramidal shape that makes it a good stand-in for rice or pasta. Buckwheat seed may be sold crushed and hulled under the name of saracen corn. The whole seeds can be eaten raw and need very little cooking, during which they stay crunchy, so you can use them as a topping on baked or pan-fried fish or chicken. When buckwheat is roasted, it's called kasha and has a rich colour and flavour. Cooks and bakers often use buckwheat flour in pancakes, blinis, biscuits and muffins – but be aware that it's almost always in combination with wheat flour, so shop-bought and restaurant versions of these foods contain gluten, even though the labels may describe them as 'buckwheat pancakes' for example. It's the same with the Japanese noodle known as soba, which is made from buckwheat but often with wheat flour.

Carob

Carob comes from a Mediterranean tree, a member of the pea and bean family. The trees may be male, female or both at once, but only female trees produce fruit pods. These begin life as bright-green pods and ripen to a dark brown.

Carob pods can be roasted and ground to produce flour, which is rich in fibre, natural sugars, vitamins and minerals. You can use carob in baking alongside other gluten-free flours and as a dairy-free alternative to chocolate.

Chestnut

A familiar smell on Christmas shopping trips is roasting chestnuts, and you'll have seen them as *marrons glacés* in French and Swiss cuisine. Chestnuts are available whole, fresh, roasted, dried and ground into flour, and cooked and pureed in tins. You can even pick them up in late summer and autumn in most British parks and fields, if you can get to them before the squirrels do.

You must cook chestnuts, and in gluten-free cooking it's the puree and flour you're most likely to use. The flour is largely starch and a touch heavy in cakes on its own, so mix it with other gluten-free flours like rice flour and fine cornmeal. It's great in fruit cakes like carrot cake and banana loaf. The puree is a useful addition to fillings for desserts, usually with whipped cream.

By the way, water chestnuts aren't the same thing, although they're also gluten-free. They're a crisp, white vegetable popular in Chinese cooking, served raw or boiled and also ground into flour to make water chestnut cake, which features in dim sum.

Chickpeas and chana dal

These two pulses are different varieties of the same plant, chickpeas being larger, paler in colour and containing less fibre than chana dal. Chickpeas are known as garbanzo beans and ceci, and are widely eaten whole and ground into a paste in hummus. Flour milled from chickpeas – farina di ceci – is creamy in colour, light and fine in texture, and suitable for baking. Gram flour, milled from chana dal, is pale yellow and a little stickier and heavier than chickpea flour. It's commonly used in Middle Eastern, North African and Indian cooking, and is rich in protein and fibre. It has a beany flavour, making it most suitable for savoury dishes such as falafels, bhajis and pakoras.

A small amount of gram or chickpea flour added to gluten-free flour mixes for pastry makes it deliciously crisp and golden-brown. Look for a gluten-free declaration on the pack to ensure it's been tested, because these products are often milled in small factories alongside gluten-containing cereals.

Coconut

Coconut is widely used in South East Asian savoury meals to enrich and thicken sauces. It's high in saturated fat, so you need to use it sparingly. We find that a resealable pack of coconut powder in the kitchen lasts for ages and doesn't separate or go rancid. These packs let you whip up a quick sauce with just a tablespoon or two of powder mixed into water and the other ingredients, so you use less coconut and get less fat than you would if you opened a pack of coconut milk or cream and used the lot. You can also buy coconut flour for baking. This is coarser than the powder and not as good in sauces.

Cocoyam

This is an interesting flour from Africa and the Caribbean. Its other name is elephant's ear plant, which thankfully describes the leaves of the plant. No elephants are harmed in the making of the product! Mixed with water, you can use it to make fu-fu, a starchy pillow served as part of a main meal. You can use cocoyam flour in bread and other baked goods, where it adds to the open texture and helps them to rise.

Fu-fu is so named after the sound it emits when it's made in the traditional way, in a shallow pot on the ground, kneaded by two people standing and pushing the dough alternately with long paddles. As the air escapes with each push, it makes a 'fu' sigh. You can make it more simply in a pan using a wooden spoon. We've seen claims that fu-fu itself is gluten-free, but this isn't always the case: in some countries people make it with semolina.

Kuzu root

From the mountains of South East Asia comes kuzu (also known as kudzu and kuzuku), a plant with starchy roots that yield flavourless, white granules useful for thickening liquids and making jellies. Buy organic kuzu because the plant is so invasive it's widely treated with herbicides.

Lupin

Dried lupin seeds look like yellow broad beans. They're popular in Eastern Europe in breads, in Italy as a salty snack and, increasingly, in Australia in baked goods and pasta. They're very high in protein – around 40 per cent – and low in fat, at about 7 per cent. With very little starch and lots of fibre, lupin has the lowest glycaemic index of any commonly used flour. Lupin is one of a dozen or so foods to which many people are allergic, particularly those who are allergic to peanuts, so suppliers in the UK must declare it on food labels.

Maize or corn

You may run across maize (or corn) with different names or in different forms, all of which are gluten-free. They include polenta, cornstarch, corn-flour and cornmeal – you can get both yellow and white types.

A-maize-ing grains

Maize originated in North America and dates back thousands of years. Its cultivation was a remarkable feat. Native Americans (Hopi) developed as many as 24 different kinds of maize adapted to the length of growing season, altitude, rain, sunlight and soil type. To ensure a full season's yield, the people grew both early- and late-ripening crops, and the corn came in a variety of colours.

Maize played an important role socially as well as nutritionally. A Hopi bride-to-be would grind corn for three days at her future husband's house to prove she had 'wifely skills'. At birth, a Hopi child received a special blanket and a perfect ear of corn as a welcome gift.

Early American settlers quickly came to depend on corn, which is easy to grow and store and needs little maintenance.

Christopher Columbus and Sir Walter Raleigh first brought maize to Europe.

Polenta is a doddle to make as an alternative to pasta. You can serve it simply boiled or boiled and then grilled in a flat dish, perhaps with some toppings like sliced onions or a dredging of paprika, and cut into wedges. With beaten egg, both cornmeals make a light, crispy batter on pan-fried foods. (Coat the food with the meal first, then egg, then meal again.) The batter seals the food inside so that it stays moist, it doesn't burn, so you can cook the food thoroughly, and it absorbs less fat from the pan than wheat-flour batter. What's not to like?

Cornflour (or cornstarch) is a fine white powder used to thicken sauces and custards and to bind ingredients. It's used in gluten-free flour mixes and makes cakes tender and light.

Millet

Millet is a member of the grass family with small, round, yellow grains, similar in appearance to mustard seed, which swell when cooked in water, to make a tasty alternative to cous cous. Millet is packed with B vitamins and iron, magnesium, phosphorus and potassium; it's also loaded with fibre and protein. Millet is easier to digest than many traditional grains.

You can add millet flakes to muesli and flapjacks, although you need to experiment with the other ingredients to overcome millet's dry texture. You can add millet flour to your home-baked breads for an intriguing and satisfying quality.

Millet has been a staple food in Africa and India for thousands of years, and people grew it as early as 2,700 BC in China, where it was prevalent before rice became the dominant staple. Today, millet is still a significant part of the diet in northern China, Japan and various areas of the former Soviet Union, Africa and India. Grown today in Western countries mostly for cattle and bird feed, millet is also gaining popularity as part of the human diet.

Nuts and peanuts

No doubt you're familiar with many varieties of nuts and peanuts in their whole, flaked, roasted and ground forms, but did you know that several Italian cakes rely on ground nuts instead of flour? Also, it's a common practice to thicken sauces in South East Asia with a few ground peanuts or cashews.

Oats

Do please read the sidebar 'Notes on oats' before introducing oats into your gluten-free diet. Oats are a healthy option because they can lower blood cholesterol, they're filling, they help to control blood sugar levels and help with digestion. Gluten-free oats are available whole, rolled, as pinmeal or flour. They look and taste exactly like ordinary oats. Not surprising because they're the same thing, just kept well away from other cereals and tested to ensure no gluten has slipped in. You can grind your own rolled oats to make flour, using a coffee mill or processor, but you need to do it in small batches no bigger than a cupful to avoid clogging up the blades.

Plantain

Essentially large, green, banana-like fruits, plantains are available fresh and as flour for making fu-fu (see the section 'Cocoyam' for more on fu-fu). The flour is a useful one to have at the ready for baking light, fluffy cakes, waffles, pancakes and scones.

Potatoes, potato flour and potato starch

Potatoes are edible underground tubers and were originally native to the Peruvian Andes, probably first taken to Europe in the 16th century by Spanish explorers. The popularity of the potato spread quickly in temperate climates, where it grew well.

Potatoes make useful and thrifty staples in the gluten-free diet. In addition, you can use potato flour, which is made from cooked, whole potatoes, dried and ground. Potato flour has quite a strong flavour and heavy texture, and its ability to absorb and retain moisture means that it's not appropriate on its own in baking. However, potato flour is useful in a mix with other gluten-free flours such as maize or rice flour, in recipes where the moisture-retaining properties are a bonus, for example for cakes, bread and pizza bases.

Potato starch is a fine, flavourless powder made from dehydrated raw potato. It absorbs moisture on cooking, making it useful as a thickening agent in soups, sauces and gravies.

 If you're making mashed potato, make some extra and keep it covered in the fridge, where it will keep for a few days. Use it to thicken soups, gravies and sweet or savoury sauces just by whisking in a spoonful at a time, or add it to batters for pancakes, cakes, scones, fritters or farls.

Psyllium husk

Not really a flour, but rather a useful substitute for wheat bran for boosting the fibre in anything cereal-based. You can even eat it raw sprinkled onto your breakfast cereal or blended into smoothies.

Pulses

The peas, beans and lentils won't need any introduction, so we'll just highlight to you that several of them are available as starches or flours. Pea starch in particular is a substitute for breadcrumbs and thickeners in processed foods such as sausages. This and the testing the manufacturers do make these foods gluten-free. It's great to see manufacturers taking these steps without any fanfare. It all goes to make living gluten-free much easier and opens up plenty of new options for you. The products aren't in the free-from section, so it pays to keep an eye on your former favourites, which may be reformulated to suit you at any time.

Quinoa

Quinoa (pronounced keen-wa) isn't really a grain; it's a seed of a relative of the common weed known in the UK as fat hen. The American National Academy of Sciences describes quinoa as 'the most nearly perfect source of protein from the vegetable kingdom'.

Because the uncooked seeds are coated with saponins – sticky, bitter-tasting stuff that acts as a natural insect repellant – you need to rinse quinoa thoroughly before cooking. Most quinoa that you buy has already been rinsed or hulled, and it's available as flour, grains and flakes. It has a subtle cabbage-like taste, so is probably best mixed with other flours if you're adding it to anything sweet.

People in the South American Andes have cultivated quinoa since at least 3,000 BC. Ancient Incas called this annual plant 'the mother grain' because it is self-perpetuating and ever-bearing. They honoured it as a sacred food, because a steady diet appeared to ensure a full, long life. The Inca ruler himself planted the first row of quinoa each season with a golden spade.

Rice and rice flour

Rice is believed to be the oldest cultivated grain and is a staple of many cultures throughout the world. Indeed, it grows on every continent. All types of rice are gluten-free, including wild rice. Even so-called 'glutinous' rice doesn't contain gluten! It's a sweet, high-starch, short-grain variety, available whole and ground. It thickens sauces and desserts in Asian cooking and is often the rice used in sushi and Chinese dumplings.

Rice flour can be white (ground from polished rice) or brown (ground from the grain without the very fibrous outer husk). Both types are available on prescription. Rice flour is easy to digest and is commonly used in Indian cooking for puddings, biscuits and the Southern Indian pancakes known as idlis and dosas. White rice flour is often the basis of gluten-free flour mixes. You'll find white rice flour is the better bet for sauces, because it behaves very similarly to wheat flour, whereas brown rice flour is great for baking.

Rice bran is a useful source of gluten-free fibre and originates from the outer layer of the rice seed. Rice noodles, sticks and Italian rice pasta are delicious alternatives to wheat noodles and pasta. Actually, the Asian rice noodles and sticks are more authentic in some dishes and they're easy to prepare: they only need a few minutes soaking in hot water.

Sago

Sago is extracted from the pith inside the trunk of the sago palm tree, *Metroxylon sagu*, also known as the tree of a thousand uses – 1,001 if you count providing another food for a gluten-free diet. It's a staple in the diet of many people around the Pacific and Indian Oceans. Sago is high in carbohydrate and a reasonable source of fibre, vitamins and minerals. Locals bake the flour into bread, pancakes and even noodles, but we're more familiar with it as the coarse pearls, rather like tapioca, used in milk puddings.

Sorghum

Sorghum is one of the oldest known grains – though it's not a true cereal grain – and it's been a major staple of nutrition in Africa and India for centuries. Sorghum is generating excitement as a gluten-free source of insoluble fibre. The body digests the protein and starch in sorghum more slowly than that of other cereals, and it's high in iron, calcium and potassium.

Sorghum is now the world's fifth most widely grown cereal and third in the USA after wheat and maize. You can find it online as white sorghum, certified gluten-free, and as a component in some gluten-free mixes. We predict it will soon be available in the free-from section of major supermarkets. It's also available as cholam or juwar flours in ethnic food shops, but you'll need to check with the millers as to whether they also mill wheat at the same facility, because these aren't tested and labelled gluten-free as yet. These flours are a little darker than the white sorghum. Fans of white sorghum enjoy its bland flavour and light colour, which don't alter the taste or look of foods when you use it in place of wheat flour.

Soya beans

Although soya beans are pulses, we're treating them separately because they're available in a much wider range of versions than other beans. Soya beans and most ingredients derived from them are naturally gluten-free. Textured soy protein has long been a vegetarian alternative to meat, and now bean curd, soya bran and soya flour are widely available in the UK. Soy sauce, however, continues to be thickened with wheat flour in China, and so it's not suitable for you. Neither are any of the Chinese sauces that contain soy sauce, such as hoisin. Luckily, tamari, which is a type of soy sauce from Japan, is gluten-free, and several brands of gluten-free Chinese soy sauce are now on sale.

Starchy fruits and vegetables

As with potatoes, several fruits and vegetables make good thickeners for sauces and ingredients in cakes and puddings. Carrot cake is well known, and you can make similar cakes with pumpkin, beetroot or sweet potato.

Aubergine and courgette make filling additions to pasta sauces, omelettes, salads and quiches. Parsnip and broccoli are two of the simplest soups to make because they both thicken when cooked and blended. Although they're not starchy, tomatoes perform a similar function and add intense flavour if you use puree or sun-dried versions. And all these help you achieve your five a day.

Sugar beet fibre

As the name suggests, sugar beet fibre is the fibre extracted from sugar beet pulp once the sugar has been removed. It's free from gluten and has an especially good balance of insoluble fibre, which helps alleviate constipation, and soluble fibre, which can help lower cholesterol levels.

Tapioca

Tapioca is the dried and treated starch extracted from the inner root of the cassava or manioc plant. Cassava is widely grown as a staple crop throughout Central and South America, Africa and the West Indies, because it produces a high crop yield even in relatively poor soils. Tapioca is available as flakes, flour, starch or white pearls. The flour is used in mixes along with other gluten-free flours such as rice and potato. The pearls are virtually flavourless and so combine well with a range of other cooking flavours. Generally, they need soaking, but on cooking they swell and become transparent – anyone remember frogspawn at school lunch? You can use tapioca in puddings, soups and casseroles to give texture and body.

Teff

Brown and white teff flours are really useful additions to the gluten-free store cupboard. We say flours, although really these are the intact whole grains of teff, which are so tiny that about 150 of them take up the same space as just one grain of wheat. Both types have a lovely flavour, pleasing toasty colour and work perfectly in all manner of baked goods. They're both available on prescription and if you scout about in health food shops and online. You may see raji in ethnic shops, which comes from the same plant, but this is unlikely to be tested or labelled as gluten-free.

Getting into gums

Gums, such as xanthan (pronounced 'zanthan') gum and guar gum, contain no gluten. They're used frequently in processed foods such as sauces and salad dressings, as emulsifiers and stabilisers. They're also really useful in home-cooked gluten-free baked goods, offering the elastic texture, softness and volume in baking that you usually get from gluten. Gums are also added to some commercially available gluten-free mixes.

Xanthan is made by fermenting sugar with a friendly bacterium, *Xanthomonas campestris*. The gum is later pasteurised to kill the bacteria. Guar is extracted from the seeds of the locust bean, a leguminous shrub that normally grows in India.

Many health-food shops stock these gums as powders, which dissolve in water, and you can add them to flour. For some people, guar gum may have a slight laxative effect.

Yam

Yams are tubers, somewhat similar in appearance to sweet potatoes. They come in various sizes and in colours from white to orange. You can cook them like potatoes, including frying, boiling and baking. For the gluten-free cook, an exciting arrival in the shops is pounded yam. This is a creamy white flour, somewhere between white rice flour and cornmeal – very slightly grainy, but light and free-flowing enough to give a soft, tender and airy texture to gluten-free baked goods.

Maybe: Checking Up on Certain Foods

The diet gets a little trickier when it comes to processed foods which are made from several different ingredients and during multiple manufacturing stages. Here, we look at processed foods you should question and those you don't have to worry about.

Knowing which foods to question

Some processed foods often but don't always contain gluten. These include:

- ✓ Baking powder
- ✓ Blended seasonings and curry powder blends

✔ Gravy mix and browning

✔ Quorn, a meat substitute made from mycoprotein (gluten-free but either coated in or contaminated with gluten-containing ingredients)

✔ Ready-made mustard

✔ Soy sauce

✔ Stock cubes and bouillon powder

Putting an end to the controversy over certain foods

People used to question certain foods which were on the 'have-to-dig-deeper-to-make-sure-this-is-gluten-free' list. They were questioned because of rumours, misinformation and misunderstanding, or even ambiguous labelling laws. But today, thanks to new laws and more definitive research, the following ingredients are no longer in question – we know they *are* gluten-free:

Alcohol (distilled)

Artificial sweeteners

Balsamic vinegar

Bicarbonate of soda

Caramel

Citric acid

Coconut cream/coconut milk

Cream of tartar

Dextrin, dextrose, glucose syrup and maltodextrin (may be derived from wheat, but refined to contain negligible gluten)

Fish sauce

Gelatine

Hydrolysed vegetable protein (HVP)

Isomalt

Mixed herbs, mixed spice

Modified maize starch, modified starch

Monoglycerides and diglycerides

Monosodium glutamate

Potato or rice starch

Rice malt or corn malt

Rice rusk

Textured vegetable protein

Vanilla and vanilla extract

Vinegar, including malt vinegar

Xanthan gum

Yeast (except brewer's yeast)

The gluten-free status of these ingredients applies to those on sale in the EU. Countries outside the EU may have different manufacturing processes and labelling rules.

Getting Gluten-Free Food on Prescription

After you have a diagnosis of coeliac disease, or the closely related condition dermatitis herpetiformis, a range of gluten-free alternatives to your everyday staple foods are easily available on prescription. The range in the UK is excellent and has greatly improved the ability of people with coeliac disease to follow a strict gluten-free diet. A recent study of over 1,000 adults in the UK shows that those who receive regular gluten-free products on prescription lapse much less frequently than those who don't. Getting these products on prescription may help you stick to your diet, and is certainly cheaper and easier than buying them individually.

Prescription foods are only for the patient and not for anyone else. So if you cook for a coeliac as well as others, you need plenty of naturally gluten-free and free-from foods on hand, particularly flour mixes and pasta, for making one big dish for everyone.

Getting your gluten-free products on prescription

In most parts of the UK, the GP writes and signs each prescription. Most people find that getting a monthly repeat prescription is easiest. Some surgeries require notice for repeat prescriptions or any changes to the prescription, so thinking ahead helps. We suggest having all the products you like listed on the system at the surgery in suitable quantities, so that you can simply tick your choices on the repeat slip. Your pharmacist may be able to deal with repeat prescriptions by getting the order sent directly to the pharmacy, but will need some notice if you're requesting something new.

England is the only part of the UK where prescriptions aren't free for everyone, and here you're exempt from the charges if you're under 16, over 60, pregnant, on certain benefits or have certain health conditions. People with coeliac disease aren't exempt from the charges in England. You pay a prescription fee for each different line on each prescription – a line can be several packs of the same product. For example, six loaves of bread and four packets of pasta would be two lines with two fees to pay.

Using a pre-payment certificate may be cheaper if you choose more than one line per month. You can include any drugs you're prescribed at no extra charge. You can buy a certificate quarterly or annually for a fixed fee and pay for an annual one in ten monthly instalments. Ask your pharmacist or visit the NHS website at www.nhsbsa.nhs.uk/ppc for details.

Appreciating the range of prescribable products

You can find a full list of all the gluten-free foods on prescription at the front of the *Food and Drink Directory* produced by Coeliac UK, and on their website (www.coeliac.org.uk). The range extends to over 200 products.

Changes are underway to the prescription guidelines, due to the wide availability of gluten-free foods by other means and the NHS's need to cut costs. Prescriptions are supposed to be for items that are necessary for health. Because you can't seriously argue that sweet biscuits and cake mixes are strictly necessary, Coeliac UK no longer supports these being available on prescription, and GPs only prescribe them in exceptional circumstances. It's up to your GP to decide how much food and which ones to allow on prescription.

Several primary care trusts are trialling pharmacy-led prescribing in order to free up GPs' time. If you live in one of these trial areas, your pharmacist will explain the system to you, and you'll probably find it more convenient than popping into and out of the surgery. However, the pharmacist isn't a doctor and can't discuss your symptoms or treatment. You must still go to your doctor for that.

The range of prescribable products includes:

Bread – loaves, rolls, baguettes (fresh, part-baked or vacuum packed; white, brown, high fibre, multigrain or wheat-free)

Crackers and crispbreads, including plain, flavoured and high-fibre

Flour, including plain, white, self-raising, brown, high-fibre

Oats and breakfast cereals

Pasta, including tagliatelle, macaroni, lasagne, penne, spaghetti

Pizza mix and bases

Bread and flour mixes for home cooking

Most manufacturers offer taster packs or samples of their products so you can try them before you decide which ones to order on a regular basis. Products vary considerably, so experimenting to find the ones you like is worthwhile.

The availability of fresh bread delivered directly to the pharmacist has revolutionised gluten-free eating and led to an improved diet for many people with coeliac disease. In one recent survey of adults who switched from longlife to fresh gluten-free bread, over two-thirds said they had increased their consumption of bread, and 65 per cent of them were eating eight or more loaves a month.

You may want to vary your prescription to avoid boredom, because of a change in the season or your lifestyle, or to try a new addition to the prescribable list. Changing your order is generally straightforward, but you may need to make the request by letter, consultation or telephone. Check in advance with your GP practice on its procedure.

Deciding how much gluten-free product you need

Patients vary considerably in their need for gluten-free products, so guidelines govern the normal monthly amounts allowed for different age groups and genders, including pregnant and breastfeeding women. These guidelines are based on typical eating habits and dietitians' recommendations for a balanced diet in which prescribable foods make up about 15 per cent of the total calorie intake. Table 4-1 gives the number of units you're entitled to on prescription each month, and Table 4-2 translates these units into food groups. When ordering, think about storage, because some products have a short shelf life, but remember that you can freeze many of them.

Table 4-1	Recommended Monthly Allowance of Prescribable Gluten-Free Items
Sex/Age	*Suggested Number of Units Per Month*
Child 1–3 years	10
Child 4–6 years	11
Child 7–10 years	13
Child 11–14 years	15
Child 15–18 years	18

(continued)

Table 4-1 *(continued)*

Sex/Age	Suggested Number of Units Per Month
Male 19–59 years	18
Male 60–74 years	16
Male 75+ years	14
Female 19–74 years	14
Female 75+ years	12
Breastfeeding	Add 4
Third trimester of pregnancy	Add 1

Table 4-2   What Constitutes a Unit?

Food Item	Number of Units
400g bread: loaf/roll/baguette	1
500g flour mix	2
200g biscuits/crackers	1
250g pasta	1
500g oats	1.5
300g breakfast cereals	1.5
2 x 110–180g pizza bases	1

How does the allowance in the tables translate into prescribed foods? As an example, for a 19- to 74-year-old woman, the normal monthly allowance is 14 units. She could make this up as follows:

- 7 loaves of bread (7 units)
- 1 pack of pizza bases (1 unit)
- 500 grams of pasta (2 units)
- 1 box crackers (1 units)
- 1 box breakfast cereal (1.5 units)
- 1 pack of oats (1.5 units)

Indulging in Some Non-Prescription Products

The gluten-free market in the UK is massive and growing. It's a lucrative opportunity for retailers, and all the big players have responded by launching own-brand gluten-free ranges and stocking several other brands. Suppliers' details and products are listed in the *Food and Drink Directory* from Coeliac UK. This growth in the market is good news for you. It means more choice and it has encouraged some manufacturers to improve their products in order to compete with new entrants to the market.

The free-from section isn't cheap, so it pays to shop around. Look in the other aisles of the supermarket, specialist food shops and online. Cooking from scratch is almost always a cheaper option. If you shop online, check the delivery charges and buy in bulk from one site to get the best deal. Then the only problem is storing the food!

Not all products in the free-from category are gluten-free. You also find foods that are dairy-free, egg-free, nut-free and so on. Check the labels to be certain your choices are gluten-free. Bakers often sell cakes such as meringues and macaroons that don't contain gluten, but these are often contaminated by other foods. We suggest you opt for packaged and labelled products, so that you can be sure they're produced separately and aren't in contact with flour or with ordinary cakes displayed nearby.

Getting the Buzz on Booze: Choosing Alcoholic Beverages

We cover food and drink in this chapter, but now we take a look at something a little stronger – alcohol. Many alcoholic drinks are gluten-free – and you can now find gluten-free beers.

Booze you can use

The choice of gluten-free alcoholic drinks is far wider than of those that are off limits. Here we list the basics of the booze you can use:

Most alcopops	Schnapps
Brandy and cognac	Sherry
Cider	Tequila
Gin	Vermouth, such as Martini
Liqueurs	Vodka
Perry	Whisky including malt
Port	Wine (all types except barley wine)
Rum	

Step away from the bottle

A few types of alcoholic beverage aren't allowed on the gluten-free diet. Technological advances show that measurable amounts of gluten remain in all beers traditionally brewed from barley, so you're safer excluding all types that aren't labelled gluten-free. This includes:

Beer, including bitter, barley wine and shandy	Home-brewed beers
Lager	Low-alcohol beers and lagers
Real ale	Stout, including Guinness

The distillation process completely eliminates any traces of gluten, which is why you can safely consume distilled vinegar and many alcoholic beverages made from distilled alcohol. If you're still not sure that your favourite tipple is gluten-free, check the drinks chapter in the Coeliac UK *Food and Drink Directory* or get confirmation from the manufacturer.

The good news is that a few enterprising brewers have started to manufacture gluten-free beers. A quick online search should turn up several options, and you can find them on the free-from shelves at supermarkets. If you like to make your own home-brew, you'll find recipes involving rice or buckwheat, instead of the barley or wheat normally used, on the Internet.

What you need to know about non-food products

Apart from food and drink, one or two other products contain gluten in amounts large enough to cause a problem if they get into your mouth. These are children's play-dough, which surprisingly is made up of about 40 per cent wheat flour, and home-made craft pastes such as those used in papier mâché and old-fashioned wallpaper paste (the type recommended for hanging porous wallpapers, such as sisal or natural linen).

Play-dough and craft paste are a worry if you have young children, particularly if these products are used at nurseries and play schools, where the supervisors may not appreciate the risk to your children. We provide a gluten-free recipe for play-dough in Chapter 18, along with guidance for when you send your gluten-intolerant little ones out into the world without you. As far as the craft paste is concerned, plenty of alternative products are on the market, so you may find it's just a question of briefing the craft supervisors as well as your child, who should be able to remind adults about the danger of coming into contact with gluten.

You may have read that gluten is a component of other non-food products such as food-storage containers, medicines, make-up and the glue used on envelopes and stamps. In fact, all prescribable medicines in the UK are gluten-free, as are all over-the counter medicines that carry a product licence (PL) number, which is most of them. If you don't see a PL number on an over-the-counter medicine, check with the pharmacist or read the ingredients list carefully yourself. Some drugs contain gluten-free wheat starch, so if you're allergic to wheat, these aren't suitable for you. Your doctor can almost certainly prescribe another manufacturer's version of the same medicine.

Equally, materials used to make storage containers and glues do not contain gluten. You're very unlikely to encounter a gluten-containing lipstick, lip balm or dental product, and even less likely to swallow enough to cause a problem. Occasionally, you do see wheatgerm and oat soaps, cleansers and creams, but the gluten in them can't be absorbed through the skin, even if you rub them in.

Chapter 5

Scrutinising the Evidence: Making Sure It's Gluten-Free

• •

In This Chapter

▶ Finding out why 'gluten-free' is becoming clearer

▶ Understanding labelling laws

▶ Shopping and eating out gluten-free

▶ Using product listings and ingredient labels to find suitable foods

▶ Getting help from food suppliers

▶ Searching for other sources of reliable information

• •

A product is gluten-free or it isn't, right? End of story. Yes, if it's in a pack with a label stating 'Gluten-free'. No, if the label states 'Contains gluten', 'May contain gluten', or shows wheat, rye, barley or ordinary oats in the ingredients list. Maybe, if it's not in a pack or if the label says nothing specifically about gluten, or your only source of information is the waiter or a chalked menu with no details of ingredients.

Maddening, isn't it? But the situation is better than it was before 2012 when new labelling regulations came into force throughout the European Union (EU). Even better news: the legislators have come to your rescue with a whole new piece of legislation that mostly clears up the 'gluten-free or not?' question and covers all information about food, including verbal descriptions and websites.

The bad news is that the food industry has until December 2014 to comply with this legislation, and after that can still sell products that don't comply until stocks that are already on sale have run out. So in the meantime, you may still have to take an extra step (or two) before you know for sure whether a product really is gluten-free.

In this chapter, we show you ways to help ensure that the food you're eating is as gluten-free as possible. We take you through the art of reading labels, we explain why 100 per cent gluten-free may not really mean 100 per cent gluten-free, and we offer a crash course in double- and triple-checking products.

Understanding Labels

Wouldn't it be great if you could just know which types of processed foods contain gluten and which don't? Well, unfortunately, some food items and ingredients aren't consistent: sometimes they contain gluten and sometimes they don't. That's why reading labels and asking questions are useful in gluten-free living.

Living gluten-free has been getting a lot easier thanks to food-labelling laws. Lucky us: we gluten-avoiders have even got our very own set of regulations. And there's more to come with new laws that apply to all information about food at every stage in the supply chain. This includes information in restaurants, cafes and takeaways – even burger vans and kiosks – and applies to verbal information as well as virtual and written.

The relevant laws fall neatly into two categories:

✔ Laws for foods that do contain gluten

✔ Laws for foods that don't

Laws for foods that contain gluten

In 2005, a new EU directive on labelling foods with details of allergens became mandatory, and it's been updated several times since then. This ruling is amazing progress for consumers, because it makes the identification of foods that can cause food intolerances so much easier.

The directive states that food manufacturers must highlight the presence of gluten-containing cereals whenever they're in packaged food products. The rule covers even minute amounts of these troublesome cereals, even if they've only been used as processing aids, as well as foods in very small packs with no ingredients list. The manufacturer must indicate the presence of the cereal, for example as 'wheat flour' or 'malt from barley'. Products that don't comply with the directive are no longer available for sale within the EU.

Cereals containing gluten are listed as wheat, rye, barley, oats, spelt, kamut and triticale, so look out for these words rather than the word *gluten* as such. No requirement exists for labels to indicate that gluten itself is in the product, although many do.

Some ingredients are derived from cereals that contain gluten, but have had it thoroughly removed. These ingredients don't pose a risk to you, so they're exempt from the requirement to alert you to the potential presence of gluten. They are:

- ✔ Cereals used in distilled products like whisky and vinegar

- ✔ Maltodextrin and dextrose

- ✔ Glucose syrup

The law doesn't apply to food that's sold loose or out of a labelled pack, although suppliers may voluntarily label these in the same way as packaged foods. Therefore, restaurants, takeaways, delis and salad bars in shops may or may not show an ingredients list or a 'Contains gluten' alert. So you need to double-check these products with the supplier. This is all set to change, and by 2014 new rules will help you to choose food when you're out and about.

These new rules on labelling came out in late 2011 and replace the old laws. Food suppliers have until December 2014 to comply, but the good news is that the existing rules have been toughened and greatly extended. The key points that will make it even easier to spot foods which contain gluten are these:

- ✔ Catering outlets including restaurants, pubs, cafes, self-service canteens, buffets, hotdog stands, sandwich bars, chip shops, takeaway services and burger vans must provide information on cereals that contain gluten in each dish they serve. They might have a separate display or leaflet to provide the information, or they can simply tell you verbally, but they must let all their customers know, not just those who enquire about it.

- ✔ Manufacturers must show cereals that contain gluten in the ingredients list in larger or bolder type than other ingredients, so that they stand out clearly. If a product doesn't have an ingredients list, it must show a 'Contains wheat' type of alert.

- ✔ All food suppliers in any setting can only use a 'May contain wheat' type of statement if it's based on scientific fact. So if you see 'May contain wheat', you can be sure there's a substantial risk that it does and avoid eating that food.

- ✔ Food sold loose, for example on market stalls and in butchers' shops, must be labelled in the same way as other foods, so if it contains a cereal that includes any gluten, there must be a warning to that effect.

The rules apply to all information about food and drink, not only to labels. The presence of cereals containing gluten must be made clear to you both before you buy and at the point of delivery. This applies whether you're shopping online, ordering a take-away, choosing from a menu, buying food at service counters, receiving meals on wheels, using a vending machine, chatting to the waiter or bartender . . . even looking at brochures and websites about food or when you're being served it in a public place such as a hospital, school canteen or the village fete.

The rules are designed to make living gluten-free easier. You still have to put in the effort to read the label and ask about gluten if you're not sure, but the information you get will be far more reliable than in the past. Suppliers have been given time to comply with these rules, to amend their labels and to train their staff. Most of them have made a fast start, and we're already seeing the new style of ingredients declaration, as shown in Figure 5-1.

Shepherd's Pie

Figure 5-1:
This is how the ingredients lists on food labels will look.

Ingredients
Lamb (45%) gravy, potato, butter, cheese crumb, spinach, salt, white pepper **Lamb gravy** contains lamb, onion, **celery**, carrot, turnip, lamb stock, **wheat flour**, tomato puree, sherry vinegar, Worcester sauce, corn oil, **soya flour**, rosemary, salt, black pepper, bay leaf **Lamb stock** contains lamb, water, salt **Worcester sauce** contains water, spirit vinegar, onion, sugar, molasses, salt, tamarind concentrate, lemon juice, black pepper, chilli, yeast extract, allspice powder, ginger **Cheese crumb** contains breadcrumbs, Red Leicester cheese **Breadcrumbs** contain **wheat flour**, water, yeast, salt

The familiar 'Contains gluten' alert will disappear from labels that have an ingredients listy. Showing these alerts has always been voluntary for manufacturers, and very helpful they were too, speeding up shopping no end. However, the legislators have prohibited them if there's an ingredients list. Confusingly, you'll see the alerts on foods with no ingredients list and where the cereal containing gluten is not an ingredient but a contaminant. In these cases, the alert may say: 'Contains wheat', 'May contain wheat' or 'Contains traces of wheat'. Some manufacturers are using alerts along the lines of 'Contains allergens. See ingredients list'. Inconvenient though this may be, it forces you to read the ingredients list if there is one, where you'll see the dangerous cereals highlighted in bold.

Keeping an eye open for gluten-free symbols

The Crossed Grain symbol is known globally as a symbol of gluten-free food, and is time-saving and reassuring for people on a gluten-free diet. Coeliac UK owns the trademarked symbol in the UK and Europe, and licenses it to manufacturers, distributors and retailers to use on their gluten-free products. Currently, more than 80 companies in the UK have adopted the symbol, and the list continues to grow.

Coeliac UK also licenses the GF and NGCI symbols you see here to catering establishments to use on their menus and around their premises to show they're accredited by the charity. On menus, the GF fork symbol indicates that the item is gluten-free and the NGCI symbol indicates that the food includes no gluten-containing ingredients.

Reproduced with the permission of Coeliac UK

If you need reading glasses, get yourself a lightweight fold-up magnifying glass to carry in your pocket or handbag. These are great for reading the tiny fonts on some packaging, especially the ones in three languages and rendered virtually illegible to the naked eye by poorly registered print in colours like brown on a beige background. You very quickly save the small cost of the magnifying glass by not buying unsuitable products by mistake only to spot gluten in them when you get them home. You can get these magnifying glasses at camera shops and outdoor pursuit stores.

Laws for foods that don't contain gluten

A regulation that helps make your life easier concerns 'the composition and labelling of foodstuffs suitable for people intolerant to gluten'. Although this regulation was feared by coeliacs, who thought all their old favourites would be withdrawn from the market and that they'd never be able to eat out again, it's turned out rather well.

The law applies to both packaged and loose foods and also those in catering outlets. And it applies not only to labels and menus, but also websites, advertisements, leaflets, product lists, shelf labels and customer care lines.

You may see three phrases about the absence of gluten, or rather its presence in amounts far below those likely to cause a problem. All three statements mean you can safely eat the product:

- ✔ Gluten-free
- ✔ Very low gluten
- ✔ No gluten-containing ingredients

Gluten-free

Any food or drink labelled as gluten-free can contain no more than 20 milligrams of gluten per kilogram of the product as sold to you, the final consumer – in other words, just 20 parts per million. This rule applies whether the food has been specially prepared for gluten-intolerant people or not. This level of gluten is just 10 per cent of the previous permitted level in foods labelled gluten-free in the UK.

The 'Gluten-free' label is reserved for foods and drinks that you might expect to contain gluten. Suppliers can't use the label where all other foods of the same type are also gluten-free, implying that there's something special about their particular brand. So they can't describe unprocessed foods like fruits and vegetables, milk, honey, fresh meat and baby formula as gluten-free, even though they are according to the test. For example, you won't see gluten-free labels on fresh meat at one butcher's shop and not at others. You'll certainly see it on burgers and sausages where appropriate, because by no means all these products are gluten-free. Baby formula must not contain gluten anyway, so manufacturers can't label it as gluten-free and mislead customers into thinking that other baby formulas might contain it.

If you're weaning your baby using processed weaning foods like baby cereal and jars of prepared meals, you'll find plenty of products labelled as gluten-free. Officially, this means they've been tested and found to contain no more than 20 parts of gluten per million, although best practice for manufacturers of weaning foods is to apply a much lower maximum of just 3 to 4 parts per million, which is the lowest level at which you can detect gluten.

Very low gluten

At the time of writing, we don't know of any products on sale in the UK labelled 'Very low gluten'. But suppliers can make the claim, so we want to explain it in case it crops up in future.

Suppliers can apply the 'very low gluten' label only to products specifically intended for people who are intolerant of gluten that are made from cereals that did contain gluten but have been specially processed to reduce or remove it. In these circumstances, the maximum level of gluten permitted is 100 milligrams of gluten per kilogram of product as sold, or 100 parts per million.

Looking out for product recalls

When a supplier launches a product specially prepared for gluten-intolerant people labelled either 'Gluten-free' or 'Very low gluten', it has to notify the legal authorities in the UK so that they can monitor the product. This is on top of the ongoing checks that food safety and Trading Standards officers do to verify that foods are labelled accurately. If a product labelled gluten-free is found to contain more than 20 parts of gluten per million, the supplier must recall it and widely publish the affected batch numbers.

You occasionally see notices in the shops about product recalls. If you've recently bought these products, check the batch numbers. If they match, return the products to the shop for a refund or replacement. Recalling a product is a costly and damaging procedure for a supplier, so you can be sure they take proper precautions before their products get to the shops.

In the early months of the new gluten-free labelling laws, there were just eight product recalls of foods labelled gluten-free that turned out to contain low levels of gluten.

When the legislation was being drafted, everyone thought that this claim of 'Very low gluten' at 100 parts per million – which, by the way, is half the level previously permitted for a gluten-free claim – would be a workable and safe maximum for manufacturers and consumers alike. In the event, manufacturers found that because they were required to perform the laboratory testing for gluten, it was preferable to go all the way down to 20 parts per million or less and label their products 'Gluten-free'.

No gluten-containing ingredients

This is a factual statement, not strictly covered by the law. It can only be used for foods which haven't been tested for gluten that are made with naturally gluten-free ingredients and if controls are in place to avoid contamination with gluten.

When it comes to minimising cross-contamination, just taking care in the kitchen would not pass muster at a Trading Standards audit. The supplier would have to demonstrate that it prepares the food with no gluten-containing ingredients in a separate kitchen or at a different time to other foods, and stores the food separately.

You're likely to see this label where loose food is served to you without a labelled pack, such as in a restaurant. Many manufacturers of packaged foods in this category have opted to test for gluten and make a definite statement about it one way or the other. But caterers aren't usually in a position to do the test. If they make the statement 'No gluten-containing ingredients', you can take it at face value and be reassured to know that the caterer has gone to great lengths to minimise the risks of cross-contamination with gluten from other foods. If you ask, the caterers should provide you with detailed information about their procedures for minimising contamination and should be more than willing to answer your questions.

However, keep in mind that this statement is optional. Suppliers don't have to adopt it if they don't want to. Even if they're not deliberately adding gluten-containing ingredients to their food, they may not be able to control cross-contamination adequately.

Other relevant descriptions

Only gluten-free foods that have been specially prepared for people intolerant of gluten can use phrases such as 'Suitable for coeliacs' or show symbols that mean the same thing.

Knowing which foods to be cautious about

Clearly, foods labelled 'Gluten-free', 'Very low gluten' or 'No gluten-containing ingredients' are safe for you. Unfortunately, you can't live on these alone. Even if you could afford it, you wouldn't be eating a very healthy diet if you restricted yourself to these and only these.

Equally clearly, you can't eat anything labelled 'Contains gluten' or 'May contain gluten'. Nor can you eat foods that contain wheat, rye, barley or 'normal' oats (that is, not pure), except for the highly processed derivatives of them such as glucose syrup (see the list in the earlier section 'Laws for foods that contain gluten').

Up until the end of 2014, you'll find foods and drinks around that contain gluten but aren't labelled as such. These are foods sold loose or served in restaurants without specific information. Ask questions and satisfy yourself that the food is suitable for you.

After 2014, whether packed and labelled or loose and unlabelled, and in all public situations, if a food contains a cereal that is a source of gluten, that information will be explicitly stated.

Keep in mind that laws and rules don't apply in private, such as in the home, at parties and at private functions like catered wedding receptions and banquets. You won't be able to call in Trading Standards when you're at your mum's for tea and she's not sure about the baking powder she used in the 'gluten-free' cake. We cover what to do in all these situations in Parts III and V.

Being aware of contamination risks

If only every food in every situation had to be labelled to show that it either did or didn't contain gluten. Unfortunately, society demands that terms like gluten-free be reserved for foods and drinks that you might otherwise expect would contain it. The legislators don't want the term bandied about to the extent that it loses its impact.

So, we need to examine situations and foods where you can't see any ingredients to worry about, or where you find no information about the ingredients but also nothing to suggest that the food is gluten-free.

Cereals and seeds

If it's flour, flakes or meal, or it's been ground, be cautious. Although the food itself may not contain gluten, it may well be contaminated with other cereals that do. More and more manufacturers are labelling these flours gluten-free, having done the appropriate tests. Others haven't got around to it yet or perhaps have started testing and found gluten to be present in some batches but not others. Go to the manufacturer's website or telephone to ask specifically about this issue. If you suspect contamination may exist, don't eat the food.

Grain processing

Contamination can occur at several points during processing. Commercially grown grains can contain trace amounts of other grains, because preventing cross-contamination is nearly impossible. The cross-contamination starts at the farm, where growers often rotate crops between fields each year, so crops from previous years can pop up where they're least expected. Contamination can also occur in grain storage, transportation and during milling.

Shared equipment or facilities

Many suppliers produce several different products on one production line. For instance, a company that produces several types of flour may mill them all on the same equipment. Although the UK and many other countries have strict laws about cleaning lines between products, sometimes traces of gluten remain on the lines – or in the facility – and contaminate the gluten-free products that are made there. For this reason, some foods with no obvious source of gluten don't make it into gluten-free listings.

The only time you know that no cross-contamination exists is when the grains are from suppliers who label food 'Gluten-free', 'Very low gluten' or 'No gluten-containing ingredients'. In this case, the food is safe.

Other packaged foods

You find lots of packaged processed foods labelled without any reference to gluten one way or the other. The golden rule for these is to examine the ingredients list and satisfy yourself that it doesn't include any source of gluten. You can also look at lists of suitable products, such as the *Food and*

Drink Directory and the other tools we describe in the later section 'Using Product Listings to Find Gluten-Free Foods'. The directory and Chapter 4 of this book include a reassuring list of all the unprocessed foods you can choose from, such as fruits, vegetables, fresh meat and fish, eggs, cheese and milk.

We recommend checking the ingredients every time you buy the product, in case there's been a change.

Loose, unpackaged foods

Wherever food is offered loose, you need to weigh up the risks of cross-contamination. We're thinking here of deli counters, help-yourself salad bars, buffets, open displays, the cake stand at the school fete, cookery demonstrations and classes, markets, pick and mix, and ice-cream parlours. No doubt you'll encounter many more.

We don't mean to put you off visiting these, but you need to be aware of other foods sitting alongside the ones you want.

At the deli counter, steer clear of cooked meats that have been through the slicer, if other sliced items such as stuffed and breaded cooked meats are on offer. Prepared items openly displayed near pastries and battered foods may have picked up a few crumbs from their neighbours, either directly or indirectly via serving tongs and the hands of the staff.

On the salad bar, it's often the croutons, cous cous salad and tabbouleh that get into your gluten-free choices, particularly where customers help themselves and put the serving spoons down in the wrong bowl. In a supermarket, you're bound to find similar or identical foods offered in sealed packs or unprocessed for you to take home and prepare yourself, so you don't need to go without.

At the ice-cream parlour or maybe the kiosk in the park or at the pictures, ice creams containing pieces of brownie and biscuit are a problem if the server uses the same scoop without washing it carefully before serving you with your gluten-free choices. And of course the wafers and cones are almost certainly made from wheat. Here you should be able to select gluten-free ice creams to have in a tub and insist that the server uses a clean scoop, or else select from the packaged ice creams on offer.

It's the same with pick and mix, whether sweets, nuts or snacks. Some of them contain gluten, and if these may have strayed into your choices, head for the packaged products instead.

Eating out

Chapter 17 has more guidelines about eating out, but we think it is worthwhile discussing the possibilities of cross-contamination here. The main problems are to do with shared cooking utensils, preparation areas and cooking liquids such as stock and oil.

Frying oil is contaminated with gluten if it's been used for battered, bread-crumbed or dough-based foods. So although your chips may be made from fresh sliced potatoes, they still pose a risk to you if they've been fried in oil used for the chicken nuggets, for example. Most smaller kitchens and take-away places have only one deep-fat fryer. Many fish and chip shops have separate fryers, so the chips might be okay, but check each time you visit. Take care with equipment such as draining racks used in chip shops and burger bars. We've even been offered gluten-free pasta in a restaurant, only to find it's been boiled in a big vat of water previously used for wheat pasta.

Breakfast buffets in hotels are fraught with danger areas for the gluten intolerant. You're very unlikely to be offered a gluten-free breakfast cereal, and don't even think of asking the staff to toast your gluten-free bread for you. You could take along some toaster bags, but if the toaster is the type with a conveyor belt in it, your bread is likely to fall out in the toaster. If you're in a bed and breakfast, an ordinary domestic toaster may be available for guests to use at the buffet. You could risk using your own toaster bags in this as long as you do it yourself and wash the bags carefully afterwards inside and out. It's probably easier and safer to take along some crackers or wrapped rolls instead, or take some gluten-free cereal. Breakfast buffets almost always have milk, yoghurt and fruit you can add too.

Salad bars and buffets in restaurants present the same problems as they do in the shops, so you're safer to ask the chef to prepare and plate up your meal separately. And do make sure that the chef does exactly that and doesn't just take food from the buffet and make it look nice on your plate!

Be alert to chefs' tricks such as serving ice cream on biscuit crumbs. They do so to stop the ice cream sliding around on the plate, but often the waiter isn't aware of the practice. Similarly, chefs can add gluten-containing garnishes or drizzles of sauces and gravies in the kitchen, even though they're not mentioned on the menu, no matter how carefully you've briefed the waiter. Often, a different person serves you when it comes to desserts, and you must of course explain your needs again to avoid slip-ups.

Crumbs are also a problem in takeaway places and sandwich bars. You may be offered a gluten-free roll, but as well as asking about the fillings available, you need to ensure the roll is sliced on a clean board with a clean knife by someone with freshly washed hands. As with bread in toasters, you can't eat sandwiches that have been in contact with grills and racks used for ordinary bread.

When it comes to food preparation, bear in mind, like the manufacturers have to, that flour is powdery and floats about in the air when it's disturbed, settling on every horizontal surface over a wide area. Chefs demonstrating their prowess at tossing pizzas about and rolling out filo pastry should send you running for the door, because it's a certain bet that flour has dusted your otherwise gluten-free food.

We could go on, but the idea here is simply to alert you to some of the danger signals that your food may be contaminated with gluten. When you get into the swing of living gluten-free, your antennae are tuned to these signals and you can confidently sidestep the pitfalls.

Using Product Listings to Find Gluten-Free Foods

Several product listings, such as Coeliac UK's *Food and Drink Directory*, are available that cover everything from baby foods to ready meals. These are great references because all the hard work has been done for you. You just need to remember to take the list with you when you go shopping, or have it to hand when you're shopping online.

Always use an up-to-date listing, because manufacturers have an annoying habit of changing the ingredients in their products. In addition, takeovers occur in the food sector and subsequent consolidation of product ranges takes place. So an item can be gluten-free one day, appearing on the list, and the next thing you know the ingredients or the brand name have been modified and the product's off the list. Any product listing is only up to date at the time of printing.

If you want to use product listings, you have several choices.

The Food and Drink Directory

The *Food and Drink Directory*, produced by Coeliac UK is invaluable for anyone following a gluten-free diet. Produced annually, the booklet is sent free to members of Coeliac UK, and non-members can buy it from the charity's online shop. The booklet is small enough to fit into your pocket but manages to list thousands of foods you can eat on a gluten-free diet. This includes the whole range of prescribable products, including their pack sizes and prescription codes for doctors and pharmacists. The information makes it easy for you to add items to your prescription list and work out the number of packs to request within your monthly allowance. The directory alerts you to new foods that have become prescribable for the first time. It also lists branded products by category and own-label products from the major supermarkets. You even find a list of brands supplied to caterers, which helps when you're eating out.

Access monthly updates on Coeliac UK's website or in its monthly e-newsletter. You can also source updates via the telephone helpline or even by post (if you send a self-addressed envelope to Coeliac UK). Full details are at www. coeliac.org.uk.

Requesting product lists from companies

Many of the large supermarkets and fast-food outlets produce lists of own-brand items that don't contain gluten, covering everything from breakfast cereals to yoghurts. These organisations are usually happy to send you a list on request, and increasingly are making them available for download from their websites. Such lists can be useful if you always shop in the same place, but make sure that you're shopping with the most current list.

We suggest you use these lists before you start shopping or put in your pre-scription, to get ideas about what gluten-free foods are available and what's new. Then when you shop, you can choose what category of food you're after and select a gluten-free version of it. At this stage, you can examine the label or details of the product if you're online and then use the listing again as a check if you're still not sure.

Testing for Gluten in Foods

With so many questions about what does and doesn't have gluten, you'd think there'd be a test that tells you for certain. And there is, but it's questionable whether it's worthwhile or practical for home users.

Several laboratory-based gluten tests are available commercially, which manufacturers use to make sure that their foods comply with labelling laws. A few test kits are also available for domestic use. These tests take about 15 minutes to carry out and should be highly sensitive to gluten, with some able to detect it at 20 parts per million. You can test cooked, raw or processed foods. You mix some of the food with a special liquid in a test tube, place a few drops on a testing pad, and after a short wait a series of coloured dots or lines, depending on the make of kit you're using, appear if gluten is present. The depth of colour gives you a measure of how much gluten is in the food.

Kits cost around £10 a go, which is more than the extra cost of buying products that have been professionally tested and labelled gluten-free. Plus, a gluten-free result on one batch doesn't mean every batch of the same product will be gluten-free. You even get different results when testing samples from different parts of the same pack. Also, you have to be very careful to follow the instructions for the tests to get an accurate result, and you need to make sure that the sample you take is a good reflection of the whole meal.

Many professional laboratories refuse to supply their kits to consumers, because you can't test lots of different foods with one type of kit. The kits need to be set up for the particular foods to be tested, and the tests need to be controlled and repeated to ensure they're accurate. For example, a kit for a chocolate manufacturer would be different to one for a baker. Consumers find it frustrating that they can't use one kit for a variety of foods or get precisely the same result for the same food each time.

Basically, tests like this are not a good way to choose foods to eat. You're much better off choosing foods labelled gluten-free, because that shows that the manufacturer has invested time and money to test the food accurately.

We've even heard people request that the kits be made to work faster so that you can use them at the table in restaurants, while the waiter . . . well . . . waits. They're really not suitable for this purpose. For one thing, for the test to be accurate you'd need to liquidise the whole meal and then test perhaps four or five samples. Whatever you found out, you could neither eat the meal nor return it to the kitchen.

Researching Gluten-Free Food

The good news is that tons of information on gluten and gluten-free foods is available. The bad news is that some of the information is rubbish.

No matter what the source, always question the credibility of the authors, and remember that even seemingly credible sources can give false or misleading information.

Unless you're using reliable sources, you may get information that's conflicting. Here are a few tips to help you sort out the real from the ridiculous:

- ✓ **Check the publication date.** Information on the Internet and in books and magazines can become outdated very quickly, so make sure that what you're reading is current.

- ✓ **Look for credentials.** Are the authors qualified to give advice, or are they just sharing personal experiences and opinions? Where do they get their information? You don't need a licence to publish, and some writers don't let the facts get in the way of a good story.

- ✓ **Compare the information with what you find from other sources.** Some of the information out there is conflicting, so compare all the sources and decide which stands up to closer scrutiny. The sources of information that we cite in this chapter are reputable and reliable.

- ✓ **Check what country the writer is based in.** Food labelling laws, eating habits, healthcare, food manufacturing and catering standards are as varied as the food is from country to country, so you may find that what you're reading just doesn't apply in the UK.

The Internet: For better, for worse

The Internet is very convenient. You can be in your pyjamas, cup of coffee in hand, before the sun even rises, and find out more about gluten than you ever knew you didn't know. The problem is that you can't always trust what you read online, and checking credibility can be difficult. Furthermore, people publish information on the Internet and forget about it or don't take the time to update it. What you're looking at may be several years old – and a lot has changed in the past several years in the gluten-free world.

Nevertheless, websites can be invaluable if you know you can trust the information they deliver. What we look for is accurate and up-to-date information, written and edited by qualified health professionals or others with relevant practical experience in the field.

Websites about gluten-free foods

Here are some of our favourite gluten-related websites:

- ✔ **Coeliac UK (**www.coeliac.org.uk**):** You've probably realised by now that we're big supporters of the patient-support charity Coeliac UK. In fact, we devote the whole of Chapter 21 to ten reasons why you should become a member. The charity's fantastic website covers a huge range of reliable and current information on healthcare, diet, families, shopping, cooking, research and support groups. We could go on, but why not take a browse yourself? You can also sign up to Coeliac UK's social media networks.

- ✔ **Gluten-Free OnTheGo (**www.gluten-free-onthego.com**):** This site was originally set up by Coeliac UK but is now run privately by a commercial organisation. It's an advertising site for gluten-free-friendly hotels, restaurants, pubs, fast-food outlets and even coffee shops by geographical region, including some in the USA and mainland Europe. Consumers are able to recommend venues and review them, although no special training or accreditation of the chefs is involved. The advertising is paid for, so it's likely to be up to date.

Websites of suppliers of gluten-free foods

All the main food manufacturers, online suppliers and retailers within the UK have their own websites providing information on their product range, including prescribable products. You can see news of product developments, recipe suggestions and even details of events such as product tastings and cookery demonstrations. You can often subscribe to receive email updates, newsletters and recipe cards.

If you're just starting out living gluten-free, we recommend contacting manufacturers, because they often provide free sample packs of products, which enables you to try before you buy. This is particularly useful for prescribable products, because the manufacturers are very generous with their samples. Samples can save both you and your doctor a lot of chopping and changing of your prescription list.

International support groups

If you're planning to travel abroad, you can find some useful information by looking up the international gluten-free patient-support group serving the local community before you go. Argentina, Australia, Canada, Israel, South Africa and the USA all have their own organisations. Within Europe, you find similar groups in Austria, Croatia, the Czech Republic, Denmark, Finland, Germany, Holland, Hungary, Ireland, Italy, Portugal, Slovenia, Spain, Sweden and Switzerland. You can find contact details by searching on the Internet or via Coeliac UK's website (www.coeliac.org.uk).

Social media sites

A quick Internet search turns up a great many discussion boards, blogs and chat rooms about living gluten-free. You can often pick up useful tips on these sites, which may also include videos of cooking techniques for some of the more challenging gluten-free recipes like fresh pasta. Gluten-free ingredients can be expensive and at first unfamiliar, so seeing pictures and videos and reading reviews by people who've tried the products helps you decide whether you want to buy them.

Needless to say, much of the health advice on social media sites is dodgy or even downright dangerous, so we don't recommend you use the sites for that.

Apps

Numerous apps (digital applications) – some free of charge and some paid for – are available to help you live gluten-free. Coeliac UK has a mobile app for members; check the charity's website for details. These apps provide many of the items available on websites, such as recipes, daily menus, tips and product news and reviews. Many include a scanner to quickly run over barcodes to check whether foods are gluten-free. If you're an app freak, apps save a lot of time and can encourage you to try new foods regularly, rather than getting stuck with the same ol' same ol'.

Chapter 6

Acquiring a Taste for Nutritious Gluten-Free Health

*W*hether you're a salad-dodger or suffering from orthorexia (an extreme desire to eat only healthy foods), eating a gluten-free diet that's nutritious and appetising is simple. You don't have to weigh portions, keep a food diary or count calories – and you're not limited to deprivation-dining.

We have more than just a passing passion for nutrition: after all, three of us are dietitians, including a coeliac living gluten-free for real, and we're all foodies. Our interest extends far beyond whether something is gluten-free or not. We love to eat, and we believe food is to be respected and revered – partly for the diversity of flavours and textures; partly for the buzz you get from enjoying a delicious, nutritious meal; partly for the energy it gives you; and most definitely, as a way to nourish your mind and body.

In this chapter, we share our quest for promoting food as being more than just fuel. We explain why gluten-free doesn't always mean guilt-free – although it can – and why paying attention to the glycaemic load is crucial to health. And with a few gentle nudges, we hope to steer you towards eating gluten-free nutritiously.

If the subject of nutrition seems intimidating or overly complex, don't worry. We focus on food rather than nutrients – and make this a lesson in nutrition that's easy to digest.

Eating Well, Eating Healthily

We may be preaching to the converted, because if you've been following a gluten-free diet for a while, you probably already pay attention to what you eat – faithfully reading labels and scrutinising the ingredients, acutely aware of where gluten can be lurking, and avoiding it like the plague. If you're just starting out on living gluten-free, now's a great time to look at your eating habits as a whole and fine-tune the balance of your diet. As well as replacing the gluten-containing cereals, you could look at whether you eat enough fruits and vegetables, get enough variety in your food, how often you snack, how much salt you eat, and whether your portions of lean meat, fish, eggs and dairy foods are enough, or maybe too big. If you want to be healthy and gluten-free, you may have to modify your thinking about what you're eating.

Most people focus on their gluten-free diet with one thing in mind: keeping it gluten-free! And of course that's vital, but so is meeting all your other nutritional needs. Having a gluten-related disorder doesn't mean you can ignore your risk of other health problems to which a poor diet contributes. Food can fuel your body, help prevent disease, improve your skin's appearance, keep you in a better mood, help you sleep, exercise and manage your weight, decrease symptoms of premenstrual syndrome (PMS) and the menopause, and maybe even help you live longer! It can keep you feeling great on the inside and looking fantastic on the outside. And luckily, it can do all that and be gluten-free.

Food is obviously essential – without it, you'd starve. But it's the *amount* and *type* of food you eat that has the most powerful effect on preventing disease and on maintaining good health.

Balancing foods that provide energy

Firstly, a little nutrition for you. Well, we did warn you we're passionate about it. The nutrients that deliver the vital energy – fuel or calories, to put it in other ways – that sustains the life of every cell in your body are carbohydrate, fat and protein. (Alcohol provides energy too, but of a type that's not useful to your body, and it comes with a risk to your health if you overdo it.)

- ✓ **Carbohydrate:** In a balanced diet, about half of your total energy intake should come from carbohydrate in the form of starches plus sugars that are still encased in whole fruits and vegetables and in dairy products.

   'Free' sugars that have been released from fruits and vegetables by refinement (such as granulated sugar), extraction (such as maple syrup) or by crushing (such as the sugars in fruit juice) can be harmful to your health, as we explain later in this chapter. So, this type of sugar should only make up a maximum of a tenth of the total calories you eat.

Starches and sugars are known as *available carbohydrates*, meaning you can digest and absorb them into the body. Another type of carbohydrate, fibre, provides very little energy, because it's not digested, but is fermented in the gut.

Apart from lactose, the sugar in milk, all carbohydrate, including fibre, comes from plants.

✔ **Fat:** To eat a balanced diet, you need to get no more than a third of your total energy from fats. These come from vegetable oils, animal foods like cream, and visible fat in meat. In this group, the saturated fats are unhealthy, so should contribute only about a tenth of your total calories, at most. That's why you see saturates declared on labels within the total fat, to help you keep an eye on the quantity of saturates you're eating.

✔ **Protein:** Your remaining energy, about a fifth or less, needs to come from proteins, which come largely from meat, fish, eggs, milk and some plant foods like beans, grains and nuts.

If you had these pure nutrients lined up on the table in front of you in amounts proportionate to their contributions to a healthy calorie intake, you'd see that the fat portion would look way too small considering it's supposed to deliver up to a third of the total calories. That's because fat has more than twice the calories weight for weight than the starches, sugars and proteins. For the record, fat has 9 kilocalories per gram, and the others only 4 kilocalories per gram. And by the way, all fats and oils have the same calories in them, whatever their appearance, taste, texture or health properties. Sorry to disappoint you if you were hoping that olive oil was somehow less calorific or fattening than other fats and oils.

A final word about available carbohydrate, fat and protein: although they all provide energy, that's only one of their functions. They also each have their own contributions to make to your metabolism and health, so they're not interchangeable.

Using the eatwell plate as a guide

You don't need to worry about keeping a tally of each nutrient you're eating, counting calories or working out whether your carbohydrates are starchy or sugary. The eatwell plate, shown in Figure 6-1, sets out a healthy daily balance of food in five groups and shows you the proportion of your total daily diet that each group should make up.

The Eatwell Plate

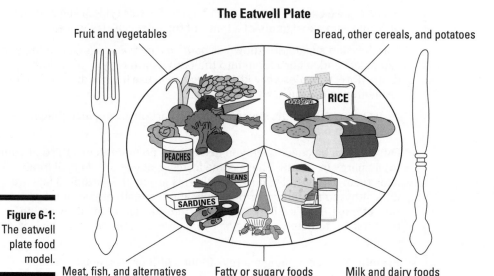

Fruit and vegetables

Bread, other cereals, and potatoes

RICE

PEACHES

BEANS

SARDINES

Meat, fish, and alternatives   Fatty or sugary foods   Milk and dairy foods

Figure 6-1:
The eatwell
plate food
model.

As you can see in the picture, about a third of the food you eat each day should be starchy foods like bread, pasta, cereal foods (all gluten-free, of course), rice and potatoes. Roughly another third should be fruits, vegetables and salads. About a sixth should be lean meat, fish, eggs, beans, peas, lentils, nuts and vegetarian meat-substitutes. About another sixth should be the dairy foods: milk, cheese and yoghurt (not butter and cream, which come into the fatty food group). The proportion of fatty or sugary foods to eat is a maximum of about one-twelfth of the total volume of food you eat daily – the less of these foods, the better.

You don't have to stick to the eatwell plate proportions at every meal, although doing so helps to ensure you get the balance about right by the end of the day. We suggest that you base all your meals on the two big food groups: the fruits and vegetables and the starchy staples.

You can easily eat this way while staying gluten-free by choosing gluten-free starchy staples and grains in the cereal and potato food group, and making sure no gluten slips in if you opt for processed foods from the other groups.

Weighing up wheat

In the typical British diet, cereal foods, principally wheat but also rye, barley and oats, make a very significant contribution to the average intake of a great many essential nutrients, as shown in Table 6-1.

Table 6-1	What We Get from Wheat and Other Cereals	
Nutrient	*Importance of Cereal Foods in the Average British Diet*	*How Much Comes from Cereal Foods?*
Calories	Top source	A third
Protein	Second source	A quarter
Carbohydrate	Top source	Half
Fibre	Top source	Almost half
Minerals	Top-two source of calcium, iron, phosphorus, magnesium, zinc, copper, manganese, selenium and iodine	About a quarter to a third
Vitamins	Top-three source of vitamins D, E, B1, B2 and B6, niacin and folate	About a fifth to a third

In nature, gluten comes packaged in grains of wheat, rye and barley together with other valuable nutrients. In fact, it's a surprisingly minor component of these grains, considering the trouble it causes for people who can't tolerate it. In wheat, which is the most widely consumed source of gluten in the UK, the gluten comprises only about 5 to 10 per cent of the whole grain, depending on the variety. About three-quarters of the grain is carbohydrate, including about 10 per cent fibre, over 60 per cent starch and just a little sugar. The rest is made up of vitamins and minerals, fat and moisture. When it comes to wheat that's been milled into white flour, the carbohydrate fraction is almost four-fifths of it, with only a small amount of fibre and sugar and about three-quarters starch. Whole barley and rye both contain even more carbohydrate and fibre than wheat – 79 and 88 per cent respectively – and less gluten.

You're eliminating gluten, so you need to consider the impact this is going to have on the balance of your diet. The trick is to eat the five food groups in the proportions shown in the eatwell plate (see the preceding section), and for the starchy foods, to pick replacements for gluten-containing cereals that supply not only the protein but also the other nutrients that you've previously been getting from wheat and probably occasionally rye and barley. This means eating naturally gluten-free grains and seeds – see Chapter 4 for a list of these.

You can also go a long way to getting some of the nutrients you've previously relied on wheat to deliver by eating a wide variety of salads, fruits and vegetables, including their skins when appropriate, and by choosing whole, unhulled peas, beans and lentils.

Going for grains

When it comes to gluten-free grains, the goal is whole because whole gluten-free grains contain all the nutrients of whole gluten-containing grains, but with different proteins. Look for wholegrain maize, millet, sorghum, quinoa and buckwheat, along with brown rice (which isn't strictly the whole grain, but comes nearer to it than white varieties), and also teff, which is always wholegrain even if it's not labelled as such, because the grains are too small to mill.

A grain has three parts: the germ, the endosperm and the bran. *Wholegrain* foods contain all three parts in their natural proportions, but not necessarily as intact grains:

- ✔ **Germ:** A new plant sprouts from this part of the grain, and it's where you can find a lot of niacin, thiamine, riboflavin, vitamin E, magnesium, phosphorus, iron and zinc. The germ also has a little protein and some unsaturated fat.

- ✔ **Endosperm:** The endosperm is the bulk of the seed. Because the seed stores its energy in the endosperm for the growing seedling, it has most of the protein and starch, as well as some vitamins and minerals.

- ✔ **Bran:** This part contains most of the fibre and forms a protective coat around the outside of the grain.

Refining grains strips them of their bran and germ, so all that's left is the endosperm. They still contain some nutritional value, but most of the good stuff gets thrown out during the refining process. The nutrients in wholegrains – vitamins, minerals, fibre and others – work together to help protect against chronic diseases such as type 2 diabetes, heart disease and certain cancers.

Manufacturers usually add synthetic vitamins and minerals back into refined grains after processing, but they're still not as nutritious as wholegrains and they lack the fibre that wholegrain provides.

Considering Carbohydrates

As a major part of a healthy balanced diet, carbohydrates are pretty important, particularly the starches, fibres and the sugars in dairy products and intact fruits and vegetables. Many different types of starches and sugars exist, and they all have their own unique characteristics, both in your food and in your body. What's more, they come mixed together in most foods, and their characteristics depend on other components in the food and the degree of processing they've been subjected to. All processing – in the factory and in your kitchen – like chopping, milling, blending, refining, mixing and cooking has an effect. It's this fascinating area we're going to cover next, to show you how you can reap big rewards from making a few careful choices.

Introducing the Glycaemic Index and Glycaemic Load

Hey! Put down that remote control! We know you're tempted to skip this section because the heading sounds complicated, tedious, boring or all the above. Please don't! This section is really important because it forms the basis of what we talk about in the rest of this chapter, so bear with us.

To start, here's a quick quiz. True or false: a potato is worse for you than a chocolate bar? Surprisingly, the answer is *true*, at least it is if you're talking about a large, floury, white baked potato versus a bar of high-cocoa-solids chocolate, and the effect these can have on your blood sugars. Now have we got your attention? Read on. . . .

Beating the low blood-sugar blues

You may be wondering what blood-sugar levels have to do with eating a gluten-free nutritious diet. The answer is lots. Your blood-sugar level can have a profound effect on your health in many ways: disease risk and prevention, weight loss and weight gain, moods and energy levels.

In order to keep your gluten-free diet well-balanced, you need to consume a wide range of non-gluten-containing foods, many of which are high in carbohydrates. Foods that contain carbohydrate aren't all composed in the same way, so they don't all have the same effect when your body breaks them down. Starches and sugars are digested and broken down into *glucose* molecules. Glucose is a sugar, so when it's absorbed from your gut into your blood, your blood-sugar level rises.

Certain foods – such as white bread, pasta, pizza, sweets, biscuits and cakes – make your blood sugar shoot up rapidly. These sorts of foods are classified as *high-glycaemic*, which means they don't take long to digest and quickly release sugar into your blood (see the later section 'Measuring the sugar rush with the glycaemic index (GI)'). When your blood-sugar level rises, it immediately causes your body to release *insulin*, a hormone produced by the pancreas.

Glucose is the fuel that your body uses to function. Insulin is in charge of getting the glucose from your blood into the cells of the tissues in your body where they can use it as fuel. Think of insulin as the delivery person – bringing glucose to the cells, opening the door and depositing the glucose inside. When insulin delivers the glucose from blood into the cells, it *lowers* your blood-sugar level. (The sugar isn't in the blood any more; it's in the cells.)

Whenever your blood-sugar level is high, your body makes bigger batches of insulin to try to bring that level down. The problem is that insulin is sometimes a little *too* good at its job. It can work so well that your blood sugar drops too fast, so you crash. You get fatigued, sometimes a little dizzy, and hungry.

Eating a lot of high-glycaemic food in one go and the resulting action of insulin causes your blood-sugar level to spike, that is to shoot up to a peak and then fall just as rapidly, wreaking havoc on how energetic or lethargic you feel and even on your moods. If you do this all day long by taking frequent sugary snacks and drinks, you'll feel frequent spikes.

Feeling the high cost of high insulin

People who habitually eat a lot of high-glycaemic food for years can develop a condition called insulin resistance. This is when the body has so much insulin all the time that it doesn't respond to it as it should. Usually, just releasing a little insulin can bring blood sugar down, but in someone who's insulin resistant, this doesn't happen. So in an effort to lower the blood-sugar level, the body keeps producing more insulin, resulting in an elevated level at all times. This state can be very hard on the body.

Syndrome X, or *metabolic syndrome*, is a cluster of conditions and symptoms caused by insulin resistance. These conditions include:

✔ Raised blood-glucose or blood-sugar levels (hyperglycaemia)

✔ High blood pressure

✔ A high level of bad or *low-density lipoprotein* (LDL) cholesterol and a low level of good or *high-density lipoprotein* (HDL) cholesterol

✔ Weight gain, especially around the middle, and obesity

✔ An excess of triglycerides (fat) in the bloodstream

Excess insulin is also blamed for deficiencies of calcium, magnesium, zinc, vitamins E, C and the B-group, and essential fatty acids.

Measuring the sugar rush with the glycaemic index (GI)

The *glycaemic index* (GI) is a measurement of how much your blood sugar increases in the two hours after you eat. Foods that are high in fat and protein don't have a significant effect on your blood-sugar level (if anything, they stabilise it), so we concentrate on using the glycaemic index for foods that are high in carbohydrates. However, all food types have a glycaemic index.

To measure the glycaemic index of food, you need a reference point. To determine that reference point, someone had to find a food that had a super-high glycaemic index – one that turns to sugar the minute you eat it. And the winner was . . . white bread! The glycaemic index of white bread (made from wheat flour) is set at 100, and we compare all foods to it.

A food's glycaemic index is how much that food increases your blood-sugar level compared with how much white bread would increase it. Whether foods contain gluten or are gluten-free doesn't help you predict where they fall on the index.

The lower a food's glycaemic index, the slower its effect on blood-glucose levels. The higher a food's glycaemic index, the more it causes a rapid spike in blood sugar.

The glycaemic effect of foods depends on a number of factors, including the type of starch it contains, whether that starch is cooked, how much fat is present, and the acidity. For example, adding vinegar or lemon juice (which are acidic) to a food lowers the glycaemic index. And fat and fibre inhibit the absorption of the carbohydrates, which also lowers the glycaemic index. That, by the way, is why a chocolate bar – which has fat in it – has a lower glycaemic index than a big white baked potato. Processing affects the glycaemic index of a food too. The more highly processed a grain such as rice or corn – in fact any of the gluten-free ones – the higher its glycaemic index and the more quickly your blood sugar rises. The same applies to overcooked food.

Glucose versus white bread reference points

Physiologists test and compare portions of foods that each contain 50 grams of carbohydrate. Some GI charts use pure glucose as the reference point instead of white bread. Different charts have different glycaemic indices for the same food, depending on whether they use the white bread or the glucose scale. Charts should tell you which food they use as a reference point. In the white bread index, glucose has a glycaemic index of 140. So to convert to a white bread scale, you multiply the score on the glucose scale by 1.4.

People with diabetes used to think they had to avoid sugar – as in granulated or table sugar. But eating ordinary sugar in some foods doesn't make your blood-glucose level rise any faster than eating some starchy foods. That's why the glycaemic index is a more valuable tool for controlling your blood-sugar level than cutting down on your sugar intake.

The glycaemic index value tells you how fast a carbohydrate turns into glucose, but it doesn't tell you how much of that carbohydrate is in a particular food. That's where the glycaemic load comes in.

Taking stock of the glycaemic load (GL)

Using the glycaemic index alone can be misleading. Watermelon, for example, has a high glycaemic index, but because watermelon's mostly water, you have to eat a lot of it to raise your blood sugar significantly. The glycaemic load (GL) measurement is actually a lot more valuable. *Glycaemic load* looks at how many grams of available carbohydrates a food provides as well as its glycaemic index.

The GL gives you an accurate and sensible picture of the real effect that foods in realistic portions have on your blood sugars. Glycaemic load is measured by serving size, which not only standardises the numbers so that you can compare one food with another, but also allows you to add up your total glycaemic load for each meal and for the whole day. Less than 80 glycaemic load units per day is a low-glycaemic-load diet; more than 120 is high.

The glycaemic load puts the glycaemic index into context. It shows you what foods in what portion sizes you can enjoy as part of a well-balanced, healthy diet, without giving yourself a sugar rush. Table 6-2 explains what we mean by high, medium and low glycaemic index and load. Remember, whether it's GI or GL you're looking at, the rule is: the lower the better.

Table 6-2	High, Medium and Low Glycaemic Load and Index	
	Glycaemic Load	*Glycaemic Index*
Low	Below 11	Below 56
Medium	11 to 19	56 to 69
High	20 and above	70 and above

You can further lower the overall GL of your meal, especially if you're eating relatively high-GI foods, by combining them with other foods, such as by sprinkling Parmesan cheese on your pasta, including beans in your soup or drizzling olive oil on your salad. For more on the intricacies of GL, check out *The GL Diet For Dummies* by yours truly, Nigel Denby and Sue Baic (Wiley).

Useful glycaemic loads (GLs) and indices (GIs)

Here are the GLs and GIs of some cooked gluten-free (gf) starchy foods. We've used the glucose scale (glucose has a GI of 100) and typical portion sizes.

Food and Portion	GL	GI
Rice (white), 150g	33 high	88 high
Rice/corn gf pasta, 150g	31 high	75 high
Millet, 150g	27 high	75 high
Rice (brown), 150g	27 high	57 medium
All-corn pasta, 150g	26 high	69 medium
Potato (jacket), 150g	23 high	85 high
Rice (Basmati), 150g	23 high	58 medium
Rice noodles, 150g	19 medium	60 medium
French fries, 125g	19 medium	75 high
Sweet potato, 125g	19 medium	54 medium
Buckwheat, 150g	16 medium	54 medium
Rice cakes, 25g	16 medium	77 high
Sweetcorn, 100g	15 medium	55 medium
Mashed potato, 150g	14 medium	70 high
Quinoa, 150g	13 medium	51 medium
White gf bread, 35g	12 medium	70 high
Potato new, 150g	10 medium	57 medium
Baked beans, 135g	10 low	48 low
Tortilla chips, 20g	9 low	74 high
Chickpeas, 100g	7 low	42 low
Porridge, 150g	6 low	49 low
Kidney beans/lentils, 100g	5 low	29 low
Butter beans, 100g	4 low	31 low

Many databases and calculators online let you keep an eye on your GIs and GLs. By the way, you'll find the spelling 'glycemic' on international websites. It's the same thing. If you can't find the GL for the food you're interested in but you have the GI, look at the nutritional information on the label for the carbohydrate content and work out the GL as we show you here:

1. **Take the GI rating of the food.**

2. **Divide that number by 100.** For example, carrots have a high GI of 75 (75 ÷ 100 = 0.75).

3. **Multiply that number by the carbohydrate in the portion.** For example, 100 grams of carrots contain just 7 grams of carbohydrate (0.75 × 7 = a low GL of 5.25).

Eating the slow-carb way

You can think of a diet based on foods with a low to medium glycaemic load as the slow-carb diet. It's a healthy, practical, enjoyable and affordable way to eat that's perfectly suited to your gluten-free lifestyle. Here are our tips for slow-carb, gluten-free eating:

✔ Keep your diet absolutely and completely gluten-free.

✔ Ensure that you include plenty of slow-energy-releasing carbohydrates such as fruits and vegetables, peas, beans, lentils and gluten-free wholegrains.

✔ Try to select low- or medium-glycaemic-load foods, which raise your blood sugar level gradually, without the roller-coaster effect of high-glycaemic foods.

✔ If you want to eat high-glycaemic-index starchy foods like gluten-free white bread and rice, eat them in small portions to keep the glycaemic load in check, and eat low-glycaemic-load foods at the same meal.

✔ Eat slowly and chew your food thoroughly, taking frequent sips of water while you eat, and if possible, making the meal a social occasion with other people or a change of scene from the rest of your day. If you bolt your food down, it won't start to fill you up as quickly, and you're more likely to eat too much before you realise you've had enough.

✔ Make sure that the foods you eat offer nutritional value. Don't rely on foods that are basically *empty calories*, that is with plenty of calories but not much in the way of valuable nutrients.

✔ Enjoy your food. Occasionally indulging in your favourite gluten-free pudding is a good thing and is part of enjoying life's little pleasures.

✔ Axe the snacks. Eating three satisfying meals a day and avoiding sugary snacks and drinks in between helps keep your weight in check, your teeth healthy and your blood sugar levels steady.

Knowing About Other Nutrients

A chapter on healthy eating wouldn't be complete without a few other suggestions for how you can make healthy choices and stay gluten-free.

Figuring out your fats

You can make a big difference to your calorie intake and overall health by limiting all fatty foods and by choosing healthier fats. The eatwell plate in Figure 6-1 earlier in this chapter shows you that fatty (and/or sugary) foods should make up only a very small proportion of your overall intake of food each day. A fatty food is one with more than 20 grams of fat per 100 grams, or 21 grams of fat per portion. Examples are deep-fried foods, pastries, cakes, cream, butter, oils, biscuits, fried snack foods, mayonnaise, oily dressings, sausages and fatty meats.

Check out food labels for the number of grams of fat per 100 grams of the food and per portion. You'll also see the guideline daily amount of fat and the percentage that comes from a portion of the food. The guideline daily amount is actually a maximum, and in the UK has been set at 70 grams of fat a day. That includes the fat you can't see in low- and medium-fat foods in a healthy diet.

Labels also show you the amounts of saturated fat in foods. You really need to cut your saturated fat intake as low as you can go, along with that of hydrogenated oils, in order to reduce your risk of heart problems. The maximum daily guideline amount advised for saturated fats is 20 grams.

Healthier types of fat to choose are monounsaturated fats and polyunsaturated fats, although keep in mind that these are still fats with the same calorie content as all other fats. Omega-3 fatty acids – like the ones found in fresh and canned salmon, mackerel, pilchards, sardines and fresh tuna – are particularly beneficial. Not only do they keep your arteries clear, but they also affect your *neurotransmitters* – the chemical messengers in your brain – which are linked to reducing depression and improving your moods. Most people don't eat nearly enough fish, and the guideline amount to aim for is at least two portions a week, with one of those being an oily fish rich in omega-3s.

Table 6-3 gives examples of common sources of different categories of fats.

Table 6-3	Fat Categories	
Saturated Fats	*Monounsaturated Fats*	*Polyunsaturated Fats*
Meat and meat fat	Olives and olive oil	Fish oils
Cream, butter and cheese	Rapeseed oil	Sunflower seeds and oil
Coconut and coconut oil	Peanut oil	Sesame seeds and oil
Cakes, biscuits and pastry	Margarines made from olive oil and rapeseed oil	Nuts
Palm oil	Avocado	Corn oil

Keeping hydrated

Adults typically need about 1.5 to 2 litres of water a day, but you get a lot of this in drinks and in your food, so you don't need to drink it all as plain water. Of course, your need for water depends on a lot of other factors, such as the weather, indoor heating and air-conditioning, what you've eaten and how active you are. Our advice is to have a glass of water with every meal, plus one first thing in the morning and another during the evening. Then keep an eye on the colour of your urine, and if it goes any darker than pale yellow, drink more. But never drink so much that your urine goes almost colourless.

Cutting down on salt

Sodium is one of the essential minerals, but in the UK most people eat far too much of it as salt, or sodium chloride, which can cause high blood pressure and other health problems. Studies estimate that in the UK the average salt intake is over 8 grams a day and some people eat up to 12 grams. Adults should eat no more than 6 grams (1 teaspoon) a day – for children, the maximum is 4 grams a day – and yes, that includes all sources of salt, not just salt you can see.

Up to three-quarters of salt comes from processed foods and savoury snacks, so eating fewer of these products and enjoying fresh foods in their natural state is one of the best ways to keep your salt intake in line with health guidelines.

Tippling moderately

Although all alcoholic drinks apart from barley- and wheat-based beers and lagers are gluten-free, bear in mind that alcohol itself provides 7 calories per gram, almost as much as fat, and it's in a form that your body can't use as fuel directly, so it goes straight to fat. Modest regular alcohol consumption seems to protect against heart and other health problems, compared with being teetotal, as long as you don't get intoxicated. So experts have drawn up guidelines for safe levels of alcohol intake as follows:

- ✔ For women, up to 2 to 3 units a day, but not every day. Have no alcohol on 2 or 3 days each week.

- ✔ For men, up to 3 to 4 units a day, but not every day. Have no alcohol on 2 to 3 days a week.

What's a unit? Less than you might think, especially as drinks are getting more alcoholic these days, particularly wine and beer. One unit is:

- ½ pint beer, lager, cider
- ⅓ pint strong beer, lager, cider
- 85 millilitres (½ glass) wine
- 1 single pub measure of spirits
- ⅔ standard bottle of alcopop

Getting your five a day, every day

Reading about nutritious food is one thing, but actually *eating* it is another. Some people want the nutrients that good foods offer, but they (or the people they're feeding) don't like the taste, cost or even the idea of healthy options. If there's one food group that this applies to more than others, it's fruits and vegetables, which is a shame because this group ticks every box when it comes to healthy gluten-free eating.

But don't worry. You don't have to love Brussels sprouts to eat well (although even these once-loathed vegetables have been bred to taste sweeter and remain crisper on cooking, so try them if you haven't eaten any for a few years). You just have to be creative about how you work fruits and vegetables into your meals, and try to eat a wide variety of different ones. If cost is an issue, choose seasonal produce, and make the most of your freezer at times of the year when different fruits and vegetables are cheap.

Here are a few ideas to inspire you:

- Hide fruits and vegetables in smoothies: cut them into small pieces and blend well.
- Sneak cauliflower, spinach, asparagus, peppers, green beans, courgettes and other vegetables into pasta dishes like lasagne. Even macaroni cheese is colourful with broccoli and peas added. Grating vegetables makes them harder for people to recognise but they still retain all their nutrients.
- Serve a few crudités (sticks of carrot, celery, peppers and so on) with dips and nibbles.
- Add a layer of salad to your sandwich or chop some vegetables into the filling.

- ✔ Throw in a few extra dried fruits with your porridge or muesli.

- ✔ Make an effort to create delicious and great-looking vegetable side dishes. A quick sprinkling of shredded garnishes like pickled ginger, sun-dried tomato, gherkins, capers, olives, sweet white onions, mild chillies, citrus peel and herbs can really liven things up, and there are no end of dressings and sauces you can add to salads and hot vegetables too.

- ✔ Add vegetables to your starchy staples, like lentils in rice, parsnip in mashed potato, diced vegetables in a quinoa 'risotto', and roasted vegetable toppings on polenta.

- ✔ Why not give vegetables the starring role? With all the different fruits and vegetables on offer now all year round, creating all-vegetable main courses like bakes, pastas, curries, casseroles, gratins and quiches is easy. We give you some ideas to start you off in Chapters 12 and 13.

- ✔ Homemade soups and sauces are another good way to get extra vegetables into your diet without you having to wade through bowls of steaming cabbage. Cut vegetables into tiny pieces or blend the mixture until smooth. We give some recipes for soups in Chapter 12 and sauces in Chapter 14.

Getting enough fibre on a gluten-free diet

Fibre is an important part of a healthy diet for many reasons. The best-known benefit of fibre is that it helps keep the gastrointestinal system moving smoothly (that's right, fibre keeps you regular), and that's good for the whole gastrointestinal tract. Fibre can also help reduce blood cholesterol levels and lower your risk of heart disease and some cancers.

People who give up gluten and eat a diet consisting mostly of foods made of gluten-free starches, such as cornflour and tapioca, are sometimes at risk of consuming too little fibre, because gluten-free starches are virtually fibre-free zones. Here are some ways to boost fibre in your diet:

- ✔ Incorporate gluten-free flours made from pulses, such as chickpea or gram flour, which contain much more fibre than white or even brown rice flour.

- ✔ Eat plenty of fruit, vegetables, pulses and naturally gluten-free wholegrains such as buckwheat, oats and millet, which are all good fibre providers.

- ✔ When you're choosing gluten-free mixes and free-from foods, go for the ones based on wholegrains or with added fibre, such as muesli, porridge, high-fibre breads and crackers.

✔ Add gluten-free brans, husks and fibres, such as toasted soya bran, rice bran and psyllium husk, to your cooking, smoothies and breakfast cereals.

✔ Use gluten-free seeds such as linseed, chia, caraway and hemp in your baking, casseroles and breakfasts.

Don't forget that you need to drink plenty of fluid (at least six to eight glasses a day; more in hot weather) to ensure that the fibre works.

Winning the Weight Wars

Nothing's particularly fattening or slimming about the gluten-free diet. You can eat gluten-free and either gain or lose weight or maintain a steady body weight. It's all a matter of making healthy choices in what you eat, how often and how much.

Losing weight on the gluten-free diet

Lots of people gain weight when they first go gluten-free. It's a good thing if you've got too skinny, but it's important not to let it get out of hand and give yourself a weight problem. This gain usually happens for three reasons:

✔ People suffering from untreated gluten intolerance often aren't absorbing all their nutrients – or all their calories. To maintain a healthy, steady body weight, they get into the habit of eating a little more than they'd otherwise need, to make up for the daily loss of unabsorbed calories. After they go gluten-free, their health begins to improve, their gut heals, and they're able to absorb nutrients – and calories – fully again. So if they continue to eat the same calorie intake as before, they gain weight simply because they're taking in more than they need, and the slight excess is turned into body fat. The number of calories needed to make this difference each day is small and the extra food often goes unnoticed.

An excess intake of just 50 kilocalories a day over your needs results in a weight gain of about 2.6 kilograms or 6 pounds in a year. A small cake or cookie, a few crisps and a teaspoon of oil contain 50 kilocalories each. Happily, the same is true in reverse. If you want to lose about 6 pounds in a year, you only need to cut out 50 kilocalories a day or burn off 50 kilocalories more by getting a little more active. But you do need to do so every day.

✔ Some people gain weight when they go gluten-free, because they're eating lots of rice, corn and potatoes in large portions, which are high-glycaemic-load foods that immediately turn to sugar. (You can read more about glycaemic load in the earlier section in this chapter 'Considering Carbohydrates')

✔ People often eat more than their fair share of gluten-free treats such as biscuits, snacks and cakes, in an effort to stave off feelings of deprivation, to explore the range of choices available or to eat up their home-baked delights.

Getting back in trim

If you've packed on a few unwanted pounds since going gluten-free, take action as soon as you can. Stick to a low-glycaemic-load approach and you should have an easier time controlling your weight. If you feel you're already eating a healthy, balanced diet and keeping your glycaemic load in check, the simplest way to lose weight is to trim back your portions a little.

Keeping a food diary is a good way of looking at what you eat, how often, in what situations and how much. The diary can help you to spot your 'danger times' during the day, when you reach for an unhealthy snack, so that you can apply the necessary willpower. In addition, you should feel a little more energetic now that you're absorbing your nutrients properly, so now's a good time get out and get active.

Tackling hunger and cravings

Your blood-sugar level affects hunger and cravings. White bread, biscuits, cakes, sugary drinks and sweets are most likely to send you into the roller-coaster effect of peaks and troughs in blood sugar. Those foods cause a rapid rise in blood sugar, which sends signals to your body to produce insulin.

Insulin does its job to bring down your blood-sugar level, but it can bring it down so low that you get hungry and, in fact, crave more of the same foods that made your blood sugar rise in the first place. Insulin also tells your body to store fat.

On the other hand, when your body absorbs sugars slowly, as when you eat low-glycaemic-load foods and proteins, the rise in blood sugar is gradual, and so is its descent after insulin begins doing its job. The gentle decline in blood sugar means your cravings are less.

Making too much insulin causes you to store fat and stimulates the liver to make more cholesterol, increasing blood cholesterol levels. Excess insulin also inhibits the breakdown of fat that's already stored in your body, so even if you're working out like a fiend, losing those extra pounds is extra hard.

Utilising the power of protein

Eating protein makes you feel fuller than fats or carbohydrates on their own do, and so you tend to eat less. Try to include some lean meat, fish, poultry, egg, pulses, milk, cheese, yoghurt or nuts in all your meals.

Protein also plays a critical part in the production of new cells, and so is important for the process of healing the *villi* (small projections that line your gut to absorb nutrients) as you recover from the effects of untreated coeliac disease. (Refer to Chapter 3 for more on how coeliac disease affects the villi.)

Gaining weight on the gluten-free diet

Some people who've suffered malabsorption as a result of being gluten-sensitive or having untreated coeliac disease are underweight and actually need to gain a few pounds.

When these people go gluten-free, their gut usually heals quickly, and they begin to absorb nutrients and calories. Their weight usually normalises quickly as a result of being gluten-free, without them needing to eat to excess.

Understanding Other Special Dietary Considerations

Certain lifestyles, life stages and other health conditions increase your nutritional needs or mean you're more likely to be deficient in certain nutrients. In this section, we give you the low-down on how to stay gluten-free and eat healthily in these situations.

I'm pregnant or breastfeeding my baby

Producing a little bundle of joy can put quite a strain on the body, so you may not be surprised to hear that the physical stress of pregnancy can cause a slight worsening of gluten intolerance symptoms. Receiving regular health checks, monitoring and support throughout pregnancy becomes particularly important.

Just as in any pregnancy, a balanced and varied diet for both you and your baby is important, but you don't need to heed the old chestnut about eating for two. Strangely, your actual energy requirement only increases slightly, and not until the last three months of pregnancy (and afterwards if you decide to breastfeed). If you're coeliac, your doctor will prescribe extra gluten-free food in the last three months of your pregnancy and while you're breastfeeding. Check out Chapter 4 for more details on obtaining foods on prescription.

You need folic acid for the healthy development of your baby's brain and spinal cord and to help reduce the risk of problems such as spina bifida. The UK Department of Health recommends that women trying for a baby should start taking a daily 400-microgram supplement of folic acid as soon as they stop using contraception, right up until the 12th week of pregnancy, or a larger supplement if they're found to have lower-than-normal levels of the vitamin in their blood. Your GP can advise you on this. This dosage is over and above the usual daily recommended intake of 200 micrograms, which you can get from your diet. This requirement becomes especially important on a gluten-free diet, because not all gluten-free cereal products are fortified with folic acid. So, unlike with gluten-containing counterparts, you can't rely on these foods to supply your needs. Some gluten-free sources of folic acid include:

- Brown rice
- Dark green vegetables such as broccoli and spinach
- Fortified gluten-free bread, breakfast cereals and pizza bases (check the label to find suitable brands)
- Oranges, whole and juiced
- Potatoes
- Yeast extract

Depending on your nutritional status, your healthcare team may also advise you to take additional supplements of other key nutrients such as calcium, vitamin D, iron or vitamin B12 during pregnancy if they have any doubt about you getting an adequate intake.

If anyone in the immediate family has coeliac disease, your baby has a one in ten chance of developing it. (You can read advice on feeding your baby to lessen this risk in Chapter 3.) Other gluten-related disorders besides coeliac disease aren't hereditary, but you can still apply the baby-feeding advice. Expectant mothers who don't have a gluten-related disorder can continue to eat gluten during the pregnancy as usual.

I'm vegetarian or vegan

It's possible to get everything you need from a vegetarian or vegan diet that's also gluten-free. However, you need to ensure you get enough protein, calcium, iron and vitamins B12 and D, which are the most likely to be deficient in your vegetarian or vegan diet, particularly in the latter. If you've been suffering from undiagnosed coeliac disease for some time or if you're anaemic or have low bone density, you need extra calcium, iron and vitamin D above average requirements.

Many vegetarians eat dairy products and eggs, so are at less risk of nutritional deficiencies than are vegans, who don't. You need to plan your meals carefully and look for foods that are naturally rich in protein, calcium, iron and vitamins B12 and D, or those that the manufacturers have fortified. We show suitable gluten-free sources of these nutrients that are appropriate for you in Table 6-4. We mark foods that are vegetarian but not vegan with an A for animal-derived product. Those foods marked with an asterisk (*) are not all gluten-free, so do check labels.

Table 6-4	Gluten-Free Sources of Nutrients Suitable for Vegetarians and Vegans
Nutrient Likely to Be Deficient in Gluten-Free Vegetarian and Vegan Diets	*Suitable Sources*
Protein	Textured vegetable protein made from soya
	Tofu*
	Soya milk, yoghurt and cheese
	A: Eggs
	A: Milk, cheese, yoghurt
	Nuts
	Beans and lentils
	Quinoa, buckwheat, lupin, teff, millet, amaranth, sorghum

(continued)

Table 6-4 *(continued)*

Nutrient Likely to Be Deficient in Gluten-Free Vegetarian and Vegan Diets	Suitable Sources
Calcium	A: Milk, cheese and yoghurt
	Tofu*
	Dark green vegetables such as kale and broccoli
	Calcium-fortified soya milk, yoghurt and cheese
	Seeds, especially sesame and sunflower
	Pulses – peas, beans and lentils
	A: Eggs
	Oranges
	Dried apricots and figs
	Nuts, especially almonds, brazils, hazelnuts and walnuts
	Hard tap water and some mineral waters
	A: Calcium-fortified foods and drinks (many contain milk and egg, especially breads and flour mixes)
Iron Increase your absorption of iron from these foods by eating them with vitamin C-rich foods like citrus fruits, blackcurrants and potatoes.	Pulses – peas, beans and lentils
	Dark green vegetables
	Dried fruit, especially apricots, figs and prunes
	Nuts, especially cashews and walnuts
	Seeds, especially sesame
	Tofu*
	Textured vegetable protein
	A: Eggs
	A: Fortified foods
Vitamin B12	Fortified foods such as margarine, yeast extract, vegetable stock, soya products and bouillon*
Vitamin D Try to allow sunshine onto your bare skin (without sun protection) for 15 minutes a day in the summer.	Fortified products such as margarine
	A: Eggs

Do seek the advice of your dietitian if you're bringing up your child on a gluten-free vegetarian or vegan diet, or if you're thinking of having a baby. A dietitian can help ensure that you meet all the dietary requirements for both a healthy mother and baby.

I'm an active sportsperson

If you're involved in sport, either as a participant or as a fan, you can't fail to have noticed that a great many world-class sportsmen and women are going gluten-free these days, although very few have been diagnosed with a definite gluten-related disorder. More and more of them attribute improved performance and even domination of their sport to the diet, so it's catching on fast.

Some are doing it to overcome occasional feelings of bloatedness, gassiness and tummy aches brought on by loading up with starchy foods like bread and pasta before training, which builds up body stores of glycogen (a carbohydrate), so that they can perform for longer. They seem to have blamed the gluten for the symptoms, rather than the sheer bulk of the food eaten. Others seem to have noted the improved performance following their diagnosis and treatment of athletes who really are gluten-intolerant, and simply want to see whether they can achieve the same.

Whatever the thinking, the gluten-free diet doesn't appear to be doing athletes any harm; this has spawned a plethora of gluten-free sports foods, which of course you can enjoy. But do note that high-profile sportspeople often have their own dietitian on hand to guide their food choices, accurately assess their intake and fine-tune their diets down to the last nutrient. You probably don't have such a resource of your own, so we don't advise that you take up some of the wackier elements of sports nutrition unsupervised, such as excessive intakes of protein, no-carb regimes and unnecessary supplements.

The main concern for active sportspeople living gluten-free is getting enough carbohydrate to fuel those active muscles. Eating carbohydrates before, during and after training or competition is essential to maintaining energy levels and speeding recovery after the event. This is where all those gluten-free grains we outline in Chapter 4 come into their own. Think about basing your meals around brown rice, potatoes, corn, other gluten-free grains or gluten-free pasta and pizza. (For more information, check out the earlier section 'Considering Carbohydrates'.)

If you're coeliac and very active in your job or in a sport or hobby, you're entitled to a higher monthly allowance of gluten-free prescribable items. Do tell your doctor, who can work out whether you qualify, by comparing your physical activity with your metabolic rate. (Read more about getting gluten-free food on prescription in Chapter 4.)

Refuelling after a training session or event is crucial for recovery. You may need to take your own gluten-free snacks to eat after an event, such as bananas, gluten-free crackers, biscuits or a sandwich. Most sports drinks and carb gels (carbohydrate-rich solutions that absorb quickly in the mouth to provide instant energy) are gluten-free, but some meal-replacement drinks and energy bars designed for sportspeople contain wheat and cost a fortune! You're better off eating real foods, but if you do buy sports ones, check the labels carefully.

I'm an older person

As you get older, a poor diet can make you more susceptible to illness or affect your quality of life. If you're on a gluten-free diet, iron intake is especially important to prevent anaemia as you get older. Include rich natural sources of iron (red meat, offal, pulses, oily fish, eggs) or gluten-free products that are iron-fortified (such as breakfast cereal) in your diet, along with vitamin C to help with absorption. Where possible, try to avoid having tea with your meals, because the tannins in tea can impair iron absorption.

Getting enough calcium (especially from dairy foods) and vitamin D (to help absorb it) remains important as you get older for the prevention of osteoporosis. This is a common condition in which the bones become thin and brittle, making them liable to break easily if you have a minor accident or a fall. About half of older coeliacs are at risk of osteoporosis, rising to three-quarters of those who don't stick to their gluten-free diet. It's never too late to start rebuilding healthy bones, and even a small improvement in the density of your bones makes them more resistant to breaking. People aged 65 years and over and people who aren't exposed to much sun can take a daily supplement containing 10 micrograms of vitamin D. You can get vitamin D in your food from meat, oily fish, eggs, evaporated milk and fortified foods, as well from getting out into the sun during the summer. Try to allow sunshine onto your bare skin (without sun protection) for 15 minutes a day in the summer.

Getting enough fibre to prevent constipation and diverticular disease can also be difficult on a gluten-free diet. See the earlier section 'Getting enough fibre on a gluten-free diet' for a range of ways to add fibre into your diet.

In the UK, a worryingly high number of older adults admitted to hospital from home are found to be undernourished. If you find shopping for, or preparing, meals hard, you may benefit from receiving meals delivered to your home.

Various systems for meal provision exist around the UK, ranging from the local social service provision of hot 'meals on wheels' to home deliveries of frozen foods from private companies. Several home delivery companies manufacture a range of meals and desserts that they guarantee to be free from gluten-containing ingredients and from contamination during manufacture.

If you're unwell and can't easily manage to digest foods, milk-based supplement drinks can be a useful addition to your diet. You can buy these drinks in both sweet and savoury flavours, and the majority are gluten-free and available in the shops or on prescription from your GP.

The sad fact of life is that the older you are, the more likely you are to have to pay a visit to hospital. If you are admitted, the nurse or doctor admitting you will probably ask whether you're on a special diet. We're really glad to say that nowadays most healthcare staff don't throw their hands up in horror if you say you're gluten-intolerant. Instead, they reach calmly for the gluten-free hospital menu. Seriously, most hospitals can provide at least one gluten-free choice from the main menu, and even if they don't, they're likely to have some frozen gluten-free meals in stock. Due to the speed of food ordering in most hospital systems (think of an oil tanker turning) you're probably wise to take some of your own foods in with you to cover the possibility of your first meal being delayed. If you know you're being admitted, ring the ward in advance. You can also bring in some gluten-free bread and crackers in case the ward doesn't have any when you're first admitted.

I'm diabetic

If you have diabetes, you're not producing or not responding correctly to insulin, the hormone that converts digested carbohydrate from food into energy for use in your body. As a result, your sugar levels may have built up in your blood, leading to a variety of symptoms. Of the two quite distinct types of diabetes, type 1 diabetes generally develops in children or younger adults, and is an autoimmune condition in which destruction of cells of the pancreas leads to a lack of insulin production. Type 2 diabetes tends to develop later in life and is due to a resistance to circulating insulin. Type 2 is more often related to being overweight or inactive.

Roughly 5 per cent of people with coeliac disease also have type 1 diabetes, more than in the rest of the population. This occurrence is probably due to a shared genetic risk for both conditions. If you have both together, a gluten-free diet can help you control your blood-sugar levels.

If you have either type of diabetes, aim to follow a healthy diet to keep your blood-glucose levels as near to normal as possible and reduce the risk of other problems such as heart disease and putting on unwanted weight.

Eating the right types and amounts of fat, fibre, protein, carbohydrate and salt is especially important, as is paying attention to the glycaemic load of your food. For more information on this, see the section 'Considering Carbohydrates' earlier in this chapter.

If your two conditions are managed by separate teams of specialists, ensure you attend your regular check-ups with both of them, and keep them both informed of your overall progress. Ideally, the same dietitian can advise you on both conditions and help you to eat a diet that fully meets your needs.

I'm intolerant to lactose

If you have an as-yet undiagnosed gluten-related disorder or you've only recently started on your gluten-free diet, you may be unable to tolerate lactose, the sugar in milk and other dairy products. If that's the case, you'll probably notice a lot of wind and diarrhoea a few hours after eating dairy foods, especially raw milk; you may have been avoiding these foods for a long time for this reason.

To digest lactose, you need the enzyme lactase, and lactose intolerance is caused by an inability to produce enough lactase. The enzyme is made by the lining of your small intestine, in the very area which has probably been damaged by eating gluten. Once you've settled into your gluten-free diet, any damage the gluten has done to this area will probably heal and you'll be able to produce lactase again and tolerate dairy products.

Lactase is produced to order only when you eat lactose, and you won't start producing it efficiently at first, even after your small intestine has healed. You need to work up your intake of dairy products gradually, starting with small portions of lower-lactose foods such as cheese, yoghurt and cooked milk, and working your way up to tolerating a latté or a glass of milk.

You may be thinking 'Why bother to eat dairy products?' Doing so is worthwhile because dairy products are the best sources of natural calcium in the British diet, and natural calcium is more likely to be absorbed and used by your body than the synthetic calcium in supplements and fortified foods. Calcium is an essential nutrient, not only for strong bones and teeth but also for metabolism in cells throughout your body. You need calcium in greater quantity than any other mineral, particularly as you get older and your bones start to thin.

If you're permanently intolerant to lactose, then obviously you won't be able to eat any dairy products, even as ingredients in other foods. Table 6-4 shows non-dairy sources of calcium; you can also eat tinned oily fish, including the soft, edible bones, and other foods which are fortified with calcium.

Part III
Taking the Plunge: How to Go Gluten-Free

Go to www.dummies.com/extras/livingglutenfreeuk for online bonus content.

In this part . . .

- ✔ Start living gluten-free – quickly and easily.
- ✔ Shop shrewdly – in-store and online.
- ✔ Enjoy the benefits of meal planning.
- ✔ Get au fait with tips and tricks for sharing the kitchen with gluten.
- ✔ Make the most of wheat alternatives, including some fabulous bread mixes.
- ✔ Go to www.dummies.com/extras/livinggluten freeuk for online bonus content.

Chapter 7

Going Gluten-Free Right Now: A Quick-Start Guide

. . . .

In This Chapter

▶ Having a positive attitude

▶ Making a fast start

▶ Working out your healthy weight

▶ Preparing the kitchen for gluten-free cooking and storage

▶ Working out what to do if you can't cook

. . . .

*Y*ou've a lot to take in about the gluten-free diet: the guidance in this book, advice you've been given by your doctor, and probably some information you've picked up from your own enquiries and from chatting to friends and family. But you've nothing to gain by delaying the start until you've digested all this info and thought about it some more, and everything to gain by getting cracking right away.

Going gluten-free means going cold turkey – that is, going completely gluten-free all at once and for ever. The gluten-free diet isn't like most diets where you cut down on something by eating less of it or eating it less often. Eating any gluten at all, even a tiny crumb of it and only occasionally, is a bad idea if you need to be gluten-free, because even a little continues to damage your health and prevents your body from recovering. And the great thing is, as soon as you stop eating gluten, your body will recover, starting right away. You'll be able to sense the difference as early as tomorrow morning, and you'll feel great knowing that your body is repairing the damage gluten has done over many months or even years.

We're not suggesting you panic, rush out and spend a fortune on gluten-free foods or stop eating while you wait for your first prescription to arrive. You've really nothing to panic about. Taking positive action today gives you a positive attitude towards your new gluten-free, healthier life. The sooner you sort out how you'll eliminate gluten and replace it with healthy gluten-free foods, the sooner you'll see that this diet isn't a huge problem in your life but an exciting and healthful change of direction.

Looking on the Bright Side

If you're already feeling positive and raring to go, skip this section. This is for you if you're feeling dejected or panicky about going gluten-free or wavering about your decision.

Saying goodbye to gluten

Gluten isn't a prop you've depended on all your life. It hasn't formed your character, made you better-looking, found you a partner, landed you a great job or got you better marks at school. It's only a minor component of certain foods, and, luckily, plenty of delicious replacements for them are available.

When we trained, gluten-free bread came in tins like large baked bean tins, only with ribs around them. The bread consisted of a snowy white foam that filled the tin end to end, so that the 'loaf' had exactly the shape of the tin. There was no crust, very little taste, and the bread disintegrated as soon as you went near it with a knife. Sorry to bring back horrible memories if you had to eat that stuff back then, but the bottom line is this: gluten-free products have moved on, and really decent gluten-free grub – even bread – is available these days (thank goodness!).

Saying hello to health

The rest of this chapter – well, the whole book, really – is about moving forwards towards a healthier, delicious diet, not looking back at the problems that led up to this point. But as you start the diet, you might be feeling low about your diagnosis and what it will mean for your lifestyle. Maybe you're worried about whether you can still eat out, go to the pub or go on holiday, or maybe you've always perceived yourself to be in tip-top health, and the diagnosis has come as a shock.

Explore your feelings with the aid of some highly specialised tools – no, just kidding. All you need is a pen, a sheet of paper divided into three columns, and a few minutes. We call this exercise 'What's stopping you?' Here it is:

1. **In the left-hand column, describe your present predicament.**

   Write down all your problems and concerns about giving up gluten.

2. **In the right-hand column, describe what you hope life will be like when you've cracked the diet.**

   Imagine yourself living gluten-free without a care in the world.

3. **In the middle column, answer the question: 'What's stopping you from getting from the left-hand column to the right-hand one?'**

   Can't afford it? Eat out all the time? Love bread? Drink a lot of beer? Can't cook? Don't believe it'll work? Just get all your thoughts down and then read the list through.

We think you'll find solutions to all the obstacles right here in this book or at Coeliac UK's website (`www.coeliac.org.uk`). And most of the obstacles will be within your own powers to overcome.

Making a Fast Start

You need to do a few things straight away. After all, you've got to eat today, tomorrow and every day. It'll be a little while before you have a larder full of options and know where to go for takeout lunches. Making a fast start helps you to stick to your resolve of not sliding back to your bad old ways. Here are our suggested first steps.

Although we address our advice to 'you', the reader, all the guidance applies equally if you're the parent, carer or partner of someone who's going gluten-free. If you're helping a young person, we've a chapter especially for you: Chapter 18.

Working out what you can eat

You're sure to have plenty of food that's gluten-free in the house right now. So before you hit the panic button and the shops, we suggest you look around your own kitchen and think about your meals for today and the next few days. Unless you have a pressing need to eat out in that time, eat your main meals and breakfasts at home for a few days while you find your feet. If you have your lunches out, say at work or school, maybe take packed ones for a few days.

These are some of the naturally gluten-free foods and drinks that are suitable for you and likely to be in stock at home: all types of rice, potatoes, cornflour, sweetcorn or maize, plain meat, plain fish, eggs, cheese, milk, yoghurt (most of them), all fruits, vegetables, plain salads and pulses (fresh, canned, frozen and dried), plain nuts and peanuts, tea, coffee, cocoa, sugar, butter, margarine, jam, honey, tomato ketchup (most brands), vinegar, salt, spices, seeds, fruit juices, most chocolate (milk, plain and white), plain crisps, wine, spirits and water.

Gluten is only in wheat, rye, barley and oats (other than pure gluten-free oats, but we're guessing you've been advised not to eat oats for the time being anyway), plus of course all the foods that are made from these grains. That still leaves a huge range of grains and starches that are naturally gluten-free. If you're a foodie, you may well have several of these already in the cupboard. Cornflour, quinoa, buckwheat and millet are the most likely. Don't forget you can eat other starchy vegetables too, such as sweet potatoes, parsnips, pumpkins, beans, lentils and aubergines.

Joining the club

Get online and visit Coeliac UK at www.coeliac.org.uk. Finding out that you're not alone is immensely reassuring. Coeliac UK isn't just for coeliacs but for anyone with a gluten-related disorder or just an interest in living gluten-free. We urge you to join the organisation today, which you can do online. You'll receive a really informative welcome pack that includes the *Food and Drink Directory*.

After you've joined, you can telephone the charity's helplines, which are staffed by people who really know their stuff and are great listeners. You can ask whatever you want, however silly you may think you sound, and if you just want to hear some reassuring words, they'll have them.

Also sign up with your nearest Coeliac UK local voluntary support group and see what events it has coming up. If you can, make contact with a member of the local group right away. The members all live gluten-free themselves and have a great deal of first-hand experience and support to offer you.

Perusing prescriptions

If you have coeliac disease or dermatitis herpetiformis, you can get some staple foods on prescription. You can find a list of these foods in Coeliac UK's directory and on the website. Have a good look at the list and check out the items you're interested in on the manufacturers' websites before you put in your first prescription. Don't expect the doctor or pharmacist to advise you on what to order. There are just too many foods to choose from.

You need to determine how much food you can get on prescription (see Coeliac UK's website and Chapter 4). Think through whether you want to 'spend' most of your allowance on flour mixes to use in your own cooking or on bread, pasta, pizza bases and crackers.

If you pay for your prescriptions, think about getting a pre-payment certificate. Go to www.nhs.uk/NHSEngland/Healthcosts/Pages/PPC.aspx for details and to apply. If you plan on getting a few different items every month, which we suggest you do in the beginning while you find out which ones you like, the certificate saves you money. But even so, we suggest not plunging in and getting the certificate right away, and if you decide to, getting one for three months.

The reason we suggest a short delay is that most of the manufacturers of gluten-free foods are extremely generous with samples of their products plus free services such as recipes, events and informative websites. Asking for samples is worthwhile so that you can try products before you put in your first prescription. Inevitably, you won't like them all, and trying them first avoids your prescription list running to several pages.

The companies send you order forms to simply tick and hand to the surgery. If you only want one or two items, that can be convenient, but if you want to order from more than one company, bin these forms and manage your own list.

Asking to see a dietitian

If you haven't been referred to a dietitian yet, request this as soon as possible, because it may be some weeks before one is available through the NHS. You can refer yourself to a freelance dietitian and pay a fee for the consultations. Go to www.freelancedietitians.org to find one near you.

A dietitian can give you individual advice, not only on eating gluten-free but also on other diet-related concerns such as being too thin, overweight or having another condition needing dietary treatment. Food is their thing and they have vast knowledge about it and its effects on your health. All their advice is based on scientific evidence not fads, celebrity diets, superfoods and commercial interest.

Before you go along for the appointment, make a note of any questions that have foxed you about living gluten-free, plus any of your normal eating habits that you've found difficult to convert to gluten-free ones.

Telling your nearest and dearest

Unless you live alone, in which case you can delay this step for a while, you need to let your nearest and dearest know what's happening in your life. Think carefully about what you want to say beforehand. Your loved ones may be thrown by your announcement, worried about the impact it's going to have on them and others in the house, concerned for you and your future health and fearful of catching what you've got – and may have a host of other emotional reactions besides. Keep in mind that most people have never even heard of coeliac disease, or if they have, have no idea what it is. Most people have only the vaguest notion of what gluten is or which foods contain it.

Obviously, you know those close to you and can put the news to them in a way that's in proportion to the problem and that everyone is comfortable with. You may be surprised to get a response of relief when others find out you can be treated just by changing your diet. Talking about your situation provides a sense of turning a corner.

Now that you know the cause of your symptoms, you know what you've got to do to avoid them. Whether you cook for your loved ones or they cook for you, your gluten-free diet is going to mean a few changes in the kitchen, but that doesn't mean that other people have to go gluten-free themselves. We offer lots of advice and tips in the book, as well as delicious gluten-free recipes in Part IV that you can all enjoy together, if you want to.

If you have any engagements coming up that will involve eating, you must let the hosts know as soon as possible that you'll need gluten-free food. That should be all you need to say. If it's a private function, you may need to explain what you can't eat, but you don't need to go into details about your health and symptoms.

Weighing In

It may not seem a priority, but you need to assess where you are weightwise compared with a healthy weight for your height. If you've been suffering from an undiagnosed gluten-related disorder for a while (and it could have been years), you may be too thin. On the other hand, plenty of gluten-intolerant people are overweight. Weigh yourself or go to a pharmacy or clinic if you don't have bathroom scales, and work out your body mass index (BMI).

Your BMI is your weight in kilograms divided by your height in metres, squared. First work out or measure your height in metres and then multiply that figure by itself. For example, if your height is 1.83 metres, the denominator is $1.83 \times 1.83 = 3.35$. If your weight is 76.3 kilograms, your BMI is 76.3 divided by 3.35 = 22.8.

Don't worry if the maths fries your brain – you can find BMI calculators online, or any health professional can show you where you are on the BMI chart. Keep a note of your starting weight and BMI. The healthy BMI range for adults is 18.5 to 24.9. If your BMI is less than 18.5, you're underweight, and if it's more than 24.9, you're overweight – seriously so if it's 30 or more. Healthy BMI ranges for children vary by gender and age, so if you're worried about your child being overweight or underweight, do see a dietitian.

Here's how to proceed, depending on the BMI result:

✔ If your BMI is in the **normal range**, you're a healthy weight for your height. To stay within this range, you need to eat a balanced diet.

✔ If you're **underweight**, you don't want to lose any more weight, which can easily happen in just a few days, so ensure you get enough starchy carbohydrate foods that are gluten-free. That means potatoes, rice, gluten-free pasta, gluten-free bread and sweetcorn, plus the lesser known gluten-free cereals like quinoa, buckwheat and millet. We assume your doctor's told you not to eat oats until your damaged gut heals, but if not, you can include pure oats in the list. For the moment, we suggest you stock up with enough of these staples to tide you over for a week or so while you settle into your new diet. Longer term, you'll probably find you put weight on as your gut heals. You don't want the weight gain to run out of control and for you to exceed your preferred healthy weight. Weigh yourself regularly from now on and adjust your total calorie intake and your physical activity to keep your weight in check.

✔ If you're **overweight**, you have the chance to solve that problem as well as eating gluten-free. Lots of low- to moderate-calorie foods are inherently gluten-free, such as lean meat, fish, eggs, low-fat dairy products, fruits and vegetables. When it comes to the starchy carbohydrate foods, opt for low-glycaemic-index ones and watch your portions. You can read a lot more about a healthy gluten-free diet and the glycaemic index in Chapter 6. Above all, if you're overweight, axe the snacks.

Kitting Up the Kitchen

Sorting out the kitchen and store cupboards is something you need to start early on, because gluten lurks there. The goal is to separate gluten-containing foods from gluten-free foods, so that no cross-contamination occurs. You also want to eat well and enjoy your food right from day one, and going gluten-free shouldn't mean going without good food.

Taking stock

Keep a shopping list on hand while you take stock in the kitchen. Gluten is in wheat, rye, barley and oats. Start by looking at labels of foods you already have in stock and putting the gluten-containing ones on separate shelves or perhaps in a separate cupboard from the rest. That's your no-go area. If you have bags of wheat flour, sort out sealable containers for them or at least put them into plastic bags with bag clips.

All the naturally gluten-free foods you already have in stock can stay where they are, because they're safe for you to eat.

Throw out any crumb-contaminated tubs, jars and packets of butter, spreads, jams, yeast extract, mayonnaise, condiments and the like – things that have been dipped into with spoons and knives that have also been in contact with wheat-containing foods. In the future, keep all tubs and jars gluten-free by assigning each with its own serving knife or spoon that doesn't touch anything with gluten in it.

Cruising the 'free-from' aisle

Depending on how much gluten-free food you've got in stock, you may need to buy in a few 'survival' items to keep you going for a week or so, but you don't need to blow the bank. A bag of flour mix, some breakfast cereal, bread, crackers or crispbreads, a packet of pasta and maybe a treat or two are really all you need for the moment from the 'free-from' aisle.

You can find plenty of naturally gluten-free foods in other aisles too. Some products require a bit of label-reading to make sure they don't contain wheat, rye, barley or oats. You'll be surprised how much of the supermarket yields gluten-free gems these days.

Avoid the biscuit aisle and the bakery section for the moment. Hanging out there at this stage can be like rubbing salt into your own wounds – it hurts and delays the healing process.

Toasting your good health

As well as the food, consider buying one or two things to make life easier:

✔ **Toaster:** A new toaster or an additional one just for you is a good idea. Don't even think about trying to clean gluten out of your old toaster, because you simply won't succeed, and anyway, someone's bound to forget and put a slice of ordinary bread into it, so you'll be back where you started. If you only want one toaster, treat yourself to one of the more upmarket ones with four slots and two separate sets of controls and, crucially, two separate crumb trays. Keep one pair of slots for gluten-free use only and place the toaster so that others aren't waving gluteny bread and toast around above your slots. A stopgap for the moment if you don't want to lash out on a new toaster is toaster bags, but they're not ideal for everyday use.

✔ **Bread bin:** Another danger area which you really can't share with ordinary bread. No matter how careful you are, breadcrumbs will stray onto your bread. Either buy a separate bin, crock or bag for your bread and buns, or plan on keeping them in the bags they came in with clips.

Other than these two items, you don't need any special utensils urgently, so there's no need to replace all your pans, gadgets and cooking and serving paraphernalia. As long as they're clean, they'll be free of gluten.

Can't Cook, Won't Cook?

If you enjoy cooking, or someone you live with does, and you're interested in food, you're already well on the way to going gluten-free enjoyably and affordably. Cooking skills and food knowledge give you the confidence to try new, gluten-free ingredients and recipes and to work these into your usual, probably wide-ranging, eating pattern. But if you're not like that, you can still eat a healthy, balanced gluten-free diet from the start.

Some naturally gluten-free foods don't need any cooking, such as salads, fruit, dairy products and tinned food, plus a lot of them only need simple cooking, such as eggs, meat, rice, potatoes and vegetables. When you get your *Food and Drink Directory* from Coeliac UK (see 'Joining the club' earlier in this chapter for details), you'll be delighted to see a long list of gluten-free ready meals available in the shops, and you can find many more online. If you've bought a survival kit of gluten-free items from the 'free-from' aisle, like bread, pasta, crackers and breakfast cereals, these can help you to extend your eating options considerably.

Try some of our gluten-free recipes in Part IV; we've written them to fit into your everyday life without needing any fancy equipment, and we explain exactly how to make them, step by step. In fact, if you've never cooked before and begin your culinary journey gluten-free, you'll have the advantage of not having to train yourself to replace gluten in your favourite foods. You'll soon be turning out delicious and easy gluten-free meals like a professional.

Chapter 8

Making Sense of Smart Gluten-Free Shopping

In This Chapter

▶ Focusing on your objectives before heading to the shops

▶ Planning your meals so you know which ingredients to buy

▶ Choosing where to shop

▶ Getting gluten-free value for money

*D*anna tells us that the first thing she did after her son Tyler was diagnosed with coeliac disease was to go shopping. No, not the head-for-the-shops-because-I'm-shattered-and-a-bit-of-retail-therapy-will-make-me-feel-better kind of shopping. She went food shopping and soon felt the roller-coaster of ups and downs that was to become all too familiar. First, she noticed there was no mention of gluten on labels anywhere, and she felt that finding foods without gluten was going to be a lot easier than she'd thought. Then she realised that everything with wheat, rye, barley or oats on the label was off limits. She thought, 'How can food shopping be so complicated? Why don't they just tell us when something's got gluten in it? Ah, here's something he can eat. Why is he spitting it out?' Now keep in mind that this was way back in the 1990s – 1991 to be exact – in the States. The Internet didn't really exist, Danna had no books on the subject and no sources of information or support.

For Hilary, in the noughties in the UK, and already equipped with the knowledge of exactly what gluten was and which foods and ingredients contained it, going gluten-free was a lot easier. But she still hit the food shops on the way home from the doctor's surgery. She made a few purchases in the 'free-from' aisles and at a health food shop ('*How* much? Are you sure?'), and then came home and hit the Internet. A couple of those purchases were okay, particularly the all-corn spaghetti that cooked up very similarly to normal spaghetti, looked the same and tasted better. Others never got finished. They were either not the sort of thing she normally ate or just not very nice.

The good news is that finding gluten-free products really *is* easier now, thanks to new labelling laws, the growing demand from consumers being met by eager food marketers, and the availability of comprehensive gluten-free food directories and listings.

In this chapter, we start by helping you work out what you want to buy. Then we offer some guidance on where to shop, how to shop and – importantly – how to avoid breaking the bank when buying gluten-free foods. We guide you down the right aisle to discover important shopping tips that can help you save time, money and frustration.

Knowing What You Want

One of the best things you can do to make shopping easier when you're enjoying a gluten-free lifestyle is to plan ahead. If you don't plan ahead, especially at first, you can end up spending hours in the supermarket and online wandering in circles – literally or virtually – trying to work out what to buy and worrying whether a product's gluten-free.

If you've read our quick-start guide in Chapter 7, you should have the basics in place pretty quickly, and you'll soon find it easier to integrate your new gluten-free diet into your preferred eating plan.

Next comes the temptation to try everything that's on offer that's gluten-free, whether you normally eat that type of food or not. Your store cupboards will soon be groaning with foods you're not sure how to cook and don't even like much when you do get to them. You end up buying the same thing twice, not realising that cereals have different names in different countries. And what was described as 'flour' on the Internet shopping site turns out to be starch when it arrives, or a naturally gluten-free grain has the dreaded words 'May contain wheat' on the pack, which wasn't mentioned over the phone.

Keeping lists saves you serious time and money when you shop for food and fill out your prescription slip. Lists can help ensure that you enjoy your food more and that it's not only gluten-free but also good for you.

Planning your meals

In our other lives, when we're not *For Dummies* authors, we follow the dictum 'plan your work and work to your plan'. For some of us, the same thing goes for meals, although 'plan your meals and eat them' isn't quite as catchy. The odd one out in our little group has a different approach. Doesn't bother to plan ahead when it comes to meals and in fact relishes the idea of cooking up whatever takes her fancy at the time. Clue there; it's not Nigel!

Most people are spontaneous and impulsive shoppers. They see something in the shop that looks particularly appealing (and because they're usually starving while they're shopping, *everything* looks good) so they toss it into their trolley. But applying a little forethought to what you'll be eating helps you focus on your health objectives, particularly if you cater for more than one person.

When you're writing lists and planning your meals, try not to think in terms of what you can't eat, but what you can. Not cutting out gluten, but what to replace it with. Consider the things you love to eat – with or without gluten – and build around those foods, making substitutions to convert gluten-containing meals into gluten-free ones. (In Chapter 9 we explain how to make *anything* gluten-free with simple substitutions.)

You may find some of these tips helpful:

- ✔ **Encourage the whole family to eat gluten-free, at least for main meals.** Even if some members of your family are gluten eaters, make your life simpler by planning most of the family meals to be gluten-free. This planning isn't hard if you follow the approach of eating meat, fish, fruit, vegetables and naturally gluten-free starchy staples (refer to Chapter 4 for more on these foods). Alternatively, if part of the meal – for example, spaghetti Bolognese – contains gluten, cook a separate portion of gluten-free pasta but serve the gluten-free sauce to everyone.

- ✔ **Plan a few days' menus at once.** Look through Part IV and other recipe books (no, they don't have to be gluten-free ones) for inspiration and map out your meal plan for the next few days, working in as much variety as you can and keeping in mind the healthy guidelines we talk about in Chapter 6.

- ✔ **Set aside a marathon cooking day.** From time to time, designate a day for cooking ahead. With several gluten-free dishes already in mind, you can prepare several meals at once and freeze them, saving yourself cooking time *and* cleaning time.

- ✔ **Choose foods that provide tasty gluten-free leftovers.** If you're planning roast chicken for dinner one night, pick a large one so that you can count on leftovers for chicken stir-fry with rice, or perhaps our Singapore noodles in Chapter 13, the following night.

- ✔ **Go for individual portions.** A lot of dishes look appealing in individual portions, like cupcakes, tartlets, scones, sliced tray bakes, bread rolls, pittas, small pizzas, lasagnes, casseroles, cottage pies and Scotch eggs. If you portion foods this way, you can segregate the gluten-free ones from the rest. And if you freeze the dishes in individual portions, they'll thaw in no time. Label the portions so you don't mix them up.

✓ **Plan meals you can cook in a slow cooker.** Slow cookers are back in fashion. They're perfect for complete one-course meals and for turning cheaper cuts of meat that are too tough for fast cooking into meltingly tender, delicious casseroles. And coming home to a house that smells like you've been cooking all day is so enticing!

Get the whole family to help with menu planning. It's frustrating to spend a weekend planning, shopping and cooking, only to hear moans and groans about how what used to be someone's favourite food is now considered 'yuck'. For that matter, enlist help with the cooking and washing up too.

Making notes and lists

Your spontaneity is exactly what food retailers and manufacturers are banking on. They want you to be impulsive, and that's why they tempt you with the naughty-but-nice foods with high profit margins situated at eye-level, and why they add those 'you might also like' messages to the online basket page. How many times have you wandered around the supermarket thinking of delicious, healthy meals to make for the week, only to get home with dozens of bags of groceries, unable to remember what inspired you to buy them in the first place? Yes, us too.

When it comes to gluten-free foods, it pays to keep notes, not only on what to buy but also on what you thought of things you've already tried. The quality is variable, particularly among prescription foods, and the pack sizes are often large. If you don't want to be stuck with a daunting amount of gluten-free food you don't like, try annotating your copy of Coeliac UK's *Food and Drink Directory* (see the next section) with your comments and preferences.

We recommend keeping a three-column list – a 'live' record, which you can adapt and keep up to date as you go. We call it the Try, Buy, Decry list. You can keep it on a computer, simply use a sheet of paper with moveable sticky notes on it, or put it on a mobile device to refer to while you're shopping. Put ingredients and brands you read about and like the look of in the Try column. Populate the Buy column with things you decide definitely to get soon or which you're running low on. Then, if you don't like something, move it to the Decry column, so that you don't inadvertently buy it again.

Deciding What to Buy

Obviously, the most important considerations when deciding what to buy are what you like, what you're going to make, and whether a food is gluten-free.

Remember that you have two kinds of gluten-free food available: those that companies make as speciality items and label as gluten-free, and those that are naturally gluten-free and not labelled as such. Foods in both these categories are scattered throughout the average shop or online store. Several food directories or product listings are available, covering both categories of gluten-free foods, including everything from baby foods to ready meals. These are great because all the hard work has been done for you.

The *Food and Drink Directory*, published by Coeliac UK, is really the gluten-free bible – we find it an invaluable reference. Produced in printed form annually, the book is sent free to members of Coeliac UK each year. Non-members can buy it for a small charge from the Coeliac UK website (www.coeliac.org.uk). It lists thousands of foods you can eat, but it's still small enough to fit into your pocket or handbag when you're shopping. The directory includes the whole range of prescribable products, plus brands and own-label foods from the major supermarkets. Coeliac UK publishes monthly updates on its website, in electronic newsletters and by recorded messages, which you can access by phone.

Most directories and listings cover complete products as well as ingredients. If you're not using a printed listing, an alternative is to print off an up-to-date list of safe and forbidden ingredients from Chapter 1 or 4 or from the Internet (try our cheat sheet on www.dummies.com/cheatsheet/livingglutenfreeuk). When you're shopping and reading ingredients on labels, a list gives you a reminder of which are gluten-free and which aren't. Lists are particularly useful if you cook from scratch most of the time and also for checking out ingredients you don't come across every day, such as buckwheat, sago, pea starch and plantain (all of which are gluten-free, by the way).

Checking out gluten-free products

The market for gluten-free foods in the UK has ballooned in recent years, which is great news for you. It means more choice, wider availability and higher quality, in most cases on a par with gluten-containing counterparts. And the foods aren't all in the 'free-from' section by any means. Many traditional foods that once contained gluten as a minor ingredient don't nowadays. And innovative launches in categories like savoury snacks and crackers mean gluten-free options are no longer shoved in as an after-thought on the bottom shelf – or would have been if they were in stock – but are up at eye level, presented to everyone as tempting options.

All the major supermarkets carry extensive ranges in their large stores – not, unfortunately, in the smaller convenience shops – and these are both own-label and brands. Online, you can find almost everything somewhere, including obscure gluten-free flours and meals, with new ones appearing all the time.

Remembering naturally gluten-free foods

Sometimes people think that the gluten-free lifestyle limits them to buying foods that say 'gluten-free' on the label. This notion is *so* untrue! Limiting yourself to those foods is restrictive and means that you're overlooking lots of foods that are inherently gluten-free, some of which are the most nutritious of all. These foods contain no gluten, although the food industry isn't allowed to market them as such. They include the obvious players – meat, fish, fruits, vegetables, eggs, milk, rice, sugar and nuts – and also some products that you may believe have gluten in them, but in fact don't, such as yoghurt, cheese, most crisps, popcorn, baked beans, jams, pickles, condiments and a lot of potato-based products like hash browns and oven chips (look for the unbattered ones made just from potatoes and oil).

In fact, many processed foods don't contain gluten, but may or may not be labelled gluten-free. Check out Chapter 5 for what exactly a gluten-free label means and when manufacturers can apply it. With processed foods, always read the list of ingredients, and if you don't see anything off limits and there are no warnings about cereals containing gluten, you're good to go.

Cruising the international aisles and independently run shops for their gluten-free options is always worthwhile. You'll find all sorts of gems. As a nation, the British have taken foreign foods to their hearts and absorbed them into their cuisine, to the point where many such foods are no longer seen as foreign. This means that foreign foods and ingredients are widely available throughout the UK. Fortunately, traditional eating habits in many of the countries these foods come from are based on staples which are naturally gluten-free, such as rice, potatoes, corn and quinoa.

Getting other people's views on gluten-free foods

The last thing you want to do is spend loads of money on gluten-free speciality items only to find that they taste more like cardboard than cake. Gluten-free foods can be pricey, and most people pay dearly for prescriptions. Because some foods are great and some are not so great, asking around and getting opinions from others who've tried them is a good way to circumvent the trial and error. Of course, opinions vary, and what one person loves, another may loathe, but opinions can be valuable, especially if you hear several of them.

If you want to access reviews of products, you have a lot of options. Try some of these places:

✔ **Support groups:** Attend your local support group meetings. Coeliac UK has over 90 local voluntary support groups which are a great way to get together, share experiences and tips and have fun. You can ask the members whether they've ever tried a particular product or whether they have suggestions for, say, gluten-free birthday cake. Ask them where they shop too. Some groups organise product tastings and store tours, often sponsored by one of the manufacturing companies or retailers. You can get lots of helpful ideas (and freebies!) this way.

✔ **Exhibitions and shows:** A big exhibition about food allergy or gluten-free living is a wonderful place to sample foods, see what's new, watch gluten-free cookery demos, exchange recipes, pick up vouchers and buy products cheaply, as well as to meet other people living gluten-free. Coeliac UK local groups organise food fairs across the country. You can check their website to find one near you: www.coeliac.org.uk.

✔ **Exchanging information online:** Reading and posting online questions and comments about gluten-free products can be valuable. You can subscribe to emails and e-zines for people living the gluten-free lifestyle, read and write blogs, read reviews, look at videos of gluten-free cooking and learn what people living gluten-free elsewhere in the world like to eat. Other countries' labelling laws might be different, but online exchanging is still an eye-opener and gives you ideas, recipes and cooking tips. Coeliac UK's Facebook, Twitter and YouTube channels are all good places to start. Thousands of people contribute to these regularly, so you're sure to find lots to interest you.

✔ **Shoppers:** If you see someone in a shop buying a gluten-free product you haven't tried before, ask for an opinion about it. At the same time, if you've tried a product and see someone looking at it, speak up.

✔ **Shop staff:** Sometimes shop staff are knowledgeable about the gluten-free products they stock. Ask them what sells well, and whether they or other customers they know have tried a particular product and enjoyed it.

When you find a product that you and your family love and have confirmed to be gluten-free, save the label. File these labels in envelopes or a plastic wallet under sections such as 'Soup' and 'Desserts', along with any gluten-free recipes given on the packs or the manufacturers' websites. Then refer to the file when you're making your Try, Buy, Decry list (see the earlier section 'Making notes and lists').

Look at the food sections in the newspapers (especially at the weekends) and foodie magazines for news of novel ingredients, recipes and artisan suppliers. Coeliac UK has its own magazine and electronic newsletters that include information about new gluten-free products on the market. Check out the organisation's favourite chefs too.

Deciding Where to Shop

So you've decided what meals you want to prepare, you have at least some idea of what foods you want to buy, and you may even have written out a shopping list. Now where do you go to buy all this stuff (some of which you may never have heard of before)? Well, you're not as limited as you may think.

Independent specialists

Butchers, fishmongers, greengrocers, delicatessens, cheese shops and the milkman should be your first ports of call. Almost all their products are naturally gluten-free, and these artisan suppliers are willing and able to accommodate your requests. For example, we often take a gluten-free stuffing mix to our local butcher and ask him to debone, stuff and roll a joint of top-quality fresh meat just for us. Fishmongers really do know how to scale and fillet fish properly and have their personal selection of the freshest fish and seafoods on offer daily. If you don't have a fishmonger locally, see whether anyone has a fresh-fish round in your area. Ask your neighbours. Independent specialists always know how to prepare and cook their products and take a keen interest in what their customers say.

Markets

If you're lucky enough to have access to a permanent or temporary food market, use it. If the market doesn't have stalls of the type you're looking for, talk to the council or market owners. If you don't ask, you won't get.

Farmers' markets and farm shops

These are popping up everywhere, offering fresh produce, dairy goods, eggs, meat, game, fish, honey, nuts, oils, home-made jams and chutneys and other (inherently gluten-free) items. If farms offer pick-your-own, go for it for the cheapest and freshest fruit, vegetables and salads, aside from growing your own.

You can quiz the farmers about what's on offer and feel good knowing that you're supporting local food producers and the environment. The food is sold without unnecessary packaging, and food miles are kept to a minimum because stallholders at farmers' markets are only allowed to sell their own produce. These are good places to try foods and varieties you haven't had before and to get tips, recipes and cooking techniques.

Supermarkets

Like them or loathe them, supermarkets have their place in the gluten-free supply chain. They're convenient, and most offer a wide choice of suitable foods. The gluten-free diet can seem restrictive and even daunting to some people, and some feel somewhat isolated by it (although hopefully not when they've read this book). Having to rely on prescription foods or to shop only at health-food stores or online can reinforce those feelings of isolation. Being able to buy the 'regular' brand-named foods that everyone else is buying is really liberating for people who feel this way.

If you have children on a gluten-free diet, considering the psychological impact of shopping at regular supermarkets is even more important. Kids want to be like all the other kids and eat the branded food (and junk food) that all the other kids eat.

We're excited to see that the major supermarkets are selling a variety of gluten-free speciality products in their 'free-from' aisles, but do visit the rest of the shop too and look around. You'll be surprised what you can find.

Online shopping

Online shopping can have a number of benefits. You can shop at your convenience, in your dressing gown, at any time of day or night, without interference, and you can take your time. This allows you to concentrate on the task in hand, making you less likely to buy on impulse. There is, of course, a charge for delivery, so it doesn't pay to buy only one or two items at a time.

All the websites have search facilities, so you can quickly pull up a list of gluten-free products. Do note that the list will often not include inherently gluten-free products, but only those where the label specifies gluten-free. Shopping websites generally show full details of the foods, including ingredients lists, so you can be sure that what you're buying is suitable for you. You can build wish-lists and save your basket to add to later. You see the total cost before you pay, and can put things back if you change your mind.

Most gluten-free speciality food manufacturers have websites with online shopping facilities, including those manufacturers better known for prescription products. If you know a specific brand you want to buy, you can go to the manufacturer's website and see what it has to offer.

If you don't have a computer, many suppliers have a customer phone number you can call for information or to place an order, and some are happy to send you a gluten-free-products list.

Health-food shops

Independent health-food shops are good places to find unusual gluten-free products, and many of them will buy in products for you on request. Some larger chains have a 'free-from' section, but it's a good idea to browse around the whole shop. All health-food shops are good for nuts, seeds, grains and dried fruits.

International food shops

For an exotic shopping experience, why not visit an international market or grocery store – the more authentic, the better – and discover a whole new world of gluten-free products? In some areas, all the small shops in the street are international with brands and produce you never see in the supermarkets. In these areas, the prices are usually competitive and the shop owners helpful. In fact, they love it if you ask for details of how to prepare and cook their products, and other customers often chip in with their expertise and opinions. One shop owner we know cheerfully rang his mother in Poland on his mobile to ask for a recipe. How's that for service?

Planning impulse purchases

High-powered psychologists have spent millions on studies that finally concluded with a shocking revelation: shoppers are impulsive. Many supermarkets capitalise on your impulsiveness by planning your impulsive purchases. 'Planned impulsiveness' may at first seem to be a contradiction, but that's exactly what supermarkets are creating when they develop strategies for everything from stock placement to the muzak and even the smell in the shop.

Don't tell us you haven't fallen for the marketing. You're in the shop for just a few items ('I'll just use a basket'), and you walk out with a trolley full of things that you didn't even know you wanted. You're captivated by the free samples or the 'buy one get one free' offers. And don't forget the fact that your children are the primary targets, because they tend to be quite influential when you make your impulsive purchases.

Rarely is this so-called *impulse generation* directing you towards healthy foods, much less gluten-free ones. If you're having a hard time sticking to the diet, or if you're tempted by the array of gluten-containing products out there, be aware of the efforts to ensnare you at the supermarkets, and have your guard up against impulsively adding gluten-containing samples and purchases to your trolley.

The selection in these places is amazing. Sauces, rice sticks, blue corn, tapioca noodles, fish sauce, cheeses, weird-looking vegetables, coffee, tisanes, oils, vinegars – things you may have wondered about for years; all gluten-free. Of course, they're not labelled as such, but that's okay. There should be a label in English, so you can check for yourself that gluten isn't in the food, and if in doubt, ask. Finally, these shop owners are often willing to stock particular brands for you.

If you allow it to, your gluten-free diet can open up a whole new food culture for you to explore without ever having to get out your passport.

Living Gluten-Free – Affordably

One of the most common complaints we hear about the gluten-free diet is that it's more expensive than buying standard food – but it doesn't need to be. Yes, we understand that a loaf of regular bread is less than half the cost of a loaf of gluten-free bread. And the fact that packs of gluten-free cakes, breakfast cereals and biscuits are often smaller *and* twice the price of regular ones isn't lost on us. And yes, we know that you may pay more than your fair share in delivery charges for online purchases too. But you have ways to save significant amounts of money when you're enjoying a gluten-free lifestyle. So before you take a second mortgage on your house to finance this diet, take note of these tips that can save you a lot.

Making the most of prescribable products

If you have a confirmed diagnosis of coeliac disease (or dermatitis herpetiformis), a large range of gluten-free alternatives to your everyday staple foods are easily available to you on prescription from your GP. Getting these products on prescription is cheaper than buying them individually, if you get your full monthly allowance. Prescription foods are intended for use only by the patient and aren't for other family members. Chapter 4 tells you more about your entitlement to prescription foods.

Scaling back on 'free-from' foods

Most of the extra expense incurred on a gluten-free diet is due to the high cost of special 'free-from' items that aren't available on prescription. We're not suggesting that you celebrate your birthday with rice cakes to save the expense of buying a gluten-free cake. You may need to have *some* non-prescription speciality items on hand, and cakes or occasional treats are definitely among them. Also, you need some 'free-from' food that you haven't got on prescription for sharing with other people, such as gluten-free pasta for making into a pasta bake or macaroni cheese for the family, or some gluten-free flour mix to knock up a quick treat for guests. But in general, people buy more 'free-from' items than they need, and these unnecessary extras can put a burden on your budget.

If you find that you're spending far too much money to accommodate this diet, take a look at how many and what types of 'free-from' items you buy. Gluten-free chocolate biscuits, cakes, pizzas, pies, pasties and mince pies – they're pricey, you don't need them every day, and they're all easy to make yourself at home at a much lower cost. Most of the speciality items aren't that healthy anyway – they're often high-fat, high-glycaemic-load foods (they raise your blood sugar quickly) that provide very little nutritional value. If you follow the healthy approach to gluten-free eating that we outline in Chapter 6, you'll find very little room for these expensive indulgences.

Avoid buying 'free-from' items unnecessarily. For instance, if you're indulging your taste for chocolate, many of the normal brands that you can get at any sweet shop are suitable and far cheaper than chocolate bars specifically labelled as gluten-free. In fact, the confectionery section of Coeliac UK's *Food and Drink Directory* stretches to over ten pages (we know, we counted!).

Saving on postage

If you buy food online, you can find ways to save on postage. For example, ask your local supermarket or independent store to stock the product you want; that way the shop, not you, pays for the postage.

If you're ordering online, order from a company that sells many different types of product; you pay one postage charge and can order several different items. Many websites deliver free of charge once the total order exceeds a certain sum, especially if you don't need an express service, whereas buying products in small amounts from individual manufacturers can cost you a fortune in shipping.

Selecting supermarket own brands

You can save money by buying supermarket own-label branded foods, especially from their economy ranges. Don't always assume that own brands are unsuitable for a gluten-free diet. These items are as clearly labelled as the major brands with details of what they contain and are included in the supermarkets' own product listings available in-store or downloadable online.

Choosing fresh produce

Some people think that eating more fresh food is expensive. Not true. Fresh produce, meat and especially fish seem expensive – they can be! But compare them to ready meals and think about how many portions you'll get out of your purchases. Many highly processed foods that are high in fat, sugar and salt are poor sources of other nutrients, so they're not good value for money.

When you buy fresh fruit and vegetables, choose what's currently in season. Select a mixture of ready-to-eat and not-so-ripe items to ripen later, thus avoiding waste. The cheapest way to buy fruit and vegetables is loose from your local greengrocer or street market. You can even grow your own.

Eating in

Eating out gluten-free is fun and easier to do than ever (head to Chapter 17 for more information). However, eating out on a regular basis can shrink your budget in no time. Eating at home not only guarantees that your meal is gluten-free, but also saves you money.

Planning and preparing home-cooked meals certainly takes time (we give some time-saving tips in Chapter 9), but saving money and benefiting from the peace of mind that your meals are healthy and gluten-free makes it well worth the effort. Part IV gives you lots of delicious and easy-to-make recipes, from breakfasts to fancy dinners.

Shopping on a budget

In addition to what we cover in this chapter, you can do other things to save time and money when you shop. For starters, try the following:

✔ **Don't shop when you're hungry.** If you shop on an empty stomach, you're more vulnerable to falling victim to impulse purchases.

✔ **Stock up when you can.** Buying non-perishable food in larger quantities is almost always cheaper, if you can afford to do so and if you have somewhere to store the food. However, don't assume that the big packs are cheaper than the same quantity in several smaller packs. It's often the other way around.

✔ **Make the most of your freezer.** Remember that some gluten-free foods have a short shelf life, so if you're going to stock up on fresh products, such as fresh bread, make sure you've got room in your freezer. And do freeze anything you don't eat straight away, and use it another time.

✔ **Club together.** Team up with other people who live gluten-free nearby and buy in bulk between you. You can also share the delivery costs if you shop online.

✔ **Dare to compare.** Always look at the unit price of a product (the price per 100 grams), not just the package price. Shops list unit prices on the price tags on the grocery shelves. The package price sometimes tells you only the cost of the entire item, whereas the unit price shows the cost per unit weight. This way, when you compare the price of one item to that of another, you're comparing like with like. Next time you're in the fruit and vegetable section, have a look at the price of the loose items compared with the same thing in a pack. You'll be amazed how much extra you pay just to have the items put it in a pack for you.

✔ **Check your receipt.** Sometimes shops make mistakes. And on many occasions, those mistakes aren't in your favour.

✔ **Get your prescriptions if you're entitled to them.** If you have been offered prescriptions for gluten-free food, take them and ensure you get your full entitlement every month. Keep an eye open for new prescribable products and new improvements to existing ones, and ask the manufacturers for samples.

✔ **Create a budget and stick to it.** If you don't know how much you already spend on groceries, you won't see the effects of your new gluten-free diet on your wallet. Having in mind a monthly budget for food and then comparing your actual expenditure with it at the end of the month helps you to control your overall spending. If you've gone a bit overboard one month, you can cut it back the next. Keeping your receipts and buying your food with a debit card helps you see the figures in black and white.

Chapter 9

Tips and Techniques for Gluten-Free Cooking and Eating at Home

• •

In This Chapter

▶ Allowing gluten into the gluten-free kitchen safely

▶ Making anything gluten-free

▶ Exploring how to cook gluten-free grains

▶ Baking gluten-free – wholesome, home-made and heart-warming

• •

First and foremost, this book helps you adjust as simply and smoothly as possible to living a gluten-free lifestyle. We go to great pains to make sure that the tips and recipes we give you for gluten-free foods follow the same line – unfussy, uncomplicated and straight to the point. In this chapter, you find practical tips for keeping your gluten-free food from mixing with foods containing gluten, together with useful ingredients and cooking techniques that let you eat the foods you want with confidence.

You don't need to be a Michelin-starred chef to cook this food – we're not masterchefs and we don't expect you to be. Don't get us wrong. We like to cook – a lot. In fact, we love to cook, but we hate the washing up. With experience, we've worked out how to serve up really good gluten-free food, sometimes simultaneously with gluten-containing food for our partners and families, without using every pot, pan and plate in the place, which would all need washing up afterwards. We do it our way. We guess that, like us, you're pretty busy too, which can necessitate making use of convenient ingredients and work-arounds to adapt a recipe to your needs. And speaking of recipes, don't think you'll have to throw out all your old favourite cookbooks. You can make almost everything in them gluten-free with a few adjustments.

If you like the more technical approach, that's okay as well. The tips and techniques in this chapter apply to any preferred cooking style.

Sharing the Kitchen with Gluten

If you'd created a delicious, gluten-free meal, you wouldn't garnish it with a dusting of wheat flour, would you? Of course not. Yet sometimes the *way* you cook food can contaminate it as though you had intentionally added wheat flour, although you may not be aware that you're contaminating your food.

Some people think that the only way to be 100 per cent gluten-free is to make the entire household and everyone in it gluten-free (take a look at Chapter 18 for the pros and cons of this idea), but this really isn't necessary. Doing so would make things easier – menu planning and cooking would be simpler, and you'd have no worries about mix-ups or contamination. But is changing the whole family to a gluten-free lifestyle really practical, affordable or realistic? No, especially if prescription foods and ingredients are involved, because you can't give these to other people.

At the same time, you can't be expected to cook two versions of everything. No one likes cooking *that* much, not even us. You can make plenty of dishes gluten-free with non-prescription foods. For that reason, you can get all the ingredients in the recipes in this book quite easily without a prescription. Everyone enjoys the recipes, and in many cases people won't even notice the difference. Alternatively, you make a largely gluten-free meal for everyone, with gluten-free accompaniments like pasta and bread for those who need it and gluten-containing accompaniments for everyone else.

When one person is gluten-free and others aren't, it's not just the food but the kitchen itself plus the equipment and utensils in it that need attention. The following sections help you avoid contamination with gluten.

Limiting flying flour

Gluten-containing flour is dry, dusty and light, liable to fly around when disturbed and to settle onto everything over a very wide area. For example, if you're putting flour into the processor or mixer, dusting the work surface with it to roll out pastry and shaking it from the bag into the scales, you have a lot of gluten to clear up afterwards. Taking care when moving flour around is key: spooning it out gently rather than tipping it, putting the lid on the mixer or processor before turning it on (probably a good idea anyway) and not using it to dust anything (you can use rice flour to roll out wheat pastry).

Take care opening and storing flour, too, because the paper bags it comes in are easy to rip. You're best sliding the unopened bag into a labelled sealable storage container – you can even get containers in the appropriate size and shape.

Dodging creeping crumbs

If you think bacteria are your biggest contamination problem in the kitchen, think again. In the gluten-free-friendly kitchen, the humble breadcrumb is a major contamination risk. Crumbs can fly off bread like sparks in a fireworks display. Even a few crumbs from glutenous breads, cakes or crackers can turn gluten-free food into a harmful experience.

Pay particular attention to spreadables. We're talking about mayonnaise, butter, margarine, jam, marmalade, peanut butter, honey, yeast extract and condiments. You can buy some of these in squeezy bottles, which is great, but most products still come in jars and tubs, so you need to adopt a different approach when using them. People dip their knives into the containers, scooping out some of the spreadable to spread onto their bread, cracker, scone or whatever. Each time the knife goes from something containing gluten back into the spreadable, gluten crumbs get a free ride into the container, contaminating the whole lot.

Jam spoons, butter knives and honey spoons are cheap as chips and reduce the mess and the risk. Use them to dish out spreadables onto the plate. Avoid putting any utensil used for spreading something on a gluten-containing item back into the jar or tub. Be prepared to get through a lot of cutlery (and washing up) this way!

You may prefer to simply have separate tubs of things you use a lot, like margarine or butter; children are likely to forget the no-crumb rule!

Be diligent about avoiding crumbs and remember the golden rule: when in doubt, leave it out. If you're not sure that your meal is uncontaminated, don't eat it.

Frying safely

When you fry breaded or battered products in oil, bits of the breadcrumbs or batter stay in the oil after you've finished frying. This applies even if you cool and filter the oil. So if you fry gluten-containing foods in oil, don't use the same oil to fry gluten-free foods. Fry the gluten-free foods first or use completely separate pans and fresh oil for the gluten-free foods.

If you cook both glutenous and gluten-free foods in your frying pan (separately, not at the same time!), you need to be extra diligent when you're cleaning the pan to make sure that you get all the gluten out before using it for gluten-free food. If your frying pan isn't easy to clean thoroughly, you may want to consider having separate pans.

Thinking about kitchen equipment

When you cook both gluten-free and gluten-containing food, use separate cooking utensils. This goes for everything that's in contact with the food at any time during the cooking and serving, even for a fleeting moment. All your pans, bowls, spoons, mixers, racks, tongs, knives, chopping boards, work surfaces, scales . . . everything. Even dishcloths and hands. When we say separate, we mean a different utensil altogether. Don't be tempted to use one large pan and try to keep the food separated inside it. Luckily, gluten isn't volatile, even when you heat it, so it won't vaporise into the air or in steam, but it will disperse in water and fat and be left on any surface it touches. So a pan of boiling water with wheat pasta in it will contain a large measure of gluten. If you stir this pan and then put the same food into gluten-free food, the spoon isn't gluten-free any more.

You don't necessarily need to stock up on new pots, pans and utensils, but you do need to pay attention to how you use the ones you have. Generally, if you clean your kitchen items well, you get the gluten off them. Non-stick surfaces that clean easily and thoroughly are especially safe.

Be thorough with colanders and sieves, making sure you clean the holes. A stainless steel colander that's small enough to go into the dishwasher is a good idea, and if you wash up by hand, we suggest you do so straight after using the colander or sieve, or at least rinse it out. Pasta tends to leave a residue that's sometimes tricky to get off. The same applies to the pasta servers.

Breadboards are another contamination culprit, especially ones with fancy carving and grooves in them. Keep a separate board for gluten-free bread and don't store it alongside one that's been used for ordinary bread.

We also suggest buying a new utensil if you have a favourite old one that you just can't get clean – a special cast iron pan, for instance. If you can see (or sense) that traces of gluten may remain on the surface and you don't want to replace the pan with one that cleans more thoroughly, just don't use it for your gluten-free cooking.

We encourage you to mark your separate items. Using a permanent marker or coloured tape may not be the latest trend in kitchen design, but this method can save you from being unsure and may even spare you health-threatening mix-ups. A big, bold 'GF ONLY' or 'GREEN FOR GLUTEN-FREE' on your gluten-free utensils reduces the chance of inadvertently using the wrong one and contaminating your gluten-free foods.

A tale of two toasters

Have you ever looked inside your toaster? What do you see? Crumbs. Lots of crumbs. If you're sharing a kitchen with gluten, some of the crumbs are of the gluten-containing variety. That means your gluten-free bread has lost its 'free' status.

Your safest option is to buy a second toaster and use it only for gluten-free bread, which may seem extreme but is really the only way to ensure that you're not getting gluten-containing crumbs on it. Toasters are quite cheap these days, and you also find pukka ones on the market that are two toasters joined together, but each with its own slots, controls and, importantly, crumb tray. If you only have one toaster, keep it for gluten-containing toast and use the grill for gluten-free stuff – but you need to make sure that everyone in the house knows the rules. The cost of the burnt gluten-free toast you throw out will soon outweigh the cost of a new toaster, however.

Another option is toaster bags, which you keep for gluten-free toast. These are all right for occasional use, say when you stay over at someone else's house, but they're not ideal for everyday use, because the bread doesn't become crisp the way bread toasted without the bag does, and they need to be washed and dried after every use. They also get fearsomely hot and emit scalding steam.

Storing foods separately for convenience

Keep gluten-free foods separated from anything containing gluten. See-through sealable containers are great, and you can use them in the cupboards, fridge and freezer. Be sure to label cooked foods carefully, because it can be impossible to tell them apart later on, especially when they're frozen.

Look around your kitchen and think about where the gluten is. You'll need a separate bread bin or crock and separate cake and biscuit storage tins. A vacuum sealer can be a boon for things you're about to freeze. Food-safe bags, clingfilm, bag clips and rezippable pouches all come into their own here.

Because you're likely to have some leftovers that are gluten-free and some that aren't, consider using brightly coloured stickers or labels to identify storage containers so that you can easily tell which leftovers are gluten-free. This idea is especially helpful if you have babysitters, lodgers or visitors in the house who are likely to grab the wrong container.

Generally, you don't need to have separate storage spaces for gluten-containing and gluten-free foods, but you may want to for convenience. After all, simply reaching up to the gluten-free section of your cupboard for a gluten-free flour mixture is easier than sorting through the shelves.

If you have children on a gluten-free diet and others in the family still eat gluten – or if some people in the home just aren't likely to exercise the same caution as you – then having separate storage areas can be a very good idea. Any gluten-free loved ones may be overwhelmed by seeing all the things they can't eat in the cupboard. By separating gluten-containing and gluten-free foods, not only do you make it quite easy for those on a gluten-free diet to quickly choose from their 'safe' shelves, but also the number of things they can eat becomes more obvious to them. This method can be a big psychological boost in what can otherwise be a daunting experience.

Nobody knows the people you live with as well as you do – so this decision really needs to be yours.

Consider marking a newly purchased gluten-free food with a 'GF' as soon as you get it home from the shops, so that children have an easier time helping you put everything away in the right place.

Having a system

Get systematic in your approach to cooking:

- **Keep track of which is which.** When you're cooking both with and without gluten, always put the gluten-free pan, utensils and so on onto the same side of the hob or on the same shelf in the oven (the one on top, for extra safety). Also plate up the food with the gluten-free version on the same side every time.

- **Prioritise the gluten-free food.** Remember: *gluten-free first*. If you're making two varieties of a meal – cheese on toast, for example – make the gluten-free one first. That way, the preparation surface, knives, grill-pan and rack stay uncontaminated. If you prepare the gluten-containing portion first, you need to wash everything thoroughly before making the gluten-free cheese on toast, or use an entirely separate set of tools. It's the same with strainers. You can use the same pasta strainer as long as you do the gluten-free pasta first and put it safely onto the plate or into the bowl before straining the wheat pasta.

- **Minimise interference.** Having too many cooks in the kitchen is bad enough, but when you're trying to keep your foods safely gluten-free and your visitors are especially 'helpful', maintaining a gluten-free zone can be more than a tiny bit stressful. If your visitors are occasional guests, let them lend a hand by pouring the drinks or laying the table. But if they're regular visitors who are sympathetic to your need for a gluten-free life, you probably need to invest the time to show them the method for keeping your containers free from contamination. Your spreadables are at risk! Your other options are to hide the tubs and jars and buy squeezables for the guests' visit, or to buy separate containers and clearly mark which ones are gluten-free.

Improvising Creatively in the Kitchen

If you love recipes, you'll be delighted to know that this book includes seven chapters of them – all gluten-free, of course. We hope these give you a springboard into confident gluten-free cooking, but also that you'll come back again and again to make your favourites. If you've got lots of recipe books already, they'll include numerous dishes that don't contain gluten. And you can adapt almost all those that do to make them gluten-free.

If you want to eat gluten-free but still make some of your old favourite recipes, chances are that you're going to need to experiment with some new gluten-free ingredients. When it comes to baking, not everything will turn out perfectly first time, but don't let this put you off. The more you play around and experiment with these new ingredients, the quicker they become old friends. And like old friends, you get to know their personalities and quirks. When a recipe does work, keep a note of which gluten-free flours you used in what proportion.

Adapting any dish to be gluten-free

You have two ways of turning a dish gluten-free: with a recipe and without. You'll soon develop your own creativity. The substitution ideas in this chapter are just that – ideas. You'll soon be thinking up substitutions that work for your convenience and to match your preferences and budget.

Starting with a recipe

If you're following a recipe for something that's not gluten-free and you want to convert it, start by reviewing the list of ingredients. Using the substitutions that we suggest throughout this chapter (see the next section 'Using standby substitutions') or some of your own, simply substitute gluten-free ingredients as necessary.

Generally, when you make substitutions, measurements convert equally – with the exception of flours, which we discuss in the later section 'Substituting gluten-free flours'.

If you don't have the right substitutions, improvise. For instance, if a recipe calls for dipping something in flour before sautéing and you don't have any gluten-free flour, maybe you have gluten-free bread or breakfast cereal that may work. Either will make fine crumbs.

Cooking without a recipe

If you're not using a recipe, creativity once again prevails. What if you want to make your own chicken nuggets? You certainly don't need a recipe for that; just slice some chicken and think about what you want to coat it in before frying or baking. You can use crushed potato crisps, rolled oats and raw buckwheat to make a crunchy coating.

Using standby substitutions

Generally, with the exception of the baking flours, the substitutions are simple – just swap one for the other. Here are some ideas:

- **Beer:** Battered and deep-fried foods often call for beer in the recipe, as do several English and Belgian casseroles, pies and even a chocolate cake we know of. You can use gluten-free beer or try cider instead. If you want the taste and colour of stout, add a teaspoon of black treacle along with the gluten-free beer.

- **Binders:** A binder is just something that holds foodstuff together. Gluten-free ones include xanthan gum, guar gum, gelatine, vegetarian jelly powder and eggs, particularly the whites, fresh or dried.

- **Breadcrumbs:** No rocket science required here. Anyone who's ever eaten a piece of gluten-free bread (especially without toasting it) knows that breadcrumbs aren't hard to come by. You can buy gluten-free bread-crumbs or make your own by grating or processing any gluten-free bread. You can toast the crumbs if you want added crunch or need dry bread-crumbs instead of fresh ones. Crushed gluten-free breakfast cereals work well in place of breadcrumbs too. Also consider using cooked rice, potato, millet or quinoa, or their dried flakes.

- **Buns and rolls:** Try a leaf wrap, gluten-free crêpe, frittata or, of course, gluten-free bread. Recipes for the crêpe and frittata are in Chapter 10. Many good gluten-free buns and rolls, including wholegrain and multi-grain, are available in the shops, online and on prescription.

- **Coatings:** If a recipe calls for some type of coating, you have several options. You can consider using seeds like sesame, ground nuts or any of the gluten-free flours we list in the following sections. Cornmeal with added seasonings gives an interesting texture. Crushed crisps (gluten-free, of course) also work well, but these add a lot of fat.

✔ **'Cream of' soups:** Use a combination of chicken broth or stock and crème fraîche instead. Then add your preferred soup ingredients.

✔ **Croutons:** Home-made croutons are actually very easy to make. Cut gluten-free bread into bite-size cubes, brush them with a little oil and bake in a hot oven. When the croutons are cooked, you can roll them in Parmesan cheese, spices or any other flavourings you like. (Head to Chapter 12 for low-fat and alternative crouton substitutions.)

✔ **Fillers:** *Filler* is a highly technical culinary term for something that adds bulk. Generally not something you hope to see on a label, filler isn't always a bad thing; it may be in home-made burgers or sausages, for example, where the recipe often calls for breadcrumbs, crushed crackers and other filler-type materials to add, well, filling. Gluten-free bread or breadcrumbs are obvious substitutions here, but also consider leftover cornbread, chestnut purée, mashed potato or cooked gluten-free pasta.

✔ **Flour:** Many recipes call for flour to act as a thickener, as opposed to a key baking component. The gluten isn't important for thickening purposes, so you can use any gluten-free flour or starch. For flour as a baking component, see the section 'Trying Your Hand at Gluten-free Baking' coming up.

✔ **Flour tortillas:** The obvious substitution here is home-made tortillas, and we give you a recipe for these in Chapter 15, or you could switch to crispy taco shells or corn chips. Other wrap substitutions include rice wraps, lettuce or vine leaves, blanched cabbage leaves or leeks.

✔ **Pie crust and pastry:** One of the easiest ways to make a sweet pie crust is to take your favourite cereal and smash it into tiny crumbs, add some butter (and sugar, if the cereal isn't sweet enough) and then press the mixture into the bottom of a pie pan. Some good gluten-free crackers and biscuits work well the same way. Also check out some of the gluten-free pastry mixes available on prescription, online and in the 'free-from' aisle, or follow our recipes for both sweet and savoury pastries in Chapters 16 and 11 respectively. You can also invert the whole thing and top with sponge, crumble, streusel or shortcake. The recipes are all in Chapter 16 and are easy as pie – in fact, easier.

✔ **Sauce for seafood:** You can make your own Marie Rose sauce with just mayo and ketchup, both of which are usually gluten-free (check the ingredients).

✔ **Soy sauce:** Most soy sauce has wheat in it, but you can find brands that are wheat-free. (By the way, *tamari* – a thicker Japanese soy sauce – is often but not always wheat-free, so check the label.) Use a wheat-free soy sauce or switch to similar sauces like fish sauce, Worcestershire sauce, mushroom ketchup, balsamic vinegar, anchovy sauce, BBQ marinade or brown sauce, but do check the label of the latter, because some leading brands contain rye flour so are not gluten-free . . . no, we don't know why either.

Cooking Gluten-Free Grains

You'll soon find your gluten-free diet opens the door to a whole range of grains you may not have tried before. These bring different flavours and textures to your plate and make delicious accompaniments to main courses. Of course, you'll still have familiar potatoes, other root vegetables and rice to enjoy, plus good-quality gluten-free pasta. If you've been living gluten-free for a while and haven't tried the latest pastas in the shops, we urge you to give them a try, because they've improved dramatically in recent years. We include a recipe for fresh gluten-free pasta suitable for filling, in Chapter 15.

You can find other gluten-free starchy carbohydrates to try in Table 9-1, along with our suggested cooking times and the approximate amounts of water or stock they'll need. These are for cooking in a tightly lidded pan over a low heat after getting to the boil, apart from polenta, which needs constant stirring. Cooking times vary according to how old the grain is and how dry it's become in storage. If all the liquid is absorbed before the grain is cooked, just add a little boiling water and continue to cook. If liquid remains when the grain is cooked, simply drain it off.

Table 9-1	Cooking Alternative Grains	
Gluten-Free Grain (240 g*)	*Water or Chicken Stock*	*Cooking Time*
Amaranth	120 ml	20–25 mins
Brown rice (long or short grain)	520 ml	40 mins
Buckwheat	480 ml	15–20 mins
Polenta	420 ml	5–10 mins
Millet, whole	720 ml	35–45 mins
Millet, golden	420 ml	15 mins
Quinoa	480 ml	15–20 mins
White rice	480 ml	15 mins
Red rice	520 ml	30 mins
Wild rice	960 ml	45 mins

* 240 grams is enough for four portions as a side dish.

Other ideas for using alternative grains, whether you pre-cook them or simply add them to the other ingredients, are as follows:

✔ **Snacks:** Using a little oil in a pan, you can pop amaranth grains on the hob like popcorn and eat them seasoned or plain.

✔ **Soups:** Use buckwheat, quinoa or millet in soups instead of barley or noodles. No need to pre-cook the grains; just add them to the soup during cooking. Remember, they absorb liquid and double in volume. Whole amaranth grains are small and may seem gritty in soups, although amaranth can work well to thicken soups if you use it in flour form.

✔ **Stuffing:** Use the larger alternative grains, such as cooked quinoa, millet or buckwheat, or try chestnuts instead of breadcrumbs in stuffing. Season to your taste and then stuff vegetables, poultry or pork tenderloins.

Thickening with gluten-free flours

People often use starchy thickeners such as cornflour, arrowroot and tapioca to thicken sauces and gravies. These give food a transparent, glistening sheen, which looks great for pie fillings and glazes, but doesn't look quite right in gravy or sauce, so knowing what to use when is important.

To thicken with gluten-free starches, mix the starch with an equal amount of cold liquid (usually water) until it forms a thin paste. Then stir into the liquid you're trying to thicken. After you add the thickener to the liquid, cook it for at least 30 seconds or so to get rid of the starchy flavour. But be careful you don't overcook it – liquids thickened with these starches can get thin again if you cook them too long or at too high a temperature.

Take a look at your options for thickeners:

✔ **Arrowroot:** If you're looking for that shiny gloss for dessert sauces or glazes, arrowroot is a good bet. Use it if you're thickening an acidic liquid but not if you're using dairy products (it makes them slimy). Arrowroot has the most neutral taste of all the starches, so if you're worried that a thickener may change or mask the flavour of your dish, use arrowroot. You can freeze sauces you make with arrowroot.

✔ **Cornflour:** Cornflour is the best choice for thickening dairy-based sauces, but don't use it for acidic foods. Cornflour isn't as shiny as tapioca or arrowroot. Don't use it if you're freezing the sauce, because the sauce goes spongy.

✔ **Instant jelly powder:** Usually a modified starch, this works especially well for fruit pie fillings because it blends well with acidic ingredients, tolerates high temperatures and doesn't cause pie fillings to 'weep' during storage. It also doesn't begin thickening until the liquid begins to cool, which allows the heat to be more evenly distributed.

✔ **Potato starch:** Usually used to thicken savoury sauces, potato starch doesn't work well in liquids that you boil for a while. Potato flour and potato starch are different. Potato flour is heavier, slightly grainy and tastes very much like potatoes. Potato starch is very fine, with a bland taste, and is great to mix with other flours for baking or to use as a thickener for soups or gravies. The starches creak when you rub them between your fingers or squeeze the bag.

✔ **Tapioca:** You can use tapioca pearls or granules to thicken puddings and pies, but they don't completely dissolve when you cook them and so you end up with tiny gelatinous balls. If you like the balls, you can also use instant tapioca to thicken soups, gravies and stews. If you don't like them, you can get tapioca starch that's already finely ground. It gives a glossy sheen and can tolerate prolonged cooking and freezing.

When you're using alternative flours or starches as thickeners, substitution amounts are a little different. Instead of 1 tablespoon of plain flour, use:

✔ **Agar:** ½ tablespoon

✔ **Arrowroot:** 2 teaspoons

✔ **Cornflour:** ½ tablespoon

✔ **Gelatine powder:** ½ tablespoon

✔ **Rice flour:** 1 tablespoon

✔ **Potato flour:** 1 tablespoon

✔ **Tapioca starch:** ⅓ tablespoon

Trying Your Hand at Gluten-Free Baking

We aren't going to beat about the bush: baking is the trickiest type of gluten-free cooking, especially yeasted bakes like bread and buns. But cakes, tray bakes, muffins, biscuits, scones, crumbles, sponges and pastries really aren't difficult. You'll soon be turning out delicious, light, fresh-tasting treats that are so good you can proudly serve them to anyone.

Normally, gluten is what makes baked goods stretchy, springy and doughy. It forms a support structure to hold the gases that expand during cooking, and then holds the structure up without sinking. The keys to getting the same effect without the gluten are adjusting the non-flour ingredients, mixing gluten-free flours according to the result you want, sometimes making individual sizes, like cupcakes, and often adding the baking aid xanthan gum.

Xanthan gum: The star of the dough

Boasting unique properties that enhance the consistency of foods, *xanthan gum* is often a key ingredient in successful gluten-free baking. It adds stretch and elasticity and a slight chewiness, but still allows a soft, tender texture.

Here's a guide on how much xanthan gum to use for each 115 grams or 4 ounces of gluten-free flour:

- **Biscuits:** ¼ teaspoon
- **Bread:** 1 heaped teaspoon
- **Cakes:** ½ teaspoon
- **Muffins:** ¾ teaspoon
- **Pizza:** 2 teaspoons

You can find xanthan gum in the 'free-from' section of most supermarkets. It costs about half as much again as baking powder, but you don't use much at a time. If you get prescriptions, it's available that way and doesn't use up your monthly allowance.

When you're baking gluten-free, use non-stick tins and grease them thoroughly, or use baking parchment. Otherwise, the sticky gluten-free batter around the rim of large cakes can remain stuck to the tin as it cooks, creating a gap underneath, while the middle falls down a little, creating a dip.

Substituting gluten-free flours

Several gluten-free flours work well for baking. But they don't always work in a one-to-one ratio. In other words, you can't just replace 240 grams of plain flour with 240 grams of potato starch – at least not for best results.

This list gives you a starting point for how you can use gluten-free flours. Play around with substitutions to find the flavours and consistencies that you like best. Our recipes in subsequent chapters give you more ideas.

Each substitution is instead of 240 grams of plain flour:

- **Amaranth flour, arrowroot flour, rice flour (white or brown), sorghum:** 220–240 grams
- **Buckwheat flour:** 210 grams
- **Cornflour or cornmeal, gram or chickpea flour, potato starch, soya flour, teff (white or brown):** 180 grams
- **Millet flour, quinoa flour, tapioca flour or starch:** 240 grams
- **Potato flour:** 120 grams

Combining gluten-free flours

If you mix a variety of flours together, they produce baked goods that have a better consistency and taste. The different combinations of gluten-free flour mixtures are endless, and you'll find that different blends work better for different recipes. That's why we prefer to blend them while we're cooking, but you can pre-mix them, label them up and have them ready for whenever you get the baking bug.

You can also buy many ready-mixed packets of combination gluten-free flours and get them on prescription. If you're using these in a recipe that includes gums and raising agents, check whether your ready-mixed flour already has these added and if so, don't add extra. The prescription ones are available in white and fibre-enriched versions. The shop-bought mixes are good for people who cook gluten-free only now and again or who don't want a cupboard full of obscure flours.

 You can't give prescription foods to anyone other than the person they were prescribed for. With baking, you're likely to be making treats to be served to the whole family or to guests, so you need a stock of non-prescription flours at the ready to avoid handing the gluten-free person at the table something different from everyone else's.

Here are some suggestions for blends of flours:

Bette Hagman's Plain Gluten-Free Flour Mixture

- ✔ 2 parts white rice flour
- ✔ ⅔ part potato starch flour
- ✔ ⅓ part tapioca flour

Gluten-Free Pulse Flour Mixture

- ✔ 1 part gram or chickpea flour
- ✔ 1 part brown rice flour
- ✔ 1 part cornflour
- ✔ 1 part tapioca starch
- ✔ ¾ parts white rice flour

Tips for great gluten-free baking

Here are a few general guidelines to help take your gluten-free baking from good to great:

- Look for recipes in which flour isn't the major component, or is absent altogether. Dense, moist chocolate cakes, fondant puddings, meringues, flapjacks, cakes made with ground nuts, carrot cake, rich fruit cake and macaroons are all easy options.

- Think small. Dividing your mix into cups, muffins, cookies, madeleines, scones, mini loaves and bars make for more consistent results. Any flawed ones won't be noticed, because you can simply leave them out

or scoff them yourself . . . just for testing purposes, you understand.

- Use good-quality tins made of thick metal or flexible silicone.

- Make the most of extracts and spices to add additional flavours.

- Save your gluten-free mistakes or stale bread, because one bad batch is another meal. If the bread didn't rise, the cake crumbled and the biscuits fell apart, save the crumbs and use them for stuffings, casseroles, coatings or breadcrumbs.

Carol Fenster's Cornflour Blend

- 1½ cups sorghum flour

- 1½ cups potato starch or cornflour

- 1 cup tapioca flour

- ½ cup cornmeal

Baking bread the gluten-free way

Those who've attempted the sometimes taste-defying feat of experimenting with gluten-free breads know that at times the word *bread* is a euphemism for *brick* and the word *edible* is an overstatement. But never fear, help is here; whether you're a die-hard baker or a newbie to the kitchen, freshly baked, great-tasting, fabulous-smelling, gluten-free bread is easier than ever to make. We must fess up, though: gluten-free breads look a little different to wheat loaves. In spite of great strides to make them fluffier, they're still a tad denser and turn out best if you make them in smaller loaves. They don't rise as much, so the tops are sometimes flat or even concave.

You may want to toast your gluten-free bread to give it a better consistency and make it less likely to crumble. Gluten-free bread is great for toasted sandwiches, because the butter and grilling process gives it a crispy texture and seals the bread so that it doesn't crumble. Freshly baked gluten-free bread is probably the most palatable bread to eat untoasted. Here are a few general bread-making tips:

- ✔ All the ingredients, except water, should be at room temperature. The water must be lukewarm. Too hot, and you kill the yeast. Too cold, and you don't activate it.

- ✔ Adding extra protein in the form of egg, milk powder or cottage or ricotta cheese is important for helping the yeast to work properly.

- ✔ Vinegar – usually cider vinegar – lemon juice or a touch of vitamin C powder helps the yeast ferment and promotes the flavour of the bread.

- ✔ Use small loaf tins for gluten-free bread to reduce drying out.

- ✔ Gluten-free bread needs to cook for longer, so cover your loaf with foil for the last 15 minutes to stop it from burning.

- ✔ Wait until the bread has cooled to room temperature before slicing it.

Given the choice of doing something by hand or using an efficient, made-for-the-job, tried-and-tested tool to do it, we're likely to opt for the tool. If you want to use a bread maker, bear a few things in mind:

- ✔ Gluten-free bread needs only one kneading and one rising cycle. If you have a setting that allows you to do only one kneading and one rising, select it, or remove the paddle after the first mixing. Bread makers have special settings for gluten-free bread. Give them a try.

- ✔ You really shouldn't share your bread machine bucket and paddle with gluten-containing recipes, so invest in spares.

- ✔ Keep dry ingredients separate from wet ingredients, and add them in the order that the machine's manufacturer recommends. Whisk together wet ingredients prior to mixing them with dry ingredients.

- ✔ A few minutes after the bread maker has started, use a rubber spatula to scrape the sides and corners of the bucket. Gluten-free doughs aren't very doughy; in fact, they're more like cake batters. They won't form up into a ball to be kneaded by the machine.

- ✔ After baking, remove the bucket and leave the loaf in it for 15 minutes to cool before shaking it out. It comes out much more easily and you don't tear a hole in the bottom.

Part IV
Scrumptious Recipes for Gluten-Free Food

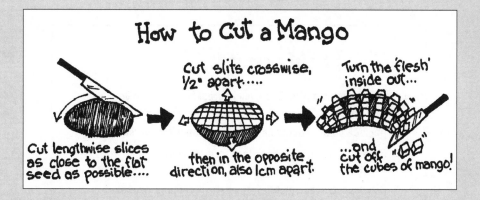

In this part . . .

✔ Welcome the day with fab, filling breakfasts to keep you going until lunch.

✔ Replace your favourite sauce with a gluten-free version.

✔ Rustle up mouth-watering starters, main courses and desserts.

✔ Discover fantastic gluten-free pasta, bread and wraps.

✔ Go to www.dummies.com/extras/livingglutenfreeuk for online bonus content.

Chapter 10

First Things First: Breakfast and Brunch

In This Chapter

▶ Making the most of hectic mornings – quick and nutritious breakfasts

▶ Enjoying protein-packed breakfasts, including eggs

▶ The fruity way to start your day

▶ Discovering gluten-free breakfast bakes

▶ Brunching at leisure

*W*hen most people think of a typical breakfast, images of croissants, pancakes, toast or muesli often come to mind. So what are those of us on the gluten-free diet supposed to do? Dig in, that's what! Yes, you can enjoy delicious traditional breakfast foods that may at first seem to be off limits on the gluten-free diet.

If you don't have much time to prepare foods in the morning, check out Coeliac UK's *Food and Drink Directory* for gluten-free breakfast cereals that provide a quick grab 'n' go breakfast. Most gluten-free breads and rolls – whether home-made or shop-bought – are improved by toasting or warming in the oven.

If you've got more time, why not try one of our delicious recipes? Not all these options are necessarily 'healthy' (some are higher than others in sugar and saturated fat), but alternating these recipes with healthy breakfasts or with healthier foods throughout the day is what balance is all about.

Don't be afraid to think beyond the traditional breakfast fare, especially when you've got more time to turn it into brunch. Smoothies are delicious and nutritious, and a plate of spicy peppers stuffed with egg and cheese can perk up any morning – or afternoon, for that matter. Use this chapter as inspiration for exploring alternatives to the old standby breakfast routines. When you start to think outside the cereal box, you may discover a whole new world of wholesome, gluten-free options to start your day off on the right foot.

Throughout our recipes, we use ingredients which are widely available gluten-free, but some brands of certain ingredients do contain gluten or may do so, particularly baking powder and flours, meals and mixes. As with all your food, always check the labels carefully and avoid anything that contains gluten, even a trace.

Getting Off to a Gluten-Free Start

If mornings are rather chaotic in your house, taking the time to prepare a healthy, gluten-free breakfast may seem like a luxury you can't afford. But in reality, breakfast really is, as your mum probably told you, the most important meal of the day. Not only does breakfast help with weight management by stopping you snacking later on, but breakfast-eaters also have a more positive attitude, and they concentrate and perform better at work and school. Starting your day with a nutritious, gluten-free breakfast has a beneficial impact on your entire day.

Breakfast is the first meal you eat after waking up – after you've 'fasted' for eight or more hours (hence the name!). Your body is literally starved of nutrition and in need of restoration to get going for the day ahead. Yet many people aren't hungry, or at least they think they aren't – and most people are frantically rushing to get themselves or others out of the door. Usually, a healthy breakfast is sacrificed in this whirlwind of chaos.

Stash 'n' dash standbys

If you're limited for time, you still have plenty of nutritious gluten-free foods to choose from. The trick is to build up your stash of wholesome foods that are easy to eat standing up or while you're getting ready, or that you can take with you as you dash out. And the foods don't have to be traditional breakfast foods. Here are some suggestions:

- Cartons of cottage cheese (with or without flavouring)
- Fresh or dried fruit or mini cans of fruit cocktail
- Gluten-free crackers with cheese slices
- Hard-boiled eggs and a pot of salsa
- Home-made granola bars – such as our gluten-free ones, later in the chapter
- Leftover gluten-free pizza
- Low-fat yoghurt

Muesli is a fancy way to describe a simple, uncooked mixture of flaked or rolled cereals, nuts, dried fruit, seeds, a little bran and maybe some bought breakfast cereals such as popped rice, popped corn or multigrain flakes. Pick and mix your preferred gluten-free options. In a small, lidded pot with a dollop of low-fat yoghurt and a swirl of runny honey or pomegranate molasses, muesli makes a great portable breakfast. When you have more time, muesli makes a super topping for fruit or simply as a bowl of cereal with milk. You can buy pre-made gluten-free muesli, but being foodies, we like to mix up our own, vary it each time and keep a stash handy in an airtight jar. Our favourite gluten-free cereals, seeds and bran ingredients include:

- Flaked brown rice, millet and quinoa
- Psyllium husk
- Rolled gluten-free oats
- Toasted rice and soya brans
- Whole buckwheat, which is crunchy just as it is
- Whole or milled seeds of flax, linseed, sesame, sunflower, poppy and pumpkin

If you know you're going to be rushed in the morning, prepare a breakfast-to-go the night before. Pack muesli, yoghurt, an apple and a small juice or water bottle into a lunch box and put it in the fridge – don't forget a spoon!

Granola

On the face of it, granola is simply muesli combined into crunchy pieces with oil and something sticky and sweet like honey or syrup, and then baked and broken into pieces. You can make it this way from bought or home-made gluten-free muesli, but we've found it's easy to overbake and goes soggy if it has fruit in it. The flakes and seeds benefit from different baking. Here's our take on it. If you're making it for one, keep the quantities modest so that you don't feel tempted to eat it every day just to use it up before it goes stale. Granola is more calorific than muesli because of the sugar and fat, so if you're watching your weight, don't over-indulge.

Preparation time: 30 minutes • **Cooking time:** 20 to 30 minutes • **Makes:** 8 servings

Ingredients	*Directions*
170 grams/6 ounces rice flakes	*1* Preheat the oven to 170°C/Gas Mark 3.
55 grams/2 ounces whole buckwheat	*2* Toast each of the cereals separately in a tray for about 15 minutes. The flakes should take on a pale beige colour and the whole cereals should darken just slightly. Don't overdo it, because you'll be cooking them again in a moment.
40 grams/1½ ounces whole quinoa	
30 grams/1 ounce millet flakes	
55 grams/2 ounces nuts or peanuts	*3* In a large saucepan, heat the honey and oil gently. They just need to warm through and mix so that they flow easily; don't overheat. Stir the mixture.
15 grams/½ ounce rice bran	
30 grams/1 ounce mixed seeds	*4* Add the remaining ingredients and stir thoroughly so that everything gets a coating of the oil and honey.
170 grams/6 ounces honey (preferably runny)	*5* Spray a large baking tray with vegetable oil. Spread the granola mixture onto the tray and pat it down firmly. A potato masher is handy for this job.
55 grams/2 ounces vegetable oil	
Vegetable oil spray, for greasing the baking trays	*6* Bake for 20 to 30 minutes until golden brown.
	7 Cool completely in the tray and then break into bite-sized pieces and store in an airtight container.

Tip: Add dried or fresh fruit when you serve this.

Nutrient analysis per serving: Calories 319; Protein 6g; Carbohydrate 46g; Sugar 17g; Fat 13g; Saturated fat 1.3g; Fibre 1.4g; Salt 0.8g.

Crunchy Munchy Bars

We've tried to give you the maximum choice of the principal ingredients in this recipe, so that you can tailor it to your preferences and whatever you have in store in the way of cereal flakes, nuts, seeds, dried fruit and nut or seed butters. For example, if you're newly diagnosed and off oats for a while, just substitute other cereal flakes such as rice, and the result will be similar.

Preparation time: 15 minutes • **Cooking time:** 30 to 35 minutes • **Makes:** 9 bars

Ingredients	*Directions*
Non-stick oil spray, for greasing the pan	*1* Grease and line an 18-centimetre/7-inch square tin or tray, using baking parchment.
2 tablespoons rapeseed oil	*2* Preheat the oven to 170°C/Gas Mark 3.
30 grams/1 ounce unsalted butter	
30 grams/1 ounce honey (preferably runny)	*3* Melt the fats, honey, sugar and nut or seed butter in a large saucepan placed over a low heat. Remove from heat as soon as everything melts, and mix thoroughly.
85 grams/3 ounces soft dark-brown sugar	
30 grams/1 ounce crunchy peanut butter or tahini	*4* Add the remaining ingredients and mix again, making sure all the dry ingredients are well coated in the sugary mixture.
115 grams/4 ounces gluten-free flakes; your choice from rolled oats, millet or rice flakes	*5* Put the mixture into the prepared tin and flatten down lightly with your fingers.
85 grams/3 ounces flaked nuts and seeds; your choice from almonds, hazelnuts, walnuts, pumpkin, sunflower, pinenuts, peanuts or cashews	*6* Bake for about 30 minutes until golden brown. Cool in the tin before slicing into nine squares. Keep the bars in an airtight container.
85 grams/3 ounces dried fruit; your choice from raisins, cranberries, figs, apricots or dates	
½ teaspoon ground cinnamon	

Nutrient analysis per serving: Calories 244; Protein 4g; Carbohydrate 29g; Sugar 19g; Fat 13g; Saturated fat 3g; Fibre 1g; Salt 0.9g.

Power-Starting Your Gluten-Free Day with Protein

Protein really does pack a nutritional punch, working alongside carbohydrates to regulate blood-sugar levels and provide lots of slow-releasing energy throughout the day. By starting your day with a meal containing some protein, you're giving yourself a nutritional boost that can keep you going for hours.

Fortunately, high-protein foods are plentiful in the gluten-free diet. In fact, many of the foods found on traditional breakfast menus that aren't gluten-free, such as croissants and toast, actually offer very little in the way of protein. In contrast, many foods that are inherently gluten-free, such as egg and bacon, are very high in protein.

Thinking outside the egg box

From a gluten-free standpoint, whether your protein is from plant or animal sources really doesn't matter. Eggs are an obvious source of protein for breakfast, but you can incorporate plenty of other protein sources into your first meal of the day:

- ✔ Bacon, ham and other meats
- ✔ Beans and lentils, including dahls and tinned baked beans in sauce
- ✔ Dairy products like milk, cheese, yoghurt, fromage frais and quark
- ✔ Fish – smoked ones like salmon, haddock and kippers are popular
- ✔ Gluten-free sausages – the leaner the better
- ✔ Nuts, peanut butter and seeds

Morning eggs-ercises

Eggs offer more value than many people realise. They're extremely nutritious, containing all the essential amino acids and several important vitamins and minerals. They're also convenient, inexpensive, quick to cook and easy to eat. Eating eggs rarely causes an allergic reaction, and they play an important role in a variety of recipes, particularly in gluten-free baking, where they replace the protein normally present as gluten.

Eggs in a Bread Basket

This recipe is a fun way to serve eggs and toast, especially if you have kids in the house.

Preparation time: 5 minutes • **Cooking time:** 5 minutes • **Makes:** 4 servings

Ingredients	*Directions*
Butter, for spreading **4 thick slices gluten-free bread** **4 large eggs**	*1* Heat a griddle or large non-stick frying pan over a medium-high heat. While the pan is heating up, butter both sides of each slice of bread.
	2 In the centre of each bread slice, cut out a circle about the size of an egg. You can use a knife to cut the circle or a biscuit cutter to make cute shapes. Retain the bread cut-outs.
	3 Make sure that the pan or griddle is hot enough by testing it with a drop of water; it sizzles when hot. When ready, place the bread – slices and cut-outs – on the pan or griddle.
	4 Fry for approximately two minutes or until the underside of the bread is golden brown, and then flip over each slice and cut-out.
	5 Carefully crack an egg into the hole in each slice of bread. You may find that the egg overspills onto the bread. That's okay.
	6 After a further two minutes, when the second side of the bread is golden, flip over the slices to cook the other side of the eggs. When the eggs are cooked to your preferred firmness, serve the 'eggs in a basket' decorated with the fried cut-outs.

Nutrient analysis per serving: Calories 247; Protein 7g; Carbohydrate 12g; Sugar 0.5g; Fat 19g; Saturated fat 8g; Fibre 0.5g; Salt 0.7g.

Athenian Eggs

If you're in a Mediterranean mood, try these eggs with sun-dried tomatoes, olives and feta cheese. This recipe is an especially low-fat egg dish because it uses only the egg whites. To see how to separate whites from yolks, go to Figure 10-1.

Preparation time: 10 minutes • **Cooking time:** 15 minutes • **Makes:** 2 servings

Ingredients	Directions
30 grams/1 ounce sun-dried tomatoes (use the dehydrated kind, not in oil) Vegetable or olive oil spray, for greasing the ramekin Whites of 4 large eggs Several large handfuls of fresh basil leaves 4 pitted Kalamata olives 1 teaspoon crushed garlic (about 1 clove) 30 grams/1 ounce feta cheese, crumbled 2 slices toasted gluten-free bread	**1** Soak the tomatoes for a few minutes in enough boiling water to just cover them. Spray a 10-centimetre (4-inch) ramekin or bowl with olive oil. Place it in a large saucepan and fill the pan with cold water to halfway up the sides of the ramekin.
	2 Place the pan over a high heat. Mix the egg whites together and then add to the ramekin. As soon as the water boils, turn the heat to low and cover the pot. Set an egg timer for 15 minutes. (If you have an egg poacher, oil the cups and pour the egg whites into four cups to roughly the same depth. They should poach firmly in about five minutes.)
	3 While the eggs are cooking, combine the tomatoes, basil, olives and garlic in a small food processor. Pulse the ingredients until finely minced. Stir in the feta cheese.
	4 Check the eggs. They're cooked when they're no longer runny. When the eggs are done, carefully remove the ramekin from the hot, simmering water.
	5 Toast the bread. Spread two tablespoons of the basil–tomato–cheese mixture on each slice of toast.
	6 Loosen the eggs from the dish with a knife, and spoon half the egg onto each piece of toast. Decorate the eggs with the remaining basil–tomato–cheese mixture and serve.

Figure 10-1:
Separating
eggs.

Nutrient analysis per serving: Calories 185; Protein 9g; Carbohydrate 15g; Sugar 1g; Fat 10g; Saturated fat 2g; Fibre 1g; Salt 1.4g.

Frittata Rolls

One well-beaten egg, spread thinly and cooked quickly on both sides in a buttered omelette pan the way you'd cook a pancake, makes an easy roll-up with sweet or savoury fillings. You can cook the frittatas ahead of time and let them cool while you make the filling. They won't crack or split and will be reheated by the hot fillings, or you can return them to the pan after rolling them up or give them a few minutes in a warm oven. Or even eat them cold. When you make an omelette or scrambled eggs, one egg per person always looks stingy, but this way, it doesn't. You'll see frittatas again in our Singapore noodles in Chapter 13, where we slice them into strips before adding them to the wok.

Vegetables aren't well represented in British breakfasts. Apart from tomatoes and occasional baked beans with fry-ups, you don't often see veggies in the morning. This is a shame because they're just as nutritious in the morning as they are at other times of the day, and they're sadly lacking in our typical diet. Here's a tempting way to get one of your five a day before you've even left the house.

Preparation time: 15 minutes • **Cooking time:** 15 minutes • **Makes:** 4 servings

Ingredients	*Directions*
1 dessertspoon olive oil **1 red pepper, thickly sliced** **1 onion, thickly sliced** **2 courgettes, quartered lengthways and cut into 5-centimetre/2-inch lengths** **Sprinkling of salt and black pepper** **A few chilli flakes** **Sprinkling of fresh or dried herbs such as parsley, oregano and marjoram** **4 tomatoes, cut into wedges** **30 grams/1 ounce butter cut into 4 pieces** **4 large eggs**	*1* Heat the olive oil in a lidded frying pan then add all the vegetables except the tomatoes. *2* Season with the black pepper, chilli flakes and herbs. Cover and cook on a medium heat until the vegetables are softened – about ten minutes. Add the tomatoes and warm them. Don't allow them to break down. *3* Meanwhile, make your frittatas. Heat a 16- to 18-centimetre/6- to 7-inch omelette pan and add a knob of butter. When it melts, tilt the pan to butter the entire base. Whisk one egg thoroughly and when the butter is sizzling, pour the egg into the pan. Immediately tilt the pan again to spread the egg evenly over the base. You don't want it too thick. When the egg sets and begins to brown underneath, which takes about a minute at the most, loosen the edges, shake the pan to make sure the frittata hasn't stuck and turn it over with a spatula. Cook the other side briefly, just enough to set it. Slide the egg out and repeat for all four eggs.

4 Divide the cooked vegetables between the frittatas, laying them out in lines near the centres. Roll up each frittata to enclose the filling and to make a neat roll.

Tip: To add nutritional value and flavour, add drained tinned or frozen vegetables such as sweetcorn, red kidney beans, green beans or asparagus. Alternatively, you could add slices of cooked meat such as roast pork or chicken or grill the rolls with a little grated cheese on top.

Tip: Don't be tempted to fry the vegetables in your omelette pan, even if you tip them out and clean the pan before you make the frittatas. There's a law written somewhere that if you cook anything other than eggs in an omelette pan, the next few times you use it, the eggs will stick.

Nutrient analysis per serving: Calories 210; Protein 10g; Carbohydrate 9g; Sugar 8g; Fat 15g; Saturated fat 6g; Fibre 2.5g; Salt 0.27g.

Quick Quiche

'Real men' may not eat quiche, but gluten-free people can – with a few modifications, of course. The beauty of this dish is that with a few tricks, it's incredibly easy – and with a little creativity, it can be exceptionally nutritious. This dish is also easily adapted to suit vegetarians – just leave the meat out and add extra veg.

Preparation time: 15 minutes • **Cooking time:** 45 minutes • **Makes:** 8 servings

Ingredients	*Directions*
185 grams/6½ ounces frozen hash browns, thawed	*1* Preheat the oven to 170°C/Gas Mark 3.
55 grams/2 ounces butter, melted	*2* To prepare the crust, carefully break up the hash browns into small chunks and mix with the melted butter, making sure that the potatoes don't turn to mush.
Non-stick oil spray, for greasing the pan	
5 large eggs	*3* Spray a 23-centimetre (9-inch) pie tin or quiche pan with non-stick oil spray. Press the potato–butter mixture evenly into the bottom and sides of the pan.
185 millilitres/6½ fluid ounces skimmed milk	
55 grams/2 ounces onion, diced	*4* In a large mixing bowl, beat the eggs with an electric mixer for two minutes on low speed. Add the milk, onion, Swiss cheese, quark and basil, and season with pepper. Stir until well mixed.
130 grams/4½ ounces Swiss cheese, grated	
30 grams/1 ounce fat-free quark or cottage cheese	*5* Pour the egg mixture into the potato crust. Place the tomatoes cut side up into the top of the mixture. Scatter over the Cheddar cheese. Bake for 45 minutes. To test whether the quiche is done, insert a knife in the centre. If it comes out clean, the quiche is ready.
Handful of fresh basil leaves, chopped	
Freshly ground pepper to taste	
200 grams/7 ounces cherry tomatoes, halved	
30 grams/1 ounce Cheddar cheese, grated	

Tip: To add nutritional value and flavour, add your favourite combinations of any chopped up vegetables or meat.

Nutrient analysis per serving: Calories 247; Protein 12g; Carbohydrate 8g; Sugar 3g; Fat 18g; Saturated fat 9g; Fibre 1g; Salt 0.6g.

The Fruity Way to Start the Day

Smoothies are a great way to start the day. These thick, smooth drinks use a base of fruit juice with fresh ripe fruit and yoghurt. No need for any fancy equipment – any blender or hand-blender works. Not only are smoothies delicious and easy to whip up, but also you can sneak a lot of nutritious things into them without anyone knowing. Refreshing and energising, smoothies suit any taste and mood. The only thing limiting your options is your creativity.

Simple Fruit Salad

If your idea of a fruit salad hails from school domestic science, think again because you don't need the syrup and you don't need to cook anything. Just trimming and cutting the fruit into bite-sized pieces with a sharp knife, and adding any juice that runs out while you're cutting and choosing fruits with a variety of colours and textures makes for an appetising breakfast starter. And you're getting all the fibre of the fruit, which gets left behind when it's juiced. As you add each new chopped fruit to the bowl, mix the chunks in with your fingers to ensure the juices coat the new addition, particularly if it's pear or apple, which go brown very quickly otherwise. You can add a squeeze of lemon juice, which also stops this happening and adds a real tang to get your taste buds going. You can also mix in dried fruits for different textures and tastes.

Fruit Smoothie

This recipe is the foundation from which all smoothies are born – simple, delicious and just waiting for you to enhance it with nutritious ingredients and a creative style all your own. This smoothie combines the sweetness of bananas and honey with the slight tartness of juice and yoghurt.

Preparation time: 2 minutes • **Makes:** 1 glass

Ingredients	Directions
140 millilitres/5 fluid ounces any fruit juice	*1* Place all the ingredients in a blender.
55 millilitres/2 fluid ounces low-fat yoghurt	*2* Mix until smooth.
1 ripe banana	

Vary It! Remember, you can make a smoothie in countless ways – use ingredients you have on hand, especially fruits that are past their best. Play with the portion sizes and types of ingredients to get the taste and nutritional value that suits you.

Nutrient analysis per serving: Calories 195; Protein 5g; Carbohydrate 44g; Sugar 42g; Fat 1g; Saturated fat 0.4g; Fibre 1.5g; Salt 0.15g.

Spiced Buttered Fruit

Yes, we know. Something of an indulgence this one, but still one of your five a day, quickly made and absolutely delicious with waffles, pancakes or French toast, with or without bacon. Bananas, pears, eating apples and any of the stone fruits like peaches, nectarines and sweet plums work best. Warm a knob of butter and a small amount of any vegetable oil in a non-stick frying pan over a medium heat. Prepare your fruit, leaving the skins on (other than for the bananas, of course) and removing the cores or stones neatly. Quarter the large fruits and halve the smaller ones. Put them cut sides down in the pan and fry gently, just enough to soften the cut surfaces and let them take on a little colour. Then turn them carefully and warm them through from the other side. Serve up and dust very lightly with ground cinnamon or grated nutmeg.

Waking Up to the Smell of Baking

Ah . . . few things get a morning off to a better start than waking up to the smell of fresh baking. Perhaps you think that you have to do without this experience on the gluten-free diet? Not a bit of it. This section proves that opportunities abound for those gooey breakfast foods that you feared were a thing of the past.

We've suggested the flours that we've found are the best for each recipe. You can buy all these in the shops or online without a prescription. You can substitute prescription flour mixes if you're prepared to go to the trouble of making up a separate batch for the person they were prescribed for, because you can't give prescription products to anyone else. Equally, some of the shop-bought gluten-free flour mixes work well in place of the combined weight of all the flours we specify.

Drop Pancakes or Waffles

Pancakes and waffles have been cherished as favourite breakfast staples around the world for years. Serve them with sliced bananas, berries or hot buttered fruits (see the recipe in the preceding section). With pancakes, you can add small berries like blueberries to the batter just after you've put it into the pan.

The following recipe calls for a cast-iron griddle or electric waffle iron. You'll only ever need to buy one each of these in your life, so we suggest you splash out and treat yourself to a good quality one. Homemade gluten-free pancakes and waffles are simply delectable. If you don't have a griddle, you can make pancakes in a thick-bottomed frying pan.

Preparation time: 10 minutes • **Cooking time:** 5 minutes per batch • **Makes:** 8 servings

Ingredients	*Directions*
Vegetable oil spray, for greasing the griddle or waffle iron	*1* Heat a griddle or pan over a medium heat, or turn on the waffle iron. Coat their surfaces lightly with the non-stick oil spray, or brush on oil using a silicone brush.
55 grams/2 ounces brown rice flour	
55 grams/2 ounces white teff	*2* In a medium-sized mixing bowl, combine the flours, xanthan gum and baking powder. Add the vanilla, eggs, oil and milk. Stir the batter until well combined, using a whisk to remove lumps.
1 teaspoon xanthan gum	
1 teaspoon baking powder	
Few drops of natural vanilla extract	*3* Use a large spoon to drop about two spoonfuls of batter onto the hot griddle or pan, or fill the lower waffle iron with the batter and close it.
2 large eggs, beaten	
2 tablespoons vegetable oil	*4* The pancake should begin to bubble after about three minutes. When it does, lift it slightly with a spatula to see whether the underside is golden brown. If it is, flip the pancake over. Usually, the pancake takes two to three minutes to become golden brown on the second side. For waffles, wait until they've stopped steaming before you check them. If you lift the lid too soon, you risk splitting the waffle in half.
240 millilitres/8½ fluid ounces skimmed milk	

Tip: Try using 'melted' berries for a healthy syrup option. Put fresh or frozen whole strawberries or blueberries in a saucepan with a little sugar, mash the berries slightly and add a little water. Heat the mixture slowly until the sugar dissolves in the juice.

Nutrient analysis per serving: Calories 114; Protein 3.5g; Carbohydrate 12g; Sugar 3g; Fat 6g; Saturated fat 1g; Fibre 1.5g; Salt 0.46g.

Versatile Blueberry Muffins

You have lots of room for creativity here – hence the name *versatile* muffins.

Preparation time: 15 minutes • **Cooking time:** 15 minutes • **Makes:** 6 servings

Ingredients	*Directions*
55 grams/2 ounces white rice flour	*1* Preheat the oven to 180°C/Gas Mark 4.
55 grams/2 ounces fine cornmeal	*2* In a large bowl, combine the dry ingredients. Add the vanilla, eggs, oil and milk. Stir until the batter is well mixed (using a whisk to remove lumps). Fold in the blueberries.
¼ teaspoon xanthan gum	
55 grams/2 ounces caster sugar	
1 teaspoon baking powder	*3* Pour the batter into six muffin cases or parchment-lined tins.
½ teaspoon ground cinnamon	
2 teaspoons natural vanilla essence	*4* Bake the muffins on the middle shelf for 20 to 25 minutes. Check to see whether they're cooked by inserting a cocktail stick into the centre of a muffin. If the cocktail stick comes out without any batter on it (it may have blueberries on it), the muffins are done. Remove from the tin and leave to cool on a wire rack.
2 large eggs, beaten	
1½ tablespoons vegetable oil	
2 teaspoons skimmed milk	
55 grams/2 ounces fresh blueberries	

Vary It! Instead of blueberries, consider using chunks of apples, banana or other soft, sweet fruit.

Nutrient analysis per serving: Calories 158; Protein 3g; Carbohydrate 22g; Sugar 11g; Fat 6g; Saturated fat 1g; Fibre 0.5g; Salt 0.5g.

Crêpes

The word *crêpe* is French for *pancake* and is derived from *crêper*, meaning 'to crisp'. Basically thin pancakes with a crisp rim, crêpes are most delightful with just lemon juice and sugar in the classic British fashion, but are also great filled with a variety of stuffings or smothered in garnishes or syrups. Although creating crêpe batter is simple, actually cooking crêpes can take a little practice. The technique starts with using the right kind of pan. You can buy pans made specifically for crêpes, but you really don't need one. Any non-stick frying pan from 18 to 20 centimetres (7 to 8 inches) in diameter is fine. Make sure that the pan is non-stick and shallow with curved sides.

Preparation time: 10 minutes • **Cooking time:** 20 minutes • **Makes:** 4 servings

Ingredients	Directions
70 grams/2½ ounces brown rice flour	*1* In a large mixing bowl, whisk together the flours, xanthan gum and eggs. Gradually add the milk, stirring to combine.
30 grams/1 ounce tapioca starch	
1 teaspoon xanthan gum	*2* Add the salt and melted butter; beat the mixture until it's smooth. The consistency should be like that of cream.
2 large eggs, beaten	
240 millilitres/8½ fluid ounces skimmed milk	*3* Heat a pan over a medium-high heat. Check the pan's temperature is correct by sprinkling a drop of water on it. If the water sizzles and bounces, the pan is hot enough. Spray the pan liberally with the oil.
Pinch of salt	
30 grams/1 ounce butter, melted	
Non-stick oil spray, for greasing the frying pan	*4* Pour just enough batter into the pan to be able to make a thin coating on the bottom. Lift the pan off the heat and quickly tilt it so that the batter thinly covers the entire bottom.
	5 Return the pan to the heat. When the crêpe is light brown on the bottom and firm on the top, after about one minute, gently loosen it with a spatula and flip it. Start checking the bottom of the crêpe when the sides become crispy and slightly loosen themselves from the pan. When both sides are light brown (the second side browns more quickly than the first), your crêpe is ready.

Tip: Working out how to make crêpes is a matter of trial and error, and the pan temperature is important. The batter should cook as soon as it touches the pan but shouldn't sizzle. If your crêpes are thick or bubbly, turn down the heat or lift the pan off for a while. If they stick or aren't browning or setting quickly enough, turn up the heat or return the pan to the hob.

Vary It! Dress to impress. Without toppings and fillings, crêpes are just, well, thin, crispy pancakes. The fun and impressive way to wow guests is with fillings and toppings. The key is creativity. You can choose to spread fillings on your crêpes and then roll them up, or spread the filling and cover it with another crêpe, sandwich style. You can make as many layers as you like, and even alternate fillings. Here are some ideas to get you started, which also work well with pancakes and waffles:

Peaches 'n' cream: Combine fresh sliced peaches with cream cheese, sour cream, whipped cream and brown sugar.

Banana sundae: Not exactly on the slimmers' menu, this indulgence calls for using sliced bananas as a filling and then topping the crêpes with your favourite ice cream and sauce (caramel, butterscotch, chocolate, hot fudge and so on). Top it off with whipped cream or even banana liqueur.

Strawberry style: In a hurry? Mix a little strawberry conserve with ricotta or cream cheese and top with fresh strawberries.

Nutrient analysis per serving (crêpes only, not fillings): Calories 164; Protein 7g; Carbohydrate 24g; Sugar 3g; Fat 5g; Saturated fat 1g; Fibre 1.5g; Salt 0.6g.

French Toast

French toast makes us think of easy elegance, and it's ridiculously simple to make despite somehow boasting an air of sophistication, especially if you serve it with icing sugar and strawberries. Don't forget the maple syrup!

Preparation time: 5 minutes • **Cooking time:** 6 minutes per slice • **Makes:** 6 servings

Ingredients	Directions
4 large eggs **55 millilitres/2 fluid ounces skimmed milk**	*1* In a medium bowl, combine the eggs, milk and cinnamon (if desired). Beat the mixture with a whisk or fork until well blended.
¼ teaspoon ground cinnamon (optional)	*2* Melt the butter in a large frying pan or griddle over a medium heat.
30 grams/1 ounce butter **6 slices gluten-free bread**	*3* Dip each slice of bread in the egg mixture, coating the bread well on both sides.
	4 Place the bread in the hot pan. Cook the bread until golden brown on both sides – about three minutes per side.
	5 Serve the French toast warm, accompanied by your favourite topping.

Nutrient analysis per serving: Calories 152; Protein 5g; Carbohydrate 13g; Sugar 1g; Fat 9g; Saturated fat 4g; Fibre 0.5g; Salt 0.5g.

Serving Up Savouries

Whether freshly prepared in the morning or left over from the night before, sometimes the best breakfast is a savoury hit to balance the sweet or neutral regulars.

Potato Cakes

You can make these fluffy delights in minutes from leftover mashed potatoes. They're particularly good with savoury foods like bacon, smoked salmon, scrambled eggs, sausages and mushrooms. And they don't need butter or syrup. They make an interesting new texture at other meals too, or as starters made half the size and topped decoratively with wafer-thin air-dried ham, salad leaves, cherry tomatoes and a creamy dressing.

Preparation time: 5 minutes; more if you need to peel, boil and mash the potatoes first •
Cooking time: 5 minutes • **Makes:** 4 servings

Ingredients	Directions
2 large eggs, separated	*1* In a medium bowl, combine the egg yolks with the potatoes, flour, baking powder, herbs, nutmeg and pepper.
255 grams/9 ounces mashed, cooled potato	
30 grams/1 ounce white rice flour	*2* Bring the milk to the boil and stir it in. The mixture should be quite thick at this stage. If you think it's too sloppy, add a little extra white rice flour.
½ teaspoon baking powder	
1 tablespoon chopped fresh parsley or dill	*3* Whip the egg whites until they're fluffy and fold into the potato mixture. Don't beat them in, but make sure no patches of egg white are visible.
A little grated nutmeg and black pepper	
55 millilitres/2 fluid ounces skimmed milk	*4* Heat a heavy frying pan, or better still a cast-iron griddle. Brush with a little oil.
Oil for frying	*5* Divide the mixture into four or eight and spoon four portions onto the hot surface. You can either make four rustic-looking cakes of about 7½ centimetres/3 inches diameter or eight daintier ones of about 5 centimetres/2 inches diameter, in two batches. Just spoon the mixture in and flatten the tops slightly. Cook the undersides until rich brown, and then flip over and cook the other sides to the same colour. They'll puff up as they cook.

Nutrient analysis per serving: Calories 160; Protein 6g; Carbohydrate 15g; Sugar 1g; Fat 9g; Saturated fat 3g; Fibre 1g; Salt 0.3g.

Chilli Cheese Casserole

Whether for breakfast, lunch or dinner, here's a great gluten-free meal that couldn't be much easier to make. When you eat this for breakfast, you're bound to have an *olé* kind of day. Fresh chillies of all colours and heats are available throughout the UK, so choose whichever you fancy from among the larger types. Serve the casserole with warm corn chips or taco shells and salsa, topped with guacamole for a creamy, flavoursome touch (see Chapter 11 for our guacamole recipe).

Preparation time: 10 minutes • **Cooking time:** 25 minutes • **Makes:** 8 servings

Ingredients	*Directions*
Vegetable or olive oil spray, for greasing the casserole dish	*1* Preheat the oven to 180°C/Gas Mark 4. Spray a 23- by 33-centimetre (9- by 13-inch) casserole dish with non-stick oil.
6 large eggs	
Freshly ground pepper to taste	*2* Separate the egg whites from the yolks (use any of the methods shown in Figure 10-1). With an electric mixer on medium speed, whip the whites in a medium bowl until they're stiff. In a small bowl, beat the yolks with a fork or whisk until smooth. Fold the yolks into the whites. Add salt and pepper to taste.
8 large, mild chillies, deseeded and finely sliced	
1 400-gram/14-ounce tin of red kidney beans, drained	
1 340-gram/12-ounce tin of sweetcorn, drained	*3* Mix the chillies, beans and sweetcorn.
225 grams/8 ounces Cheddar cheese, grated	*4* Spread about a third of the egg mixture onto the bottom of the dish.
225 grams/8 ounces mozzarella cheese, grated	*5* Layer the vegetables on top of the egg mixture. Then combine the cheeses and sprinkle a layer of mixed cheese on top. Continue layering – egg, vegetables, cheese – until all the ingredients are used. You should end up with about three layers of each ingredient, finishing with the egg mixture.
	6 Bake for 25 minutes or until golden brown. Cut into slices to serve.

Nutrient analysis per serving: Calories 336; Protein 23g; Carbohydrate 14g; Sugar 3g; Fat 21g; Saturated fat 11g; Fibre 3g; Salt 0.9g.

Kedgeree

Another quick, tasty treat making the most of leftovers – this time, leftover boiled or steamed rice, white or brown. Even if you have to cook it from scratch, white basmati, long grain and Thai rice only take about 15 minutes tops from start to finish. Purists will no doubt grumble at our choice of fish, which traditionally should be the smoked white type, but our recipe is an excellent way of sneaking in a portion of the healthier oily fish without anyone turning a nose up.

Preparation time: 5 minutes • **Cooking time:** 10 minutes, not counting boiling or steaming the rice • **Makes:** 4 servings

Ingredients	*Directions*
2 large eggs **1 tablespoon oil**	*1* Hard boil, cool and peel the eggs. Then quarter them lengthways.
1 onion, chopped fairly finely **2½-centimetre/1-inch cube of fresh ginger root, grated**	*2* Meanwhile, heat the oil and soften the onion and ginger, without browning. Add the rice and spices and mix to disperse the colours evenly.
500 grams/18 ounces cooked rice, or cook a third of this quantity with water **Cayenne pepper to taste** **1 teaspoon ground cumin**	*3* Add the peas and continue to heat and stir until they thaw. Add water if the mixture starts to stick or looks too dry – but not too much, otherwise the rice will go sticky.
1 teaspoon ground turmeric **115 grams/4 ounces frozen peas** **255 grams/9 ounces skinned oily fish fillets, such as salmon, mackerel, trout or Cornish sardine**	*4* Cut the fish into small chunks and fold into the rice. Let the fish cook thoroughly and gently turn the kedgeree, without breaking up the fish flakes completely. Fold in the egg quarters and heat them through.

Nutrient analysis per serving: Calories 400; Protein 22g; Carbohydrate 46g; Sugar 4g; Fat 16g; Saturated fat 3g; Fibre 2g; Salt 0.2g.

Chapter 11

Stylish Starters

In This Chapter

▶ First-course finger and fork foods

▶ Sexy spreads and top toppings

▶ Dipping into dips

▶ Creating delicious fillings for gluten-free rice rolls and wraps

A really great get-together begins with a great-tasting starter, whether you're at a casual gathering of friends and family or an elegant dinner party. Not only does a good starter whet the appetite, but it also whets the imagination, setting the stage for the meal to come.

But anticipation can quickly turn to disappointment for someone on a gluten-free diet, because more often than not, starters turn out to be one enormous glutenfest. And party planners perusing starter recipes for inspiration find that they're likely to contain flour, breadcrumbs or a myriad other gluten-containing ingredients, striking fear into hosts and hostesses everywhere: what can I serve that's impressive and gluten-free?

If you find yourself stumped for ideas, never fear: gluten-free starters are here! Just don't blame us if everyone's too full for the main course.

Throughout our recipes, we use ingredients which are widely available gluten-free, but some brands of certain ingredients do contain gluten or may do so, particularly flours, meals, starches, ketchups and soy sauce. As with all your food, check the labels carefully and avoid anything that contains gluten, even a trace.

Fashioning Fab Finger- and Fork-Lickin'-Good Food

People love to eat with their fingers. And as long as everyone's wearing jeans, so they can wipe their hands off, what's the harm in dining with your digits? On the other hand, if your guests have shown up smartly dressed or carrying suede clutch bags, forks and napkins are a must, if not small plates. Cocktail sticks, mini kebab sticks and those flat ceramic spoons that Chinese restaurants serve soup with all make useful serving tools that help your guests to help themselves. If you're also serving any gluten-containing starters, you can distinguish the gluten-free ones by using tools of different colours, and of course discreetly tipping off your gluten-intolerant guests before they wade in. In this section, we bring you some of our favourite recipes that help get the party started with fun finger and fork foods.

Spicy Corn Fritters

This delicious dish uses polenta, which is simply large-grained cornmeal. You can find dried polenta in most supermarkets or continental shops. Simply mix this up with water, following the directions on the packet. We've seen ready-made polenta in the shops, but often with a warning that it may contain gluten. You can find fresh kaffir lime leaves in the Thai sections of Asian markets, and dried ones with the herbs and spices in supermarkets.

Preparation time: 15 minutes • **Cooking time:** 25 minutes • **Makes:** 4 servings

Ingredients	*Directions*
155 grams/5½ ounces sweetcorn (canned in water; drained) 2 fresh red chillies, seeded and finely chopped 1 teaspoon crushed garlic (about 1 clove) 10 kaffir lime leaves, finely chopped or crumbled if dried, leaving the central vein out 3 tablespoons chopped fresh coriander 2 large free-range eggs, beaten 115 grams/4 ounces made-up polenta 55 grams/2 ounces green beans, finely sliced 115 millilitres/4 fluid ounces rapeseed oil (for frying)	*1* Place the sweetcorn, chillies, garlic, lime leaves, coriander, eggs, made-up polenta and green beans into a large bowl; mix them thoroughly. Use your hands to form balls about the size of golf balls. Put them on a plate. *2* Heat the oil in a wok, frying pan or deep fryer on a high heat. You know that the oil is hot enough when you add a fragment of leftover mix from the bowl and it starts to sizzle immediately. *3* Turning the fritters occasionally, cook them in the oil until they're brown and crispy on the outside (about seven minutes). Remove the fritters from the pan with a slotted spoon and let them drain on kitchen paper before serving.

Nutrient analysis per serving: Calories 302; Protein 5g; Carbohydrate 12g; Sugar 2g; Fat 26g; Saturated fat 5g; Fibre 1.1g; Salt 0.1g.

Triple Whammy Combo

This combination is our all-time favourite mix of appetisers. You can serve up this combo as a choice of starters or all together as an alfresco lunch. You can mix and match the fruits or vegetables to suit your taste, but we urge you to try this combination first time around – we're pretty sure that after you've tasted our suggested combination of ingredients, you aren't going to want to change a thing!

Preparation: 30 minutes • **Chilling time:** 10 minutes • **Makes:** 4 servings of each dish

Ingredients	Directions

Parma Ham with Figs

Ingredients	Directions
12 small, fresh, ripe figs 12 thin slices Parma ham	**1** Using a sharp knife, cut the figs into quarters lengthways without cutting right through the skin at the base.
	2 Gently pull the flesh of the fruit away from the skin, leaving the central part of the pulp still attached to the skin.
	3 Stand the figs on a serving plate and drape the Parma ham between the figs. Keep refrigerated until ready to serve.

Nutrient analysis per serving: Calories 120; Protein 9g; Carbohydrate 14g; Sugar 14g; Fat 4g; Saturated fat 1g; Fibre 2g; Salt 1.26g.

Stuffed Avocados

Ingredients	Directions
2 ripe avocados 1 onion, peeled and chopped	**1** Cut the avocados in half, remove the stones, scoop out a little of the flesh around the holes and put into a small mixing bowl.
2 tomatoes, chopped 2 hard-boiled eggs, shelled and chopped	**2** Add the remaining ingredients to the bowl and mix gently.
115 grams/4 ounces cooked skinless chicken breast, chopped	**3** Pile the chicken mixture into the centre of each avocado half.
2 tablespoons mayonnaise	**4** Refrigerate until ready to serve.

Nutrient analysis per serving: Calories 342; Protein 12g; Carbohydrate 4g; Sugar 4g; Fat 31g; Saturated fat 6g; Fibre 3.4g; Salt 0.33g.

Asparagus Cocktail

225 grams/8 ounces fresh asparagus

4 pineapple rings, canned or fresh

115 grams/4 ounces ham, diced

4 large iceberg lettuce leaves

4 tablespoons mayonnaise

½ teaspoon brandy (optional)

2 tablespoons fresh lemon juice

Pinch of cayenne pepper

1 Prepare the asparagus by cutting off any woody stems, trimming them and rinsing under cold running water. Chop into 25-millimetre (1-inch) lengths then boil in water for ten minutes or until just tender. Drain and cool.

2 Meanwhile, chop the pineapple rings and mix with the diced ham.

3 Add the asparagus to the ham and pineapple.

4 Divide the asparagus, ham and pineapple mixture between each of the lettuce leaves.

5 In a bowl, mix the mayonnaise, brandy (if using), lemon juice and cayenne pepper, and spoon over the asparagus mixture.

6 Fold the leaves to make a parcel.

Nutrient analysis per serving: Calories 285; Protein 6g; Carbohydrate 6g; Sugar 6g; Fat 26g; Saturated fat 4g; Fibre 0.6g; Salt 1.2g.

Cheese Shortbreads

These can be either delicately lacy or crisply biscuity, depending on how thickly you roll them. Either way, they spread out in the oven, so don't go to the trouble of cutting out precise shapes. They make great nibbles to take along to informal gatherings where you're expected to contribute to the buffet. Think in terms of five or six shortbreads per person, although some people have been known to double that!

Preparation time: 15 minutes • **Cooking time:** 10 minutes • **Makes:** About 60 shortbreads, 10 servings

Ingredients	*Directions*
45 grams/1½ ounces brown rice flour	*1* Preheat the oven to 170°C/Gas Mark 3. Process the flours, spice and butter in the food processer to the 'breadcrumb' stage. Tip it out.
45 grams/1½ ounces fine cornmeal	
Pinch of cayenne pepper or hot paprika	*2* Break all the cheese into chunks and process it until it becomes coarse crumbs.
55 grams/2 ounces butter	
30 grams/1 ounce gram flour	*3* Add the flour mixture and process again until the whole thing forms a ball of dough. Roll this out with a dusting of cornmeal to about 5 millimetres/⅕ inch thickness, more if you want biscuits, and cut with a 2½-centimetre/1-inch round cutter.
55 grams/2 ounces Cheddar cheese	
55 grams/2 ounces Lancashire, Caerphilly or Cheshire cheese	*4* Place onto a non-stick baking sheet or silicone mat – no need to grease or spray it – and bake for ten minutes. Keep an eye on them after about six minutes, because they can easily burn.
	5 Allow to cool a little before carefully moving them with a spatula to a wire rack, where they'll crisp up. As soon as they're cold, store in an airtight container.

Nutrient analysis per serving: Calories 132; Protein 4.5g; Carbohydrate 8g; Sugar 0g; Fat 9g; Saturated fat 6g; Fibre 0g; Salt 0.3g.

Helpful hints if you're relying on frying

Although far from being one of the healthier modes of cooking, frying is, nonetheless, a common method for cooking many finger foods. Here are some important tips to help you create the perfect crunch:

✔ **Use oil you designate for gluten-free foods.** If you're preparing gluten-containing foods and gluten-free ones, make sure that you cook the gluten-free foods first or change the oil in between batches. Breadcrumbs and batters can contaminate the oil, turning your gluten-free goodie into a hidden source of wheat.

✔ **Choose the right oil.** Some oils, like olive, pumpkin, hemp and sesame oil, aren't meant to be heated to the very high temperatures that deep frying requires. Corn, rapeseed, sunflower, peanut, grapeseed and rice bran oils are some of the best deep-frying oils, because they have a high smoking point. The oil is hotter and so the food seals more quickly and absorbs less oil. Find an oil that matches the flavour profile of the food you're cooking, and turn down the heat if it begins to smoke, which indicates the oil is degrading. Degrading oil can affect the flavour of the food.

✔ **Don't overload the basket.** If you're impatient, like we are, you may be tempted to hurry the cooking process by cooking as much as you can at once. Overloading the basket can result in uneven or incomplete cooking and may cause the food to absorb extra oil.

✔ **Filter and clean often.** If the oil gets smoky or has debris in it, change it for new oil and start again. Clean your frying pans and deep-fat fryer regularly.

When you've finished deep frying your favourite gluten-free goodies, you need to decide what to do with the used cooking oil. You can't just pour it down the sink; that's not only bad for the environment, but it's also bound to clog the pipes. After the oil has completely cooled, pour it into an empty rigid plastic container with a lid. Seal the lid tightly and throw it in the bin or take it to your local civic amenity, where they may have disposal facilities. Alternatively, if you have a compost heap, the micro-organisms in that will break down oil, but it's best not to flood it in all at once.

Unlike wheat pastry or shortbread, gluten-free doughs tolerate the off-cuts being gathered up, re-rolled and re-cut. You can even press any scraps into holes and tears without water. They'll hold in place and no one will notice the join. So nothing needs to go to waste. Without gluten, the dough doesn't have the elasticity of wheat-based pastry, but that's helpful because it means it doesn't shrink out of shape when it bakes.

Spicy Buffalo Wings

These savoury snacks are actually chicken wings, named *Buffalo* after the city in New York where they originated in 1964. Serve them with celery sticks and a salad dressing.

Preparation time: 5 minutes • **Cooking time:** 10 minutes • **Makes:** 24 wings

Ingredients	*Directions*
For the chicken: **155 grams/5½ ounces fine, yellow cornmeal** **1 teaspoon celery or garlic salt** **24 fresh chicken wings (or defrosted if frozen)** **Rapeseed oil, for frying**	*1* Put the cornmeal and salt in a large plastic bag, and shake the bag to mix. Add the wings (about five at a time) and shake the bag to coat them well.
	2 Heat the oil over a medium-high heat in a heavy-based frying pan. Fry the wings in about 5 centimetres/2 inches of hot oil for approximately five minutes, until they're crispy on the outside. Break a wing open to make sure that the meat inside isn't pink. Drain the wings on kitchen paper.
For the sauce: **115 millilitres/4 fluid ounces red wine vinegar** **115 millilitres/4 fluid ounces runny honey** **2 tablespoons black treacle** **3 tablespoons tomato ketchup**	*3* Prepare the sauce by mixing together the red wine vinegar, honey, treacle, ketchup, hot chilli sauce and salt and pepper in a medium bowl.
3 tablespoons your favourite hot chilli sauce **Salt and pepper to taste**	*4* Dip the cooked wings in the mixture to coat them with the sauce.

Nutrient analysis per serving: Calories 200; Protein 10g; Carbohydrate 16g; Sugar 6g; Fat 11g; Saturated fat 3g; Fibre 0.2g; Salt 1.1g.

Latin American Marinated Seafood (Ceviche)

Ceviche poses an imponderable question – is it cooked or not? *Ceviche* is a delicious Latin American seafood dish that people prepare by using an ancient method of 'cooking' that uses the acid from citrus juice instead of heat. The acid actually changes the protein structure in the fish, and you can watch the fish turn from translucent pink to opaque white. Ceviche is usually a mixture of chunks of fish, lemon and lime juices, chopped onion and chilli peppers. The fish cooks in the citrus while the flavours blend into a spectacular dish that you can serve as a starter or main course.

Preparation time: 15 minutes plus 6 hours in the fridge • **Refrigeration time:** 6 hours •
Makes: 8 servings

Ingredients	*Directions*
1 kilogram/2¼ pounds fresh red snapper, hake or plaice fillets, cut into 12-millimetre/½-inch pieces	*1* Place the fish, onion, tomatoes, chilli pepper, salt, coriander, Tabasco and cumin in a glass or ceramic dish.
40 grams/1½ ounces sweet white-skinned onion, finely diced	
185 grams/6½ ounces fresh tomatoes, peeled, seeded and chopped	*2* Pour over the lemon and lime juices, cover the dish in foil or clingfilm, and place in the fridge for at least six hours.
1 red chilli, seeded and finely diced	
1 teaspoon salt	*3* Stir the mixture frequently, ensuring that the citrus liquid covers the fish.
2 teaspoons chopped fresh coriander	
Dash of Tabasco sauce	*4* Serve the ceviche with heated tortillas and avocado slices or with tortilla chips for dipping.
Pinch of ground cumin	
115 millilitres/4 fluid ounces freshly squeezed lime juice	
115 millilitres/4 fluid ounces freshly squeezed lemon juice	

Tip: You can use prawns, scallops or squid instead of or in addition to the fish. You can also use any type of white fish you like – just make sure that it's firm, like sole or haddock.

Vary It! Get creative and add diced fruit such as mangos, and serve the ceviche rolled in a fresh, warm tortilla with lettuce and a little salsa, or with corn chips for dipping. See our recipe for tortillas in Chapter 15.

Nutrient analysis per serving: Calories 121; Protein 25g; Carbohydrate 2g; Sugar 2g; Fat 2g; Saturated fat 0.5g; Fibre 0.3g; Salt 1g.

The sweet white-skinned onions we suggest don't give you onion breath or an onion taste in your mouth for the next couple of days, like ordinary onions do when eaten raw. They're available throughout the summer, when you're most likely to be eating ceviche. If you can't get hold of white-skinned onions, use red onions chopped and blanched in a little boiling water for a minute before being refreshed with cold water.

Indulging in Dips

Whether you're dipping vegetable crudités, or fluten-free crackers or flatbreads, a few good dips go a long way, and you can vary your repertoire of basic recipes to create exciting gluten-free graze-ables. Although many dips are inherently gluten-free, others require just a few tweaks here and there to make them safe for anyone avoiding gluten.

Double-dipping is *not* allowed, especially if some of the guests are eating gluten-containing foods. After people have dunked gobs of gluten into the dip, it's no longer gluten-free.

By the way, dips aren't just for dipping. Use them as fillings for hollowed vegetables or halved hard-boiled eggs, or spread them on crêpes (you can find a recipe in Chapter 10). You can roll the filling into a wrap and eat the whole thing as a tasty picnic snack or slice it into a stylish roulade.

Artichoke and Spinach Dip

You aren't going to find this recipe in *Dieting For Dummies,* but it is gluten-free! Serve this cheesy dip with corn tortilla chips, rice crackers, vegetable sticks or deep-fried potato skins. Or if you have a favourite gluten-free bread, slice it thinly, toast it and spread the dip on top.

Preparation time: 10 minutes • **Cooking time:** 25 minutes • **Makes:** 12 servings

Ingredients	*Directions*
225 grams/8 ounces light cream cheese	*1* Preheat the oven to 180°C/Gas Mark 4. Let the cream cheese warm to room temperature.
4 tablespoons mayonnaise	
½ teaspoon crushed garlic (about 1 small clove)	*2* In a large bowl, cream together the cream cheese, mayonnaise, garlic, basil and salt and pepper. Setting aside a few teaspoons of each cheese to use as a topping, add the Parmesan, Manchego and mozzarella cheeses. Mix until well blended.
Handful of fresh basil leaves	
Freshly ground salt and pepper to taste	
100 grams/3½ ounces Parmesan cheese, grated	*3* Add the artichoke hearts and spinach, and mix again.
100 grams/3½ ounces Manchego cheese, grated	*4* Spray an ovenproof serving dish with non-stick oil spray, pour in the dip and top it with the cheese that was put aside in Step 2.
40 grams/1½ ounces mozzarella cheese, grated	
400 grams/1 x 14 ounce jar artichoke hearts, drained and chopped	*5* Bake the dip for about 25 minutes or until the top begins to brown and the cheese has melted. Serve the dip from the dish with a selection of dippers.
100 grams/3½ ounces tinned spinach, drained and chopped	
Non-stick oil spray, for greasing the dish	

Nutrient analysis per serving: Calories 159; Protein 9g; Carbohydrate 2g; Sugar 0.5g; Fat 12g; Saturated fat 6g; Fibre 0.1g; Salt 1.3g.

Guacamole

Guacamole is an avocado-based dip that originated in Mexico. Most guacamole recipes start with fresh peeled avocados and add lime (or lemon) juice, tomatoes, onions, coriander, garlic and spices. The lime juice keeps the guacamole from turning brown when you expose it to the air. Leaving the avocado stone in the guacamole until just before serving also decreases browning. For this guacamole, feel free to kick it up a notch with your favourite hot chilli sauce.

Preparation time: 15 minutes • **Makes:** 6 servings

Ingredients	*Directions*
2 ripe avocados	*1* Peel the avocados, remove the flesh from the stones and cut into cubes. Save the stones. (Check out Figure 11-1 if you're not sure how to remove the stone from an avocado.)
1 small to medium ripe tomato, diced	
½ small red onion, chopped	
½ teaspoon finely cut jalapeño pepper	*2* In a medium bowl, combine the avocado flesh, tomato, onion, jalapeño, lime juice, coriander, salt and pepper.
4 tablespoons fresh lime juice	
2 teaspoons chopped coriander	*3* Mix all the ingredients well, but keep the guacamole lumpy. Place the avocado stone in the dip, removing it just prior to serving.
Freshly ground salt and pepper to taste	

Nutrient analysis per serving: *Calories 95; Protein 1g; Carbohydrate 1g; Sugar 1g; Fat 9g; Saturated fat 2g; Fibre 1.8g; Salt 0.5g.*

How to De-seed and Peel an Avocado

Figure 11-1: De-stoning an avocado.

Slice avocado in half lengthwise and pull apart.

Firmly strike the seed with a chef's knife.

Lift the seed out with a gentle twist of the knife.

GENTLY scoop out the meat with a spoon.

Chop or slice according to your recipe.

Hummus

Freshly made hummus is so much better than the shop-bought variety, which always seems to go too thick while it sits in the fridge. Anyway, it's a lot cheaper, can be made in a few minutes with tinned chickpeas and allows you to get the flavour just right for your taste. Served with our home-made flatbreads (see Chapter 15) or bought gluten-free pittas and some colourful sticks of crisp vegetables, such as carrot, red pepper, celery, chicory and mouli (Japanese radish), it makes a lovely lunch as well as a crowd-pleasing dip for parties.

Preparation time: 10 minutes • **Makes:** 2 servings for lunch, 4 as a starter, more as a dip

Ingredients	*Directions*
1 x 400-gram tin of chickpeas **Juice of one lemon** **2 cloves of garlic** **2 tablespoons of tahini paste** **3 tablespoons of light olive oil** **1 teaspoon ground cumin** **Dash of Tabasco sauce**	*1* Drain the chickpeas into a cup and keep the liquid. Put the chickpeas, about 3 tablespoons of lemon juice and the other ingredients into the food processor and blend until smooth.
	2 Add some of the drained chickpea liquid if you feel the hummus is too thick, re-blend and taste. Now adjust the seasoning, thickness, lemony-ness, sesame-ness and spiciness until you get it just the way you like it.
	3 At the table, serve the hummus in individual bowls or ramekins, decorated with a drizzle of olive oil, a sprinkling of paprika and a few pitted black olives. These garnishes get a bit messy when a group of people are dipping in, so they're best left out in that situation.

Nutrient analysis per serving as 4 starter portions: Calories 133; Protein 7g; Carbohydrate 10g; Sugar 0g; Fat 8g; Saturated fat 1g; Fibre 3g; Salt 0.4g.

Simple but sexy spreads

The difference between a dip and a spread lies in its consistency. A dip is creamier, so even a fragile dipper can withstand the pressure of a good dig through a dip. On the other hand, you usually serve a spread with spreading knives and load on to crackers or tortillas.

Today, several widely available varieties of rice cakes, corncakes, oatcakes and seeded crackers make the perfect gluten-free bases for spreads. Consider using these ideas to impress your guests but still have plenty of time left to enjoy your own party:

✔ **Brown sugar on baked brie:** Place a wedge or round of brie cheese on an ovenproof serving platter. Top the cheese with a layer (about 6 millimetres, ¼ inch, thick) of light brown sugar. Bake at 180°C/Gas Mark 4 for eight minutes or until the inside of the cheese appears to be soft.

✔ **Crab cream cheese brick:** Set a brick of cream cheese on a serving platter. Drain a can of crab meat and spread the meat evenly over the top of the cream cheese. Drizzle a tasty, spicy sauce over the top (make a cool design if you feel so inclined).

✔ **Roasted mushroom spread:** Slice large field mushrooms finely and toss them in olive oil with chopped parsley, salt, Worcestershire sauce and crushed fresh garlic. Bake at 180°C/Gas Mark 4 for 20 minutes until they're soft. Then mash or blend to a spread.

✔ **Smoked mackerel pâté:** Flake smoked mackerel fillets finely and simply mix with soft butter, ricotta cheese, French mustard, black pepper and lemon juice.

Substantial Starters

Sometimes a meal needs more than an appetiser at the beginning. Here are two suggestions that will fill the gap and fill your guests. You'll only need a light main course after either of these, particularly the tarts, which also make a good lunch or supper with salad. These dishes both lend themselves to being transported and they taste great cold, so they're perfect for picnics.

Flanafel

An intriguing and impressive cross between flan and falafel, this is easier to make and less oily than home-made falafels, but it has the same flavours. Traditionally, Egyptian falafels are made not from chickpeas but white beans, which you can easily get in tins to save you all the bother of soaking and pre-cooking. It tastes divine.

Preparation time: 10 minutes • **Cooking time:** 45 minutes • **Makes:** 16 buffet-sized wedges, 8 as sit-down starters

Ingredients	*Directions*
1 large onion	*1* Preheat the oven to 190°C/Gas Mark 5.
4 large garlic cloves	
A bunch each of parsley and coriander leaves (a supermarket small pot or large pack of each)	*2* Chop the onion, garlic and herbs, stalks and all, finely in the food processor. Add the other ingredients and blend until smooth.
3 x 400-gram tins of butter beans, drained	*3* Oil a 26-centimetre/10-inch shallow dish thoroughly with olive oil and pour in the mix. Bake for 45 minutes. The top will become dark brown and the flanafel will set firmly.
2 large eggs	
2 teaspoons ground cumin	
1 teaspoons bicarbonate of soda	*4* Cool completely and slice into wedges. Serve as part of a buffet or with our tzatziki (see Chapter 14) or another yoghurt dressing and some salad leaves.
Dash of Tabasco	
Salt and black pepper	
2 tablespoons olive oil, plus a little extra for oiling the dish	

Nutrient analysis per serving (as 8 starter portions): Calories 130; Protein 7.6g; Carbohydrate 12g; Sugar 1g; Fat 6g; Saturated fat 1g; Fibre 4g; Salt 1.4g.

Leek Tarts

What's that? Gluten-free pastry? Have we gone mad? Actually, it's easier without gluten than with it. This is a savoury pastry suitable for tarts of all sizes: these generous individual ones, smaller ones to serve as finger foods, quiches for cutting into wedges or even 10-pence-sized discs to bake and then top with goodies like our spreads, wafer-thin smoked fish or ham, chopped devilled eggs and morsels of chutney.

You'll find gluten-free pastry is crisper, darker and more appetising than conventional wheat-based pastry and also easier on the cook, because it's more tolerant of technique. When you've mastered the art of tarts, you can vary the fillings to your heart's content.

Preparation time: 30 minutes • **Cooking time:** 35 to 40 minutes •
Makes: Four 11-centimetre/4-inch tarts or one 17-centimetre/7-inch quiche

Ingredients	Directions
For the pastry:	*1* If you have a facility in your oven to use the fan with bottom heat only, preheat the oven to 170°C/ Gas Mark 3. If not, preheat it to 180°C/Gas Mark 4.
85 grams/3 ounces brown rice flour	
85 grams/3 ounces fine cornmeal	*2* For the pastry, mix the dry ingredients and rub in the butter by hand, or mix in a food processor. Beat the egg and mix it in until you have a ball of dough. Add a spot of water if you can't get the dough to stick together, and then remix.
55 grams/2 ounces gram flour	
1 teaspoon xanthan gum	
100 grams/3½ ounces butter	
1 egg	*3* Roll the dough out on a light dusting of brown rice flour. If you're making four individual tarts, then cut the dough into four equal pieces before roll- ing. Place the pastry into the buttered tart tins. Patch up any gaps or splits and trim off any excess at the rims.
For the filling:	
1 thick leek or 2 thinner ones, about 425 grams/15 ounces	
30 grams/1 ounce butter	*4* Wash, trim and finely slice the leek. Melt the butter in a sauté pan and gently cook the leek, uncovered, with the seasoning. It shrinks down as it softens and cooks.
Salt and white pepper	
Pinch of mace	
1 large egg and 1 egg yolk	
70 millilitres/2½ fluid ounces single cream	
70 millilitres/2½ fluid ounces milk	

5 Beat the egg, yolk, cream and milk together in a jug.

6 Place the tarts on an oven tray and fill with the leek. Pour in the egg mixture, dividing it equally between the four individual tarts, or pouring it all into the large one. It mustn't brim over, but the tarts should be full.

7 Place the oven tray on the lowest rung if you're using the fan plus bottom heat, or in the middle of the oven if you're cooking conventionally. Cook for 35 to 40 minutes. Cool in the tins. Serve warm or cold with salad.

Nutrient analysis per serving: Calories 557; Protein 15g; Carbohydrate 41g; Sugar 4g; Fat 38g; Saturated fat 21g; Fibre 3g; Salt 1.4g.

Soggy bottoms are pretty unappealing in any circumstance! To avoid this with wheat-based pastry, you often cook tart shells *blind* – that is, without the filling, possibly with ceramic beans instead – and then cook the tart again with the filling. This technique doesn't work so well with gluten-free pastry, because the sides tend to collapse, leaving no room for the filling. If your filled, cooked tarts come out with soggy bottoms, you can easily finish them on a hot griddle for a few minutes. You can do so at any stage, even after they've gone completely cold, and this tip works for cut wedges as well as intact tarts.

Wrapping and Rolling

As one of today's most popular food trends, wraps offer never-ending possibilities for gluten-free dishes, many of which make great starters or main dishes. The only limits to what you can make into a wrap are your creativity and your sense of adventure. Choose your wrap from our suggestions below, and then let your imagination run wild as you concoct clever, flavourful fillings for the wrapper you're using.

Our favourite wraps include:

- ✔ Egg frittatas; the recipe is in Chapter 10
- ✔ Crêpes; also in Chapter 10
- ✔ Soft flour tortillas, or corn tortillas; in Chapter 15
- ✔ Sushi Nori – a deep green, dried sea vegetable that comes ready to roll
- ✔ Rice wraps, aka rice paper or galettes de riz (a bit thicker than rice paper for macaroons)
- ✔ Leaves such as lettuce, vine and green cabbage

A word of advice, though: you may want to skip the wraps on a first date or when you have the boss over for dinner. They're delicious, but attempting to eat them doesn't always make the best impression. A serving of these finger foods usually turns into a fistful.

If you're having trouble deciding what to put in your wraps, we give you some recipes to impress all your guests in the following sections. But here are some ideas to get you started:

- ✔ **Caesar salad wrap:** Actually, any salad works well in a wrap.
- ✔ **Fajita:** Fajitas are basically a Mexican blend of marinated meat and sautéed onions and peppers wrapped in a tortilla. Feel free to get creative, though, and use any meat, vegetable or bean combination you like. You generally serve the fillings separately from the tortillas so guests can load up their wraps themselves.

✔ **Fish wraps:** In California, these wraps are called fish tacos. The taco or wrap is a tortilla stuffed with cooked fish. Add some mango salsa from the recipe given in Chapter 14, and you've got yourself a gourmet meal!

✔ **Leftovers wrap:** Seriously, every fridge on the planet has something in it that you can make into a wrap. Go for it. Mix. Blend. Be wild and crazy, and clean out the refrigerator at the same time.

✔ **Quesadilla:** A *quesadilla* is simply a folded tortilla with melted cheese inside.

✔ **Shredded pork wrap:** You can use a barbecue sauce, salsa or flavoured mayonnaise to add more flavour to your pork in this wrap.

Perfecting rice rolls

Rice rolls are a great type of wrap. Available in ethnic markets or the ethnic sections of larger supermarkets, rice-paper wrappers are made from a paste of ground rice and water which is stamped into rounds and dried. When moistened, the brittle sheets of rice paper become flexible, making rice paper perfect for wraps. Rice-paper wrappers can be tricky to use, but they're well worth the effort after you've mastered working with them.

Pre-made wrappers and bottled dipping sauces are readily available in Asian markets and the Asian section of most supermarkets, but do check the labels, because many sauces with soy sauce in them contain wheat flour. The secret to making great rice rolls is to use the freshest ingredients, moisten the rice-paper wrappers until they're pliable but not too wet, and roll the bundles tightly. Try these tips and tricks:

1. **Soak 'em.**

   To make the rice-paper wrappers pliable for folding, you need to soak them one at a time for about four to five seconds until they're soft. Although some people simply use hot water for soaking, others believe the key to making a rice wrap that's pliable but doesn't fall apart is in the soaking liquid. If hot water makes your wrapper fall apart, try this for your soaking mixture:

   115 millilitres/4 fluid ounces warm water

   30 grams/1 ounce sugar

   4 tablespoons cider vinegar

2. **Drain the wrappers on a flat surface.**

   You can use your hands to take the wrappers out of the water and lay them flat on a chopping board or plate. Don't put them on top of each other, though, or they stick together and you never get them apart. Pat them dry. Handling rice-paper wrappers can be tricky, because they tend to stick to themselves and seem to rip in all the wrong places. Be patient. With a few attempts, you can get the hang of handling them.

3. **Layer the ingredients in the wrapper.**

   To avoid ripping, don't overfill the softened wrappers. The easiest way to prevent tearing is to layer the filling mixture.

4. **Fold with finesse.**

   Check out Figure 11-2 to see how to fold these wraps.

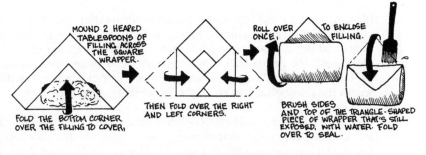

Figure 11-2:
Rolling and folding rice-paper rolls.

MOUND 2 HEAPED TABLESPOONS OF FILLING ACROSS THE SQUARE WRAPPER.

FOLD THE BOTTOM CORNER OVER THE FILLING TO COVER,

THEN FOLD OVER THE RIGHT AND LEFT CORNERS.

ROLL OVER ONCE, TO ENCLOSE FILLING.

BRUSH SIDES AND TOP OF THE TRIANGLE-SHAPED PIECE OF WRAPPER THAT'S STILL EXPOSED, WITH WATER. FOLD OVER TO SEAL.

COVER THE SPRING ROLLS WITH A TOWEL TO PREVENT DRYING.

To give your rice wraps an extra special look, garnish them with a few strips of chive or spring onion poking out one end of each roll. You can also tie them with thin strips of leek or spring onion cut lengthways.

Vietnamese Rice Wraps, or Summer Rolls (Goi Cuon)

Get on a summer roll. Goi cuon (pronounced *goy koong*) is a fresh counterpart to the spring roll, which is fried. Summer rolls are delicious, nutritious and gluten-free. You can make them with the rice-paper wraps we talk about in the preceding section and fill them with raw vegetables such as shredded iceberg lettuce, carrots, cucumber, spring onions, bean sprouts, mint and basil. Add shiitake mushrooms and tofu for another variation. The pork inside these rolls can be replaced with cooked chicken, more seafood or fish.

Preparation time: 30 minutes • **Makes:** 1 roll

Ingredients	*Directions*
1 sheet of rice-paper wrapper	*1* Soak a single rice wrapper in hot water or in a soaking mixture (see the numbered steps at the beginning of the 'Perfecting rice rolls' section) for four to five seconds. Drain the wrapper on a flat surface and pat dry.
2 peeled and cooked prawns, cut lengthwise and sliced	
3 iceberg lettuce leaves, washed and dried and then torn to about the size of playing cards	*2* Layer the ingredients in the rice wrapper: prawns first, followed by the lettuce, mint, bean sprouts, vermicelli and pork.
3 fresh mint leaves	
1 tablespoon bean sprouts	*3* Fold the right side of the wrapper towards the centre and then fold the short ends over the filling. Roll the wrapper gently – but firmly and tightly – towards the left until you form a neat oblong bundle. Slice each roll in half at a slight diagonal.
2 tablespoons rice vermicelli, soaked in warm water until soft	
5 very thin slices of cooked pork	

Vary It! For a vegetarian summer roll, substitute tofu for the prawns and pork.

Tip: This recipe makes one wrap. If you're going to make several wraps at once, you may want to put the ingredients into separate bowls. You can refrigerate the ingredients for up to three hours before putting the wraps together.

Nutrient analysis per serving: Calories 143; Protein 12.3g; Carbohydrate 15.3g; Sugar 1g; Fat 3.6g; Saturated fat 1.2g; Fibre 0.8g; Salt 0.03g.

Pork Spring Rolls

Although many spring rolls use a wheat-based wrapper, rice wrappers work really well and make a gluten-free version of this delicious treat. Because you fry spring rolls, they're not quite as healthy as the fresh summer rolls, but they're definitely delicious.

Preparation time: 30 minutes • **Cooking time:** 10 minutes • **Makes:** 8 servings

Ingredients	*Directions*
8 rice-paper wrappers **115 grams/4 ounces ground pork, cooked and drained** **340 grams/12 ounces cabbage, shredded** **3 carrots, shredded** **85 grams/3 ounces onion, diced** **1 teaspoon crushed garlic (about 1 clove)** **1 teaspoon minced fresh ginger** **Freshly ground salt and pepper to taste** **Corn oil, for frying**	*1* Soak the rice wrappers, one at a time, in hot water or in a soaking liquid (see the numbered steps at the beginning of the 'Perfecting rice rolls' section) for four to five seconds. Drain the wrappers on a flat surface and pat them dry. *2* In a large bowl, combine the pork, cabbage, carrots, onion, garlic, ginger, salt and pepper. *3* Drop 2 tablespoons of the mixture into a softened wrapper. Fold the right side of the wrapper towards the centre. Fold the short ends over the filling. Roll the wrapper gently – but firmly and tightly – towards the left until you form a neat oblong bundle. Place the rolls seam-side down onto greaseproof paper or baking parchment until you're ready to cook them. *4* Heat the corn oil in a frying pan over high heat to about 180°C (check using a cooking thermometer or dip a corner of a roll into the oil. If the oil bubbles, it's ready). Fry the rolls two at a time in the oil until they're golden brown, for approximately four minutes. *5* Carefully remove the cooked rolls from the oil with a slotted spoon and then place on sheets of kitchen paper to drain.

Tip: You can freeze these rolls to use later. To reheat, bake them in a preheated oven at 190°C/ Gas Mark 5 until warmed through, for about ten minutes.

Tip: If the rice wrapper tears while you're preparing a roll, don't start all over again. Just use a second wrapper over the first one. You end up with a thicker skin, which you may prefer anyway.

Nutrient analysis per serving: Calories 173; Protein 5g; Carbohydrate 13g; Sugar 4g; Fat 12g; Saturated fat 2g; Fibre 2g; Salt 0.4g.

Exploring leaf wraps

One of the coolest things about leaf wraps – besides the cool, crisp palate-cleansing wrap itself – is the versatility they offer gluten-free diners. You can stuff leaf wraps with any kind of meat, seafood, poultry, vegetable, bean and cheese combinations.

Here are a few things to ensure that your wraps make an even bigger hit:

- ✔ **Use large, pliable leaves.** Consider iceberg, radicchio or cabbage leaves. Core the head and soak it in iced water for a couple of hours to help you remove the leaves off the head without tearing them.

- ✔ **Blanch if necessary.** For cabbage leaves, you may need to blanch them in boiling water for a minute then douse them in cold running water to stop them cooking further and to retain their colour.

- ✔ **Dry and chill the leaves.** Lay them on some kitchen towel in the fridge for a couple of hours to make them crisp. Cold leaves make a great contrast to warm fillings. Also, they hold together better when they're chilled; otherwise they tend to collapse into limp, lifeless leaves.

- ✔ **Use a variety of colours, textures and flavours in the filling.** Ensure that your fillings have bold flavours and varying textures and colours. Consider using flavourful ingredients like mustard, yoghurt, plum sauce, chilli sauce, tamari and sesame oil in your fillings. When you're trying to decide what to serve, think about your stash of leftovers. They can usually inspire and delight you.

- ✔ **Make the fillings and sauces in advance.** Fillings are usually served chilled, so make them in advance, which gives you time to refrigerate them while you get on with preparing something else.

- ✔ **Let your guests assemble their own wraps.** People love to fill their own wraps, so place the leaves and fillings where everyone can reach them.

Oriental Pork Lettuce Wraps

The variety of lettuce wraps you can make is endless. This recipe follows one of the most basic approaches to lettuce wraps, featuring ground pork and an array of Oriental flavours. You can also substitute minced or ground chicken for the pork. Serve the wraps with individual containers of peanut sauce or any type of gluten-free Oriental dipping sauce.

Preparation time: 15 minutes • **Cooking time:** 2 minutes • **Makes:** 6 servings

Ingredients	Directions
450 grams/1 pound cooked ground pork	**1** In a medium glass bowl, combine the cooked ground pork, rice vinegar, soy sauce, sesame oil, spring onions, carrot and rice vermicelli. Season the ingredients with salt and pepper and mix well.
3 tablespoons rice vinegar	
2 tablespoons soy sauce	
2 teaspoons sesame oil	**2** Cover the mixture and heat in a microwave oven on high for about two minutes, until the mixture is hot.
2½ tablespoons chopped spring onions	
3 tablespoons grated carrot	**3** Serve the pork mixture in a bowl with a large serving spoon. On a separate platter, arrange a stack of chilled lettuce leaves so people can fill their own wraps.
100 grams/3½ ounces cooked rice vermicelli	
Freshly ground salt and pepper to taste	
6 large chilled lettuce leaves	

Nutrient analysis per serving: Calories 182; Protein 26g; Carbohydrate 7g; Sugar 2g; Fat 6g; Saturated fat 2g; Fibre 0.4g; Salt 1.5g.

Chapter 12

Sensational Soups, Salads and Sides

In This Chapter

▶ Getting bowled over by delicious gluten-free soups

▶ Putting salads and hot vegetables into a fresh perspective

▶ Stimulating your side dishes with mouth-watering gluten-free ideas

Soups, salads and side dishes are just as important as the main meal itself. In fact, they can be the meal itself. But many soups are thickened with flour, salads are often dressed up and garnished with gluten-laden goodies, and side dishes are sometimes seasoned with sauces that make them unsuitable for people enjoying a gluten-free lifestyle.

So should you just forget about creamy soups, crunchy croutons, Yorkshire puddings and side dishes with pizzazz? Are you stuck with boring salads of just lettuce and tomatoes? We don't think so. Are you limited to the old gluten-free standbys of rice and potatoes? No way. Stick with us, and you can whip up some scrumptious accompaniments to rival – or even serve as – the main course.

Throughout our recipes, we use ingredients which are widely available gluten-free, but some brands of certain ingredients do contain gluten or may do so, particularly flours, meals, starches, stock cubes, ready-made stock and sauces. As with all your food, check the labels carefully and avoid anything that contains gluten, even a trace.

Creating a Storm in a Soup Cup

Soup has been a versatile and important part of people's diet for about 5,000 years. Soups can be hot, cold, thick, thin, creamy, chunky, sweet, savoury, elegant or simple. You can create them from virtually anything in your cupboard, they're quick and cheap to make, and they can help clear out your fridge of leftovers. Soups are comforting, satisfying and nutritious.

However, commercial soups often contain flour, pasta, barley or other ingredients that make them taboo on a gluten-free diet. Fortunately, great-tasting gluten-free soups are easy to make, and even noodle-based soups are a breeze. And when you make soups yourself, they're generally more wholesome and less salty. Plus you get to choose what goes in them, so you're bound to enjoy eating them even more.

Taking stock

More than half of chicken soup sales in the UK take place during the cold and flu season. That's because many people believe that chicken soup has healing properties. Physician Moses Maimonides first proposed using chicken soup as a cold and asthma remedy in the 12th century, and scientists have studied the therapeutic properties of chicken soup extensively in recent decades. The jury's still out, but one thing's for sure: home-made chicken stock made from the bones after a roast is far more likely to work as a remedy than anything made with a stock cube.

We have nothing against stock cubes, as long as they're gluten-free, of course – and a market-leading cube in the UK isn't, by the way. Similarly, we have nothing against bouillon powder, which has the advantage that you can add just a little and taste, so you're less likely to over-salt your soup.

However, proper stock made from bones adds texture as well as taste, and doesn't need any extra fat or oil. You can simply throw the soup ingredients into the home-made stock and start cooking. Leave out the cream, too. This stock is also perfect for risottos.

Here's how to make the stock when you have chicken bones handy, or those of any game or poultry bird. If you have a pasta-boiling pan with a strainer that almost reaches the bottom of the pan, the job is a lot easier. As you carve the chicken, put the scraps and bones into the strainer. You can leave this covered until the next day in the fridge, or freeze the scraps and tackle them later. Add a quartered onion, a roughly chopped carrot and celery stalk, plus a few peppercorns, allspice berries and a bay leaf. Cover the bones completely with water, bring to the boil and then turn down the heat as low as you can go. It should barely simmer. After an hour or so, simply lift out the strainer, drain it and throw out its contents, or strain your stock through a colander. Freeze it or use it for soup or risotto right away.

Quinoa Vegetable Soup

This super-healthy soup suits just about anyone, whatever their dietary requirements. As well as being gluten-free, it contains no dairy or egg, so it's even suitable for vegans. You're going to be amazed at how a recipe that's so 'free from' can taste so good!

Preparation time: 25 minutes • **Cooking time:** 10 minutes • **Makes:** 4

Ingredients	*Directions*
1 tablespoon vegetable oil	*1* Heat the oil in a large saucepan, add the quinoa, carrot, celery, onion, pepper and garlic and fry gently until golden.
55 grams/2 ounces quinoa	
1 carrot, peeled and diced	
1 celery stick, diced	
2 tablespoons finely chopped onion	*2* Add the water, tomatoes and cabbage. Stir and bring to the boil. Reduce the heat and simmer for ten minutes.
½ green pepper, deseeded and diced	*3* Season with salt and pepper and serve hot.
2 cloves garlic, peeled and crushed	
960 millilitres/34 fluid ounces cold water	
2 large tomatoes, finely chopped	
55 grams/2 ounces cabbage, chopped	
Freshly ground salt and pepper to taste	

Nutrient analysis per serving: Calories 92; Protein 3g; Carbohydrate 12g; Sugar 6g; Fat 4g; Saturated fat 1g; Fibre 2g; Salt 0.75g.

Faux Pho – Thai-Namese Prawn and Chicken Soup

This soup is our simplified version of a traditional Vietnamese noodle soup called pho. Today the soup is a worldwide favourite, with many variations. Our version has a Thai influence, with the fish sauce, ginger and curry, but the rice noodles make it Vietnamese, hence the name 'Thai-Namese'.

Preparation time: 15 minutes • **Cooking time:** 20 minutes • **Makes:** 4 servings

Ingredients	*Directions*
1 litre/1¾ pints ready-to-use chicken stock	*1* Combine the chicken stock, fish stock, fish sauce, garlic, ginger and red curry paste in a large casserole, stirring the ingredients with a whisk. Add the mushrooms, and bring the mixture to a boil over medium heat.
225 millilitres/8 fluid ounces ready-to-use fish stock	
2 tablespoons fish sauce	
2 teaspoons crushed garlic (about 2 cloves)	
2 teaspoons minced fresh ginger	*2* Reduce the heat and simmer the soup for five minutes. Add the prawns, chicken and mangetout, and then bring the soup to the boil. Cover the soup, reduce the heat and simmer for five minutes.
¾ teaspoon red curry paste	
225 grams/8 ounces fresh mushrooms, sliced	
450 grams/1 pound large raw prawns, peeled	
225 grams/8 ounces fresh chicken breasts, skinned and boned, cut into 25-millimetre (1-inch) cubes	*3* Stir in the lime juice, sugar, spring onion tops, coriander and coconut milk. Cook the soup for four minutes or until it's thoroughly heated. Add the cooked rice noodles just before serving.
70 grams/2½ ounces fresh mangetout, trimmed	
Juice of 2 fresh limes	
2 tablespoons granulated sugar	
2 tablespoons spring onion tops, chopped	
2 tablespoons chopped fresh coriander	
400 grams/14 ounces (usually 1 can) light coconut milk	
255 grams/9 ounces dried rice noodles, reconstituted according to pack directions (700 grams/1½ pounds when cooked until slightly firm)	

Nutrient analysis per serving: Calories 287; Protein 5g; Carbohydrate 40g; Sugar 10g; Fat 12g; Saturated fat 1.5g; Fibre 1.5g; Salt 1.6g.

Many Thai ingredients are inherently gluten-free, although you do need to check the labels, especially for Westernised products. Fish sauce is a good example. Traditional fish sauce comes from fermented, salt-cured fish, and most fish sauce is just that – fish. But you may occasionally find a label that shows added wheat. (Authentic Oriental products are labelled in English even if they're imported.)

Creamy Broccoli Soup

Here's a quick-to-make warming soup that uses the stalks that get left out when you serve broccoli as a vegetable. The cooked stalks thicken the soup to the perfect consistency, and the florets finish it with speckles of darker green.

Preparation time: 15 minutes • **Cooking time:** 20 minutes • **Makes:** 4 servings

Ingredients	Directions
1 tablespoon oil **1 onion, chopped** **1 head of broccoli** **2 broccoli stalks or small potatoes** **1 litre/1¾ pints ready-to-use chicken or vegetable stock** **1 tablespoon crème fraîche** **White pepper**	*1* Heat the oil to moderate heat and fry the onion gently, without allowing it to brown.
	2 Separate the florets of the broccoli. Trim and roughly chop the stalks, along with the peeled potato if you have no extra stalks. Add the stalks and potato to the onion and stir.
	3 When the vegetables are coated with oil and have softened just slightly, add the stock and bring to the boil. Cover and simmer for about ten minutes until the stalks are beginning to soften. Then add the florets and continue to simmer for another five minutes or so until all the vegetables are tender.
	4 Blend the soup until it's smooth and add the cream, stirring it in thoroughly while warming the soup again and letting it thicken. Taste and adjust the seasoning.

Nutrient analysis per serving: Calories 110; Protein 6g; Carbohydrate 46g; Sugar 5g; Fat 7g; Saturated fat 2g; Fibre 4g; Salt 0.5g.

Posh Squash Soup

Sweet, savoury and satisfying all at the same time, this soup can be served hot or chilled. It's a doddle to make, yet it looks quite chic with the garnishes.

Preparation time: 20 minutes • **Cooking time:** 20 minutes • **Makes:** 4 servings

Ingredients	*Directions*
400 grams/14 ounces butternut squash (half a large one) 255 grams/9 ounces swede (half a small one)	*1* Deseed the squash and peel it and the swede. Roughly chop the squash and swede into chunks. Wash and thinly slice the leeks.
White parts of 2 leeks 1 teaspoon ground coriander seeds 1 litre/1¾ pints ready-to-use vegetable stock	*2* Put all the vegetables and the ground coriander into the pan with the stock and bring to the boil. Cover and simmer for about 20 minutes or until the vegetables are tender.
285 millilitres/10 fluid ounces semi-skimmed milk Salt and pepper A squeeze of lemon juice Smooth yoghurt and sumac or achiote to garnish	*3* Blend until smooth and then add the milk and lemon juice. Reheat and taste for acidity and seasoning. Garnish each bowl with a swirl of yoghurt and a sprinkling of sumac or achiote.

Nutrient analysis per serving: Calories 116; Protein 7g; Carbohydrate 19g; Sugar 14g; Fat 2g; Saturated fat 1g; Fibre 5g; Salt 0.6g.

Surprising Salads, Versatile Vegetables

Most plain green salads are gluten-free – and of course, you can serve up steamed or boiled vegetables – but even hard-core veggie fans get tired of these options pretty quickly. In this section, we show you ways to dress up delicious salads and suggest ideas for how to make hot vegetables that are more than just supporting acts.

Adding taste and texture to salads

Salads offer a great way to combine interesting grains, fruits, vegetables, eggs, fish, cheese and meats in one dish. Served on the side or as a complete meal, salads are nutritious and delicious, and they're especially great on a hot summer's day, when they make a welcome cool and quick dinner.

Most of these salads start with a basic bed of greens or a variety of lettuce. Pre-washed salad leaf selections make life even simpler, but of course you can use any type of lettuce you want. Remember, the darker the leaf, the more nutritious the salad – watercress and spinach are nutrient-packed dark-green leaves.

A few of our personal favourites include:

- **Caesar salad:** Chop up a head of romaine lettuce and add Caesar dressing. You can buy the dressing ready-made or make your own following the easy recipe in Chapter 14. Remember to add freshly grated Parmesan cheese.

- **Cool-as-a-cucumber salad:** In a medium-sized bowl, mix finely chopped cucumber (peeled and seeded) with plain yoghurt, some finely diced spring onions, lemon juice and black pepper. Spread over a bed of green leaves and top with freshly chopped tomatoes.

- **Grilled garlic chicken salad:** In a small bowl, mix 3 to 4 tablespoons of vinaigrette with 2 teaspoons of crushed garlic and a dash of crushed chilli flakes. Add slices of red pepper and mushrooms to the dressing, and toss to coat them. Fish the peppers and mushrooms out of the dressing, setting the remaining dressing aside, and grill them with your chicken. Place handfuls of salad greens on plates and top with the grilled vegetables and chicken. Drizzle over the remaining dressing.

- **Thai beef salad:** Start with a bed of greens and add 2 tablespoons of fresh mint leaves (torn into large pieces), half a cucumber (peeled and sliced), several thinly sliced pieces of grilled rump steak, 2 tablespoons chopped peanuts and lime wedges (for garnish). Top the salad with a gluten-free Asian salad dressing.

- ✔ **Tomato and basil salad:** Over a bed of green salad leaves, add sliced beef tomatoes topped with a scattering of freshly torn basil leaves. If you fancy, add a slice of buffalo mozzarella. Then drizzle the salad with balsamic vinaigrette dressing.

- ✔ **Warm beetroot salad:** In a large saucepan, cook some green beans in boiling water until tender (takes about eight minutes). Add a jar of sliced beetroot (drained), and cook over medium heat until heated through. Drain the beans and the beetroot. Meanwhile, in a screw-top glass jar, combine about 3 tablespoons orange juice, 3 tablespoons extra-virgin olive oil, 1 tablespoon balsamic vinegar, 2 teaspoons crushed garlic and a dash of white pepper. Shake the dressing well. Arrange some mixed greens on plates, place the beans and beetroot on top and coat the veggies with the dressing.

Sprout 'em yourself

Familiar sprouted seeds include bean sprouts, which are the very young seedlings of mung beans, and mustard and cress seedlings. You can sprout a host of other seeds indoors at any time of year, including alfalfa, broccoli, red clover, fenugreek, radish, buckwheat, aduki beans and lentils. You don't need green fingers to grow sprouts – just invest in a few basic starter items, and you can watch your sprout garden grow.

You can grow sprouts in soil, just like any other plant, but most people grow them in jars. For that, you need the following:

- ✔ A large jar

- ✔ Cheesecloth or nylon netting

- ✔ An elastic band

- ✔ 1 tablespoon sprout seeds, available at nurseries or online

- ✔ Water

Here's what you do:

1. **Put the seeds into the jar, cover with water and tighten the cheesecloth or nylon netting over the jar opening with a rubber band.**

   Let the seeds soak overnight.

2. **Drain the water from the jar through the cheesecloth. Leave the jar on the windowsill or in a cool, darkened place.**

   If you keep the jar in the dark, the sprouts grow white; if you expose the jar to light, the sprouts come out green.

3. **Rinse and drain the seeds once a day or more.**

   This step is very important, because the seeds need to be moist but not wet. If you don't rinse the seeds often enough, they may start to mould. If you notice a bad smell from your sprouting seeds, they've probably gone bad. Throw them away and start again.

In less than a week, the sprouts should be ready to eat. To harvest them, just use scissors to cut the edible sprouts away from the roots, leaving what you don't need. The rest keep growing, and you can use them later.

Energising your salad

You can add many other foods to your salad to perk it up while also providing more nutrition:

- ✔ **Beans and legumes:** Try green beans, kidney beans, black beans or chickpeas. Not only do they add flavour and provide you with slow-releasing low-glycaemic-index (GI) energy (refer to Chapter 6 for more on low-GI foods), but they also add lots of fibre to your salad.

- ✔ **Cherry tomatoes:** Several varieties of cherry tomatoes are available. Sweet, juicy and full of antioxidants, they come in all different colours and shapes.

- ✔ **Chopped ham or turkey:** A little less fatty than bacon, these meats add protein and flavour to a salad.

- ✔ **Crumbled bacon:** Of course, bacon adds fat and salt, but it also adds flavour, so you don't need a lot.

- ✔ **Crumbled cheese:** Be creative – use a variety of types from feta to Parmesan and Manchego to mozzarella.

- ✔ **Fruit:** Grapes, pineapple, melon, kiwi – adding a handful of chopped fruit can liven up a salad to make a fresh and healthy treat.

- ✔ **Greens:** Iceberg lettuce is boring and relatively worthless nutritionally speaking. Consider using radicchio, romaine, kale, spinach, rocket, watercress and other greens to increase the vitamin, mineral and fibre content of your salad – not to mention flavour.

- ✔ **Herbs:** Adding a handful of whole or chopped fresh herbs can liven up your salad, provide you with extra vitamins and introduce piquancy to your meal. Many pre-packaged, washed salad selections now include herbs in them.

- ✔ **Mushrooms:** They have a distinctive taste and texture. Finely sliced and marinated for an hour in a teaspoonful each of Worcestershire sauce and tamari, they make their own no-fat dressing.

- ✔ **Nuts and seeds:** Choose from a vast selection of fresh, unsalted nuts and seeds. They add nutrients, crunch and flavour.

- ✔ **Olives:** Try black or green olives, or both, and add them whole or chopped so you can spread the flavour throughout your salad.

- ✔ **Onions:** Red onions and spring onions are two of the most popular varieties to include in salads. Onions and other crunchy white vegetables such as white cabbage and celeriac add nutrients too.

✔ **Pak choi:** Pak choi is loaded with nutrients, and is great in salads.

✔ **Radishes:** These add zip to your salad, without calories.

✔ **Raisins:** Also try similar dried fruit, such as dried cranberries.

✔ **Raw broccoli:** Ready prepared packs of broccoli make adding flavour and crunch easy. Broccoli is loaded with antioxidants and nutrients.

✔ **Shredded cabbage:** In the same family as broccoli, cabbage contains important nutrients for good health. Use red, white and green varieties to add crunch, texture and colour.

✔ **Sprouting seeds:** Loaded with fibre and nutrients, sprouting beans and seeds are a great addition to any salad. And they're easy to grow yourself. See the 'Sprout 'em yourself' sidebar for how.

Getting creative with croutons

Okay, we don't know about you, but we've got some pretty specific requirements when considering what makes a good crouton. After all, if you're going to indulge, you may as well do it right. Personally, our crouton criteria include crunch, flavour and just a touch of decadence. For us, broccoli florets just don't cut it as a crouton; do they for you?

But croutons are usually made from bread and are therefore no good on a gluten-free diet. But don't worry – with a little creativity you can make all sorts of croutons. Try some of these ideas:

✔ **Crisps:** Break these up onto your salad.

✔ **Deep-fried veggies:** Take your favourite vegetable – sweet potatoes work really well for this – and dredge pieces in any gluten-free flour mixture. Deep-fry until crispy and golden, and you've got yourself veggie croutons.

✔ **Gluten-free homemade croutons:** Use any gluten-free bread, cut into cubes and deep-fried. Then coat the croutons with Parmesan and seasoning. If you want a lower-fat version, spread out the cubes on a baking tray and drizzle with extra-virgin olive oil. Season the bread with fresh herbs or seasoned salt and bake the croutons in a moderate oven (160°C/Gas Mark 3½) for about ten minutes until golden.

✔ **Polenta:** Polenta is a grainy form of cornmeal that you make into a stiff paste with water, following the directions on the pack. For croutons, let the polenta cool then dice it into crouton-sized pieces and deep-fry for a great salad topper.

✔ **Potato croutons:** Dice two potatoes and put the pieces on a baking tray coated with non-stick spray. Then drizzle the potatoes with oil and bake at 220°C/Gas Mark 7 for 30 minutes or until crisp and golden.

✔ **Potato skins:** Scoop out the insides of baked potatoes and save the skins. Deep-fry and season the skins with garlic or celery salt.

✔ **Tortilla chips:** Make your own from our recipe in Chapter 15 and break them up. If you buy them ready-made, check they don't contain gluten.

Now for something hot

We could have written a whole book on interesting ways to serve hot vegetables, besides simply steamed, but here are a few gluten-free ideas to get your taste buds tingling. Check out Chapter 14 too for ideas on suitable gluten-free versions of sauces that normally contain gluten, such as cheese sauce for cauliflower or broccoli.

✔ **Call it a curry.** Root vegetables, aubergine, courgettes and peppers make lovely curries you can eat either on the side or as the star of the show with rice and dahl. Start with gently roasting whole seeds such as mustard and kalonji in a little oil. Pile in your cut-up vegetables, including an onion, and ground spices, especially cumin, coriander, turmeric and chilli powder. Add enough water to more or less cover the vegetables. Cook until the vegetables are tender, season to taste and, if necessary, thicken the sauce with tomato purée and a little cornflour or tapioca starch mixed with cold water and then cooked into the sauce.

✔ **Mix them.** You can boil vegetables such as parsnip, turnip and celeriac together or with an equal amount of potato, and then either mash or crush them together for a different flavour and look.

✔ **Layer and bake.** Finely slicing firm vegetables and layering them up with herbs, onion and a little milk or stock and then baking them, either covered or uncovered, takes some advance prepping, but means they can be ready when you are, without the last-minute over-cooking that can easily happen when you're putting the finishing touches to a meal.

✔ **Get fruity.** Mixing vegetables with fruit works well, particularly with fruit you'd normally serve cooked, like Bramley apples, plums and rhubarb. Cooking them together, perhaps with brown sugar and wine vinegar, makes the fruit turn into a sauce for the vegetables – particularly good with members of the cabbage family. Dried fruits also make unexpected additions to vegetables, and we include sun-dried tomatoes in that. A tomato sauce makes a refreshing change from milky or creamy sauces. Citrus zests and juices add tang without sweetness, and don't forget preserved lemon and olives for tastes and colours all of their own.

✔ **Go to seed.** Cumin with carrot, aniseed with fennel, coriander with swede, fenugreek with sweet potatoes, fennel seed with kale, and caraway with just about any vegetable are all combinations to try.

✔ **Ginger them up.** You can grate and slice fresh ginger root over most cooked green leaves. Pickled ginger just needs cutting into shreds. And if you're after sweet heat, either preserved or crystallised ginger works well with vegetables, as does a spoonful of the syrup from the preserved ginger jar.

✔ **Very berry good.** Nasturtium, capers, juniper and clove all have their own mysterious flavours to impart to cooked vegetables.

✔ **Go nuts.** All nuts, including pinenuts, can add crunch to vegetables. Most are best chopped or slivered and lightly toasted before being tossed in with the vegetables at the last minute.

✔ **Give them a glaze.** Sliced onions browned in oil or caramelised make interesting toppings for mashed or baked vegetables, and can be mixed with seeds and chilli as well. An oily or buttery glaze with sweet sherry or honey keeps cooked vegetables looking fresh and needn't add too many calories, because you only need a little to get the effect.

We hope you've been inspired now to jazz up your greens – and your reds, purples, yellows, oranges, blacks and whites and everything in between when it comes to the stunning variety of vegetables on offer.

Starchy Staples That Strut Their Stuff

Some people think that serving starchy side dishes on the gluten-free diet is easy, and that's true to some extent. Rice and potatoes do serve as staple sides for most people new to the gluten-free lifestyle. But we say 'Move over, mash' to make way for more provocative side dishes featuring interesting alternatives such as quinoa, millet, lentils and beans.

Lemon Quinoa Crunch

You can serve this crunchy, colourful, tangy and nutritious dish at room temperature or cold (we prefer cold). This food makes a great stand-alone, side or salad substitute. In fact, because quinoa contains all the amino acids that your body can't produce on its own, this grain can be the main dish. You may want to double the quantities in the recipe, because the leftovers are fantastic – this dish gets better each day as the flavours mingle.

Preparation time: 15 minutes • **Makes:** 6 servings

Ingredients	*Directions*
For the dressing:	*1* Make the dressing by whisking together the lime juice, white pepper, black pepper, jalapeño, coarse salt and olive oil. Set the mixture aside.
4 tablespoons fresh lime juice	
¼ teaspoon white pepper	
¼ teaspoon freshly ground black pepper	
30 grams/1 ounce sliced marinated jalapeño pepper	*2* Place the quinoa in a fine sieve and rinse it under cold running water, rubbing your hands through it for a few minutes. Drain off any excess water.
¼ teaspoon coarse salt	
55 millilitres/2 fluid ounces extra-virgin olive oil	
For the quinoa:	*3* In a large pot, pour in the water and add the quinoa. Bring the mixture to the boil, lower the heat and simmer uncovered for about 10 to 15 minutes, or until the quinoa is barely tender, making sure not to overcook it. Carefully tip the quinoa into a sieve to drain thoroughly, and leave to cool. No need to rinse it.
360 grams/12¾ ounces whole quinoa	
700 millilitres/1¼ pints cold water	
85 grams/3 ounces cucumber, peeled, seeded and diced	
140 grams/5 ounces fresh tomatoes, seeded and diced	
115 grams/4 ounces red pepper, sliced	*4* Mix the quinoa in with the cucumber, tomato, red and yellow peppers, spring onions, parsley, mint and dressing. Add a little salt and pepper to taste (you don't need much, because this dish has plenty of flavour). Serve the dish at room temperature or cold.
40 grams/1½ ounces yellow pepper, sliced	
30 grams/1 ounce spring onions, white part only, sliced	
1 tablespoon chopped fresh parsley	
1 tablespoon chopped fresh mint	
Freshly ground salt and pepper to taste	

Nutrient analysis per serving: Calories 294; Protein 9g; Carbohydrate 34g; Sugar 7g; Fat 13g; Saturated fat 2g; Fibre 1g; Salt 0.4g.

Rice with Red Peppers, Chickpeas and Feta

This dish is loaded with flavour, and it's already packed with nutrients, but to add extra goodness, try using brown rice instead of white.

Preparation time: 15 minutes • Resting time: 1 hour • **Makes:** 6 servings

Ingredients	*Directions*
4 tablespoons extra-virgin olive oil	*1* In a large saucepan, warm the olive oil and cook the garlic and spring onions gently. Add the rest of the ingredients apart from the cheese and warm everything through in the oil, stirring to avoid the rice sticking.
2 teaspoons crushed garlic (about 2 cloves)	
4 spring onions, washed, trimmed, thinly sliced	
Freshly ground salt and pepper to taste	*2* When everything's hot, add the feta cheese and fold in without breaking it up further.
200 grams/9 ounces brown or white rice, cooked according to the pack directions (480 grams/17 ounces cooked weight)	
400 grams/14 ounce can of chickpeas, drained and rinsed	
115 millilitres/4 fluid ounces fresh lemon juice	
2 tablespoons chopped fresh parsley	
2 teaspoons chopped fresh dill	
55 grams/2 ounces roasted red peppers (fresh or from a jar)	
155 grams/5½ ounces feta cheese, finely diced	

Nutrient analysis per serving: Calories 354; Protein 12g; Carbohydrate 34g; Sugar 2g; Fat 19g; Saturated fat 5g; Fibre 3.5g; Sodium 1.6g.

Sweet Potato Pot

Sweet potatoes (as opposed to 'regular' ones) are very nutritious and a valuable slow-releasing energy food. Try this simple and refreshing 'potato' salad for a unique twist on an old favourite.

Preparation time: 15 minutes • **Cooking time:** 20 minutes • Refrigeration time: 2 hours •
Makes: 6 servings

Ingredients	*Directions*
1 kilogram/2¼ pounds sweet potatoes, peeled and cooked	**1** Peel and dice the sweet potatoes. Steam them for 20 minutes or until they're tender but not mushy.
2 fresh green chillies, finely chopped	**2** With the pan over a gentle heat, mix the sweet potatoes with the rest of the ingredients. Turn the mixture to warm it through and mix. Serve warm.
85 grams/3 ounces red pepper, chopped	
2 teaspoons chopped coriander	
Pinch of paprika	
75 millilitres/5 tablespoons single cream	
1 dessertspoon red wine vinegar	

Nutrient analysis per serving: Calories 240; Protein 2g; Carbohydrate 33g; Sugar 14g; Fat 11g; Saturated fat 2g; Fibre 4g; Salt 0.2g.

Vary it! For a lower-calorie version, replace the cream with low-fat smooth yoghurt and use less vinegar.

Topping off the trusty spud

Baked potatoes are a staple side dish on the gluten-free diet. But, seriously: do you think anyone ever gets a craving for a plain old baked potato with nothing on it? Not likely. Baked spuds cry out for some serious support from the wonderful world of toppings. After all, if you're going to indulge (yes, we consider a potato a bit of an indulgence, because it's a very high-glycaemic-index food; you can read more about the glycaemic index in Chapter 6), you may as well make it worth eating. Bottom line: an unadorned baked potato is too plain and simple. Try dressing it up with these toppings:

✓ Bacon or ham pieces

✓ Barbecue sauce

✓ Broccoli florets

✓ Butter or sour cream

✓ Caramelised onions

✓ Chilli (choose mild fresh ones)

✓ Chopped chives

✓ Diced chicken

✓ Gluten-free soy sauce or tamari

✓ Grated cheese

✓ Guacamole or avocado slices

✓ Pickled jalapeño peppers

✓ Salsa

Pulses to Please

The gluten-free diet can be lacking in insoluble fibre, the kind that keeps you regular. This happens because the main source of insoluble fibre in the typical British diet is wheat bran, and there are no gluten-free sources available. So you need to look for other foods that provide insoluble fibre. Peas, beans and lentils still in their skins are all good sources, and delicious too. They make interesting additions to soups, salads and hot vegetables. They can act as a filling vegetable, and you can turn them into comforting and nutritious side or even main-course dishes in their own right.

None of the lentils need to be pre-soaked, and they cook in just 15 to 30 minutes, depending on the type. You can prepare them continental style or turn them into dahls; we give a recipe for each, using dried lentils.

Dried peas and beans do need to be pre-soaked and boiled for some time, but this is worth the effort if you want to cook other flavours into them. Many are now available tinned but otherwise plain, and these are your best bet for rustling up bean-feasts on the quick. Several are now available freshly frozen, including mushy peas and soy beans, so you can ring the changes to the traditional garden peas at no notice.

Continental Lentil

Preparation time: 5 minutes • **Cooking time:** 30 minutes • **Makes:** 4 servings

Ingredients	*Directions*
2 shallots **1 tablespoon rapeseed oil**	*1* Finely chop the shallots and fry them gently in the oil in a saucepan.
285 grams/10 ounces Puy or other small green or brown whole lentils; not the split, hulled ones **A sprig of fresh thyme or a little dried** **Salt and pepper**	*2* Wash the lentils, add to the pan and stir them to coat with oil. Add the thyme. Just cover the lentils with water, bring to the boil and simmer, covered, for about 30 minutes. Check the mixture and add more water if it appears to be drying out. Towards the end of the cooking, most of the water will have been absorbed, softening the lentils, and the remaining liquid should have thickened slightly.
	3 Taste and season. Throw out the remains of the thyme sprig and serve.

Nutrient analysis per serving: Calories 260; Protein 18g; Carbohydrate 37g; Sugar 1g; Fat 5g; Saturated fat 0.5g; Fibre 7g; Salt, only what you add.

Dahl

Strictly speaking, you make dahls with split lentils, but no one will object if you use whole ones. If you decide to mix different lentils and beans in this dish, check the suggested cooking times on the packs and put them into the pot at intervals so that they'll all be cooked at the same moment. In particular, the most familiar lentil – the red, split masoor – only needs about ten minutes' cooking.

Preparation time: 5 minutes • **Cooking time:** 15 to 45 minutes, depending on the lentils used • **Makes:** 4 servings

Ingredients	*Directions*
285 grams/10 ounces any split or whole lentils or small beans such as whole green lentils, masoor, urad, mung, toovar and chana	*1* Wash the lentils and put them into a saucepan with enough water to easily cover them. Bring to the boil and skim off any foam on the top. Add the ginger and turmeric. Stir.
1 teaspoon grated fresh root ginger	*2* Turn down the heat as low as possible, cover the pot and cook until the lentils are soft – anything from 15 to 45 minutes, depending on the lentils you're using. From time to time, stir the lentils and top up the water if they go dry. Add any salt at the end.
1 teaspoon ground turmeric	
Salt to taste	
1 tablespoon rapeseed oil	*3* Meanwhile, heat the oil in a separate pan and gently fry the garlic and spices. You can leave this mixture to go cold until the lentils are done and then reheat, but do be careful not to brown the garlic.
2 cloves of garlic	
2 teaspoons whole cumin seeds	
2 teaspoons ground coriander seed	*4* When the lentils are tender and beginning to turn to a purée with the remaining water, stir in the spicy, garlicky mixture. Serve sprinkled with the coriander leaves.
Pinch of chilli powder	
2 tablespoons chopped fresh coriander leaves	

Nutrient analysis per serving: Calories 260; Protein 119g; Carbohydrate 37g; Sugar 1g; Fat 6g; Saturated fat 0.5g; Fibre 7g; Salt 0.05g, plus whatever you've added.

Puda Cakes

A cross between a savoury scone and a pancake, puda cakes are lighter than pakoras and bhajis, because they're not fried. In fact, the recipe is very nearly fat-free. Puda cakes are yummy with curries or for breakfast or as an unusual base for savoury toppings (we suggest tasty toppings in Chapter 11). The cakes do take time, although not much of that is hands-on. You can make a batch and freeze them, and then simply thaw and reheat in the oven or toaster.

Preparation time: Overnight soak, plus 10 minutes, plus an hour to stand •
Cooking time: 5 to 6 minutes per batch • **Makes:** 12 puda cakes

Ingredients	*Directions*
225 grams/8 ounces mung beans	**1** Rinse the beans and cover them with cold water. Leave to soak overnight. Then rinse them again, pat them dry with kitchen paper and grind them up in the food processor.
100 millilitres/3½ fluid ounces yoghurt	
2 large tomatoes, quartered	**2** Throw in the rest of the ingredients apart from the butter and process until fairly fine but still with visible flecks of the vegetables and herb. Set aside for an hour or so. The mixture should be thin enough to spread out when it hits the griddle, rather like a drop scone. Add a little more yoghurt or some gram flour to adjust the consistency if necessary.
1 small courgette, cut into large chunks	
½ teaspoon ground turmeric	
¼ teaspoon garlic salt	
3 green chillies	
6-8 fresh coriander sprigs	**3** Heat your griddle or a heavy frying pan and brush with butter. Drop on the mixture in large spoonfuls and fry until the undersides are mid-brown and set. Turn them over and fry the other side until mid-brown. Serve warm.
A little butter for cooking	

Nutrient analysis per 2 cakes: Calories 125; Protein 10g; Carbohydrate 19g; Sugar 2g; Fat 1g; Saturated fat 1g; Fibre 4g; Salt 0.4g.

Essentials on the Side

The phrase 'all the trimmings' can strike fear into your heart when you're eating gluten-free. It usually means tempting but off-limits stuffing, dumplings and Yorkshire puddings. Now, you don't have to go without. Here are our gluten-free recipes for these essentials on the side.

Yorkshire Pudding

You have two choices here. The first makes a traditional doughy, moist pudding, similar to the middle part of a large wheat-based one. The second is really a choux bun – crisp and puffy. They're both good, so go with whichever takes your fancy.

Recipe 1

Preparation time: 5 minutes • **Cooking time:** 25 minutes • **Makes:** 4 servings

Ingredients	Directions
30 grams/1 ounce brown rice flour	*1* Preheat the oven to 200°C/Gas Mark 6.
30 grams/1 ounce tapioca starch	*2* Blend all the ingredients apart from the dripping or oil.
1 large egg 140 millilitres/5 fluid ounces skimmed milk	*3* Divide the dripping or oil between either four 7½ to 10-centimetre/3- to 4-inch Yorkshire pudding tins or eight half-sized Yorkshire pudding tins. You may need a little more for the eight small ones. Get the tins up to heat in the oven.
1 teaspoon baking powder 4 teaspoons hot beef dripping or oil	*4* Open the oven and pour the batter evenly into the tins. Then close the oven as soon as you can to keep the tins hot.
	5 Bake for 25 minutes and serve at once.

Nutrient analysis per serving: Calories 125; Protein 4g; Carbohydrate 13g; Sugar 2g; Fat 7g; Saturated fat 3g; Fibre 0g; Salt 0.09g.

Stuffing

Most stuffings are, of course, simply bread-crumbs mixed with seasoning, herbs, spices and other flavouring ingredients like chopped onion, celery and lemon zest, all held together with either egg or water. Apart from the bread-crumbs, none of these ingredients contains gluten, so mixing up your own gluten-free stuffing can be as simple as substituting gluten-free breadcrumbs for wheat-based ones. In fact, it's a good idea to turn any uneaten gluten-free bread, including crusts and stale pieces, to breadcrumbs and then freeze them. When you need a handful, you'll find they've stayed crumbly and don't need to be thawed before use.

Stuffings for meat needn't contain any starchy ingredients at all. Dried fruit, garlic and rosemary make a fantastic stuffing for pork, for example, along with a virtually ready-made sauce. You can ring the changes with all sorts of finely chopped fruits, vegetables, herbs and spices as long as the stuffing isn't too wet.

If you want a starchy element to thicken your stuffing and make it more substantial, plenty of gluten-free alternatives to breadcrumbs exist, but you must cook them first. You can cook up sticky rice, gluten-free oats, quinoa, buckwheat, millet or any flaked grain you fancy, and then cool it, mix in your flavouring ingredients, with or without egg, and recook the stuffing.

Recipe 2

Preparation time: 10 minutes • **Cooking time:** 25 minutes • **Makes:** 4 servings

Ingredients	*Directions*
40 grams/1½ ounces butter	*1* Preheat the oven to 210°C/Gas Mark 6½.
125 millilitres/4½ fluid ounces water	*2* Put the butter and water into a small saucepan, heat gently until the butter melts, and then bring to the boil. Take off the heat.
30 grams/1 ounce brown rice flour	
30 grams/1 ounce tapioca starch	*3* Add all the dry ingredients and beat with a wooden spoon until you have a ball of dough of uniform consistency. Add the egg a little at a time and beat in each addition. You get a stiff paste.
1 teaspoon bicarbonate of soda	
1 teaspoon xanthan gum	
1 large egg, beaten	*4* Brush the fat around the same size and number of tins as in Recipe 1, and divide the dough out between them evenly. You can spread it up the sides of the tins or leave it in a mound.
4 teaspoons hot beef dripping or oil	
	5 Bake for 25 minutes, by which time the Yorkshire puds will have ballooned. If they collapse when you remove them from the oven, pierce them with a vegetable knife, put them back in the oven immediately and cook for about five more minutes to puff them up again and to crisp up the outsides. They'll be quite dark when they're crisp.

Nutrient analysis per serving: Calories 185; Protein 2g; Carbohydrate 11g; Sugar 0g; Fat 15g; Saturated fat 8g; Fibre 1.5g; Sodium 1g.

Polenta Dumplings

Traditional British dumplings are simply flour, suet, baking powder and water made into dough balls that float and poach in a meaty stew or stock. Gluten holds them together, so without that you need to put in a little more work and a few extra ingredients. The reward is tasty, textured, filling dumplings, which serve as the starchy accompaniment to your stew, without the need for pasta, rice or potatoes.

Preparation time: 15 minutes • **Cooking time:** 15 to 30 minutes • **Makes:** 6 dumplings

Ingredients	*Directions*
140 millilitres/5 fluid ounces full-cream milk 100 grams/3½ ounces dry polenta 1 large egg 1 tablespoon chopped fresh herbs 30 grams/1 ounce lean bacon or pancetta 30 grams/1 ounce gluten-free bread A little grated nutmeg	*1* Boil the milk and stir in the polenta. Continue to stir and cook until the mixture leaves the sides of the pan. Cool, and mix in the beaten egg and herbs.
	2 Finely dice the bacon and bread. Fry the bacon until it releases its fat, and then add the bread and brown it.
	3 Mix the polenta and bread–bacon mixtures together and, with wet hands, form a dough. If it's too dry, add a little more milk.
	4 Divide the ball of dough into six spherical dumplings and either put them into a casserole about 30 minutes before it's finished cooking, or boil them in a pan of salted water for about 15 minutes, by which time the dumplings will have risen to the surface.

Nutrient analysis per dumpling: Calories 113; Protein 5g; Carbohydrate 15g; Sugar 1g; Fat 4g; Saturated fat 1g; Fibre 0g; Sodium 0.3g.

Chapter 13

Mastering Mouth-Watering Main Meals

A home-cooked meal is one of life's great pleasures, whether it's just for one, for you and a significant other, the family or a bunch of friends. Making main meals gluten-free is a breeze, because most of the main-course players are already naturally free of gluten, like meat, fish, vegetables, eggs, cheese, rice and potatoes. You can easily replace those that do contain gluten with gluten-free pastas and grains, plus pastry and sauces made with gluten-free flour. So you don't need to make a separate main course for someone who's gluten-intolerant. We promise you: everyone will enjoy these recipes, whether they're gluten-intolerant or not.

In the other recipe chapters you can find lots more ideas that you can adapt to a main course, such as savoury tarts in Chapter 11, salads in Chapter 12, sauces to serve with meat, fish and vegetables in Chapter 14, and pizzas, tortillas and fresh pasta in Chapter 15. Even some of our breakfast and brunch ideas in Chapter 10 make tasty suppers and lunches too.

Throughout our recipes, we use ingredients that are widely available gluten-free, but some brands of certain ingredients do contain gluten or may do so, particularly flours, stock cubes, ready-made stock, condiments and sauces. As with all your food, check the labels carefully and avoid anything that contains gluten, even a trace.

Mains You Can Change

We start with a couple of recipes that give you the maximum choice of ingredients to add along with the basics. So you can easily make meals that are either cheap and cheerful, or luxurious and lavish.

Singapore Noodles

You have a big choice of ingredients to add to this dish, as long as you include the rice sticks or noodles, oil, garlic, spring onions, chilli, tamari and wine. You can substitute any or all of the remaining ingredients with others in the same quantity to suit your taste. Shredded cabbage, prawns, peas, sliced peppers, mangetout, baby corn, squid rings, broccoli, cashews and peanuts are just some of the other options to try.

Preparation time: 20 minutes • **Cooking time:** A few minutes • **Makes:** 2 servings

Ingredients	Directions
155 grams/5½ ounces rice sticks or noodles	**1** Soak the rice sticks or noodles according to the directions on the pack. If they only need a few minutes' soak, leave this until near the end so they don't get sticky. Put the oils, garlic, spring onions and chilli into a wok or wide, deep sauté pan.
1 tablespoon groundnut oil	
2 teaspoons toasted sesame oil	
2 garlic cloves, finely sliced	
5 or 6 spring onions, cut into short lengths	**2** Using a separate frying or omelette pan, make a thin omelette of the eggs. Roll this up and slice it into thin strips. Cut the cooked meat into strips, slice the mushrooms and cut the green beans and carrots into thin, short lengths.
Few dried chilli flakes or a fresh chilli	
70 millilitres/4½ tablespoons tamari	
1 tablespoon dry sherry or Chinese cooking wine	**3** Stir-fry all the vegetables and mushrooms gently in the wok until they're beginning to soften. Add a splash of water if necessary to keep them cooking, but boil it off before you proceed.
Variable ingredients:	
2 eggs, beaten	
100 grams/3½ ounces cooked meat	**4** Add the bean sprouts and the meat and just heat them through, before adding the drained, soaked rice sticks or noodles, the tamari and sherry or wine. Stir the whole lot together to heat it all up and distribute the liquids evenly. Add the egg just at the end. Serve immediately.
100 grams/3½ ounces mushrooms	
100 grams/3½ ounces green beans	
100 grams/3½ ounces carrots	
100 grams/3½ ounces bean sprouts	

Nutrient analysis per serving: Calories 630; Protein 34g; Carbohydrate 77g; Sugar 9g; Fat 22g; Saturated fat 5g; Fibre 5g; Salt 6g.

Baked Egg Galette

You can add a wide range of ingredients to this galette along with the oil, eggs, onion and black pepper. All vegetables, seafood, fish, meats and firm cheeses work well in this recipe. Try to use them in a similar total quantity to that in our recipe and select a colourful medley. You need to pre-cook the onion and all these additional ingredients then cool them and chop them into manageable pieces before you add them to the eggs. This allows you to slice the galette cleanly into wedges to serve. Eat the galette hot or cold.

Preparation time: 20 minutes • **Cooking time:** 25 minutes • **Makes:** 4 servings

Ingredients	Directions
8 large eggs	*1* Preheat the oven to 170°C/Gas Mark 3. Beat the eggs thoroughly with a little black pepper, using a mixing bowl that's large enough to hold all the other ingredients.
Black pepper	
1 tablespoon olive oil	
1 red onion, diced	*2* Select a wide, deep pan that can go both onto the hob and into the oven, preferably one with a lid. Heat the oil in it to medium heat and turn the pan to oil the base and sides. Now cook the diced onion, pepper and courgette in the oil until tender. Turn these out to cool slightly.
Variable ingredients: **1 red pepper, diced**	
1 courgette, diced	
1 medium potato, peeled, diced and boiled briefly	*3* Add all the ingredients except for 2 tablespoons of the cheese to the eggs and carefully fold them in so that everything gets a coating of egg but stays intact. Tip the whole mixture back into the hot pan and shake it level.
85 grams/3 ounces peas	
140 grams/5 ounces cooked salmon	
1 tablespoon chopped fresh herbs	*4* Cover with the lid if you have one, turn the heat to low, and cook on the hob without stirring for about 15 minutes. After ten minutes, ease the sides away from the pan and check that the galette isn't getting too brown underneath. It should be getting hot on the top by then, with the eggs beginning to set. Finally, strew the remaining cheese over the top and bake, uncovered, in the oven for a further ten minutes.
85 grams/3 ounces Cheddar cheese, grated	

Nutrient analysis per serving: Calories 460; Protein 32g; Carbohydrate 14g; Sugar 5g; Fat 32g; Saturated fat 10g; Fibre 3g; Salt 0.8g.

Enjoying Meaty Mains

We're not about to give you the full monty on meat and how to roast it, grill it, barbecue it or casserole it. If you're a novice, plenty of books are around to help you find your feet with meat, or just dive in and have a go. Use free-range or organic lean British meat, which is the best you can buy from the point of view of animal welfare, environmental impact, taste and nutritional quality. Our meaty mains would normally contain gluten. We've chosen them to show you how to make them gluten-free.

Spicy Indian Chicken

This has to be the easiest chicken curry recipe around, and it's delicious with Indian accompaniments like rice, flatbread and dahl (see our ideas in Chapters 15 and 12) or with a baked potato and steamed vegetables.

Preparation time: 10 minutes • **Cooking time:** 30 minutes • **Makes:** 2 servings

Ingredients	Directions
½ **tablespoon ground cumin**	**1** Preheat the oven to 190°C/Gas Mark 5. Mix all the ingredients apart from the oil and chicken with 2 tablespoons of water.
½ **tablespoon hot paprika**	
½ **tablespoon turmeric**	
½ **teaspoon ground black pepper**	**2** Brush half the oil onto a shallow ovenproof dish that's just large enough to accommodate the chicken fillets. Spoon in half the spice mixture, spreading it over the base. Lay the chicken fillets on top and spread the rest of the mixture over the top, completely coating the chicken. Drizzle a little oil on top.
2 crushed garlic cloves	
3 tablespoons lemon juice	
1 tablespoon oil	
2 skinless, boneless chicken fillets	**3** Bake, uncovered, for about 30 minutes, adding a little more water to the dish if it dries out. When the chicken is cooked (no longer pink inside) remove it to the plates. Stir the remaining spice mixture, adding more water if necessary to make a thick sauce and reheating it as needed. Serve the chicken with the sauce poured over.
2 tablespoons water	

Nutrient analysis per serving: Calories 247; Protein 38g; Carbohydrate 3g; Sugar 0g; Fat 11g; Saturated fat 1g; Fibre 0.2g; Salt 0.2g.

Lemon Caper Chicken

We happen to love lemon, capers and chicken, so this dish is definitely one of our favourites. Plus, it's easy to make but looks like you've spent hours in the kitchen. The recipe calls for rice flour for dusting the chicken, but feel free to use any gluten-free flour or baking mix that you have available. (By the way, capers are a type of pickled flower bud – look for them near the pickles.)

Preparation time: 20 minutes • **Cooking time:** 25 minutes • **Makes:** 4 servings

Ingredients	*Directions*
4 chicken breasts, boned and skinned **4 tablespoons extra-virgin olive oil, for frying** **40 grams/1½ ounces rice flour** **Freshly ground salt and pepper to taste** **For the sauce:** **3 spring onions, chopped** **1 teaspoon crushed garlic (about 2 cloves)** **55 millilitres/2 fluid ounces chicken stock** **115 millilitres/4 fluid ounces dry sherry** **55 millilitres/2 fluid ounces freshly squeezed lemon juice** **4 tablespoons capers, drained and rinsed** **30 grams/1 ounce unsalted butter**	*1* Pound the chicken breasts to an even thickness – about 13-millimetres/½-inch thick. If you don't have a meat tenderiser, you can use any other heavy, manageable object, like a heavy-based frying pan. *2* Put enough olive oil into a large frying pan to coat the bottom of the pan (about 2 tablespoons). Heat the oil over a medium-high heat. *3* Dredge the chicken breasts in flour seasoned with salt and pepper. *4* Fry the chicken breasts until brown: about three minutes on each side. If your pan isn't big enough, you may need to fry the chicken in a couple of batches. Make sure that you have enough oil in the pan to prevent the chicken from sticking, adding more if necessary. Transfer the cooked chicken to a warm serving platter and cover with foil. *5* Wipe out the excess oil in the pan with kitchen roll, or use a clean pan. Reduce the heat to low and add a further tablespoon of oil. Add the spring onion, garlic, chicken stock, sherry, lemon juice and capers. Turn the heat up to medium-high and simmer until the liquid has reduced to half (about five minutes). *6* Tilt the pan so that the liquid pools on one side, and whisk in the butter until the sauce is smooth. Pour the sauce over the chicken breasts and serve immediately.

Nutrient analysis per serving: Calories 415; Protein 42g; Carbohydrate 10g; Sugar 1g; Fat 19g; Saturated fat 6g; Fibre 0.7g; Salt 0.6g.

Steak and Ale Pies

This is one to make when you're not in a hurry, although you can cook the casserole ahead of time and reheat it just before serving. It's satisfying without the flaky pastry tops if you want to cut the calories down, although with the pastry, the pies are buttery, tasty and impressive.

Preparation time: 40 minutes • **Cooking time:** 2 to 3 hours • **Makes:** 6 servings

Ingredients	Directions
1 tablespoon corn oil	**1** Heat the oil in a casserole to medium-high heat. Cut the meat into 2½-centimetre/ 1-inch cubes.
½ teaspoon ground allspice	
Few gratings of nutmeg	
6 cloves	**2** Add the spices to the oil and immediately add all the beef cubes. Stir them about in the oil to allow them to seal and brown slightly. Add the onion, garlic, carrot and lemon as soon as liquid starts to appear in the casserole and stir again.
1 teaspoon juniper berries, chopped	
910 grams/2 pounds lean chuck or braising steak	
1 large onion, finely chopped	
2 teaspoons crushed garlic (about 3 cloves)	**3** Pour in the beer, and add the treacle and enough water to barely cover the beef and vegetables. Season, stir and bring to the boil briefly, and then cover and turn down to the lowest heat. Simmer very gently for two hours or until tender.
455 grams/1 pound carrots, thickly sliced	
¼ washed lemon	
330 millilitres/11½ fluid ounces gluten-free beer	
1 tablespoon black treacle	**4** Mix the arrowroot with a little water, stir it in and allow to thicken slightly. Add the prunes and continue simmering for about 20 minutes. Don't allow the prunes to disintegrate. Discard the lemon.
Salt and black pepper	
2 teaspoons arrowroot	
225 grams/8 ounces ready-to-eat prunes	
For the pastry:	**5** Meanwhile make the pastry by processing all the dry ingredients with half the butter. Then add the egg and process until the pastry forms up into a ball.
55 grams/2 ounces fine yellow cornmeal	
55 grams/2 ounces brown rice flour	
55 grams/2 ounces gram flour	
1 teaspoon bicarbonate of soda	
115 grams/4 ounces cold butter	
1 egg	

6 Cut the pastry into four equal pieces and roll each out as thinly as possible. The pastry will split and break up a little. Grate the remaining butter over three of the circles and layer them up on top of each other, finishing with the fourth, unbuttered circle. Roll the stack lightly to stick the layers together. Now cut the stack into six round shapes with a 6-centimetre/2½-inch cutter and pat each out with your hand to about half the thickness.

7 Preheat the oven to 200°C/Gas Mark 6 and bake the pastry circles near the top of the oven for 15 minutes, by which time they'll be flaky, crisp and golden brown. Cool them on the tray. Serve the casserole in bowls with the pastry resting on top.

Nutrient analysis per serving: Calories 607; Protein 40g; Carbohydrate 47g; Sugar 25g; Fat 28g; Saturated fat 14g; Fibre 5g; Salt 1.2g.

Steak and Peanut Pepper Pasta

In this amazing dish, you mix crunchy, colourful vegetables with some of your favourite gluten-free pasta, served as a bed for thinly sliced steak and covered in a spicy peanut sauce. Seriously, this dish is one of the most delicious, unique and impressive (shhhh . . . it's really very easy) that we've ever made!

Preparation time: 25 minutes • Refrigeration time: 2 hours • **Cooking time:** 15 minutes •
Makes: 4 servings

Ingredients

115 millilitres/4 fluid ounces rice wine vinegar

115 millilitres/4 fluid ounces extra-virgin olive oil

4 tablespoons soy sauce or tamari

4 tablespoons smooth peanut butter

2 tablespoons chopped fresh coriander

1 teaspoon crushed garlic (about 2 cloves)

½ teaspoon cayenne pepper

450 grams/1 pound lean sirloin steak in one piece

115 grams/4 ounces fine gluten-free pasta

85 grams/3 ounces Savoy cabbage, washed and shredded

85 grams/3 ounces pak choi, shredded

30 grams/1 ounce fresh spinach, washed and shredded

130 grams/4½ ounces carrots, cut into thin sticks

½ cucumber, thinly sliced (to garnish)

40 grams/1½ ounces unsalted peanuts, chopped (to garnish)

Directions

1 Combine the vinegar, oil, soy sauce, peanut butter, coriander, garlic and cayenne pepper in a blender. Whiz the dressing until well mixed.

2 Trim any fat from the meat. Place the steak in a shallow dish and pour about one-third of the peanut dressing over the meat. Cover and marinate the meat in the refrigerator for two hours, turning occasionally. Chill the remaining dressing.

3 Preheat the grill. If you're using a gas grill, heat on high for ten minutes and then reduce the heat to medium-low.

4 Lift the meat out of the marinade and drain off any excess. Discard the marinade; you don't need this any more. Grill the steak until it's cooked to your preference, turning once halfway through. This should take about eight minutes, depending on the thickness of the meat and how well you like your steak cooked. Rest the steak by keeping it warm for about ten minutes.

5 Meanwhile, cook the pasta according to the directions on the packet, making sure that it's al dente (slightly firm and not overcooked). Drain the pasta and combine it with the cabbage, pak choi, spinach and carrots in the hot pasta-cooking pan. Add about half of the remaining dressing to the pasta–veggie mixture and stir until well-mixed.

6 Cut the meat into thin slices across the grain. To assemble this dish, serve a portion of the pasta–veggie mixture on each plate. Add a few slices of meat on top of the pasta. Garnish the dish with a few slices of cucumber. Drizzle the remaining dressing over each plate, and sprinkle over the peanuts.

Tip: Instead of shredding the veggies yourself, buy a pack of stir-fry mix that includes broccoli, carrot and cabbage. Use any combination of vegetables you like, as long as they're thinly shredded.

Nutrient analysis per serving: Calories 512; Protein 38g; Carbohydrate 27g; Sugar 7g; Fat 28g; Saturated fat 7g; Fibre 4.5g; Salt 1.6g.

Resting cooked meat for about 10 to 15 minutes before you carve it allows the juices to redistribute so that your meat turns out more moist. But the meat's temperature rises by about five to ten degrees during this time, so you need to stop cooking a little early to allow for this.

Marvellous marinades

Besides adding flavour, acidic marinades also tenderise foods. The acids and enzymes in some fruits break down the muscle and connective proteins in the meat, making it less tough. Some tips for marinating follow:

✔ Refrigerate during marinating to restrict the growth of harmful bacteria. The temperature at which you marinate doesn't affect the meat's tenderness.

✔ Poultry and fish can turn to mush or become tough if you marinate them for too long. Poultry benefits when marinating for up to 4 hours, and about 30 minutes is long enough for fish.

✔ Natural tenderisers include pineapple, figs, papaya, kiwi, mango, honeydew melon, wine, citrus, vinegar, tomato, yoghurt and buttermilk.

✔ Be careful with the container you use for marinating. Never use aluminium – only glass, ceramic, stainless steel or plastic.

Marinades react chemically with most metals to produce an unpleasant metallic taste.

✔ If you're grilling or barbecuing meat or fish, you can dab a little extra marinade on during the cooking to achieve a flavoursome glaze. Equally, if you're making a casserole, use the marinade as the liquid portion, topping it up if necessary, according to your recipe. But do bear in mind that the marinade has had raw fish or meat in it for some time, and will contain harmful bacteria and juices that have seeped out of the meat or fish. So the marinade itself needs to be thoroughly cooked to destroy these bacteria.

✔ If you're going to use some of the marinade for a sauce, take out the amount you need and set it aside before you marinate the meat or seafood in the rest.

✔ Throw out any unused marinade.

Lamb Chops in Green Jackets

Crisp green rösti coatings on lamb chops; this is a gluten-free variation on the theme of pastry-wrapped meat such as beef Wellington.

Preparation time: 30 minutes • **Cooking time:** 15 minutes • **Makes:** 4

Ingredients	Directions
30 grams/1 ounce butter	*1* Melt the butter and 1 tablespoon of the oil in a large frying pan. Add the lamb chops and lightly fry for one to two minutes. Remove from the pan and set aside.
4 tablespoons extra-virgin olive oil	
8 lamb chops	*2* Place the spinach in a large saucepan and sprinkle with a little water. Blanch for three minutes, drain and finely chop.
170 grams/6 ounces fresh spinach (washed)	
340 grams/12 ounces potato, peeled and grated	*3* In a tea towel, squeeze the potato to remove any excess moisture, and then place in a bowl. Add the spinach, egg, onion, salt, pepper and nutmeg and mix well.
1 large egg	
1 onion, peeled and finely chopped	
Freshly ground salt and pepper to taste	*4* Put the reserved lamb chops into the potato mixture and toss to make sure that each chop is coated.
Pinch of grated nutmeg	*5* Add the remaining oil to the pan and fry the chops for five to eight minutes on each side or until golden brown. Remove from the pan and drain on kitchen paper. Serve immediately.

Nutrient analysis per serving: *Calories 639; Protein 44g; Carbohydrate 16g; Sugar 2g; Fat 44g; Saturated fat 21g; Fibre 2.3g; Salt 0.8g.*

Pork Steaks with Sage and Cider

Pork, sage and cider have been buddying up for centuries in cider-producing countries, and today British-reared free-range pork is one of the leanest, tastiest and most economical meats you can buy.

Preparation time: 30 minutes • **Cooking time:** 10 minutes • **Makes:** 4

Ingredients	*Directions*
½ tablespoon olive oil 1 tablespoon fresh lemon juice Freshly ground salt and pepper to taste 4 pork steaks or escalopes Sprig of fresh sage (about 12 large leaves) 2 shallots, finely chopped 115 millilitres/4 fluid ounces dry cider	*1* Combine the olive oil, lemon juice, salt and pepper, and rub both sides of each steak with the mixture. Place the meat in a grill-proof dish or pan. *2* Pull the leaves off the sage, slice them thinly and scatter all but a spoonful over the meat so that the pieces stick to both sides. Cover and refrigerate for two hours. *3* Preheat the grill to high. Grill the steaks for five to ten minutes on each side according to your taste and the thickness of the meat. Remove from the dish and keep them warm while you make the sauce. *4* Fry the shallots in the oil in the dish, browning them slightly. Add the cider and let it sizzle away while you scrape up all the crisp, meaty residues in the dish. Add the remaining sage and enough water, vegetable stock or extra cider to get the quantity of sauce you need to serve with the steaks. Taste and adjust the seasoning if necessary.

Nutrient analysis per serving: Calories 175; Protein 27g; Carbohydrate 1g; Sugar 1g; Fat 6g; Saturated fat 2g; Fibre 0g; Salt 0.4g.

Crispy coatings

You can pan-fry lots of foods in very little oil to create a crisp coating. Cut up the meat or fish beforehand into goujons or finger-sized strips, and flatten meat slices or fillets to make them cook more quickly. You can also use courgettes cut lengthways into six or eight slices, cooked potato wedges, sweet potato and even banana chunks. The idea is that the food cooks by the time the coating is crisp and lightly browned. Do serve it as soon as it comes out of the pan, because if you keep it warm, the coating goes flabby.

The best gluten-free coating in our book is fine yellow cornmeal with beaten egg. You can use the cornmeal just as it is or add ground spices, grated citrus zest, cheese and dried or fresh herbs. Cumin, hot paprika, thyme and garlic salt are particular favourites. Dip the food first into the cornmeal and then into the beaten egg and back into the cornmeal. Make sure the food is fully coated, and then into the hot pan it goes. Don't toss the food about as you would if you were stir-frying; simply cook it on each side undisturbed.

Diving into Seafood

Seafood has been an important source of protein and other nutrients in diets around the world since, well, people started eating. Although many recipes call for coatings or breadcrumbs, or are served with pasta, all of which ruin seafood for gluten-free types, you can easily modify the recipes to make them gluten-free without losing any of their delicious taste.

Tequila-Lime Prawns and Scallops

Tangy, spicy, herby and chic, this is a dish to impress. And you can cook it in the time it takes your guests to take their seats at the table.

Preparation time: 2 minutes • **Cooking time:** 10 minutes • **Makes:** 4 servings

Ingredients	*Directions*
55 millilitres/2 fluid ounces fresh lime juice	*1* In a large glass, ceramic or stainless-steel mixing bowl, mix the lime juice, lemon juice, coriander, tequila, garlic, Tabasco, cumin and oregano. Add the prawns and scallops.
55 millilitres/2 fluid ounces fresh lemon juice	
4 tablespoons chopped fresh coriander	*2* In a large frying pan over medium-high heat, cook the onion and green and red pepper slices in a tablespoon of oil until they begin to soften (about four minutes).
4 tablespoons tequila	
2 teaspoons crushed garlic (about 4 cloves)	
Dash of Tabasco sauce	*3* Add the prawn and scallop mixture to the frying pan, and bring everything to the boil. Cook the mixture, stirring, for about three minutes, until the liquid has reduced a little and the seafood is cooked.
½ teaspoon ground cumin	
½ teaspoon dried oregano	
225 grams/8 ounces raw peeled prawns	*4* Serve the seafood over rice, pasta or in the wrap of your choice, and garnish with lime wedges.
225 grams/8 ounces raw scallops	
1 large onion, sliced	
1 green pepper, cut into thin strips	
1 red pepper, cut into thin strips	
1 tablespoon extra-virgin olive oil	
4 lime wedges (to garnish)	

Nutrient analysis per serving: *Calories 430; Protein 40g; Carbohydrate 23g; Sugars 6g; Fat 6g; Saturated fat 1.5g; Fibre 2g; Salt 1.3g.*

Szechuan Scallops with Orange Peel

This simple Szechuan dish is a hit with seafood lovers, but if you're not one of those, you can use chicken instead of scallops.

Preparation time: 1 hour 30 minutes • Refrigeration time: 1 hour • **Cooking time:** 15 minutes • **Makes:** 6 servings

Ingredients	Directions
1 large orange	*1* Preheat the oven to 110°C/Gas Mark ¼.
450 grams/1 pound fresh scallops	*2* Use a vegetable peeler or sharp knife to cut the peel from the orange into 25-millimetre (1-inch) wide pieces, being careful not to cut into the pith (the white part of the peel). Cut the peel into 5-centimetre (2-inch) strips, and spread them out on a small baking tray. Bake them in the cool oven for about 30 minutes to dry them out.
2 tablespoons soy sauce or tamari	
2 tablespoons dry sherry	
5 spring onions, cut into 25-millimetre (1-inch) pieces	*3* In a medium-size bowl, mix the scallops, soy sauce, sherry, spring onions, cayenne pepper, red pepper, chilli flakes and ginger. Cover and refrigerate the mixture for an hour or so.
½ teaspoon (or to taste) cayenne pepper	
55 grams/2 ounces red pepper, sliced	*4* In a small bowl, mix the cornflour, sugar and orange juice. Cover and refrigerate this mixture for about an hour.
1 teaspoon dried chilli flakes	*5* When you're almost ready to serve the meal, heat 2 table-spoons of the oil in a large frying pan over a medium heat. Stir-fry the orange peel for about two minutes until it's crisp and the edges are slightly browned. Drain the peel on kitchen paper.
1 teaspoon grated fresh ginger	
1 tablespoon cornflour	
¾ teaspoon granulated sugar	*6* Using the same frying pan, turn up the heat to high. Use the remaining oil to stir-fry the scallop mixture until the scallops are cooked through – approximately five minutes. Stir the orange-juice mixture prior to adding it to the scallops. Cook the mixture, stirring all the time, until the sauce thickens slightly and coats the scallops.
115 millilitres/4 fluid ounces fresh orange juice	
4 tablespoons extra-virgin olive oil	*7* Spoon the scallop mixture onto a serving platter and sprinkle with the orange peel.

Nutrient analysis per serving: Calories 176; Protein 13g; Carbohydrate 5g; Sugars 3g; Fat 11g; Saturated fat 2g; Fibre 0.3g; Salt 1g.

Baked Lemon Fish

This delicious fish dish is high in protein and low in fat and carbs. You can use any mild white fish fillet. Serve it on brown rice for extra fibre and nutrients.

Preparation time: 10 minutes • **Cooking time:** 30 minutes • **Makes:** 8 servings

Ingredients	*Directions*
Non-stick oil spray, for greasing dishes	*1* Preheat the oven to 190°C/Gas Mark 5.
8 white fish fillets, boneless and skinned	*2* Using the non-stick oil spray, lightly grease two medium-sized baking dishes. Wash and pat dry the fish fillets, and lay them in a single layer on the baking dishes.
4 tablespoons fresh lemon juice	
45 grams/1¾ ounces butter, melted	
½ teaspoon grated fresh ginger	*3* Mix the lemon juice, butter, ginger, garlic, black pepper, paprika and coriander in a small bowl. Drizzle the lemon juice mixture over the fillets.
½ teaspoon crushed garlic (about 1 clove)	
½ teaspoon freshly ground black pepper	*4* Place an orange slice over each fillet. Drain and discard about three-quarters of the juice from the canned pineapple, and pour the crushed pineapple and remaining juice over the fillets.
½ teaspoon paprika	
2 tablespoons chopped fresh coriander	
8 fresh orange slices	*5* Bake the fillets for about 20 to 30 minutes or until they are opaque. Be careful not to overcook. Serve with brown rice.
560 grams/20 ounces (usually 1 large can) crushed pineapple	

Nutrient analysis per serving (with 100g brown rice): Calories 325; Protein 28g; Carbohydrate 37g; Sugar 8g; Fat 7g; Saturated fat 4g; Fibre 1.1g; Salt 0.4g.

Giving Vegetables the Starring Role

Many people eat meat and fish less often these days or choose to cut them out altogether. It's no problem at all to do this without eating gluten, as long as you make the vegetables the stars of the show. If you opt for shop-bought meat substitutes like burgers and cutlets, check that the products are gluten-free, because many of them have coatings, toppings and thickeners derived from wheat. If you allow it to, living gluten-free encourages you to try new vegetables and get into the habit of adding more of them to your main-course dishes. These vegetarian dishes are so delicious that even die-hard carnivores can't resist them.

Vegetable Lasagne

This dish is easy to make and a hit with guests, who may never guess that what they're eating is gluten-free. Our fresh pasta from Chapter 15 would make it extra special; and it's so easy – it's less effort than pre-boiling dried lasagne.

Preparation time: 15 minutes • **Cooking time:** 1½ hours • **Makes:** 10 servings

Ingredients	Directions
680 grams/24 ounces passata	**1** Preheat the oven to 190°C/Gas Mark 5.
2 teaspoons fresh basil, chopped	
Freshly ground black pepper to taste	**2** In a medium bowl, mix together the tomato sauce, basil, black pepper and salt.
Freshly ground sea salt to taste	
30 grams/1 ounce fresh spinach, washed and chopped	**3** Heat a large frying pan over a medium-high heat. Cook the spinach, courgettes, olives, mushrooms and onions in the vegetable stock for four minutes or until the onion starts to soften, being careful not to overcook the vegetables.
70 grams/2½ ounces courgettes, diced	
40 grams/1½ ounces black olives, sliced	
30 grams/1 ounce mushrooms, sliced	**4** Spray a shallow 23-x-33-centimetre (9-x-13-inch) baking dish with non-stick oil. Layer the ingredients in the baking dish, starting with one-third of the tomato sauce on the bottom, followed by a layer of lasagne. Mix the cheeses together and add half to cover the lasagne, followed by half the remaining vegetable mixture. Repeat the layers with another portion of the sauce, lasagne, most of the remaining cheese and the rest of the vegetables. Finish with the last of the tomato sauce, a final layer of lasagne and a thin covering of cheese.
40 grams/1½ ounces onion, chopped	
1 tablespoon vegetable stock	
Non-stick spray oil, for greasing	
285 grams/10 ounces gluten-free dried lasagne cooked according to instructions on the pack; or 350 grams/12½ ounces uncooked fresh lasagne	
225 grams/8 ounces mozzarella, grated	**5** Cover with aluminium foil and bake for one hour. Remove the foil and bake for a further 30 minutes or until the top is golden brown. Cool the lasagne for at least 15 minutes before cutting.
115 grams/4 ounces Parmesan cheese, grated	

Tip: Be creative with your choice of vegetables or alternative ingredients, such as by adding roasted vegetables, lentils or cannellini beans to the sauce. If you prefer more flavour to your sauce, add a teaspoon of crushed garlic.

Nutrient analysis per serving: Calories 243; Protein 8g; Carbohydrate 32g; Sugar 8g; Fat 9g; Saturated fat 1g; Fibre 0.6g; Salt 2.2g.

Fresh Harvest Penne

This recipe is an easy-to-prepare vegetarian meal in one and a great way of serving fresh vegetables.

Preparation time: 30 minutes • **Cooking time:** 50 minutes • **Makes:** 6 servings

Ingredients	*Directions*
450 grams/1 pound gluten-free penne (or any short pasta shape)	*1* Cook the pasta, following the directions on the packet, being careful not to overcook it.
2 tablespoons extra-virgin olive oil, for frying **½ medium red onion, finely chopped**	*2* Meanwhile, in a large frying pan, heat the olive oil over a medium heat. Add the onion, courgettes and peppers to the pan, and sauté, stirring often, for about five minutes.
100 grams/3½ ounces courgettes, thickly sliced **100 grams/3½ ounces yellow pepper, thickly sliced**	*3* Add the garlic and aubergine to the pan, and continue to sauté, stirring frequently.
1 tablespoon crushed garlic (about 6 cloves) **85 grams/3 ounces fresh aubergine, cut into 12-millimetre (½-inch) cubes**	*4* After about five minutes, when the aubergine begins to soften, reduce the heat and add the tomato. Continue stirring the mixture for three to four minutes.
2 fresh medium-size tomatoes, chopped	*5* Drain the pasta. In a large serving bowl, combine the pasta and vegetables, and sprinkle over the basil and Parmesan.
2 tablespoons fresh basil, chopped	
40 grams/1½ ounces vegetarian Parmesan cheese, freshly grated	

Nutrient analysis per serving: Calories 365; Protein 9g; Carbohydrate 64g; Sugar 5g; Fat 8g; Saturated fat 3g; Fibre 3g; Salt 1.3g.

Cheese Enchiladas

You have to be careful with enchiladas, because most shop-bought and restaurant-prepared kits have wheat flour in them – in the tortillas, seasonings and sometimes the sauces. But with Mexican food being so popular, you can easily find gluten-free tortillas online from specialist suppliers in the UK, along with other unusual items such as masa harina, tomatillos and cactus leaves. Plus, we give you a recipe for making tortillas at home, in Chapter 15. You can dress up this quick and easy recipe with your favourite veg, other types of cheese, salsas, sour cream or cooked meat.

Preparation time: 25 minutes • **Cooking time:** 1 hour • **Makes:** 6 servings

Ingredients	Directions
225 grams/8 ounces Cheddar cheese, grated	**1** Preheat the oven to 180°C/Gas Mark 4. Combine the grated cheeses, garlic powder and 2 teaspoons of cumin.
225 grams mozzarella cheese, grated	
3 teaspoons ground cumin	**2** To make the enchilada sauce, heat the olive oil in a large frying pan over a medium-high heat. Add the chopped onion, and sauté until soft, for about four minutes. Add the chopped tomatoes, chilli powder, oregano, hot chilli sauce and the remaining teaspoon of cumin. Cover the pan and simmer for about 30 minutes.
1 tablespoon extra-virgin olive oil	
1 small onion, finely chopped	
2 teaspoons crushed garlic (about 4 cloves)	**3** When the sauce is cooked, spray a 23-x-33-centimetre (9-x-13-inch) baking dish with oil, and pour approximately two-thirds of the sauce into it.
1 kilogram/35 ounces (usually 2½ cans) chopped tomatoes	**4** Soften one corn tortilla by sprinkling it with a little water on both sides and heating it in a hot, dry pan or griddle for a few seconds on each side, or you can do this in a microwave. Dip it into the enchilada sauce, coating both sides. Lay the tortilla flat on a plate and sprinkle about ⅓ cup of the cheese mixture down the centre of the tortilla. Roll it up, and place it seam-side down into the sauce in the baking dish.
2 tablespoons chilli powder	
1 teaspoon oregano	
2 tablespoons hot chilli sauce	
Non-stick spray oil, for greasing	**5** Repeat for each tortilla. Pour the rest of the enchilada sauce over the rolled-up enchiladas, and sprinkle over any remaining cheese. Add the sliced black olives on top of the cheese.
12 gluten-free soft tortillas	
30 grams/1 ounce black olives, sliced	**6** Bake the enchiladas for 20 to 30 minutes, until the cheese melts and bubbles.

Nutrient analysis per serving: Calories 558; Protein 25g; Carbohydrate 54g; Sugar 6g; Fat 27g; Saturated fat 14g; Fibre 7.2g; Salt 1.8g.

Black Bean Veggie Burgers

Gluten-free veggie burgers are hard to find – so why not make your own? This recipe uses black beans, but you can use a combination of any beans and even add grains such as millet and buckwheat. Wrap one of these burgers in a large iceberg lettuce leaf, top with salsa and guacamole, and you have a delicious, nutritious vegetarian meal.

Preparation time: 10 minutes • **Cooking time:** 10 minutes • **Makes:** 8 servings

Ingredients	*Directions*
4 x 400-gram tins black beans, drained and rinsed (960 grams/34 ounces cooked beans)	*1* Put the beans, onion, red pepper, cayenne, cumin, egg or egg substitute, quinoa and coriander into a food processor or blender. Process the mixture until it forms a stiff consistency but isn't so smooth that it doesn't contain any chunks.
40 grams/1½ ounces onion, chopped	
85 grams/3 ounces red pepper, chopped	*2* Shape the mixture into eight rounds.
1 teaspoon cayenne pepper	
1 teaspoon cumin	*3* Heat 1 tablespoon of olive oil in a large frying pan over a medium heat. Add as many burgers to the pan as possible, and fry them for two minutes per side, turning once. Add the remaining tablespoon of oil and cook the remaining burgers.
1 large egg	
170 grams/6 ounces cooked quinoa	
2 tablespoons fresh coriander, chopped	*4* Wrap each burger in a lettuce leaf, topping with salsa and guacamole.
2 tablespoons extra-virgin olive oil	
8 crisp lettuce leaves	
Salsa and guacamole (if desired)	

Nutrient analysis per serving: Calories 237; Protein 13g; Carbohydrate 34g; Sugars 1.4g; Fat 6g; Saturated fat 1g; Fibre 12.3g; Salt 0.1g.

Chapter 14

The Sauce Resource

In This Chapter

▶ How a good sauce can transform an everyday gluten-free meal into something special

▶ Savoury sauces and dressings for quick and easy main courses and starters

▶ Sweet sauces for luscious puddings and cold desserts

good sauce can make a simple meal special. The sauce alone can unite the meal's components into one harmonious whole. It can hide shortcomings too: meat a little dry, vegetables a bit overdone, boring salads and desserts hastily mustered from tinned fruit and ice cream.

Once you've got a few delicious gluten-free sauce recipes at your fingertips, your gluten-free cooking repertoire explodes. You can serve your sauces with the vast range of naturally gluten-free foods available, including meat, fish, vegetables, salads, fruit, eggs and cheese, along with the other recipes you find in this book.

In this chapter, you have both savoury and sweet sauces and dressings you can whip up from scratch; just two of them start from the point at which you've cooked meat, and use the juices. And we explain what foods each sauce goes with best. But don't be constrained by our ideas. This chapter's just a springboard you can use to devise your own great gluten-free meals.

In all our recipes, we use ingredients that are widely available gluten-free, but some brands of certain ingredients do contain gluten or may do, notably stock powders and cubes, flours, some condiments, and even chocolate and cream cheese. As with all your food, check the labels carefully and avoid anything that contains gluten, even a trace.

Sauces for Courses: Starters and Mains

Many traditional sauces and ready-made ones are thickened with wheat flour, which is a shame because this is sometimes the only source of gluten on the plate. In this section, you find old friends like gravy and cheese sauce, new ways to thicken sauces without flour, some intriguing and unusual dressings plus tips and techniques to help you turn all your old recipes gluten-free.

Gravy

So you've gone to the expense and trouble of roasting a joint of meat or a whole bird, probably with roast potatoes, vegetables and other trimmings. Now for the crowning glory – the gravy. But after all that effort, and with everything coming together at the last moment, it's not the time to start making two lots of gravy. With this recipe, you only need one gravy for everyone at the table. We defy even the most ardent traditionalist to notice it's gluten-free.

Preparation time: 5 minutes • **Makes:** 6 servings

Ingredients	*Directions*
The juices left in the meat-cooking pan **30 grams/1 ounce white rice flour** **115 millilitres/4 fluid ounces dry cider or wine** **500 millilitres/17½ fluid ounces water or stock** **1 tablespoon redcurrant jelly or tomato purée (optional)** **Salt and pepper**	*1* Put the meat to rest in a warm place for at least ten minutes before you carve. Meanwhile, drain all the liquid from the roasting dish or pan into a cup, preferably one of those fat-separators with a spout opening near the bottom. Let the liquid sit for a minute or two to allow the fat to rise to the top. Tip about a tablespoonful of the fat back into the meat-cooking pan. Add the white rice flour and stir it thoroughly into the fat, scraping up all the crispy, dark deposits on the pan as you go.
	2 Pour in the dark juices from under the fat in the cup, without letting any of the fat run in. Here's where the fat-separator comes into its own. If you're using an ordinary cup, tip off the fat layer first and then pour the juices into the pan. Stir in the liquid to achieve the same consistency throughout the mix.
	3 Heat the pan slowly on the hob whilst stirring. Add the cider or wine a little at a time and thoroughly stir in to achieve an even consistency throughout. If you add more liquid before you've mixed in the previous lot, you'll get lumpy gravy and will have to blend it.
	4 Now add the water or stock in dribs and drabs while continuing to mix and simmer. If you used wine, you may want to add the redcurrant jelly and melt it in to counterbalance the tartness of the wine. Cider is generally sweet enough. The tomato purée is also optional, depending on the colour you want. Adjust the seasoning to your taste.

Nutrient analysis per serving: Calories 41; Protein 1g; Carbohydrate 4g; Sugar 0g; Fat 1.7g; Saturated fat 1g; Fibre 0g; Salt 0.1g.

Wine Sauce for One (or Two)

If you've cooked one or two steaks, chicken breasts or chops in a frying pan on the hob, here's a quick way to make a wine sauce that will go with them beautifully.

Preparation time: 5 minutes • **Makes:** 1 or 2 servings

Ingredients	*Directions*
115 millilitres/4 fluid ounces red or white wine **1 tablespoon tomato purée** **140 millilitres/5 fluid ounces water** **Seasoning of your choice, such as salt, pepper, stock cube, bouillon powder, tamari, lemon juice, mushrooms, ketchup, chilli sauce, honey, jam or marmalade**	*1* If your meat was fatty, there'll be a lot of fat in the frying pan. Remove the meat to a warm oven to rest for a few minutes, and drain off most of the fat from the frying pan. Pour the wine straight into the hot pan and stir vigorously while it boils furiously. The aim is to scrape all the tasty meat residues from the pan into your sauce. *2* Add the tomato purée and about half of the water and bring it back to a simmer. Stir and taste. At this point you can add more water and any seasoning you like. Keep tasting until you get the sauce the way you want it. You can also add ingredients like sliced mushrooms, finely chopped shallot, red pepper, peppercorns (from a jar, not the dry sort), chopped herbs or crème fraîche. It all depends on your meat and what you feel will go best with it.

Nutrient analysis per serving if the above quantity serves 2: Calories 35; Protein 1g; Carbohydrate 1g; Sugar 1g; Fat 2g; Saturated fat 1g; Fibre 0g; Salt 0.4g.

Savoury White Sauce

This sauce goes well with chicken, fish, vegetables and pasta. It's the basis of macaroni or cauliflower cheese, the topping for lasagne and other pasta bakes and, with onions, a classic accompaniment to lamb. We give you recipes for gluten-free fresh pasta and gnocchi in Chapter 15.

Preparation time: 10 minutes • **Makes:** 4 to 6 servings

Ingredients	*Directions*
40 grams/1½ ounces butter	*1* Melt the butter in a saucepan and stir in the white rice flour thoroughly. Cook over a medium heat, stirring continuously, while you add a few tablespoons of the milk. Mix the milk in completely, making sure you have the same consistency throughout the mix.
40 grams/1½ ounces white rice flour	
570 millilitres/1 pint milk	
Salt, white pepper, ground mace	*2* Now add the rest of the milk a little at a time, mixing each addition in thoroughly and heating the sauce. If you add more milk before you've incorporated the previous addition, you can never get a smooth sauce. Bring to a slow simmer. Add the salt, pepper and mace. Taste and adjust the seasoning if necessary.

Nutrient analysis per serving: Calories 128; Protein 4g; Carbohydrate 10g; Sugar 5g; Fat 8g; Saturated fat 5g; Fibre 0g; Salt 0.8g.

Roux in reverse

The mixture of fat and flour in our gravy and white sauce recipes is known as a roux and it's a simple way of thickening a sauce. If you make a sauce without thickening and then decide it's too thin, you can add a little starch pre-mixed with cold water and then stir it in and simmer the liquid. Gluten-free options include cornflour, tapioca starch, potato starch and arrowroot. You must use a starch – not a flour or meal, which will simply stay in dry lumps in your sauce.

But you won't get a rich, smooth, opaque sauce with starch. For that you need to make a *beurre manié*, or worked butter. This is like adding a roux at the end of the process instead of at the beginning. Take a tablespoon of white rice flour and 15 grams or half an ounce of soft butter. (If the butter's hard, you can melt it to oil first, but soft, solid butter is easier.) Mix the two thoroughly and whisk a little at a time into your simmering sauce. The butter helps disperse the flour so that it can do its job of thickening.

Varying a white sauce

Once you've mastered the basic gluten-free white sauce, you can adapt it to make lots of other sauces by varying the liquid element and adding other ingredients. Here are some ideas to get you started.

Other liquids you can use in place of the milk are:

- **Dry cider** to produce a light, sweet sauce for fish or white meats.
- **Dry white wine** to make a sophisticated sauce with a slight acidity.
- **Gluten-free beer** for an intriguing sauce with characteristic bitter, hoppy flavours.
- **Stock** – vegetable, fish or chicken, for example – to give a velvety sauce known as a velouté.

You can add a number of other ingredients to either our savoury white sauce recipe or any of its variations made with stock, wine, cider or beer; for example:

- **Capers, hot red peppers, black olives and gherkins:** Jars of these keep in the fridge after opening. About 15 grams or half an ounce of each, rinsed and very finely chopped before being stirred in, makes a zingy, sophisticated sauce for fish, seafood, pork or chicken.
- **Chopped herbs:** About 2 tablespoons of chopped fresh herbs looks and tastes divine. The herbs must be the soft-leaved types, but don't think you must stick to parsley; tarragon, chervil, coriander, basil, dill, chives, sorrel and fennel fronds all work well.
- **Cooked seafood:** Cooked crab meat, chopped prawns, baby clams or brown shrimps stirred in, together with a dash of brandy or Calvados and a few drops of Thai fish sauce, and just heated through without cooking gives you the fastest seafood sauce we know.
- **Cream:** If you used full-cream or semi-skimmed milk, you probably won't need this, but a dash of single cream, maybe with the herb or mustard variations in this list, enriches your sauce.
- **Egg:** Two hard-boiled eggs, roughly chopped, give interesting texture and taste, and a beaten raw egg stirred into the sauce with grated cheese after you take it off the heat makes a lovely topping for moussaka. The sauce sets and browns in the oven as the moussaka bakes.
- **Grated cheese:** Try 115 grams or 4 ounces of Cheddar, Red Leicester, Fontina, Gruyère or Emmenthal cheese, or even a mixture of a couple of them, to make a Mornay sauce for gluten-free macaroni, cauliflower, broccoli, leeks or poached or baked white fish. You can allow any left-over Mornay sauce to go cold and then spread it on toast and grill under a low heat for a quick rarebit.
- **Leek, onion, spring onions or shallots:** Finely slice either a whole leek, an onion, four spring onions or three shallots and soften them in the butter before you add white rice flour and make up the sauce.
- **Mushrooms:** Use 115 grams or 4 ounces of white mushrooms sautéed in a little butter or oil first. The large ones with black gills taste great, but be warned: they make your sauce a rather unusual grey.
- **Mustard:** Just a tablespoon should be enough, but you can always add more if you wish. Dijon or grainy types are best.
- **Tomato ketchup:** Just a tablespoon is enough to make a rosy sauce.

Better-than-Bread Sauce

Bread sauce is a traditional accompaniment to turkey, chicken and pheasant. You can, of course, use gluten-free breadcrumbs, but the result is a bit gloopy. Here's our version, which won't raise a disapproving eyebrow – even your mother-in-law's. Make this shortly before you serve it because it goes on thickening if you leave it standing.

Preparation time: 10 minutes • **Makes:** 4 servings

Ingredients	*Directions*
15 grams/½ ounce butter **1 shallot, finely chopped** **1 bay leaf** **4 whole cloves** **225 millilitres/8 fluid ounces milk** **30 grams/1 ounce white rice flakes** **Salt and white pepper** **Dash of Tabasco**	*1* Melt the butter in a saucepan and soften the shallots gently without browning. Add the bay leaf and cloves and pour in the milk. Heat to almost boiling and add the rice flakes. *2* Turn the heat to low. Allow the mixture to cook for five to ten minutes, stirring only occasionally. Add more milk if it's too thick for your liking. Taste the sauce and add seasoning.

Nutrient analysis per serving: *Calories 81; Protein 2g; Carbohydrate 9g; Sugar 3g; Fat 4g; Saturated fat 2g; Fibre 0g; Salt 0.3g.*

Fresh Cranberry Sauce

We thought you'd like this recipe for fresh cranberry sauce to go with that Christmas turkey. It's so much better than the shop-bought jammy sauces, and you can make it well in advance.

Preparation time: 10 minutes • **Makes:** 6 servings

Ingredients	Directions
Grated zest and juice of a large orange	*1* Simply put all the ingredients into a saucepan and heat slowly while stirring until all the sugar dissolves.
85 grams/3 ounces sugar	
170 grams/6 ounces fresh cranberries	*2* Bring to the boil for a second and then turn down and simmer slowly for a couple of minutes or until the cranberries start to pop. Store in an airtight container. The sauce will keep in the fridge for a few days.
Pinch each of ground cinnamon and nutmeg	

Nutrient analysis per serving: *Calories 65; Protein 0.4g; Carbohydrate 17g; Sugar 17g; Fat 0g; Saturated fat 0g; Fibre 1.5g; Salt 0g.*

Old English Tomato Sauce

This is a reduced sauce with concentrated flavours that go well with hearty roasts. *Reducing* a sauce means giving it time, starting with what seems like far too much liquid, and then letting the excess steam off while the sauce thickens and the flavours intensify.

Preparation time: 30 minutes • **Makes:** 6 servings

Ingredients	*Directions*
1 onion, trimmed but not skinned, chopped	*1* Brown the onion and carrot in the oil in a large sauce-pan. Add the flour, stir in and allow it to darken a little. Add the rest of the ingredients and stir to incorporate all the browned residues from the pan.
1 carrot, finely chopped	
1 tablespoon of oil	
15 grams/½ ounce white rice flour	*2* Bring to the boil and lower the heat to a simmer. Continue to simmer, not too briskly, uncovered, until the sauce has reduced by about half, stirring occasionally.
30 grams/1 ounce mushrooms, chopped	
1 tablespoon tomato purée	
2 teaspoons sweet paprika	*3* Strain through a sieve, pressing the vegetables through with a soup ladle and scraping the pulp from the outside of the sieve into the sauce. Eventually, you're left with a dryish mix in the sieve, which you can throw away. It seems criminal, we know, but by then the vegetables have done their job and you have a flavoursome, full-bodied sauce. Reheat the sauce when you're ready to serve it, and adjust the seasoning if necessary.
140 millilitres/5 fluid ounces red wine	
140 millilitres/5 fluid ounces dry ruby port	
570 millilitres/1 pint chicken or vegetable stock	
225 grams/8 ounces fresh tomatoes, chopped	
Sprig of fresh thyme or a pinch of dried	

Nutrient analysis per serving: Calories 101; Protein 1g; Carbohydrate 10g; Sugar 7g; Fat 3g; Saturated fat 0g; Fibre 1.4g; Salt 0g.

Mango Salsa

Salsas come in endless forms and flavours. Fresh mango salsa is versatile and easy to make. You can serve it as a dip or use it to jazz up grilled pork, chicken or salmon. You can also use it to make fish tacos – just spoon this salsa over cooked fish and wrap the mixture in a corn tortilla.

Preparation time: 20 minutes • **Makes:** 6 servings

Ingredients	Directions
1 ripe mango, peeled, stoned and diced	**1** Combine the mango, onion, jalapeño, tomato, coriander, lime juice and salt and pepper in a bowl; mix until well blended. Don't mix so hard that you mash the mango – the salsa should be chunky.
½ medium red onion, finely chopped	
1 jalapeño pepper, minced	**2** Chill the salsa for an hour or more to infuse the flavours.
1 large tomato, diced	
2 tablespoons fresh coriander, chopped	
4 tablespoons fresh lime juice	
Freshly ground salt and pepper to taste	

Tip: Figure 14-1 shows you how to dice a mango. With that big seed in the middle, mangoes aren't easy to work with, but you can find a special mango stoner among the gadgets in kitchen shops.

Vary it: Try this with extra tomatoes and red peppers in place of the mango, and with a teaspoon of sugar. For an authentic Mexican flavour, add a touch of chipotle (smoked chilli paste).

Nutrient analysis per serving: Calories 26; Protein 0.8g; Carbohydrate 5.3g; Sugar 5.2g; Fat 0.2g; Saturated fat 0.0g; Fibre 1.1g; Salt, only what you add.

How to Cut a Mango

cut slits crosswise, ½" apart.....

Turn the 'flesh' inside out...

Figure 14-1: How to cut a mango.

Cut lengthwise slices as close to the flat seed as possible....

then in the opposite direction, also 1cm apart.

...and cut off the cubes of mango!

Oriental Salad Dressing

Most commercial Oriental salad dressings use soy sauce, so they nearly all contain wheat. Making your own is easy, though, and to keep it gluten-free, just use any type of gluten-free soy sauce. This dressing can also double as a marinade for meats or tofu.

Preparation time: 5 minutes • **Makes:** 8 servings

Ingredients	*Directions*
115 millilitres/4 fluid ounces rice vinegar	**1** Combine the vinegar, soy sauce, water, sesame oil and sesame seeds in a jar with a tight-fitting lid, and shake the mixture well.
4 tablespoons gluten-free soy sauce	
2 tablespoons water	**2** Add the rapeseed oil and shake again.
1 teaspoon sesame oil	
1 teaspoon toasted sesame seeds (simply dry-roast them in a hot frying pan for a couple of minutes)	
85 millilitres/3 fluid ounces rapeseed oil	

Nutrient analysis per serving: Calories 101; Protein 0.3g; Carbohydrate 1g; Sugar 1g; Fat 11g; Saturated fat 1g; Fibre 0g; Salt 1.3g.

Caesar Salad Dressing

For a classic Caesar salad, all you need is this dressing, Cos lettuce and garlicky croutons. We've lots of ideas for you for the croutons in Chapter 12.

Preparation time: 5 minutes • **Makes:** 8 servings

Ingredients	*Directions*
1 large egg, soft-boiled, cooled and peeled	**1** Combine the lot in a processor or blender. Process the dressing until smooth. If it's too runny, add a little more Parmesan cheese. If it's too thick, add a little more lemon juice or olive oil.
115 millilitres/4 fluid ounces fresh lemon juice	
115 millilitres/4 fluid ounces extra-virgin olive oil	
2 teaspoons crushed garlic (about 4 cloves)	
2 tablespoons gluten-free Worcestershire sauce	
85 grams/3 ounces Parmesan cheese, grated	
50-gram/2-ounce can anchovies	
1 teaspoon freshly grated black pepper	

Nutrient analysis per serving: Calories 202; Protein 6g; Carbohydrate 1g; Sugar 1g; Fat 19g; Saturated fat 4g; Fibre 0g; Salt 1g.

Creamy Green Anchovy Salad Dressing

This dressing is one of our all-time favourites. You can make a vegetarian version by leaving out the anchovies and adding a little salt instead. Alternatively, add a few chunks of avocado for a creamy twist. Spoon it onto your favourite salad or greens. Because the dressing is green and creamy, we especially like to serve it on a colourful salad full of tomatoes, yellow, green and red peppers and avocados.

Preparation time: 5 minutes • **Makes:** 8 servings

Ingredients	*Directions*
450 millilitres/15 fluid ounces (1 large jar) mayonnaise	*1* Mix the mayonnaise, anchovies, spring onion, parsley, chives, rice vinegar, tarragon and lemon juice in a blender or food processor.
5 anchovy fillets, finely chopped	
1 chopped spring onion	*2* Process the mixture until smooth. Refrigerate the dressing until you're ready to serve the salad.
2 teaspoons freshly chopped parsley	
2 teaspoons freshly chopped chives	
1 tablespoon rice vinegar	
1 teaspoon chopped fresh tarragon	
2 teaspoons lemon juice	

Nutrient analysis per serving: Calories 411; Protein 2g; Carbohydrate 0g; Sugar 0g; Fat 45g; Saturated fat 7g; Fibre 0g; Salt 0.5g.

No time for following complicated recipes? Check out these quick and easy dressings to add to your salads (simply adjust the amount of oil, vinegar or lemon juice to achieve your desired consistency and taste):

- **Roasted red pepper vinaigrette:** Mix chopped roasted red peppers with white wine vinegar, crushed garlic, chopped flat-leaf parsley, extra-virgin olive oil, salt and pepper.

- **Chickpea vinaigrette:** Mix coarsely mashed chickpeas with sherry vinegar, a good handful of finely chopped shallots, chives and parsley, and combine with a few glugs of olive oil. Season to taste with freshly ground salt and pepper.

- **Lemon Parmesan dressing:** Mix fresh lemon juice and freshly grated Parmesan cheese with mayonnaise, crushed garlic, extra-virgin olive oil, salt and pepper.

- **Pesto vinaigrette:** Simply blend a good handful of basil or coriander leaves with garlic, olive oil and a tablespoon each of pinenuts and Parmesan cheese. Taste the mixture and add pepper and white wine vinegar.

Tzatziki

This is a cool dude of a sauce to serve with any Indian, Middle Eastern or North African meal, such as our flanafel from Chapter 11 or spicy Indian chicken from Chapter 13. Why not try our flatbreads from Chapter 15 with it too? Being cold, tzatziki goes with any salad, and being practically fat-free, it makes the ultimate dressing for dieters.

Preparation time: 5 minutes • **Makes:** 6 servings

Ingredients	Directions
10-centimetre/4-inch piece of cucumber	**1** Grate or finely chop the cucumber and mix with the rest of the ingredients.
225 grams/8 ounces smooth plain yoghurt	
2 tablespoons chopped fresh mint leaves	**2** Let the sauce stand for a few minutes and taste. Adjust the seasoning if necessary.
1 teaspoon ground cumin	
Dash of Tabasco sauce	
Salt, pepper and sugar to taste	

Nutrient analysis per serving: Calories 27; Protein 2.5g; Carbohydrate 3.6g; Sugar 3.5g; Fat 0.5g; Saturated fat 0g; Fibre 0g; Salt 0.2g.

And Now for Something Sweet

When it comes to puddings – hot, cold, dainty and robust – almost all benefit from a sauce alongside. Dessert sauces often get forgotten, coming as they do at the end of the meal, when you don't want to start cooking again. Plenty of shop-bought custards, yoghurts, bottled sauces and ice creams are available that you can fall back on, and many are gluten-free and very good. But we couldn't have a chapter on sauces without including a few of our sweet favourites. If you've gone to the trouble of making your own dessert, you want to set it off with a final, triumphant flourish. These sauces fit the bill.

Hot Custard

Custard goes with any hot pudding, including stewed fruit and all our suggestions in Chapter 16 for crumbles, streusels, shortbreads and sponges.

Preparation time: 10 minutes • **Makes:** 4 servings

Ingredients	Directions
450 millilitres/16 fluid ounces milk **1½ tablespoons cornflour** **1 tablespoon sugar** **1 large egg** **1 egg yolk** **½ teaspoon vanilla extract**	*1* Mix a little of the milk with the cornflour until smooth. Heat the rest of the milk in a saucepan with the sugar. When the milk and sugar mixture is nearly boiling, pour it over the cornflour mixture and stir. Pour the combined mixture back into the pan and reheat, stirring continuously until it thickens and starts to boil. Reduce the heat to the lowest setting.
	2 Beat the egg, yolk and vanilla extract well enough to fully disperse the egg white. Pour a little of the hot custard onto the egg while still beating. Pour this mixture back into the custard in the pan. Allow the custard to reheat slowly, stirring all the time.

Nutrient analysis per serving: Calories 99; Protein 6.5g; Carbohydrate 11g; Sugar 9g; Fat 3.4g; Saturated fat 1g; Fibre 0g; Salt 0.2g.

Chocolate Pouring Sauce

You can use white, milk, dark or flavoured chocolate – mint, orange, chilli – in this recipe, but do get the best quality you can run to. Serve with ice cream, hot or cold fruit, crêpes, waffles or drop pancakes (see the recipes in Chapter 10) or as a double-chocolate treat with our chocolate cake or zebra meringues in Chapter 16.

Preparation time: 10 minutes • **Makes:** 6 servings

Ingredients	*Directions*
115 grams/4 ounces chocolate 30 grams/1 ounce butter	*1* Using a heavy-based saucepan or a bowl over a pan of simmering water, melt the chocolate and butter together. If using dark chocolate, add the golden syrup and melt it.
2 tablespoons golden syrup (with dark chocolate) 200 millilitres/7 fluid ounces milk	*2* Now start to add the milk while heating gently and stirring, and continue until you get the consistency you like. Serve warm or at room temperature.

Vary it: Try replacing the milk with water or single cream and a slug of rum or liqueur.

Nutrient analysis per serving: Calories 163; Protein 2g; Carbohydrate 19g; Sugar 19g; Fat 9g; Saturated fat 5g; Fibre 0.5g; Salt 0.1g.

Fruit Coulis

For a refreshing cold sauce to serve with meringues, sponges, dense chocolate cakes, pancakes and ice cream, go for a fruit coulis. It's a complete change from custard and cream and it's entirely fat-free.

Preparation time: 10 minutes • **Makes:** 6 servings

Ingredients	*Directions*
225 grams/8 ounces ripe soft fruit 1 tablespoon granulated sugar (optional)	*1* If the fruit is very firm, first soften it with a little granulated sugar in a warm pan until its juices start to run, but don't cook it as such. If not, start with Step 2.
1 tablespoon icing sugar Lemon juice (optional)	*2* Blend the fruit with a tablespoon of icing sugar and taste. Depending on how tart the fruit is, you may need a little lemon juice or more sugar to get the taste you want.
Water	*3* Add a splash of cold water and reblend. Strain out any seeds through a sieve, pressing the fruit pulp through. Chill.

Nutrient analysis per serving: Calories 13; Protein 0.5g; Carbohydrate 3g; Sugar 3g; Fat 0g; Saturated fat 0g; Fibre 1g; Salt 0g.

Buttersweet

Buttersweet is an impressive sauce that takes moments to prepare, yet really lifts the most basic of desserts to new heights. It's rich and filling, so you don't need much. Serve it as a topping with fruit, meringues, ice cream or old-fashioned milk puddings like rice, sago or tapioca puddings. Several unsweetened nut butters are available now in the shops, some crunchy and some smooth. You can even make your own by processing nuts with a touch of vegetable oil to bind the mixture together into a paste.

Preparation time: 5 minutes • **Makes:** 6 servings

Ingredients	Directions
115 grams/4 ounces unsweetened nut butter	*1* In a heavy-based saucepan, gently melt the nut butter over a very low heat.
2 tablespoons lemon juice	
85 grams/3 ounces honey	*2* Stir in the lemon juice and honey.
55 millilitres/2 fluid ounces water	*3* Add the water, stir and heat through.

Nutrient analysis per serving: Calories 159; Protein 4.5g; Carbohydrate 13g; Sugar 11g; Fat 10g; Saturated fat 2.5g; Fibre 1g; Salt 0.1g.

Creamy Dreamy Sauce

You can whip up this sauce in a few moments. It goes well with cakes and cookies, particularly dark ones like our carrot cake, and it makes a dessert in itself with a streusel topping. Head to Chapter 16 for ideas.

Preparation time: 5 minutes • **Makes:** 6 servings

Ingredients	Directions
200 grams/7 ounces light cream cheese	*1* Beat the cream cheese in a bowl with a wooden spoon until it's smooth and soft. Add the lemon juice and a few spoonfuls of juice from the tin to get a sauce consistency.
1 teaspoon lemon juice	
200-gram/7-ounce tin of fruit in juice	*2* Drain and shred the fruit or chop it finely and fold into the sauce.

Nutrient analysis per serving: Calories 63; Protein 3g; Carbohydrate 4g; Sugar 4g; Fat 4g; Saturated fat 2.5g; Fibre 0.4g; Salt 0.3g.

Lemony Elderflower Sauce

A unique and unexpected flavour combination, this is the business with chocolate cakes.

Preparation time: 10 minutes, plus several hours to chill • **Makes:** 6 servings

Ingredients	*Directions*
285 millilitres/10 fluid ounces water	*1* Heat the water and sugar together, stirring to dissolve the sugar. Add the lemon juice.
70 grams/2½ ounces sugar	
Grated zest and juice of 2 lemons	*2* Snip the tiny florets from the elderflowers into the lemony syrup. Bring up to a simmer, cover tightly and allow to simmer gently for five minutes. Cool a little without lifting the lid, and then strain the mixture through a sieve. If you don't have elderflowers, which will be the case for most of the year, omit Step 2 and simply add the cordial to the syrup.
4 elderflower heads or 1 tablespoon elderflower cordial	
1 teaspoon arrowroot or cornflour	
	3 Add the lemon zest. Mix the arrowroot or cornflour with a little water until smooth, and then add it to the sauce.
	4 Bring up the heat again while stirring to thicken the sauce, but don't allow the sauce to boil for more than a few seconds. Chill and serve very cold.

Vary it: Instead of elderflower, you can add orange flower water or rose water, and you can use limes instead of lemons.

Nutrient analysis per serving: Calories 50; Protein 0.2g; Carbohydrate 13g; Sugar 12g; Fat 0g; Saturated fat 0g; Fibre 0g; Salt 0g.

Chapter 15

Making Your Own Pizza, Pasta, Tortillas and Breads

*L*iving gluten-free doesn't mean that you have to go without all your old favourites like pizza, pasta, tortillas and bread. All are available gluten-free, either in the shops or online, and the quality is improving all the time. But being cooking fanatics, we like to make our own, which allows us to make every meal exactly to our liking. It also opens the door to a huge number of recipes and variations that simply aren't available otherwise. Gluten-free stuffed fresh pastas, wraps, spicy naans, reduced-salt bread and wonderful Mexican dishes are all examples.

In this chapter, we share the secrets of making deliciously authentic yet outrageously easy gluten-free staples like pizza bases, fresh pasta, crisp and soft tortillas and good, wholesome breads. Conventionally, all these foods contain gluten, but these recipes are wholly gluten-free, made with easy-to-get, affordable ingredients and simple techniques.

Throughout our recipes, we use ingredients which are widely available gluten-free, but some brands of certain ingredients do contain gluten or may do so, particularly baking powder, flours, meals and yeast. As with all your food, check the labels carefully and avoid anything that contains, or may contain, gluten, even a trace.

Perfecting Your Pizza

The secret of a good pizza is, of course, the quality of the ingredients. The secret of a perfect one is cooking those high-quality ingredients together so that the sauce begins to sink into the base and the other toppings meld with the sauce as the pizza cooks. So to achieve the perfect pizza, you really need to start with fresh, raw pizza dough, not with a pre-cooked base. Here's how.

Pizza Margherita

A classic pizza just as it is, and also the perfect recipe for adding extra toppings of your choice. Load the extra toppings between the sauce and the cheese before baking the pizza. You can add raw, thinly sliced fruits, vegetables, fresh herbs, extra cheese, ham, pepperoni, chorizo, fish and seafood, allowing them to cook under the cheese. Other meats, eggs and chunks of fish are best cooked separately before they go onto the pizza, to ensure they're thoroughly cooked by the time the pizza is ready.

Preparation time: 20 minutes • Rising time: 1 hour • **Cooking time:** 15 minutes •
Makes: Two 30-centimetre (12-inch) pizza bases (8 servings)

Ingredients	*Directions*
For the pizza bases	*1* In a large bowl, mix the dry ingredients and add the milk, water, egg and olive oil.
155 grams/5½ ounces brown rice flour	
155 grams/5½ ounces tapioca starch	*2* Mix thoroughly and then knead by hand to incorporate all the flour into the liquid, until the dough is soft and smooth. Roll the dough into a cylinder, and divide into two.
70 grams/2½ ounces chickpea flour	
85 grams/3 ounces cornmeal	
2 teaspoons xanthan gum	
1 tablespoon dried quick-acting yeast	
1 teaspoon sugar	*3* Roll out each piece on a surface lightly dusted with cornmeal to 30 centimetres/ 12 inches. Spray or grease two non-stick oven trays or pizza pans. Slide your hands under each pizza base and slide the dough off carefully onto a tray or pan.
2 teaspoons baking powder	
55 millilitres/2 fluid ounces milk, warmed	
200 millilitres/7 fluid ounces tepid water	
1 large egg, beaten	
2 tablespoons extra-virgin olive oil	
Non-stick spray or oil to grease the tray or pizza pan	

For the sauce

1 tablespoon olive oil

2 medium onions, thinly sliced

2 plump garlic cloves, finely chopped

1 x 400-gram tin of chopped tomatoes

1 tablespoon tomato purée

1 tablespoon tomato ketchup

Pinch of chilli flakes

Black pepper

To assemble the pizzas

255 grams/9 ounces mozzarella cheese (2 balls)

255 grams/9 ounces taleggio cheese

4 Cover with a damp cloth and leave the dough to rise in a warm place for about one hour.

5 Meanwhile make your sauce. Soften the onions and garlic in the oil in a saucepan. Stir in the remaining ingredients. Bring to the boil and lower the heat. Simmer the sauce, uncovered, for about 30 minutes. Slice the cheeses thickly and prepare any other toppings that you plan to add.

6 Preheat the oven to 220°C/Gas Mark 7. Spread your sauce evenly over the bases, scatter on any extra toppings and finish with the cheeses on top. Bake for 25 minutes.

Nutrient analysis per serving: Calories 464; Protein 20g; Carbohydrate 50g; Sugar 4g; Fat 21g; Saturated fat 10g; Fibre 5g; Salt 0.9g.

Indulging a Passion for Pasta

Complaining about the taste of gluten-free pasta was once completely acceptable. Gluten-free pasta used to be either gritty and chalky, or slimy and heavy, and it went from being al dente to mush in a millisecond. We have to admit: some makes of pasta still do.

But thanks to the growing demand for great gluten-free pasta, and the attention it has attracted among the big pasta-brand-owners in Italy, who were presumably seeing their core market chipped away, gluten-free pasta has come a long, long way. We suggest you shop around and try a few makes until you find the ones you prefer, and then make a note of the key ingredients and go searching for the shapes you want with those main ingredients. If you're looking for authenticity with home-cooked pasta, you'll need several shapes including, as a minimum, spaghetti, lasagne, short tubes like penne, and ribbons such as tagliatelle.

If you're buying dried gluten-free pasta shapes, avoid those with varying widths within each piece of pasta, such as fusilli (spirals) and farfalle (butterflies). When you cook these, the thin areas cook and go flabby while the dense parts remain hard.

Thousands of recipes for pasta accompaniments and sauces exist, from the simplest to the most elaborate. Many are gluten-free already, because they're based on meat, fish, cream, vegetables, cheese, seafood, oil, butter, eggs and herbs, which are all gluten-free naturally. Numerous cookery books are dedicated to pasta dishes, and you find large sections about pasta in more general Italian recipe books. So rather than picking out a random sample of recipes for sauces, we give you recipes and methods for delicious gluten-free fresh pasta and gnocchi with guidelines for sauces and accompaniments. We suggest how you can thicken sauces, replace the few gluten-containing ingredients that do crop up occasionally, and manage the cooking and serving processes if you're also cooking a batch of wheat pasta alongside the gluten-free components.

Making your own pasta

When it comes to stuffed or baked pasta dishes, such as ravioli, agnolotti, cannelloni and lasagne, you can't beat making your own fresh gluten-free pasta. The rolling technique is a little different to that for wheat pasta, but the result is divine, and overall it's easier than pre-boiling dried gluten-free pasta, which you'd have to do before layering, filling or rolling it. With fresh pasta, you don't need to pre-boil it, because it cooks with the filling or during baking.

Fresh Pasta

You need to allow more fresh pasta per person than you would dried pasta, because it absorbs less water when it cooks, so allow for a good 115 grams/4 ounces per person. The quantity in our recipe makes about 255 grams/9 ounces, which is two generous portions when served in a bowl with sauce; four if you make it into a lasagne.

Preparation time: 10 minutes • **Makes:** 2 to 4 servings

Ingredients	*Directions*
55 grams/2 ounces fine yellow cornmeal **55 grams/2 ounces brown rice flour** **55 grams/2 ounces cornflour** **1 teaspoon xanthan gum** **1 large egg** **1 large egg yolk** **1 tablespoon olive oil** **1 tablespoon water**	*1* Mix the dry ingredients in a bowl and make a well in the centre. Break the egg and add it to the well together with the yolk, the oil and the water. *2* Mix the liquids with a fork, gradually incorporating the dry ingredients as you go, until you have a ball of dough. Now go in with your hand and knead the dough lightly to incorporate all the flour. If it won't combine into a firm but smooth ball without any cracks on the surface, wet your hand with water and knead the ingredients in. *3* Divide the dough into two and form each smaller ball into a round, flat shape. Put the ball of dough between two large sheets of clingfilm and roll it out thinly with a rolling pin. You need to press down quite hard as you roll and ensure that the top layer of clingfilm hasn't tucked underneath the dough at the edges, which stops you from rolling the pasta thin enough. *4* Cut the pasta into the shapes you want and either cook it in a stuffed, rolled or layered pasta recipe or boil it gently for two to three minutes in a big pan of lightly salted water, without too much stirring, just allowing the moving water to keep the pieces separate while they cook. Then serve the pasta with a sauce of your choice.

Nutrient analysis per serving (for 2): Calories 412; Protein 9g; Carbohydrate 61g; Sugar 0g; Fat 15g; Saturated fat 3g; Fibre 3g; Salt 0.1g.

Gnocchi

Gnocchi are light little dumplings served pasta-style with sauces and toppings. The main ingredient of these gnocchi is potato, which is of course already gluten-free.

Preparation time: 20 minutes • **Cooking time:** 30 minutes • **Makes:** 4 servings

Ingredients	*Directions*
900 gram/2 pounds floury potatoes	*1* Boil the potatoes, unpeeled, in lightly salted water until tender. Drain and cool them until comfortable to handle. Peel the potatoes and mash them or put through a potato ricer or mouli.
55 grams/2 ounces butter	
2 large eggs, beaten	
40 grams/1½ ounces white rice flour	*2* While the potatoes are still warm, add the remaining ingredients and mix together to form a sticky dough. Add extra rice flour if the dough is too sticky to handle.
40 grams/1½ ounces tapioca starch	We recommend proceeding as follows with just a couple of gnocchi to test the mixture, because the texture varies according to the potatoes. If the gnocchi fall apart in the water, add some extra of each of the flours to the mix. If the mixture is too dry and makes stodgy gnocchi, add extra beaten egg and knead again.
40 grams/1½ ounces fine cornmeal	
½ teaspoon xanthan gum	
1 teaspoon bicarbonate of soda	
	3 Dust your worktop or a marble slab with white rice flour. Take a handful of dough and roll it with both hands into a long sausage shape about 2 centimetres/¾ inch in diameter. Cut it into pieces about 2½ centimetres/1 inch long. Press each piece lightly with the tines of a fork to make a ribbed pattern on the top.
	4 Bring a large pan of lightly salted water to the boil and drop the gnocchi in, about six at a time. When they bob up to the top and have floated for a few seconds, they're cooked. Lift them out with a slotted spoon and drain off the excess water. They stick together as they cool, so serve at once or layer them up with grated cheese and a thick vegetable or tomato sauce and then brown under the grill.

Nutrient analysis per serving: Calories 444; Protein 10g; Carbohydrate 66g; Sugar 1g; Fat 17g; Saturated fat 9g; Fibre 4g; Salt 1.2g.

Making gluten-free pasta sauces

A number of the sauces in Chapter 14 are suitable for serving with pasta. If you're using a general recipe book, here are some ideas for creating gluten-free versions of sauces:

- ✔ In thick milky or cheesy sauces, use white rice flour in place of plain wheat flour.

- ✔ Thicken tomato and vegetable sauces by allowing them to simmer away uncovered as they cook.

- ✔ You can thicken tomato and meat sauces with tomato purée, passata, dried porcini mushrooms, sun-dried tomatoes, crème fraîche or, if you're going to bake the dish, an egg or egg yolk.

- ✔ The classic Italian ragù doesn't include tomatoes, but purée and milk. You add the milk bit by bit as the sauce cooks slowly for a good hour or more. Surprising, but it actually works and makes a thick sauce.

- ✔ Use popular accompaniments for pasta that aren't really sauces at all, like chopped herbs and vegetables, seafood or dressings like pesto, which is basically cheese, basil and pinenuts, blended together.

Avoiding mix-ups with wheat pasta

If you're making a gluten-free pasta sauce and cooking two lots of pasta to serve with it (gluten-free and wheat pasta), you must use two separate pans of boiling water. We suggest you get into the habit of doing everything to do with the gluten-free one on the same side, say on your right-hand side. For example, always boil the gluten-free pasta on the right-hand side of the hob and always serve it into the bowl on the right. Keep separate utensils to handle the gluten-free pasta and take care not to put the gluteny utensils into the sauce. If you want to add a spoonful of the pasta-boiling liquid to the sauce, you must take it from the gluten-free pan. Pointing this out may seem silly, but absent-mindedly throwing in some water from the wrong pan is amazingly easy. Trust us: we've done it, especially after an *aperitivo*!

Remember the rule: gluten-free first. What we mean is, handle the gluten-free pasta before the wheat pasta throughout. Weigh it first, drain it first and put it into the bowl first. If you want to mix the pasta with the sauce before you put it into the bowl, drain your gluten-free pasta and put it back into the pan it boiled in, and then add the portion of sauce and mix in the pan. Then serve straight into the bowl, and do the same with the gluteny pasta.

Making it Mexican

Tortillas feature in most Mexican meals in the guise of corn or flour tortillas, tacos, nachos, totopos, chalupas or sopes. And, of course, a flour tortilla as a wrap makes a popular alternative to bread as a sandwich. You'd think the corn tortillas and fried versions of them would be gluten-free, but in reality they're often not. Gluten-free corn tortillas are only just becoming available online, and we haven't seen any gluten-free flour tortillas available anywhere in the UK at the time of writing. Luckily, you can get hold of the special gluten-free tortilla flour you need to make your own.

Corn Tortillas

Masa harina is cornmeal that's been treated with slaked lime and then washed and ground. The flour has the characteristic taste of Mexico and allows you to make up authentic corn tortillas at home. Cornmeal and polenta just don't cut it here.

You need to cook corn tortillas twice: the first time dry and the second time in vegetable oil.

Preparation time: 20 minutes, plus 30 minutes to rest • **Cooking time:** 2 minutes each •
Makes: 8 tortillas

Ingredients	Directions
225 grams/8 ounces masa harina **½ teaspoon salt** **240 millilitres/8½ fluid ounces warm water**	*1* In a large bowl, combine the masa harina and salt and add half the water. Mix with a spoon and then knead with your hand while you add more water a drop at a time. You need a good ten minutes of kneading before you get a stiff but smooth dough that's not at all sticky. If the dough continues to split when you squeeze it, wet your hands and work more water in until it doesn't split. Wrap the dough in clingfilm and rest it at room temperature for about 30 minutes.
	2 Heat a heavy-based frying pan or griddle over a medium heat. Divide the dough into eight and knead each piece into a smooth, flat disc. Place one between two sheets of clingfilm and roll it out thinly – no thicker than a ten-pence piece – working from the middle outwards to maintain a round shape.
	3 Remove the film and cook the tortilla on the pan or griddle for a minute or so on the first side and for less time on the second side. The tortilla should have mid-brown patches on both sides and puff up as it cooks. Flatten any large bubbles that form, in order to keep the tortilla in contact with the griddle.
	4 Store the tortillas between two plates as you cook more. Tortillas are best fried until crisp in deep peanut oil, which takes just seconds. For corn chips, cut the tortillas into quarters before you fry them.

Nutrient analysis per tortilla: Calories 102; Protein 3g; Carbohydrate 30g; Sugar 0g; Fat 1g; Saturated fat 0g; Fibre 1g; Salt 0.2g.

Soft Flour Tortillas

This recipe is a gluten-free version of the creamy-white wraps or flour tortillas you see in shops. You don't need to fry them and, unlike corn tortillas, they're pliable, so you can easily use them to make parcels and roll-ups for Mexican dishes such as our enchiladas in Chapter 13.

Preparation time: 20 minutes • **Cooking time:** 1 minute per tortilla • **Makes:** 6 servings

Ingredients	Directions
140 grams/5 ounces white rice flour	*1* Heat a heavy-based frying pan or griddle over a medium heat. In a large bowl, combine the dry ingredients. Rub in the butter with your fingertips.
55 grams/2 ounces potato flour	
30 grams/1 ounce tapioca starch	*2* Slowly add the warm water to the flour mixture, stirring after each addition. Knead gently by hand to incorporate all the flour, until the dough is smooth and soft. Form the dough into six balls and flatten them slightly into thick discs.
2 teaspoons xanthan gum	
2 teaspoons granulated sugar	
½ teaspoon salt	
1 teaspoon baking powder	*3* Put a disc between two layers of baking parchment or waxed paper. Using a rolling pin, working from the middle outwards, and turning the stack frequently, roll the dough out to make an 18-centimetre/7-inch tortilla. Carefully peel back the top layer of paper. The rolling technique keeps the shape round, but if you particularly want a perfect circle, use a plate or cake tin as a pattern to cut around.
30 grams/1 ounce butter	
115 millilitres/4 fluid ounces warm water	
	4 Invert the tortilla onto the hot griddle, leaving the paper on top in place. Cook it for about 40 seconds and then carefully peel off the paper. Flip the tortilla over and cook the other side for about 20 seconds. If you intend to use the tortilla in a cooked dish like enchiladas, leave it slightly undercooked at this stage so it's more pliable and easier to roll up. Cook the other tortillas in the same way, interleaving them with a wet tea towel and keeping them covered until you're ready to use them.

Nutrient analysis per serving: Calories 225; Protein 3g; Carbohydrate 44g; Sugar 6g; Fat 4g; Saturated fat 2g; Fibre 2g; Salt 0.7g.

Baking Fresh Bread

Gluten-free bread has a bad reputation – and for years, this reputation was well-deserved. But if any food deserves to win in the 'most improved' category in the gluten-free food world, it's definitely bread. Thanks to some dedicated experimental cooking, gluten-free bread has evolved from being tasteless and brick-like to light, doughy and tasty.

If you're a home-baking fan, you'll want to make gluten-free bread for yourself. To give you a head start, we've experimented and developed some simple bread recipes for you. For some additional bread-making tips and tricks, refer to Chapter 9.

If you'd rather not buy and measure all the recipe ingredients that go into bread, you can use one of the excellent bread mixes available, especially those available on prescription. Just pop a mix in your bread machine, add a few ingredients and switch on.

Don't be surprised if the gluten-free program on your machine doesn't work very well. On some machines, it includes a second kneading or 'knocking back', which is an essential step with gluten-containing bread – but in gluten-free recipes, the bread never recovers from the knocking back, and you get a disappointingly flat loaf. You'll know whether your machine has this step or not from reading the manual, asking the manufacturer or just listening out for the sound of the blade turning before the last proving stage. If you do have this step in your machine's gluten-free program, don't use the program but follow our method below.

White Bread

You can make this recipe either in a machine or by hand, and in the latter case, you can turn out small loaves or rolls. We like this particular recipe because, unlike most gluten-free bread recipes, it doesn't need four or five eggs, vinegar or gelatine, and all the flours are readily available without a prescription, either in the shops or online. Moreover, the result is a moist, satisfying loaf or roll with a crisp, golden crust – good just as it is or toasted.

Preparation time: 10 minutes • **Cooking time:** See the recipe for details; varies according to the size of loaf or rolls • **Makes:** One 650-gram/1½-pound loaf in the machine, or two 450-gram/1-pound loaves or 10 small rolls by hand

Ingredients	*Directions*
55 grams/2 ounces gram flour	**Using a bread machine**
100 grams/3½ ounces tapioca starch	*1* Put all the dry ingredients into the bread machine. Beat the egg in a large jug, stir in the oil and milk, and add the hot water last to give a warm liquid without cooking the egg. Add this mix to the dry ingredients. Set the machine to the pizza program and start it. It will start to mix at once. After a couple of minutes, use a thin plastic spatula to scrape the flour from the corners of the bucket while the machine continues to mix. Leave it to mix for the first mixing phase – usually about 15 minutes.
155 grams/5½ ounces white rice flour	
40 grams/1½ ounces potato flour	
2 teaspoons baking powder	
2 teaspoons xanthan gum	
2 teaspoons dried quick-acting yeast	*2* When the mixing stops, remove the paddle and smooth the top of the mix to fill the hole in the middle. Do this as quickly as you can to avoid the dough cooling down too much. Now close the lid and leave the dough to prove for 1½ hours. The pizza program will finish during this time, but don't open the machine or turn it off.
1 large egg	
1 tablespoon oil	
155 millilitres/5½ fluid ounces milk	
170 millilitres/6 fluid ounces very hot water	*3* Turn off the machine after the proving and restart it on the 'bake only' program for one hour. Remove the bucket promptly, but leave the bread in it for 15 minutes to cool and seal underneath before turning it out and leaving it to cool on a rack.

Making loaves or rolls by hand

1 Put all the dry ingredients into a mixing bowl. Beat the egg in a large jug, mix in the oil and milk, and add the hot water last to give a warm liquid without cooking the egg. Add this mix to the dry ingredients and mix thoroughly with a spoon. You may need an extra 20 millilitres/¾ fluid ounce of water to achieve a smooth, spongy dough. You can add more water to make the dough easier to mix.

2 Thoroughly oil either two 450-gram/1-pound loaf tins or a large baking sheet. Divide the dough into two loaves or ten rolls. Push the dough gently into the corners of the tins. Oil your fingers or the back of a spoon and smooth the surfaces – that's unless you want a craggy crust, which does look pleasingly rustic and home-made.

3 Prove the bread for 1½ hours in an oven set to conventional heat (not fan) at 50°C, or in a warm airing cupboard. (Unfortunately, if you use a gas oven, you can't get the temperature low enough for proving the bread.)

4 Bake in the middle of a pre-heated oven at 220°C/Gas Mark 7 for 25 to 30 minutes for loaves and about 15 minutes for rolls. Turn the loaves out of the tins after allowing them to cool for about 15 minutes. Then cool them completely on a rack. If you're making rolls, simply move them to the cooling rack as soon as they come out of the oven.

Nutrient analysis per roll or two thick slices of bread: Calories 149; Protein 4g; Carbohydrate 28g; Sugar 1g; Fat 2g; Saturated fat 0g; Fibre 1g; Salt 0.5g.

You can add whole seeds to these breads or sprinkle them on top just before baking. Caraway, sesame, poppy and sunflower seeds are all good. Add about a teaspoonful of each, or mix them to make up a tablespoonful in total. Another option is to add two teaspoons of bran such as toasted soya bran or rice bran, or ground linseed. You may need to add an extra splash of water with the linseed because it tends to thicken the dough.

Flatbreads

These tasty flatbreads can double as naans or pittas. They're great fresh from the oven, or you can freeze them and then defrost in the toaster on the lowest setting.

Preparation time: 10 minutes, plus 1 hour to prove • **Cooking time:** 6 minutes • **Makes:** 8 breads

Ingredients	Directions
55 grams/2 ounces white teff	*1* Mix the dry ingredients in a mixing bowl. Beat the egg and add it along with the buttermilk and oil. Stir the mixture together until smooth, fairly stiff and springy.
115 grams/4 ounces tapioca starch	
130 grams/4½ ounces white rice flour	*2* Turn the dough out onto a board or marble slab lightly dusted with white rice flour. Knead lightly into a neat, thick roll with a non-sticky surface. Cut into eight equal pieces.
55 grams/2 ounces potato flour	
1 teaspoon baking powder	
1 teaspoon bicarbonate of soda	*3* Using the minimum amount of white rice flour to prevent the dough sticking underneath, pat and roll the dough into teardrop shapes about 5 millimetres/⅓ inch thick. Leave them to prove for an hour on the worktop or board. They'll plump up just slightly.
½ teaspoon salt	
2 teaspoons xanthan gum	
2 teaspoons dried quick-acting yeast	*4* Heat the fan grill, if you have one, to 200°C, or use the conventional oven at 230°C/Gas Mark 8. Set the oven tray on the position third from the top and, if you have one, heat a pizza stone on it, or use a griddle, non-stick tray or silicone sheet.
1 large egg	
284 millilitres/10 fluid ounces buttermilk	
2 tablespoons oil	*5* Gently lift each flatbread onto the flat of your hand without tearing it and brush any excess flour away from the underside. Slap it onto the stone or tray and grill or bake for three minutes, turning when lightly browned, and cooking the other side for three minutes.

Nutrient analysis per flatbread: Calories 211; Protein 5g; Carbohydrate 38g; Sugar 2g; Fat 5g; Saturated fat 0g; Fibre 2g; Salt 0.7g.

Cornbread

A Southern States favourite that normally contains wheat flour and cream, this cornbread is a non-yeasted, low-fat bread that tastes and looks as though you've gone to a lot of trouble. In fact, it's a breeze to make, doesn't even need to prove, and can bake along with whatever else you've got in the oven.

Preparation time: 10 minutes • **Cooking time:** 45 minutes • **Makes:** 9

Ingredients	*Directions*
30 grams/1 ounce soft butter **1 teaspoon sugar** **418-gram/15-ounce tin of creamed-style sweetcorn** **85 grams/3 ounces yellow cornmeal or polenta** **1 large egg, separated** **Extra butter for greasing the tin**	*1* Preheat the oven to 200°C/Gas Mark 6. Cream the butter and sugar in a bowl with a spoon. Stir in the sweetcorn and polenta along with the egg yolk. *2* Whisk the egg white in a separate bowl until fairly stiff and foamy. Fold this into the corn mixture, just until you've worked in the white foam. *3* Generously butter an 18-centimetre/7-inch square cake tin or a similarly sized roasting tin. Pour in the mix and bake either until risen and firm to the touch (30 minutes) or, if you prefer, golden brown on top (45 minutes). Cool completely in the tin and cut into nine squares.

Nutrient analysis per serving: Calories 98; Protein 2g; Carbohydrate 13g; Sugar 1g; Fat 4g; Saturated fat 2g; Fibre 1g; Salt 0.3g.

Chapter 16

Sweet Treats

In This Chapter

▶ Creating decadent gluten-free desserts and confectionery

▶ Baking sweet foods for packed lunches

▶ Serving up gluten-free versions of traditional tea-time treats

▶ Creating wholesome puddings for the health-conscious

*W*hen you've finished the main course, you eagerly anticipate one thing – and it's not doing the dishes. Of course, we mean the dessert. But sweet treats don't appear only at mealtimes. The British afternoon tea is one of the glories of our culinary contribution to the world: a pot of properly brewed tea with a sweet baked temptation on the side. If you think that following the gluten-free lifestyle means having to deprive yourself of such pleasures, this chapter surely proves you wrong.

If you ache to bake, we've got that covered with treats to tempt you and everyone else. They're all gluten-free of course, but you won't need to make any apologies for that, or even tell people if you don't want to. In the past, gluten-free baking has sometimes got the response 'Not bad for gluten-free,' but now it's 'Mmmm, I want that recipe!' We've got treats to tuck into the picnic basket and the lunchbox for when you're gluten-free on the go. And when you want to ease back on calories without denying yourself altogether, we've some ideas that hit the spot.

Throughout our recipes, we use ingredients which are widely available gluten-free, but some brands of certain ingredients do contain gluten or may do so, particularly baking powder, flours, meals, dessert sauces, some confectionery and baking ingredients. As with all your food, check the labels carefully and avoid anything that contains, or may contain, gluten – even a trace.

Daring to Be Decadent: Gluten-Free Indulgences

Yes, you can have your cake and eat it too. As long as it's gluten-free! We're into indulgences. We believe that if you're going to live it up from time to time, you may as well really satisfy that craving and get it out of your system. Plenty of gluten-free desserts can satisfy your cravings, but these recipes are wickedly wonderful.

Flourless Chocolate Cake

One of the most incredible desserts on the planet, this flourless chocolate cake is rich, dense, moist and surprisingly easy to prepare. It requires very few ingredients, none of which are difficult to obtain. Prepare to be amazed.

Preparation time: 30 minutes • **Cooking time:** 50 minutes • **Makes:** 10 servings

Ingredients	*Directions*
Non-stick oil spray, for greasing the tin	*1* Preheat the oven to 140°C/Gas Mark 1. Spray a 23-centimetre (9-inch) round loose-based or springform cake tin with non-stick oil. If you don't know what a springform cake tin looks like, see Figure 16-1.
225 grams/8 ounces unsalted butter	
225 grams/8 ounces 70% chocolate, broken into pieces	*2* Put the butter and chocolate in a large bowl over a saucepan of hot water. Put the pan on a low heat and allow the chocolate and butter to melt. Alternatively, microwave the chocolate and butter for ten-second intervals until melted, stirring after each interval.
6 large eggs	
200 grams/7 ounces caster sugar	

3 Separate the egg whites and egg yolks, putting the yolks and whites in separate small bowls. Whisk the yolks into the warm chocolate–butter mixture.

4 Whisk the egg whites (or beat them on low speed) for three minutes, and then add the sugar. Continue to beat or whisk the egg whites until stiff and glossy, which should take about three minutes. Gently fold the stiffened egg whites into the chocolate mixture.

5 Pour the batter into the prepared pan, and smooth over the top with a spatula.

6 Bake until the cake is set in the centre – for about 45 to 50 minutes. Let the cake cool for 15 minutes and then remove from the tin.

Tip: Cover the cake in powdered sugar or cocoa powder, or drizzle with caramel sauce or chocolate sauce. If you're watching your waistline (yeah, right!), you may want to cover the cake in raspberries instead.

Nutrient analysis per serving: Calories 418; Protein 6g; Carbohydrate 34g; Sugar 34g; Fat 29g; Saturated fat 17g; Fibre 1g; Salt 0.1g.

Figure 16-1:
The cylinder of a springform cake tin unlatches, allowing you to remove the bottom.

Peanut Butter Fudge

This incredible fudge is almost embarrassingly easy to make – it's foolproof. The hardest part of this recipe is being patient enough to wait until the fudge is cool before eating it.

Preparation time: 10 minutes • **Refrigeration time:** 2 hours • **Makes:** 100 pieces

Ingredients	*Directions*
500 grams/17½ ounces smooth peanut butter **397 grams/14 ounces (usually 1 can) sweetened condensed milk** **2 teaspoons natural vanilla extract**	**1** Put the peanut butter into a medium-sized glass bowl and add the condensed milk. Microwave the mixture on high for three minutes, making sure that it doesn't bubble over the sides of the bowl.
	2 Stir the mixture to make sure that the peanut butter has melted and the mixture's smooth. Add the vanilla, and mix well.
	3 Line a 25-centimetre (10-inch) square tin with greaseproof paper, and pour in the fudge mixture. Refrigerate the fudge for two hours (if you can wait that long!). Cut into 2½-centimetre (1-inch) squares to serve.

Nutrient analysis per piece: Calories 44; Protein 2g; Carbohydrate 3g; Sugar 2.4g; Fat 3g; Saturated fat 1g; Fibre 0g; Salt 0.05g.

Making your own desserts

Close your eyes and think of the most delicious dessert you can imagine. Is it gluten-free? No? Well, it can be – and here's how. Find a recipe in this chapter that's similar to the gluten-containing part of your dream dessert, and use our suggestions for the flour. By all means adapt our recipes; we just offer ideas to get you started.

Is it a tart or pie? Use our sweet pastry recipe. A crumbly topping? We've got crumble for hot puddings and streusel for cold ones. Sponge? No problem: we give you a basic sponge mix that you can steam or bake, and to which you can add fruit, coconut, chocolate, ground nuts – whatever takes your fancy. And if you're after a crisp, biscuity texture, we've got cookies to try.

If you only bake gluten-free now and again, you can try a shop-bought or prescription mix and simply substitute it for the wheat flour in your recipe. No pun intended, but mixes are a mixed bag in our experience. Some are brilliant for one type of recipe but a tad disappointing in others. The makers supply excellent recipes of their own that show you how to get the best results with their mixes. But if you're serious about gluten-free baking, we suggest you get in a few gluten-free flours and mix them yourself according to what you're making.

Honey Orange Cake

Moist but light cakes like this are popular in the Med, and when you try our cake, you'll see why. This one's a winner in every way. It scooped first prize in a bake-off judged by a no-nonsense WI veteran, and it wasn't even in a gluten-free category!

Preparation time: 30 minutes • **Cooking time:** 40 minutes • **Standing time:** Several hours or overnight • **Makes:** 10 servings

Ingredients	*Directions*
1 large orange **140 grams/5 ounces butter plus extra for greasing the tin** **140 grams/5 ounces caster sugar** **215 grams/7½ ounces polenta** **115 grams/4 ounces ground almonds** **2 large eggs, beaten** **2½ teaspoons baking powder** **For the syrup:** **140 grams/5 ounces honey** **2 tablespoons water** **1 tablespoon lemon juice**	*1* Line the base of a 23-centimetre (9-inch) loose-based sandwich-cake tin with baking parchment and butter the sides. Preheat the oven to 200°C/Gas Mark 6. *2* Wash and dry the orange, finely grate the zest into a mixing bowl and add the butter and caster sugar. Cream them together until the mixture is pale, using a wooden spoon or a hand beater. *3* Squeeze all the juice from the orange and add 3 tablespoons of it to the cake mixture, along with the rest of the ingredients. (Set aside the remaining juice for later.) Mix the whole lot together until you have an even consistency throughout. *4* Put the mixture into the tin and smooth the top. Bake in the centre of the oven for five minutes. Then lower the temperature to 180°C/Gas Mark 4 and continue to bake for 35 minutes. Keep an eye on the cake and cover the tin with brown paper if the cake looks like scorching. The cake will be mid-brown and will have shrunk away from the sides of the tin slightly when it's cooked. Leave it to cool completely in the tin. *5* Meanwhile, make the syrup by very gently and briefly melting the honey and other ingredients with the rest of the orange juice. You need 4 tablespoons of orange juice, so squeeze another or add juice from a carton if your orange wasn't juicy enough. *6* Select a serving plate that's not much bigger than the cake and that has a rim. The cake must sit flat on the plate. Pour about a third of your syrup onto the plate and place the cake on top. Spoon the rest of the syrup over the top and down the sides. Cover the cake loosely with clingfilm and leave it to stand for several hours or overnight to soak up the syrup.

Nutrient analysis per serving: Calories 364; Protein 6g; Carbohydrate 42g; Sugar 27g; Fat 20g; Saturated fat 8g; Fibre 1g; Salt 0.3g.

Making and Taking Sweet Treats

Some desserts are just meant for eating at home. This is fine if the get-together is at your house, but what if the party's somewhere else and the host asks you to bring a dessert? What can you bring to picnics? What packs and travels well for a sweet treat in the kids' lunchboxes? What if you just want a gluten-free sugar fix? We're glad you asked.

Chocolate Marshmallow Bars

Very few sweet snacks have withstood the test of time like marshmallow bars. But most cereals that cooks use to make those bars have gluten in them, so they're usually unsuitable. Try this simple variation using gluten-free chocolate puffed-rice breakfast cereal.

Preparation time: 30 minutes • **Refrigeration time:** 10 minutes • **Makes:** 12 servings

Ingredients	Directions
Non-stick oil spray, for greasing the dish	*1* Spray a 20-by-30-centimetre (8-by-12-inch) tin or dish liberally with non-stick oil.
55 grams/2 ounces unsalted butter	*2* Put the butter into a large saucepan to melt over a low heat. Add the marshmallows and, stirring constantly, cook until they have completely melted and the mixture is smooth. Remove the pan from the heat.
285 grams/10 ounces (usually 1 packet) marshmallows	
100 grams/3½ ounces dried fruit, preferably brightly coloured	*3* Chop the fruit into small pieces and add it to the pan along with the cereal. Mix well to coat everything thoroughly with the marshmallow mixture.
170 grams/6 ounces gluten-free chocolate puffed-rice breakfast cereal	*4* Spread the warm mixture into the tin. Using a spatula coated with non-stick spray, coax the mixture into an even layer without crushing the cereal too much.
	5 Refrigerate the pan for ten minutes and then cut the mixture into bars. If you prefer, you can put the bars back into the fridge to make them really cold.

Nutrient analysis per serving: Calories 180; Protein 2g; Carbohydrate 35g; Sugar 24g; Fat 4g; Saturated fat 3g; Fibre 1g; Salt 0.2g.

Fruity Caramel Popcorn Balls

In keeping with the cereal-makes-good-desserts theme, this recipe calls for any gluten-free puffed-rice cereal.

Preparation time: 20 minutes • **Makes:** 20 servings

Ingredients	Directions
115 grams/4 ounces gluten-free puffed-rice cereal	*1* In a large bowl, combine the cereal, popcorn and peanuts.
15 grams/½ ounce popped plain popcorn	*2* In a small microwave-safe bowl, heat the butter and caramel topping on high for one minute or until melted. Stir until smooth.
70 grams/2½ ounces peanuts	*3* Pour the caramel mixture over the cereal mixture and stir well to combine.
40 grams/1½ ounces butter	*4* Spread the mixture onto greaseproof paper and leave to cool. When cool enough to touch safely, shape the caramel cereal into balls the size of a golf ball. Cool completely and store the popcorn balls in an airtight container.
55 grams/2 ounces caramel sauce ice-cream topping	

Nutrient analysis per serving: Calories 113; Protein 3g; Carbohydrate 11g; Sugar 4g; Fat 6g; Saturated fat 3g; Fibre 0.5g; Salt 0.2g.

Sweet pastry

For individual tartlets to be filled with fresh fruit and cream or perhaps jam or lemon curd, this is the pastry to go for. It works for double-crusted mince pies too, but do be sure to get gluten-free mincemeat or make your own, omitting the suet. You could use the pastry for any of the classic sweet tarts such as lemon meringue pie, frangipane and fruit, tarte au citron, custard tart, treacle tart with gluten-free breadcrumbs, chocolate tart or Bakewell. The quantity is enough for 12 small open tartlets, 6 double-crusted ones or a 20-centimetre/8-inch flan. Here's what you need:

85 grams/3 ounces brown rice flour

85 grams/3 ounces fine cornmeal

55 grams/2 ounces chickpea flour

30 grams/1 ounce caster sugar

1 teaspoon xanthan gum

100 grams/3.5 ounces butter

1 egg

Process the dry ingredients with the butter to the breadcrumb stage. Then add the egg and process again. Roll out a little thicker than you would for wheat pastry, using a light dusting of cornmeal.

Zebra Meringues

These delicious meringue biscuits are incredibly easy to make, but they give the impression that you've spent hours in the kitchen baking them.

Preparation time: 15 minutes • **Cooking time:** 2 hours • **Makes:** 40 meringues

Ingredients	Directions
Non-stick oil spray, for greasing the trays	*1* Preheat the oven to 180°C/Gas Mark 4. Lightly grease two baking trays with non-stick oil spray.
3 egg whites	
Pinch of cream of tartar	*2* Use an electric beater to beat the egg whites at high speed until they're foamy.
100 grams/3½ ounces caster sugar	*3* Add the cream of tartar. Beat the whites until they form stiff peaks.
1 teaspoon natural vanilla extract	
185 grams/6½ ounces dark chocolate, cut into small pieces or drops	*4* Add the sugar gradually, while beating. Then add the vanilla, beating it in.
	5 Using a wooden spatula, fold in the chocolate.
	6 Use a teaspoon to drop the meringue batter onto the greased baking trays; one teaspoonful for each meringue. Place the tray in the oven and turn the oven off. Leave in the oven for approximately two hours. Remove and store in an airtight container.

Nutrient analysis per serving: Calories 34; Protein 1g; Carbohydrate 5g; Sugar 5g; Fat 1g; Saturated fat 1g; Fibre 1g; Salt 0.1g.

Tickling the Tastebuds at Tea-Time

The old song says that when the clock strikes four in England, everything stops for tea. Sometimes we stop for more than just a reviving hot drink, and 'tea' becomes a light afternoon meal or a snack. Tea-time can be a lovely occasion to socialise or to entertain, especially with children present, and a tea is so much easier to prepare and clear up than a dinner party. The only downside is that the usual tea table is loaded with gluten, yet gluten-free cakes, biscuits and scones aren't difficult to make. Here are three recipes to get you started, and you'll find more ideas in our breakfast suggestions in Chapter 10 and tips on adapting conventional recipes to be gluten-free in Chapter 9.

Sultana Scones

You may be surprised to know that these gluten-free scones are easier to make than their glutenous cousins. Why? Because when you cut the dough, it cuts cleanly without squashing the edges, so in the oven nothing stops the scones from rising. This means they're lighter and easier to split.

Preparation time: 15 minutes • **Cooking time:** 12 to 15 minutes • **Makes:** 12

Ingredients	Directions
55 grams/2 ounces sultanas 140 grams/5 ounces brown rice flour	*1* Preheat the oven to 200°C/Gas Mark 6. Wash the sultanas and pour on 3 tablespoons of boiling water and leave them to soak while you proceed.
30 grams/1 ounce potato flour 85 grams/3 ounces white teff	*2* Mix together all the dry ingredients apart from the sugar, and rub the butter in with your fingertips. You can use a processor, but it's not worth the washing up you create.
1 teaspoon baking powder 1 teaspoon bicarbonate of soda 85 grams/3 ounces butter, cubed	*3* Drain and pat dry the sultanas and stir them in with the sugar. Beat the egg and buttermilk together and mix most of it into the scone mix with a fork. Don't add all the liquid, because you want a stiff but smooth dough. If it's too wet, it won't roll out, so add a touch more rice flour. If it's dry and cracking, add extra liquid and knead in by hand.
30 grams/1 ounce caster sugar 1 large egg 4 tablespoons buttermilk	*4* Dredge a slab or worktop with a tiny dusting of rice flour and roll and pat out the dough to a thickness of 2 to 3 centimetres or around 1 inch – probably thicker than normal. Cut out the scones with a plain 4-centimetre/1½-inch round cutter or with a blade into squares and then triangles. Unlike when using wheat dough, you can gather up the scraps and re-roll them, because there's no gluten to be overworked. Place on a non-stick baking sheet or greased tray.
	4 Brush the tops only (not the sides) with the remaining egg-and-buttermilk mixture and bake for 12 to 15 minutes.

Nutrient analysis per serving: Calories 151; Protein 3g; Carbohydrate 22g; Sugar 6g; Fat 6g; Saturated fat 4g; Fibre 1g; Salt 0.4g.

Carrot Cake or Cupcakes

These are deliciously moist just as they are, but if you want to add a creamy topping, beat together 225 grams/8 ounces light cream cheese with 3 tablespoons of low-fat yoghurt and 2 to 3 teaspoons of caster sugar.

Preparation time: 20 minutes • **Cooking time:** 1 hour for large cake, 35 minutes for cupcakes.
Makes 8 to 10 servings

Ingredients	*Directions*
140 millilitres/¼ pint skimmed milk	*1* Preheat the oven to 180°C/Gas Mark 4. Line a deep 20-centimetre/8-inch cake tin with baking parchment or set out 8 to 10 large muffin cups in muffin tins.
1 tablespoon lemon juice	
115 grams/4 ounces butter	*2* Mix the milk with the lemon juice and set aside to curdle. Warm the butter and brown sugar together to melt them. Place all the dry ingredients, with the carrots, fruit and nuts, into a mixing bowl.
170 grams/6 ounces soft dark-brown sugar	
225 grams/8 ounces carrots, processed or grated finely	
115 grams/4 ounces raisins	*3* Pour in the melted mixture along with the beaten egg and milk and lemon juice mixture, and stir the lot together thoroughly. Pour the cake mix into the tin or cups. You can fill the cups fairly full but not right to the brim. You may get ten, depending on their size.
115 grams/4 ounces chopped dates	
55 grams/2 ounces chopped nuts	
170 grams/6 ounces brown rice flour	*4* Bake for one hour for a large cake and 35 minutes for cupcakes. If the large cake appears to be getting scorched, put a sheet of brown paper over the top. The cake(s) are done when a cocktail stick pushed into the centre comes out clean.
70 grams/2½ ounces tapioca starch	
1 teaspoon xanthan gum	
1 teaspoon baking powder	
2 teaspoons bicarbonate of soda	
1½ teaspoons mixed spice	
1 large egg, beaten	

Nutrient analysis per serving: Calories 356; Protein 4g; Carbohydrate 56g; Sugar 36g; Fat 14g; Saturated fat 6g; Fibre 2.5g; Salt 0.9g.

Incredibly Easy Peanut Butter Cookies

By definition, a cookie can be any of a variety of flour-based sweet biscuits. We break all the rules with this recipe, because it uses no flour. Best of all, the cookies are incredibly easy – you only need four ingredients!

Preparation time: 5 minutes • **Cooking time:** 20 minutes • **Makes:** 24 cookies

Ingredients	*Directions*
Non-stick oil spray, for greasing the baking tray	*1* Preheat the oven to 180°C/Gas Mark 4. Lightly grease two baking trays with non-stick oil spray.
2 large eggs **255 grams/9 ounces chunky peanut butter**	*2* Beat the eggs in a medium-sized bowl. Stir the peanut butter and sugar into the eggs.
200 grams/7 ounces granulated sugar	*3* Drop dollops of dough from a spoon onto a baking tray about 5 centimetres (2 inches) apart. Use the back of a fork to press them flat.
	4 Bake the cookies for 10 to 12 minutes or until the cookies spring back a little when you press them.

Nutrient analysis per serving: Calories 106; Protein 4g; Carbohydrate 9g; Sugar 9g; Fat 6g; Saturated fat 1g; Fibre 1g; Salt 0.1g.

Going Easy: Health-Conscious Desserts

'Healthy dessert' – isn't that an oxymoron? For the most part, desserts can be like land mines in the Battle of the Bulge and the Hunt for Health, sabotaging even your most determined attempts to eat well. Most of the recipes we've seen for healthy desserts usually just make for unappetising, tasteless, no-substance affairs.

But you *can* satisfy without sabotage and still keep the dessert gluten-free. In fact, some of the recipes we offer in this section are downright good for you, so you can enjoy them as part of a gluten-free, guilt-free, well-balanced diet.

Try sautéing fruits such as apples, pears or bananas over a medium-high heat in sugar (or sucralose artificial sweetener, sold as Splenda) and water until they're caramelised a little. Doing so adds a caramel flavour without the fat of a caramel sauce.

Hot Banana Crunch

Cooking bananas gives them a great texture and intensified flavour, and in this recipe you get a sweet, tangy sauce and a crunchy topping to set them off.

Preparation time: 10 minutes • **Cooking time:** 30 minutes • **Makes:** 6 servings

Ingredients	Directions
1 teaspoon soft butter **6 bananas** **3 tablespoons honey (preferably runny)** **3 tablespoons lemon juice** **85 grams/3 ounces flaked almonds**	*1* Preheat the oven to 200°C/Gas Mark 6. Select an oven-proof dish large enough to hold the bananas in one layer, and brush it with the soft butter.
	2 Peel the bananas and lay them in the dish.
	3 Spread the honey all over the bananas and drizzle over the lemon juice. Scatter the almonds evenly over the top.
	4 Bake uncovered for 30 minutes. Serve hot with your choice of cold toppings such as low-fat vanilla yoghurt, fromage frais, gluten-free chocolate or red fruit dessert sauce, ground cinnamon or nutmeg or a swirl of maple syrup or pomegranate molasses.

Nutrient analysis per serving without toppings: Calories 200; Protein 4g; Carbohydrate 30g; Sugar 27g; Fat 8g; Saturated fat 1g; Fibre 2g; Salt 0.01g.

Blueberry Parfait

No need to peel, de-seed, core, dice, slice or chop these berries. They're easy to cook, delicious and available fresh and frozen all year round.

Preparation time: 30 minutes • **Freezing time:** 2 hours • **Makes:** 4 servings

Ingredients	*Directions*
300 grams/10½ ounces blueberries	*1* In a medium-sized saucepan, stir together the blueberries and sugar.
55 grams/2 ounces granulated sugar	*2* In a small bowl, mix the cornflour and water together until the cornflour dissolves.
2 tablespoons cornflour	
55 millilitres/2 fluid ounces cold water	*3* Add the cornflour–water mixture to the blueberries and sugar, and bring to the boil over a medium heat, stirring well. Let it boil for one minute. Stir in the lemon juice, and allow to cool.
1 tablespoon fresh lemon juice	
225 grams/8 ounces low-fat plain yoghurt	*4* Gently fold the yoghurt into the cooled blueberry mixture, being careful not to crush the berries.
325 grams/11½ ounces fresh strawberries, sliced	*5* In four separate glass dishes, layer some of the blueberry mixture and then some strawberries, and then the blueberry mixture again. Keep alternating layers until the dishes are full and you've used all the ingredients.
	6 Freeze the parfaits for at least two hours. Take them out of the freezer 30 minutes before serving.

Tip: Serve your favourite gluten-free biscuits with these parfaits.

Nutrient analysis per serving: Calories 151; Protein 4g; Carbohydrate 32g; Sugar 29g; Fat 1g; Saturated fat 0g; Fibre 3g; Salt 0.1g.

Luscious-But-Light Cheesecake

Really, the best part of any cheesecake is the soft custard. This cheesecake seems decadent but it's actually quite light – the perfect indulgence.

Preparation time: 10 minutes • **Cooking time:** 20 to 30 minutes • **Makes:** 8 servings

Ingredients	*Directions*
Non-stick oil spray, for greasing the dish	**1** Preheat the oven to 180°C/Gas Mark 4.
225 grams/8 ounces (usually 1 packet) light cream cheese	**2** Lightly grease a 23-centimetre (9-inch) round loose-bottomed tin with the oil spray.
100 grams/3½ ounces caster sugar	**3** Combine the cream cheese, sugar, eggs, lemon juice, vanilla and flour. Pour this mixture into the tin, and bake for 20 to 30 minutes. The cheesecake is done when you insert a skewer in the centre and it comes out clean.
2 large eggs, beaten	
2 tablespoons fresh lemon juice	
1 teaspoon natural vanilla extract	**4** After the cheesecake has cooled completely, take it out of the tin. Meanwhile, prepare the fruit. If you're using tinned or poached fruit like peaches or apricots, or fresh strawberries, slice them. Fresh raspberries or stoned sweet cherries would be nice raw, dusted with the icing sugar and left to make a glaze. Or you could use frozen mixed berries that you thaw and cook very gently with a little sugar. These may need thickening with half a teaspoon of arrowroot mixed with water and cooked in briefly. Arrange the fruit on top of the cheesecake and chill.
30 grams/1 ounce white rice flour	
225 grams/8 ounces fresh, frozen or tinned soft fruit	
2 tablespoons icing sugar (optional)	

Nutrient analysis per serving: Calories 150; Protein 5g; Carbohydrate 23g; Sugar 19g; Fat 5g; Saturated fat 3g; Fibre 1g; Salt 0.3g.

Chocolate Trice Pudding

Made in a few minutes, this is one for the kids. Or for adults, try adding spirits or liqueur such as dark rum, whisky, brandy or an orange or cherry liqueur.

Preparation time: 15 minutes • **Makes:** 2 servings

Ingredients	*Directions*
284 millilitres/½ pint skimmed milk	*1* Warm everything except the egg together in a sauce-pan and stir. Bring the mixture briefly to the boil and then lower the heat immediately.
50 grams/1¾ ounces flaked white rice	
30 grams/1 ounce drinking chocolate powder, preferably flavoured	*2* Cook gently for about 15 minutes without too much stirring – just enough to stop it sticking. Add more milk if the mixture is too thick.
½ teaspoon vanilla extract	
1 tablespoon liqueur or spirit (optional)	*3* Add the beaten egg and stir in. Warm just enough to cook the egg. Stir in the liqueur or spirit if using. Serve warm.
1 egg, well-beaten	

Nutrient analysis per serving: Calories 223; Protein 11g; Carbohydrate 35g; Sugar 16g; Fat 4g; Saturated fat 1g; Fibre 0g; Salt 0.2g.

Fabulous fruit – cold desserts and hot puddings

Humans do love their sweets. If you give a baby a spoonful of ice cream and one of sour cream, you don't need a team of researchers and a multi-million-pound, placebo-controlled, double-blind study to guess which brings a smile and which makes the baby grimace.

We all need glucose – that's the sugar that powers the body. But you can make enough glucose from fruit, vegetables and starchy carbohydrate foods. With these foods you also get the added benefit of vitamins, minerals, fibre and antioxidants for far fewer calories than the 'empty calories' you find in sugary foods. So satisfy your sweet tooth, but try to do so with foods that pack a nutritional punch, like these:

- **Chocolate–hazelnut spread fruit dip:** Warm up the chocolate–hazelnut spread a little and dip fresh fruit in it.

- **Grapes and Chantilly-style cream:** Combine reduced-fat sour cream, icing sugar, sucralose artificial sweetener (Splenda) and a dash of vanilla extract. Mix the cream with red, green and black grapes.

- **Peaches 'n' cream:** Place half a peach or pear in a dish and add a small scoop of vanilla frozen yoghurt. Scatter with raspberries or strawberries.

- **Strawberries and yoghurt:** Slice strawberries and blend them with low-fat fruit yoghurt. Top the mixture with artificial sweetener if you like a little extra sweetness.

- **Strawberry sweet and sour:** Dip fresh strawberries into reduced-fat sour cream and then into artificial sweetener or honey.

For hot fruit puddings, it's hard to beat a homely sponge, crumble or shortcake topping, served with custard. You can find a recipe for custard in Chapter 14, and for the puddings, here are some ideas to go with enough cooking fruit for six people. Try apples, gooseberries, rhubarb, pears and plums. You need to part-cook the fruit with sugar on the hob, using the bare minimum of water, if any, because you don't want the fruit too watery. Then top with one of the following and bake in the oven at 190°C/Gas Mark 5 for about 35 minutes.

- **Sponge:** Beat together 85 grams/3 ounces each of butter, caster sugar and brown rice flour with a large egg, ½ a teaspoon xanthan gum and 1½ teaspoons of baking powder. Butter the sides of the dish above the fruit, put spoonfuls of the mix on top of the fruit (any gaps will close up in the oven) and bake.

- **Crumble:** Briefly process 55 grams/2 ounces each of brown rice flour, cornmeal and demerara sugar with 30 grams/1 ounce of chickpea flour and 85 grams/3 ounces of butter, leaving the mixture slightly lumpy. Sprinkle it over the fruit and bake.

- **Streusel:** You can turn crumble into streusel using our crumble recipe with a little extra butter left in visible pieces, plus 55 grams/2 ounces finely chopped nuts mixed in. Try baking this separately in a tray and then strewing it over cold fruit for a bit of extra crunch.

- **Shortcake:** Briefly process 30 grams/1 ounce each of white teff, brown rice flour and cornmeal, with a pinch of cinnamon, 55 grams/2 ounces butter and 40 grams/1½ ounces soft brown sugar. Add an egg yolk and process again until it forms a dough. Roll this out thickly or just pat it out with your hands and lift it carefully onto the fruit. Don't worry about sealing the edges. Bake. If you prefer, you can bake the shortbread separately in a sandwich cake tin and serve it in wedges with the fruit.

Part V
Living – and Loving – the Gluten-Free Lifestyle

 Go to www.dummies.com/extras/livingglutenfreeuk for online bonus content.

Living – and Loving –
the Gluten-Free Lifestyle

In this part . . .

- ✔ Avoid gluten pitfalls when dining out, at parties and at friends' houses.
- ✔ Speak gluten-free when you're abroad.
- ✔ Help your child to go gluten-free safely and happily.
- ✔ Involve the family in gluten-free meal times.
- ✔ Get back on track when you feel derailed.
- ✔ Go to www.dummies.com/extras/livingglutenfreeuk for online bonus content.

Chapter 17

Getting Out and About: Gluten-Free Eating Away from Home

*F*or many people, following a gluten-free diet at home isn't their biggest challenge – the problem is managing that diet away from home. Even people who've been gluten-free for years can find that eating out is difficult at times, but the good news is that it's getting easier.

We believe that eating out is an important part of life. And it appears most Brits agree. British people buy 11 billion meals a year – on average 180 per person – out of the home in restaurants, hotels, workplace canteens, pubs, sandwich shops, cafés, grab 'n' go outlets and takeaways. And that doesn't include meals at schools, in hospitals, in care homes or at Her Majesty's pleasure. Nor does it include eating out at conferences, corporate entertainment events or private functions. And eating out has become a 24/7 activity, with quick-service breakfasts now one of the fastest-growing markets.

And if you have the enticing prospect of overseas travel, that will definitely involve eating out at some stage, from grabbing a quick snack at the airport to eating out for the whole trip.

___

Phew – eating out is getting easier!

Gluten-free eating out really has been getting easier in recent years – at least in the UK.

When just diagnosed with coeliac disease, Hilary had an invitation sitting on the mantelpiece to a big catered birthday dinner, and she knew about a hundred people would be there. The hosts had thoughtfully asked guests to indicate any special dietary needs in the RSVP, and so Hilary rather apologetically replied that she needed a gluten-free meal. It was a surprise and a relief when her friends called to say she'd be one of three people eating gluten-free that evening, and that they'd already agreed the necessary and very minor alterations to the menu with the caterer. On the night, a fabulous gluten-free meal was served with no fuss whatsoever and no need to explain anything to anyone, because it looked very similar to everyone else's.

The point is, you're not alone or even all that unusual. The demand for gluten-free food out of the home has meant that the food-service industry is now well-served with gluten-free options to put on menus and, on the whole, it understands your needs and the importance of keeping your food strictly free of gluten. After all, food providers want your business. The market value of gluten-free diners and others eating with them has been estimated at £100 million a year. Food providers want you to enjoy the dining experience, feel safe, come back again and again, and recommend them to other people. And although home entertaining does require a little forethought, the trend now is to serve an entirely gluten-free meal to everyone, or at least one that you can make gluten-free by substituting or leaving out just one or two minor items. In fact, keen cooks seem to enjoy the challenge.

___

So whether you're having lunch with clients, enjoying a romantic dinner for two, travelling for business or touring the world for pleasure, you're sure to be eating out sometime. And unless you want to miss out, you need to know how to cope with eating away from home gluten-free.

Eating Out Gluten-Free – Tips and Tricks

Imagine that you've just arrived at the party of the year. You're feeling energised, looking fabulous and are eager to spend a great evening chatting with friends. And you're famished. You head for the buffet table, and it's loaded with the most amazing spread; then slowly you begin to realise that you can't eat any of it. Your mood plummets as fast as your panic rises, because you realise you're going to be there all night with nothing to eat.

In this section, we give you some tips about eating out gluten-free. Planning ahead should prevent such a depressing scenario from happening, because you have no reason to let a little food (or lack of it) ruin a good time. Armed with these practical guidelines, your gluten-free social experiences can be as good as ever.

Don't be a diet bore

Whatever the occasion, wherever you're eating, if you're with other people you want to try to avoid discussing your health and diet while they're eating. If you get into protracted discussions with the waiter or your host about what's gluten-free and what isn't, you inevitably end up chatting with other guests about your condition, particularly your symptoms, diagnosis and what happens if you do eat gluten. We're frequently amazed at the detail people seem to require, and once the questions start, you struggle to stop them.

Also, you may feel a subtle pressure to eat what everyone else is having and stop making an issue out of it, particularly if you didn't have any obvious symptoms before your diagnosis. Some people wonder why a little bread can be so dangerous for you if you won't even notice any ill effects. But it's best to avoid justifying your diet at the dinner table.

We find simply saying you're allergic to gluten helps to stop chitchat in its tracks. If you say you can't tolerate gluten, you imply you have a choice and are just being difficult. Being prepared with an allergy-related answer usually means you avoid an embarrassing and intrusive discussion altogether.

Relying on others to adapt to your diet

The office party is coming up in two months. Realising that food is obviously going to be provided, you arrange to meet the person planning the party and you explain your dietary restrictions, right down to the sometimes intricate details of the gluten-free diet. She's making a good show of understanding you, nodding in the appropriate places, even adding an, 'Oh, so you probably can't eat the bread rolls?' Great! She understands! Don't rely on it. And whatever you do, don't expect it. If she succeeds and you see gluten-free goodies on the table, be thankful and appreciative. She didn't have to make the effort to meet your dietary needs, but she did. And if everything goes wrong or you encounter a little slip-up, be gracious about it. Don't eat the offending food, but don't make your host feel a failure.

Really, you can't *expect* anyone to accommodate your gluten-free diet – no matter who they are. Even those closest to you – those you love most – are going to forget or make mistakes. Errors don't happen because people don't care. Often, the lack of gluten-free goodies is just an oversight, or sometimes people think that they understand the diet but they overlook some of the intricacies, and what they thought is gluten-free isn't. They didn't know that the stock cubes they used in the gravy contained wheat flour, or they just forgot and added a shake of soy sauce to the salad dressing. Accept that you mustn't rely on anyone to accommodate your gluten-free dietary requirements.

Asking what's for dinner

Asking what's on the menu isn't rude, depending on how you go about it. When you're gluten-free and attending a dinner party, asking the host what's for dinner isn't going to put you on the social circuit blacklist. Increasingly, hosts ask their guests about any special dietary requirements ahead of time, and do their best to accommodate them. So that gives you an opening to bring up the subject.

If you have to broach the subject yourself, we suggest a tactful, 'I have a dietary restriction and was wondering whether it would be okay to ask you about what you're serving so I can plan accordingly?' People are generally receptive to such an approach and may even ask for your input. The last thing they want is to serve food that doesn't agree with someone or have you sitting at the table unable to eat a bite, particularly if they've gone to a lot of trouble and expense to lay on a lavish dinner.

Filling up before you go

If you know the event won't include a sit-down meal – perhaps it's a buffet or finger-food offered around while the guests mingle – you can avoid eating altogether if nothing is suitable for you. Just saying 'Not for me, thanks' or steering clear of the buffet table won't go amiss. You can easily do so without drawing attention to yourself.

You can't expect to see gluten-free goodies at this sort of party, and you can hardly interrogate the waiters about every item on offer – they simply won't know. So fill up before you go, especially if you plan to have alcohol and you want to avoid drinking on an empty stomach. That way you're not ravenous and fixated on food, and don't feel tempted to risk it and eat something that turns out to have gluten lurking in it. You can enjoy the party for what it's really all about, which is fun and friends.

Bringing your own food

We're not suggesting that you walk into a formal soirée carrying bags of fast food, wafting the smell of fries among guests in dinner jackets. That sort of grand entrance may not go down well. Luckily, this sort of do is usually professionally catered, and you'll receive questions in advance about your needs. All that's necessary is a quiet word with the head waiter or maître d' when you arrive. If you do plan to bring any food, the setting and details such as your outfit and where you've parked do, of course, determine the type of food you bring. If it's an informal or business event, bringing along a few crackers or oatcakes just in case is generally acceptable.

If you're staying overnight in a private house or going to friends for supper, a nice gesture is to offer to bring your own bread and a gluten-free dessert or tea-time treat for everyone to enjoy – not just you – as long as your host is happy with that. Such an offer is especially welcome at Christmas and other festive weekends when cakes, puddings and pies play a big part in the celebrations. For ideas, check out our recipes in Chapter 16 and suggestions for adapting conventional wheat-based recipes in Chapter 9.

Biting your tongue

You've spoken to the hosts about their plans for the meal, and they've offered to make a few accommodations for you. You get to the party only to find nothing but filled filo pastries and deep-fried breadcrumb canapés. Do you:

A) Starve?

B) Starve, and grumble at the hostess?

C) Pick the innards out of the filo pastries (please don't, they're contaminated with gluten!)?

D) None of the above. You enjoy the party and relax. You weren't hungry anyway, because you filled up before you came out.

The correct answer, of course, is D.

Dining Out

Eating out at a terrific restaurant is a treat. Good company, a nice ambience, respectful service and delicious food combine to create an experience that's about far more than just the food.

Being on a gluten-free diet shouldn't stop you from having these experiences. Yes, eating out does involve some risk. Unless you see a gluten-free label or someone tells you a dish is gluten-free, you don't know for sure what's in it. No matter how much you try to educate the waiting staff and chef, when they're busy, staff can (and do) make mistakes, and cross-contamination is always an issue. And by the law of averages, at least once in your gluten-free dining days you're sure to receive a salad with croutons that you send back.

But with just a little extra planning and effort, you can help ensure that your meal is safely gluten-free, and you can enjoy gluten-free dining as one of life's more pleasurable social experiences.

Choosing the restaurant

We may be stating the obvious, but if you choose an outlet that deals mainly with limited types of food, you're setting yourself up for frustration and disappointment. Try to avoid restaurants that, by the very nature of their menus, aren't likely to have much (if anything) that's gluten-free.

Instead, go to restaurants that have a large and diverse menu selection, or choose one that's likely to have more gluten-free foods like steaks and salads or foods that the kitchen staff can easily modify.

Phone ahead. Give details of your dietary requirements when making your table reservation, or ring separately if someone else has made the booking. Ask what the restaurant's policy is for catering for people on a gluten-free diet. Say what foods you can't eat, in case the staff don't know what gluten is (although that's less likely nowadays). Ask whether they can email you a menu or whether it's on their website. If you feel they don't understand what you mean or you sense they're not taking you seriously, we suggest you move on to a different place. You may encounter places that tell you they simply can't cater for you. Fair enough. You'll find other places that can.

Check out Coeliac UK's venue guide on www.coeliac.org.uk. It has over 2,000 venues where you can eat out gluten-free. Note that a listing doesn't mean every-thing on offer is gluten-free, only that the venue has options for you. Also look through other databases such as www.go-gluten-free-wheat-free.co.uk, www.gluten-free-onthego.com, www.glutenfreefoodie.co.uk and www.glutenfreemrsd.com.

Finding fast food

One good thing about fast-food places is that they generally follow stan-dardised recipes and methods for food preparation. Visit their websites or call their head offices to get answers to your questions about dedicated fryers, ingredients and gluten-free items. For instance, many offer fries, shakes, salads, ice creams and sauces that are gluten-free.

If you fancy a burger, make sure that it's 100 per cent meat with no cereal fill-ers, and order it without the bun – even if you leave the bun on your plate, it has still contaminated your burger. Some fast-food places offer lettuce as a wrap instead of a bun, even when they don't advertise it, and some are happy to put a burger inside a gluten-free roll if you provide one, although you're better off doing this yourself at the table.

When you're ordering chips or roast potatoes, make sure they're not battered or coated in anything. Roast potatoes are increasingly being coated in semo-lina to give them a crisp outer layer. For anything deep-fried, ask what other foods are fried in the same oil. You don't want to order fries that have been swimming with battered onion rings or samosas.

If you eat at fast-food restaurants often, put any relevant information into a small file and keep it in your car. That way, when you're pulling in to one of your favourites, you have a handy list of its gluten-free items.

Eating international

International restaurants can be a real bonus to the gluten-free diner, but always ask how the chefs prepare their traditional fare. Double-check doubtful ingredients and consider whether cross-contamination issues are likely to be a problem. Most international restaurants are more than happy to share the secrets of their national cuisine.

Many foods from international cuisines are naturally gluten-free. You need to work out which cuisines you like and, among those, the foods that are inherently gluten-free. Then you can choose a restaurant of that variety and know what to order. Mexican, Thai, Vietnamese, Japanese and Indian cuisines are just a few that may offer gluten-free dishes. But, as with any meal, you need to make sure that the kitchen staff don't add flour to the sauces, and ask about the grains used in, for example, tortillas, noodles and flatbreads. Be careful: not all are going to be gluten-free, but they may be safe if they're corn- or rice-based. Instead of soy sauce, Thai cooking often uses fish sauce, and Japanese cooking uses tamari, so these cuisines are more likely to be gluten-free, but don't take this as read – always check.

Be wary of Chinese restaurants, because they use soy sauce in many, if not most, of their dishes, and most soy sauce contains wheat. Why? We don't know either.

Stir-fry restaurants and Pan Asian noodle bars are popping up all over the UK and, generally, they're happy to cook your dish to order in an individual wok. The rice and buckwheat noodle (soba) dishes are generally safe, but some can be mixed with wheat flour – do ask before you order.

Most sushi, including the accompaniments such as seaweed, pickled vegetables, ginger and wasabi, is usually gluten-free, but again beware of soy sauce glazes, and watch out for 'imitation' crab, which contains wheat. Any sushi chef worth his salt can tell you what's in the ingredients he uses. An alternative is sashimi, plain fish and steamed rice, which uses fewer sauces and is generally gluten-free.

Other good bets

As a general rule, other types of restaurants that are a good bet include:

- **Soup and salad bars:** Not only do these chains usually offer lots of gluten-free items, but they also often have their ingredients handy, so you can check soups and salad dressings to be certain. Sometimes, they post ingredients on placards in front of the item. If not, ask a member of staff to provide you with a list of ingredients.

✔ **Barbecues:** Although you do have to check the sauces, many barbecues are good bets because they serve traditional fare such as spare ribs, chicken, fish, corn on the cob, jacket potatoes and salad.

✔ **Greasy spoons:** Ask for freshly cooked eggs and bacon and bring your own gluten-free bread (pop it in a toaster bag, and they may even toast it for you). You can order tomatoes, mushrooms, fried potatoes (check the hash browns), fruit, yoghurt and lots of other good gluten-free breakfast foods too, but avoid the sausages.

✔ **Steak and seafood:** These restaurants have steaks and/or burgers, seafood, salads (hold the croutons), baked potatoes, rice and chips, although check that the oil hasn't been used for battered or crumbed items.

Risky restaurants

You can get gluten-free meals at some of these restaurants, but in general those that aren't going to be a good bet include:

✔ **Bakeries:** We probably didn't need to point that out, did we? Even cakes like meringues and macaroons, which are inherently gluten-free, can become contaminated during cooking or storage.

✔ **Italian:** Most Italian restaurants serve wheat-based pasta, pizza and breaded dishes. But some offer gluten-free pasta and pizza bases with a range of sauces and toppings (just ensure they use clean pans and other utensils and fresh water to boil the pasta), plus polenta, potatoes and risotto. And of course you can enjoy their wonderful (crouton-free) salads or a variety of grilled meat or fish dishes.

When ordering any dish, you still need to remind the staff that crumbs from gluten-containing foods can cause cross-contamination issues with baking trays, serving spoons and pans.

✔ **Speciality coffee shops:** The trendy coffee shops you're familiar with offer foods and snacks, and most have a gluten-free wrapped brownie, flapjack, cookie, fruit-and-nut bar or cake on offer. One or two offer wrapped gluten-free sandwiches and rolls, along with pre-packed salads. All these packs are labelled, so it's easy to give them a final check before you tuck in.

✔ **Chippies:** Usually, only one type of batter is in use, and it's not the gluten-free kind, and also one fryer for the fish and one draining cabinet for everything. At quiet times, they might do a pan-fried fish fillet for you, and the mushy peas should be okay. Having said that, some enterprising chippies are doing gluten-free nights, so keep an eye out for local promotion of these.

✔ **Motorway services:** Don't expect to find any gluten-free food in the restaurant, but you can generally find salad boxes, sandwiches, crisps, cakes and nut bars in the other outlets at the services, such as the shops, supermarkets, coffee bars and filling stations. The restaurants don't seem to mind if you take this food in to eat if you buy a drink there.

Looking out for clearer gluten info

Eating out in public places is about to get a whole lot easier in the EU, thanks to a new directive called the Food Information Regulation. This was published in 2011, but allows suppliers until the end of 2014 to comply. In a nutshell, caterers must provide information on the presence of cereals containing gluten in your food. The information must be provided at the point you're choosing what to eat and when it's delivered to you, just in case you missed it the first time around. The information might be on the menu or labels as well as on promotional items like displays, brochures and websites, many of which you can look at before you go. Suppliers can also tell you verbally, and you're entitled to ask for more detailed information if you want.

The law doesn't compel suppliers to offer gluten-free food but only to alert their customers to where gluten is present. But it's possible that if outlets see that everything on the menu contains gluten, they might want to introduce gluten-free options. And they can't get away with slapping 'may contain' warnings over everything just in case. Any 'may contain gluten' statement must be based on scientific data such as a test or obvious cross-contamination. For more information on food labelling, head to Chapter 5.

Remember: you won't always see and hear the word 'gluten' in warnings about foods that contain it or may contain it. The presence of gluten-containing cereals such as wheat must be pointed out to you, not the presence of gluten as such.

Making smart menu choices

Set yourself up for success. Choose menu items that are likely to be gluten-free or that the kitchen staff can easily modify to be gluten-free. Obviously, breaded and fried items aren't going to be your best choices, although sometimes cooks can use the same meat, season it and grill it instead.

So, do you order the fish in a beery batter? Not a good choice. The Chinese pork stir-fry with noodles? No. Fried chicken? Probably not. Grilled chicken? Quite possibly. Grilled fish? Steak? Very likely. Of course, you need to ask a few questions to be sure, but at least you're on the right track.

Ordering is a four-step process:

1. **Find the foods on the menu that are already likely to be gluten-free or that you think the chef can easily modify to be gluten-free.**

2. **Choose the item(s) you want.**

3. **Ask about ingredients and food preparation methods.**

4. **Make sure that you've made your order clear, and asked the waiter to tell the chef that your food must be gluten-free.**

Gluten-free menus

Close your eyes and imagine being at a beautiful restaurant with great company. The waitress says, 'Hi, I'm Sarah. I'll be serving you today. Would you like to see the gluten-free menu?' Okay, you can open your eyes now, because we know how hard it is to read this book with them closed. Besides, this isn't a dream. It's a reality! Today, some restaurants offer gluten-free menus – some of them are even online. You usually need to do your research in advance, though.

You can get a helping hand with food choices from some menus that carry symbols. Coeliac UK, the national charity for people with coeliac disease, has introduced trademarked symbols for licence to catering establishments, and it runs accreditation and training programmes to back them up. The symbols, shown in Figure 17-1, highlight options on offer that are gluten-free or which have no gluten-containing ingredients. Such foods are safe for you.

Figure 17-1:
Look out for these symbols when you're eating out.

The GF fork symbol on a menu means the dish is gluten-free. It means that the restaurant has verified that its processes are sufficient to produce food that is gluten-free – food that contains no more than 20 parts per million of gluten (20 milligrams of gluten per kilogramme of food). You might see this symbol on gluten-free versions of foods that normally contain gluten, such as pizzas, and also on meals made from naturally gluten-free ingredients like fresh meat, fish, eggs, fruit and vegetables.

The NGCI ('no gluten-containing ingredients') symbol on a menu doesn't just mean that the dish doesn't include any gluten, but also that significant efforts have been made to ensure it hasn't been contaminated with gluten from other foods.

Talking to the staff

Our teenage kids hate being with us when we order food at a restaurant. All we have to do is hold up the menu and say to the waitress, 'Can we ask you a question?' and the kids start fidgeting, rolling their eyes, mumbling, 'Here we go . . .' But what's wrong with getting what you want when you're paying for your food? (Certainly, our kids don't hesitate to put in their specific requests when we're the chefs!)

Here are some tips for dealing with staff:

- **Explain that you have a health issue, not a preference.** You don't need to be specific about your condition or symptoms. You're just making the point that your health issue is important; you're not being difficult.

- **Ask whether they have a gluten-free menu, and if not, what's on offer that doesn't contain gluten.** If the waiter doesn't know what gluten is, you know you're going to have more explaining to do. It's also possible that the waiter will bring in a colleague to help you or ask the chef what would be suitable. It's always better if the staff start talking about what you can have, rather than what you can't.

- **Don't be afraid to ask for what you want.** You're paying for the meal, and you should be able to enjoy it knowing that it's safe for you to eat. Gluten-free isn't a fad diet – even small amounts of gluten can upset you. Don't ever feel like you're making an unnecessary fuss – your health is important.

- **Ask how the food is prepared.** The more you know about the preparation, the better decisions you can make when ordering. If they're using any ready-made items such as sauces, ask them to check the ingredients list.

- **Send food back if it's not right.** Of course we're not suggesting that you're rude about returning your meal, but if the restaurant gives you a salad with croutons on it, don't pick the croutons out and eat the rest. That's not safe! Politely ask, 'Are these croutons gluten-free?' Or better still, 'What are these?' Open-ended questions that the staff can't answer with a yes or no generally get you a lot more useful information.

- **Remain pleasant and appreciative.** If you're very demanding, you're going to put people on the defensive. When they accommodate your requests, show your appreciation.

Watching out for the 'Whoops!'

Whatever the menu says and however carefully you've quizzed the waiter, you still need to watch out for little mistakes – things the menu doesn't mention but that chefs do to make the food look great. Biscuit crumbs are, of course, a problem, but chefs use them quite often either as a crunchy topping or underneath desserts to stop them sliding around the plate. Croutons, croutes and breadcrumbs are another issue. And often chefs don't see drizzles of sauces both on the plate and over your food as part of the dish, and they overlook them in the description, so you've no idea what's in them.

Salad bars and buffets need particular attention. Just one gluten-containing dish there can contaminate other dishes nearby, either from being transferred directly on serving utensils or from tiny pieces like cous cous and tabbouleh dropping off serving spoons and plates.

Also beware food offered free of charge, like nibbles, bread, butter, palate-cleansers between courses and petit fours and chocolates with coffee. They may well contain gluten, even where it's not obvious.

Staying Gluten-Free When Travelling

You don't have to limit or, worse yet, give up travelling for business or pleasure because you're on a gluten-free diet. In fact, you may find that some countries are more accommodating than you imagined. For example, when you order a burger at fast-food outlets in some parts of Sweden or Finland, where there's a greater awareness of coeliac disease, they ask you whether you'd like a regular or gluten-free bun, and they even cook it on a separate gluten-free grill!

Knowing the boundaries when crossing borders

If you're travelling internationally, be aware of some special considerations. Many countries don't allow you to bring in foods, and some may, understandably, subject them to rather intense scrutiny or confiscate them at customs. In particular, you can't take any meat or dairy products from the UK into any other country.

Be aware that different countries have different standards for what's allowed on the gluten-free diet. In Europe, for instance, we commonly use Codex Alimentarius wheat starch, which has the gluten removed, and products that contain it are labelled gluten-free. In the United States and Canada, however, Codex wheat starch isn't considered gluten-free.

If you follow our advice in the earlier section 'Eating Out Gluten-free – Tips and Tricks', you'll be well-prepared for wherever your travels take you. And because travelling nearly always involves eating in restaurants, also pay particular attention to the advice in the preceding section on dining out. But to ensure a great gluten-free adventure, here are a few more things that you should know before you hit the road.

Researching your destination

Do yourself a favour and spend some time researching the area before you go on your trip. You can almost always find food shops, markets, restaurants and fast-food places, all of which have at least some things you can eat. But you may do even better than that. National or local support groups and specific Internet discussion boards and blogs may be able to steer you in the direction of gluten-free-friendly restaurants and shops. (You can find more details about sources of information in Chapter 5). You can also spot local dishes and specialities that are likely to be gluten-free, and some to avoid.

Sprechen zie gluten? Speaking gluten-free in other countries

Knowing some key words in the language of the country you're visiting is important. For instance, *flour* in Spanish is *harina*. But that can refer to cornmeal or wheat flour, and so you have to distinguish further what you're talking about by saying *harina de maiz* (cornmeal) or *harina de trigo* (wheat flour).

Find out the words for *gluten*, *with*, *without*, *no* and *allergy*. If you can find someone who comes from the country you're planning on visiting to help with the language and pronunciation, this can be invaluable. We suggest you avoid free online translations, because they rarely put words into context. We once found a translation of gluten as *snot*, which, fortunately, we found out was wrong before we said it to anyone. You can download free travel and language guides from www.coeliac.org.uk. These include contact details for coeliac support organisations in a number of countries. The online shop also stocks a pocket-sized multilingual-phrase passport with over 1,200 phrases to help with international gluten-free travel.

Check out Table 17-1 for some key words in Spanish, French and German.

Table 17-1	Terms for Explaining the Diet in Foreign Languages		
English	**Spanish**	**French**	**German**
I can	puedo	je peux	ich kann
I can't	no puedo	je ne peux pas	ich kann nicht
(to) eat	comer	manger	essen
gluten	gluten	gluten	gluten
wheat	trigo	blé	weizen
flour	harina	farine	mehl
corn	maiz	maïs	mais
with	con	avec	mit
without	sin	sans	ohne
yes	sí	oui	ja
no	no	non	nein
allergy	alergia	allergie	allergie

Remember that each country has different regulations about what manufacturers must list on the ingredients label. Some countries outside the EU aren't obliged to list items such as wheat flour if they only make up a small percentage of the product. A more reliable source of information may be a product listing of suitable foods that's produced by the coeliac support group for the country, if it has one. You can find contact details at www.coeliachelp.me.uk.

Getting the message over in black and white

Some companies produce discreet, durable 'dietary alert!' cards for people with specific dietary requirements. The card explains your dietary needs in simple, clear terms for you to show to waiting staff and chefs with the minimum of fuss. This system can help avoid your message being corrupted between the table and the kitchen, and helps authenticate your request as a medical requirement rather than one for a fad diet. You can get these cards in 18 languages. For more information, visit www.dietarycard.co.uk or telephone 01506 635358.

Choosing accommodation

Where you stay can make your holiday a much more enjoyable experience. If possible, choose accommodation with some self-catering facilities. Even a small fridge and microwave can make your trip a lot easier. That way, you can go to a local supermarket and stock up on some essentials and treats, like fruit, milk, popcorn, cold meats and snack items. If you have a full kitchen at your disposal, you can prepare your own meals if you want to, sparing yourself the worry of eating at restaurants – not to mention the expense.

If you don't have a kitchen, try to find accommodation that has a restaurant attached or has several nearby. You can call the hotel restaurant in advance and have it email you the menus so you can discuss items you may be able to enjoy. Some restaurants may even work with you to accommodate your dietary needs during your stay. If your accommodation is near several national restaurant chains, you can look up their websites and see whether they have menus online. You may be delighted to find a gluten-free menu.

Packing your own provisions

Keep in mind that most food is naturally gluten-free and most foreign and British regional cuisines include fresh meats, fish, milk, eggs, fruits, vegetables and cereals other than wheat, rye and barley. The simplest and most enticing option is to plan on eating from this substantial range of foods when you're away and avoiding breads, pasta and the like. If you're self-catering and travelling in your own car, caravan or campervan, you may want to bring your kitchen-in-the-cab (everything but the kitchen sink!). Depending on where you're going and for how long, you may include some of the following items:

✔ Baking mixes

✔ Biscuits

✔ Crackers and snack items

✔ Gluten-free cereals that may be hard to find

✔ Pasta

✔ Pizza bases

✔ Sliced bread

✔ Small toaster and adaptor

✔ Toaster bags

With any luck, the food survives the trip and you arrive fully prepared to enjoy your gluten-free stay.

Think about getting toaster bags for toasting your bread when you're away from home. The bags are great for making sure that your bread doesn't get contaminated by wheat crumbs left in the toaster.

If you don't want to lug the whole kitchen and pantry with you, consider sending your foods ahead, if you're going somewhere that really doesn't have anything on offer locally and will accept food coming in from the UK. Internationally, your package must go through customs, so check up with the authorities in question what food is allowed (see the sidebar 'Knowing the boundaries when crossing borders', earlier in this chapter). An alternative is to order the food online and have it sent to where you're going, in which case the suppliers may be able to advise about any duties and customs restrictions if you're off to a foreign destination. Hotels and self-catering apartments usually accept packages if you clearly mark the guest name and date of arrival on the box.

Getting there

As Robert Louis Stevenson once said, 'To travel hopefully is a better thing than to arrive.' Well, whether you're going by plane, train, car or cruise ship, you need to consider the issue of eating on the journey itself in your gluten-free plans.

Flying high

Airports usually have fast-food restaurants, so if you know which fast foods are gluten-free, you can always go there. Some of the kiosks and cafés sell yoghurt, fruit and salads, and some airports have large restaurant chains where you can order as you would in any other restaurant.

Here are some tips for the flight:

- Order gluten-free meals when you buy your ticket, and make sure the meal choice has been registered when you check in and at the gate. Call ahead a couple of days before the trip as well.

- Have some gluten-free crackers or bread in case what they serve on the plane is limited in its gluten-free selections. (At airports in the UK, you can take solid food through security and onto the plane in your hand luggage, but not drinks, dressings, sauces or liquids, except in very small quantities.)

- Once on board, make yourself known to the cabin crew to reduce the chances of your special meal going to someone else.

Some airlines provide these meals brilliantly – we've seen delicious examples, and we were once even served gluten-free rolls, individually packaged with all the ingredients clearly labelled!

Cruising the high seas

Cruise lines are extremely good at accommodating dietary restrictions of any type. Most of the cruise lines we've looked into are very familiar with the gluten-free diet and even stock speciality items like gluten-free breads, pastas, crackers, biscuits and cakes. They also offer lots of healthy fare like fresh seafood, chicken, steaks, fruit and vegetables.

If you're planning a cruise, call ahead and ask to speak to the executive chef for the line you're going to be on. Discuss the gluten-free diet with the chef – in the unlikely event that the chef isn't familiar with the diet, email the guidelines and follow up with a phone call to discuss the specifics of what you want while you're on board, including contamination issues.

Letting the train take the strain

If you're taking the train somewhere, your best bet is to bring your own food. British rail operators usually don't have any restrictions about bringing your own food, so you can load up. The cafés or snack trolleys on trains rarely have much hot food that's gluten-free; instead, they usually serve packaged sandwiches, filled croissants, muffins, pastries and other not-even-close-to-being-gluten-free goodies. However, they may sell fruit and other suitable gluten-free snacks such as crisps and nuts – take your Coeliac UK *Food and Drink Directory* with you so you can check up. You don't want to derail your trip by starving the whole way.

If you're going to France by rail, coach or car from the UK, consider the restrictions on the foods you can take in, as outlined in the 'Knowing the boundaries when crossing borders' sidebar.

Travelling near or far by car

Driving offers you the most flexibility, so it's often the easiest way to travel, at least in terms of accommodating your gluten-free diet. (The traffic jams, or the kids fighting and asking 'Are we almost there?' the entire way, is another matter.) You can bring your own food or stop off at a service station and cross-check in your directory, or drop into a fast-food outlet that you know sells suitable items.

Chapter 18

Raising Happy, Healthy, Gluten-Free Kids

*W*hen adults need or choose to adopt a gluten-free lifestyle, making all the necessary adjustments can be hard. However, when your kids need to be gluten-free, that's an entirely different matter. As the mum of a now healthy, happy coeliac son, nobody knows that better than Danna.

Her son Tyler was almost two when he was diagnosed with coeliac disease. That was back in 1991 in America. The abridged version of Tyler's story is that he was a sick little baby, but the doctors didn't think so. They kept saying that nothing was wrong, even though he had severe diarrhoea, his tummy was distended, he was growing listless and lethargic, and his personality was changing before his parents' eyes.

Nearly a year later, having seen four paediatricians and a paediatric gastroenterologist, heard preliminary diagnoses of cystic fibrosis, cancer or a blood disease, and having washed thousands of diarrhoea-stained nappies, his parents heard the bittersweet words that changed their lives forever: 'Your son has coeliac disease.' They were shocked, panicked, angry, sad, glad, confused, frustrated, and terrified to feed their own child. And that was all within the first 2.4 seconds of hearing those words.

We've packed this chapter with information to help you deal with your roller-coaster of emotions, the practicalities of having kids on the gluten-free diet and the psychological impact this may have on your family. We also give you a glimpse into the wonderful world of terrific teenagers who are avoiding gluten.

Before you dive in, we feel compelled to give away the most important message of all (so much for teasing you into reading the whole chapter!): getting the diagnosis is a *good* thing in your child's life and in yours. If you're having trouble believing us, read on.

Forging through the Feelings

Everything's different when your child's the one on the gluten-free diet: the feelings you have, the way you communicate about the diet, the resentment you feel towards parents who don't have to make special arrangements just to feed their child, the preparations you make to go anywhere, the way you shop, the foods you buy, the school lunches. The list of potential frustrations just goes on and on.

If you're a parent – or someone who loves a child as a parent would – and your child has to (for health reasons) adopt a strict, gluten-free diet, your emotions probably resemble a roller-coaster. You know: up one minute, crashing the next, as in Figure 18-1. Just when you're feeling great about the diet, the lifestyle and all the benefits that go along with it, you find out that a party was held at school and that your child was the only one without a slice of cake to take home. Your emotions go from flying high to a terminal-velocity free-fall.

We talk in Chapter 19 about the emotional obstacles you may face when you switch to a gluten-free lifestyle. To quantify what the change feels like when your child, as opposed to you, has to go gluten-free, take the magnitude of those emotions, multiply by 100, square that and add infinity, and you're getting close.

Figure 18-1: The emotional ups and downs of dealing with your child's diet.

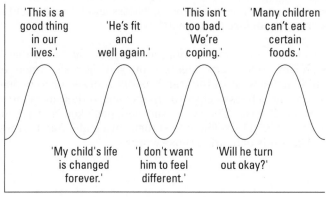

'This is a good thing in our lives.'

'He's fit and well again.'

'This isn't too bad. We're coping.'

'Many children can't eat certain foods.'

'My child's life is changed forever.'

'I don't want him to feel different.'

'Will he turn out okay?'

In addition to the emotions we talk about in Chapter 19, you face other worries – nagging concerns that distress you because it's your child who's affected. See whether some of the concerns in this section strike a familiar chord.

'My child's life is changed forever'

Yes, your child's life is changed forever. That's true. And forever seems like a really long time, doesn't it? What happened to those visions you had for your children: the perfect life, where things are easy and magical? Well, for one thing, with or without gluten, that's not the reality.

People forget to dream about the hardships their kids are going to face and how they're going to handle the difficulties in their lives. Yet, how to handle adversity is one of the most important lessons your children ever learn. This moment is a chance for them to find out at an early age how to turn adversity into advantage.

Furthermore, what you initially see as a difficulty may actually be a good thing in your child's life (and in yours). See the later section 'Focusing on the good things in life' for more information.

'I don't want my child to feel different'

You imagine your kids' lives as being smooth and painless, and part of that means fitting in. But fitting in doesn't mean being the same as everyone else. In fact, all children are different – some kids have blonde hair, others have red; some prefer cricket to ballet; some are in wheelchairs; others wear glasses. And when it comes to food, lots of children have allergies, intolerances, unusual diets, fads and foods they hate. To pine away for your child's lost conformity is to send a signal that something about being different in this (gluten-free) way is bad. The last thing you want to do is send that message.

Parents worry that their kids aren't going to fit in or be accepted, because of their 'different' diet, but kids can fit in regardless of what they're eating. Fitting in has much more to do with their attitude than anything else.

'Is my child going to turn out okay?'

All parents of gluten-intolerant children are bound to ask this question. Just remind yourself that your child is going to be better than okay, because your child is healthy! But you may still agonise about the future, when your child is first diagnosed.

A kid's perspective

We asked Danna's son Tyler what he thought about being a kid with coeliac disease – he's now in his 20s – and he said that back then he thought more about other things in his life, like friends, school, sports and family, than about gluten.

He always knew the importance of staying 100 per cent gluten-free. In fact, he only cheated a few times when he was 17 or 18, and soon found out that he still couldn't tolerate gluten. No surprise there. He felt terrible and went back to his strictly gluten-free diet with renewed determination.

At a young age, he took control of what he ate and made sure that when he'd be away from home he had access to gluten-free food. He got interested in cooking – even making his own bread – and was amazed when, in his teens, he told his friends about his diet and found they'd never even noticed he ate any differently to them. For him, it's been no big deal.

We thought his perspective was inspirational – he sounded just like any other young person we know. With very few exceptions, his approach has been mirrored by that of the coeliac kids that we've come across in our careers. In fact, the exceptions are where parents have made kids' lives revolve around coeliac disease, rather than making coeliac disease fit in with their lives.

The truth is that being gluten-free really doesn't have to be a big deal for your child, although getting kids involved with their gluten-free diet from the start is, we believe, crucial. We always maintain an optimistic yet realistic approach with families who are getting used to the idea that they have a child who needs to follow a gluten-free diet, and we find that's the best approach. We don't make false promises that everything is sure to be easy, but give plenty of practical advice to make the transition with the constant theme that, above all, now that the family knows the problem, they can understand exactly how to manage the diet together so that their child grows up just fine.

'It's harder for me than it is for my child'

If you love a child the way a parent does (even if you're not the actual parent), you can comprehend the this-hurts-me-more-than-it-hurts-you phenomenon. Seeing a bloody knee or a broken heart truly causes pain – palpable pain – for the grown-ups who love that child.

If you're agonising over the fact that your child has been diagnosed with a condition that requires a strict, lifelong gluten-free diet, look at it this way: dealing with the diagnosis is harder for you than it is for your child.

Your dreams for your child's future make you think that having to be gluten-free is hard; you envisage your child skipping merrily down the road of life, not tripping over an obstacle like food, for goodness' sake. But kids don't have visions for the future like that. To a child, a vision of the future may take in the next netball game or next week's pocket money. It's far more near-sighted than your vision.

In most cases, kids are resilient. They accept what life dishes out, and they make the best of it. We think grown-ups should take note.

If you don't believe that this diagnosis is harder on you than it is on your child, ask any children you know what they think about in their lives, and take note. They're likely to mention things like 'football', 'my best friend', 'riding my horse', 'playtime' or any number of other answers. We're reasonably certain that you won't find any who answer 'my diet'. It's just really not a priority – nor should it be.

Focusing on the good things in life

Being gluten-free may be a good thing in your child's (and in your) life for a lot of reasons. We encourage you to make your own personal list to consult when you find yourself feeling frustrated or depressed, because the reality is that once in a while you're going to feel like that. We list a few ideas here to get you started:

- ✔ **Your child has the key to better health.** Most people who have coeliac disease or gluten sensitivity never find out what's wrong with them. They don't know that a dietary modification can fully restore their health, so they continue to eat the very foods that make them ill.

- ✔ **Your child is less likely to develop associated conditions.** Your child has the advantage of being diagnosed early and going gluten-free at an early age. This means that the chances of developing associated complications in later life (refer to Chapter 2) are far lower than for someone diagnosed after years of being sick with gluten sensitivity or coeliac disease but continuing to eat gluten.

- ✔ **Your child is likely to become tolerant of other people's sensitivities and generally more aware of other people's needs.** This can encourage more empathy with others and help to hone social skills.

- ✔ **Your child isn't the only one with a dietary restriction.** If 1,000 kids attend your child's school, about 10 of them may have coeliac disease – and more may have a form of gluten sensitivity. Then you have all those with food allergies, intolerances to some food colours, diabetes, and who are over-weight or vegetarian or on a diet restricted by their ethnicity or religion.

- ✔ **Your child may well find that controlling any other dietary issues, such as diabetes and excess weight, is easier on the gluten-free diet.** Being more diet-aware than other children, those with a dietary restriction often take an interest in food and healthy eating. Gradually, making better choices about what they eat and how much becomes second nature.

Talking to Your Kids about Being Gluten-Free

Whether your child is 18 months or 18 years old, now's the time to talk, and you need to include the entire family. How you do this depends on your style, your internal family relationships and your child's ability to understand the intricacies of the subject matter. Talking to your kids is step one towards making sure that they develop healthy attitudes and habits.

Coeliac UK produces a fantastic booklet called *Me and My Tummy*, which gives some great tips on talking to children about coeliac disease, and how to make parties, eating at school and visiting friends as hassle-free as possible. It's free to members, either in hard copy format on request or downloadable from www.coeliac.org.uk, or available for a nominal charge to anyone. If you're a new member of the charity, simply ask for your free copy and you'll receive it in your welcome pack.

Including the whole family

Even if your entire family doesn't choose to go gluten-free, having a gluten-free kid in the house affects all family members. Everyone in the family needs to know about your child's condition, the diet and how to handle a variety of situations that may arise. And don't forget close relatives who see a lot of your child, especially if food's involved, which it often is.

We're not suggesting that you organise an extended family reunion and include fifth cousins thrice removed. But you do need to include your close relatives in some type of discussion. Don't think that these talks need to take place all at once; discussion is an ongoing process, and you're going to be talking about the gluten-free lifestyle for months, if not years, to come.

Kids will be kids, and sibs will be sibs. Just because the brothers and sisters understand the diet doesn't mean that they're always going to be kind. You may hear the typical taunting – you know, the 'I can eat this and you can't' type of thing. Treat this teasing the same way you treat any other act that you don't approve of between siblings. Don't let your feelings of frustration that your child has this condition make you overreact to unkind gestures. Quarrelling is quarrelling, and you should try to respond to it consistently.

Startled siblings

So you're sitting down to have a family discussion about Victoria's new gluten-free lifestyle, and before your very eyes, her sister, Mild-Mannered-Molly, turns into Bordering-on-Ballistic-Barbie. What's going on? You did your best to explain everything in a positive way. Why is she freaking out?

Don't be surprised if you see this type of reaction from other children in the family: being scared, confused and even a touch panicked is perfectly normal.

Siblings can be wondering all sorts of things. Is my sister poorly? Is she going to die? Am I going to catch it? If she has to eat horrible stuff, do I have to eat it too? (The correct answer is that *neither* of them has to eat horrible stuff!) Why does she get special attention and I don't? What if she gets better stuff than I do? Why did this happen to our family? And, most importantly, are my friends going to think I'm weird because my sister eats different food?

Being aware that these reactions are typical can help you respond in a sympathetic, understanding way. Address the feelings you suspect the other children are having, even if they're not able to articulate their anxieties, and encourage them to tell you why the situation troubles them. Before you know it, everyone can relax and you can have a more productive discussion.

Keeping the discussion upbeat

Everyone you talk to about the gluten-free lifestyle – and the conditions that require it – finds out how to feel about the gluten-free lifestyle from you. Is being gluten-free a bad thing in your life? A scary thing? A good thing? How you talk about it has a far greater impact than you may realise.

If you call a family meeting and gather sombrely, you're going to scare your children right out of their pyjamas and cast an impression of doom and gloom. This conversation should be upbeat, light-hearted and interactive – after all, becoming gluten-free is a good thing in everyone's life. If you can't remember the benefits of living gluten-free, look back to the preceding sections in this chapter or go to www.dummies.com/extras/livingglutenfreeuk.

The most important person to stay upbeat around is your gluten-intolerant child. How that child feels about living gluten-free now and in the future depends on you and your present attitude. This is all new, and because children don't know how to feel, they take their cue from you (granted, it's new to you too, but you're the grown-up). It's a big advantage to everyone concerned if you start off upbeat and optimistic. The kids will take it from there.

Little ears are listening

When you're talking to other grown-ups about your child's diet and condition, bear in mind that any children in the room may be tuning in to every word you're saying. They may seem distracted with toys or friends – and they may, in fact, be too busy to hear what you're saying. But kids have ears and they know how to use 'em (unless, of course, you're asking them to do the washing up).

Are you apologising for the complexity of the diet? That can make your child feel like a victim.

Are you complaining about the restrictions and the cost? That may give an impression that to you it's a burden. Are you feeling sorry for yourself? Your child may then feel guilty for encumbering you with the challenges this lifestyle may present.

We're not saying don't vent your feelings. If you're frustrated, exhausted or feeling overly burdened at the moment, that's fine, and having someone to confide in is therapeutic. Just make sure that little ears aren't listening.

Don't make a huge fuss out of needing to go gluten-free. As huge as it may seem to you, chances are this isn't going to be a huge deal in your child's life . . . unless you make it one.

Explaining the new lifestyle

The level of detail you get into about the condition depends on your child's age, maturity and ability to understand this type of thing. In a nutshell, you want to provide your child with the 'why?', 'what?' and 'what now?' – why to go gluten-free (to feel better), what gluten-free means, and what foods are still allowed, including a number of favourites. The latter is really the most important, because that's what matters most to your child.

Be patient and don't try to rush explaining everything in one go. Understanding and accepting may not happen all at once, but is more likely to be an ongoing process for you all.

Focusing on the benefits

Chances are that your child has had health issues that led to the need for a gluten-free diet, so start the discussion with something positive like, 'You're going to feel *so* much better now that you're going to be eating gluten-free foods!'

Kids think in specifics. Drive the point home to your child with something personal to relate to, such as, 'You know how much your tummy's been hurting lately?' or 'You know how you've been feeling so tired lately?' and then, 'You aren't going to have that any more now that you don't eat gluten!' Specifics can help children understand exactly *what's* going to be better on the gluten-free diet.

Then, a few weeks into the lifestyle, remember to point out how much better your child feels thanks to the delicious gluten-free foods on the menu.

Using big words and good explanations

Don't underestimate what your kids can grasp. When explaining the diet to your child, use the 'big' words like gluten (spare them the carboxymethyl cellulose, though, okay?). Even if your child has developmental or learning disabilities, use the proper terminology to encourage better communication with others about what foods are permissible to eat.

Of course, your child's not going to understand at first (did *you*?). Give easy-to-understand examples – explain that 'gluten is in lots of the foods we used to eat, like bread, biscuits and cereals' – and then quickly let your child know that *lots* of wonderful things don't have gluten in them.

Offering gluten-free alternatives

Always focusing on what your child *can* eat is important. Whenever your child asks for a food that's off limits, try to point out something equally as scrumptious that's gluten-free.

Of course, you're not going to say, 'You can't have those cakes any more, Oliver, but look here! You can eat all the broccoli your little heart desires!' That isn't going to win you any parent points, and little Oliver isn't likely to buy in to this new lifestyle with much zest. Instead, you can accomplish three things at once here:

- ✔ Reward your child for grasping the diet.
- ✔ Offer an alternative.
- ✔ Reinforce that your child can eat it *because* it's gluten-free.

A couple of simple sentences do the trick: 'You're right, Oliver, you can't eat that cake. But you *can* have this one instead, because it's gluten-free!'

Always be prepared to do the treat trade. When your child wants to eat a treat that contains gluten, be ready to trade it for something equally as appealing – but of the gluten-free variety. Kids are relatively easily distracted, and if you have some delectable goodies waiting in the wings as a treat trade, you're sure to turn that frown upside down.

Reinforcing the idea that gluten makes your child feel poorly

Help your child to make the connection between eating gluten and feeling poorly. Do so whenever you talk about gluten: 'You're right, you can't eat that. It contains gluten, and gluten makes you feel poorly.' This way, your child gradually discovers that gluten is the direct cause of feeling ill and so stops wanting to eat foods that contain it.

Keep any mistakes about inadvertently eating gluten in proportion and make sure that your child doesn't feel guilty about them. Point out that everyone makes mistakes and that gluten can hide in all sorts of things. It just means that you have to be extra careful in the future.

When kids who have coeliac disease get tummy aches, you may jump to the conclusion that they feel ill because they ate some gluten, and find yourself agonising over the probable culprit. But remember, all kinds of different things can cause tummy aches, but generally, they're a normal part of growing up.

Handling your child's reaction

You can't predict how your child is going to respond when you first start talking about this new gluten-free lifestyle. The reaction depends on how you present the diet and on your child's age, maturity, level of understanding, ability to express feelings and, of course, personality.

You probably realise that if your child shows anger, hostility or other 'negative' emotions, you should be soothing, understanding and supportive – those parental responses are natural.

Don't think, though, that the initial 'upset' reaction is going to persist, because it's most likely a fleeting response that, as time passes and your child becomes accustomed to the new lifestyle, evolves into a more positive outlook. Continue to remind your child of the benefits in store by avoiding gluten.

Also, be prepared for little or no response. Appearing to be indifferent or apathetic isn't unusual for kids. Don't read too much into it or assume this reaction is a cover-up for deep, disturbing thoughts – chances are, the response is an honest reaction to a somewhat confusing issue or to something that truly doesn't seem to matter much.

Helping your child talk to others about the diet

Children need to discover how to talk to other people – both adults and other kids – about the gluten-free lifestyle. They're going to be doing it for the rest of their lives, and the best time to start is the present. Of course, exactly what your child says about it depends on age, personality, the situation and who's involved in the conversation.

Explaining what children can and can't have

Come up with a phrase to use, even if your coeliac or gluten-sensitive child is too young to know what it means. Use something comprehensive, concerning food rather than health or symptoms, and make it something simple that your child can repeat to adults. For example, 'I can't eat gluten. That means I can't eat wheat, rye, barley or oats.' We know that definition isn't technically correct (oats are gluten-free, but sometimes contaminated), but it tells adults what they need to know. Maybe that phrase is too cumbersome, but if your child can handle the words, go with it. If not, find a phrase that's more age-appropriate or one that suits your child's personality. The idea behind the memorised 'sound bite' is that it covers a lot of situations with a relatively easy couple of sentences.

Of course, the more information children can add, the better. If your child can explain to people exactly what foods are suitable and unsuitable, that's terrific – and if your child can add the fact that eating any gluten results in illness, that's even better. Before long, your child is going to decide what works best.

Educate your child to be open about and conversant with being gluten-free. We're not suggesting that you and your child walk into a room, grab a microphone, clear your throats and begin preaching about the gluten-free lifestyle. Nor do you want your child to feel automatically entitled to have people accommodate the diet. But informing people (especially those who may be involved in feeding your child) is important, and you can do this in a friendly, informative manner.

Some kids feel more comfortable simplifying their explanation to something people can understand more easily, such as 'I'm allergic to gluten' or even 'I'm allergic to wheat'. Even though that explanation's not technically correct, sometimes it's easier. Just make sure that your child knows the *real* facts and doesn't get confused later on.

Getting kids to say 'no, thanks'

No matter how well children communicate the fact that they can't eat gluten, at some point, a person, usually with the best of intentions, is sure to offer them something containing gluten.

This situation can be really confusing to your child, especially if the well-meaning person is a loved one and is folding a biscuit into your child's hand and saying with a conspiratorial just-between-you-and-me wink, 'Don't tell Mummy and Daddy.' Nightmare! What's a gluten-free kid to do?

Explain to your child how and why this type of a situation may come up, and, most importantly, how to handle it. Sometimes saying 'no, thanks' or 'Eating that will make me ill' is easy for a child. Other times, just accepting the treat and not eating it is easier and more diplomatic.

Even if your friends and family don't offer your child gluten, someone out there is sure to do so. You can spare your child disappointment and confusion if you prepare the ground in advance and remember to take gluten-free treats with you when you're visiting friends and family, so you can do the treat trade – that is, offer a gluten-free treat in lieu of a gluten-containing one that's been offered.

Deciding Whether the Whole Family Should Be Gluten-Free

Many people assume that because one child is gluten-free, the entire family should adopt the lifestyle. After all, wouldn't it be cruel to be feasting on doughnuts while your gluten-free child is choking on rice cakes? Yes, it would.

But having the entire family live gluten-free isn't always the right answer. You really have to weigh up both sides of the issue and consider the practical and psychological issues.

The pros

Here are some advantages if everyone goes gluten-free:

- **You make only one version of each meal.** Rather than making a gluten-free version and a 'regular' version of some dishes at mealtimes, you can make just one gluten-free version and be done with it.

- **You shop only for gluten-free foods.** You can pass the bread and biscuit aisles altogether.

- **You cut out the risk of contamination in the kitchen.** (Check out Chapter 9.)

- **Your child doesn't feel different.** Being different is okay, but feeling the same is nice as well, especially within the family.

- **You can fill the cupboards with 'safe' foods.** You don't have to worry that you or your child will accidentally grab a gluten-laden snack, because you don't have any.

- **Your child isn't tempted to cheat.** At least not at home.

The cons

We're trying to offer both sides here, but if you sense that the cons list is a little weightier than the pros list, you're right. Ultimately, in our opinion, the cons outweigh the pros of having the entire family going gluten-free:

✔ **A gluten-free world isn't reality.** Your child needs to understand that the rest of the world eats gluten. People aren't doing it to ostracise or make your child feel bad, and no malicious or evil intentions are present. What better environment to find out that important lesson than in a loving, supportive home?

✔ **Your child doesn't find out how to make food choices.** Knowing how to choose which foods are gluten-free and which aren't is important for your child. If the cupboard's free of 'no-nos', your child doesn't need to decide and may become complacent about mindlessly grabbing food without giving a thought to whether it's gluten-free.

✔ **It can create resentment among other family members.** Siblings – even parents – can be a little bitter about having to give up bread and cakes if they don't have a health condition that requires it. They can direct that resentment towards your gluten-free child, and that sets up an unhealthy family dynamic.

✔ **Your child isn't tempted to cheat.** Although this item also appears as a pro (it's really both a pro and a con), we believe that helping your child to discover how to resist the temptation (especially because gluten is practically everywhere) is better than never offering temptation.

✔ **Eating a lot of 'free-from' foods can be more expensive.** We're not advocating eating only 'free-from' foods, but they have a place in the gluten-free lifestyle. Isn't it sensible to save the £4 pack of biscuits for the person who really needs them? The gluten-free foods on prescription are only for the person with coeliac disease and not for the whole family.

Middle ground

Sometimes a compromise is the best solution. See whether these ideas work for your family:

✔ **Make most meals gluten-free.** If you can make the majority of your meals gluten-free and still please everyone, without using up your worth-their-weight-in-gold gluten-free speciality items, do so. This makes cooking and preparation easier – and there's less washing up.

✔ **Buy gluten-free condiments.** Using gluten-free salad dressings, soy sauce, tomato ketchup, pickles and other condiments makes life a lot easier on you – and you don't have to make separate stir-fries just because one has the gluteny kind of soy sauce in it.

✔ **Choose gluten-free oven-chips.** Oven chips with just two ingredients – potatoes and vegetable oil – are the only ones to have in the freezer, unless you like making your own from the same two ingredients. Faffing about with two trays of chips in the oven isn't worth the trouble, especially because you can't see or taste any difference.

✔ **Enjoy home-made sweet treats.** In baking, gluten-free breads are a challenge, we admit, but honestly, with a bit of practice and a few types of flour in the cupboard, you can turn out fantastic gluten-free cakes, biscuits, brownies, tarts, crumbles, pancakes and other puddings for the whole family. Some of them are even better than the conventional sort. Have a go with our recipes in Chapter 16. Most of the gluten-free cake mixes these days are as good as the real thing. They're a little more expensive maybe, but cost aside, you really have no reason to make separate batches of these things. Make one batch of the gluten-free kind and let the entire family tuck in. It's good to have one or two of these in individual portions in the freezer too.

Giving Your Child Control of the Diet

If your child doesn't take control of the diet, the diet will take control of your child. No matter how young, your child needs to learn from day one how to make decisions about what to eat and what to avoid – and the importance of not cheating, no matter how tempted.

From a psychological standpoint, not letting the gluten-free diet take centre stage in your child's life is important. But when the time comes to eat, your child needs to realise that making good choices is important. Food is something to be given attention.

A wise proverb says, 'Give a man a fish, and you feed him for a day. Teach him to fish, and you feed him for a lifetime.' Your kids need to choose foods they can eat for a lifetime. Giving your child control of the diet also creates bonuses for everyone:

✔ **Your child has confidence.** Even if you're not there, your child's able to eat safely and make healthy food choices.

✔ **You can relax.** You know that even if you're not there, your child is prepared to make good food choices. And if you are there, you don't have to be doing all the decision-making.

✔ **Your child is discovering the importance of healthy eating.** How many kids read food labels or give even a first thought (much less a second) to what they're putting in their mouths? Your child is finding out at an early age how to be conscious of nutrition, which is a valuable lifelong lesson.

Working together to make good choices

When we say to give your child control, we're not suggesting that you just stand back and don't get involved – like everything else in life, children need a little guidance, especially at first. Parents and children can do lots of things together to help kids find out how to make good food choices:

- ✔ **Read labels together.** Even if your child is too young to read, pretend. Hold the ingredients label where you can both see it, and go through the ingredients out loud, one by one (just like when you're tired and reading bedtime stories, you can skip the superfluous stuff). Point to the words, and when you come to pertinent ones, like *wheat*, say something like, 'No. This one has gluten in it.' And then, because you're well-conditioned to quickly point to the alternative, follow up with, 'Let's try *this* one,' and grab something you know is gluten-free.

- ✔ **Make a game out of it.** When you're reading labels or talking about foods, see who can decide which one is gluten-free (or not) first. (Note to those of you competitive types: let 'em win a few times.)

- ✔ **Encourage your children to telephone food manufacturers.** (This works best if your child is old enough to talk!) After they've heard you query food ingredients a few times, let your children make the calls. Sometimes, being on another extension so you can take over is a good idea.

- ✔ **Get your children to plan the occasional meal.** Not only does this provide a chance to practise working out what's gluten-free and what isn't, but also you know they'll eat the food. So what if the menu consists of chips, rice, sweets and gluten-free macaroni cheese? Go with it. Remember, for that meal at least, your child's in control and this exercise is primarily to instil gluten-free thinking, not detailed knowledge of a balanced diet.

- ✔ **Allow your children to pack their own lunches.** If it's not perfectly nutritionally balanced, make some suggestions, but otherwise, go with it. One unbalanced meal isn't going to kill anyone – and this exercise helps your gluten-intolerant child to see that food can be gluten-free and tasty.

- ✔ **Let your children help with the cooking.** Kids *love* to cook, even though it usually ends up being far more work for you than if they don't help. Discovering how to cook at an early age is important for all children, especially for those who are going to require some specially prepared foods for the rest of their lives.

Trusting kids when you're not there

Letting g-g-g-go is one of the hardest things parents ever do, yet it's your job to do so. On a daily basis, you're preparing your children for life, so you can eventually set them free. If you do your job well, you can relax knowing that they have all the tools they need to make decisions that lead to safe, happy, healthy lives.

The idea behind giving your kids control of their diet is that they need to know how to feed themselves, because you aren't always going to be there, and that's true for all kids. You don't have much of a problem giving them control of certain things – toilet training, washing their hands and switching on the computer. But when it comes to choosing foods, trusting that they're going to make safe choices is hard – particularly when some foods can make them really ill.

You'll know when the time is right and you can actually relax, knowing that your children are making safe food choices. That time is most likely to come long before you expect it, and you should be prepared for it to arrive before *you're* ready.

Your children are going to make mistakes. But bear in mind that mistakes aren't going to kill or permanently harm them. With any luck the error causes some discomfort, so that they realise the importance of being more attentive next time.

Getting Out with the Gluten-Free Gang

Living life in an overprotected environment isn't healthy. Your child's life shouldn't be restricted just because of a restricted diet!

Really, getting out and about with gluten-free kids isn't much different from the way gluten-free adults do it. You follow the same golden rules of gluten-free eating out and travelling as gluten-free adults do. And ordering at restaurants isn't very different, except that you may be ordering from a kids' menu instead of an adult one. We cover all these things in detail in Chapter 17, so for the most part, if you master the general ideas of that chapter, you're going to excel at getting out and about with the kids.

We do have a few suggestions specific to eating out with gluten-free kids:

- **Let your child choose and order.** At first, this idea may be cumbersome, because you may not approve of the choices and may need to offer a steer in the right direction. Don't worry about taking a long time or bothering the waiter. Discovering how to order at a restaurant is really important for children, particularly those living gluten-free.

- **Don't be shy.** Some kids are mortified when adults 'make a scene' (ask a question) at a restaurant. All you have to do is say, 'Can I ask you about this menu item . . .' and the eyes start rolling, the 'Oh no, here she goes, it's sooooo embarrassing' comments start spewing forth. Ignore your kids and ask anyway!

- **Try letting your child call the restaurant beforehand.** In the same way you'd call if you needed a gluten-free meal yourself, encourage your child to make the call occasionally to explore what gluten-free options are available.

Party time!

Parties are supposed to be all about fun! But to parents, parties sometimes seem like they're all about food. Apparently, a new law has been drawn up that requires all children's parties to be held at pizza or fast-food restaurants. For a few pounds per child, parents can host a party that lasts all of about an hour, and stuff the kids with pizza, burgers and cake. So what about those pizzas, burgers and cakes? Do you let party time turn to pouty time? No, of course you don't. Try some of these ideas:

✔ **Check out the venue beforehand.** You may be surprised to find that gluten-free pizza bases and burger buns are on the menu after all. If the hosts are offering a set menu, check that they're happy to add gluten-free options, and if not, offer to contribute extra funds.

✔ **Make sure that your child eats before going to the party.** This only works if the party is not primarily an eating occasion, for example if it's a visit to an attraction, theatre or sporting activity. If your child's full, missing out on the food isn't such a big deal.

✔ **If you know that the only food served has gluten in it, bring your own.** If possible, bring something close to what they're serving – gluten-free pizza, for instance.

✔ **If it's your child's party, serve gluten-free foods to everyone.** There's no need to apologise, explain or make excuses. We provide lots of suitable recipes for party food in Part IV, and we defy anyone to notice anything unusual about them.

✔ **Be aware that not all the food at parties is on the table.** Food comes into play at children's parties in some surprising ways, such as prizes, picnics, midnight feasts, gifts, goody bags, treasure hunts, treats from entertainers, bowls of sweets dotted about, snacks eaten on the way to some event, and food brought in by the children themselves. If your child is confident in knowing what to look out for, and you've briefed the hosts thoroughly, these sources shouldn't be a problem

Leaving Your Gluten-Free Kids in the Care of Others

Leaving your kids with other people is scary enough, even when your kids don't have dietary limitations that can make them ill. But trusting someone else to feed your gluten-free child safely? Are you insane? Letting go of a little parental control can be frightening, but spending time apart is an important part of growing up for kids and parents.

Trusting your kids with friends, family and sitters

The most important thing you can do to ensure that your kids are in good hands from a gluten-free standpoint is to educate the people caring for them.

If you suspect the carers don't fully understand the diet, work harder to make sure that they do, or find a new carer.

When you leave your child in someone else's care, take along some gluten-free prepared food, and clearly mark on the containers that the food is gluten-free. This prevents any mix-up between your child's food and someone else's.

Sending them off to nursery and school

Sending your gluten-free little ones to nursery is a wrench, and when they get to school age, the challenge is even bigger because they'll be away for several hours at a time, day after day, with other people in charge of their food. Some important tips are to:

- **Advise your teachers, school nurse, school cook and headteacher.** Schools and nurseries don't have to provide gluten-free food, but most are well aware of gluten intolerance and coeliac disease and are willing to help as much as they can. Even if other gluten-intolerant children are at the school, it's a good idea to brief all the adults who'll be in charge of your child. Put it in writing and offer to go along to find out where food crops up in your child's day. As well as school meals, don't forget to ask about the food at social events, on trips, during evening activities, field trips and cookery classes. Repeat this process every time your child changes school or goes up a year to a new form teacher.

- **Visit the Coeliac UK website,** www.coeliac.org.uk. It has lots of information for schools that you can download and print out. The organisation also has leaflets on gluten-free living that the school might find useful.

- **Give the teacher a stash of treats for your child.** Nothing's worse than finding out from your child at the end of the day that it was a friend's birthday and your child ate nothing while the other kids smeared cake all over their faces. Bring bags of fun-sized gluten-free treat packages that the teacher can store in a special place for your child in case of a surprise party or an event that involves treats. (Head to Chapter 16 for some great gluten-free sweet treat recipes.)

- **Be aware of craft time.** Play-dough has gluten in it, and although kids aren't *supposed* to eat it, show us one kid who can resist. We know we couldn't! Other crafts involve gluten-containing cereals, and those activities often become a matter of 'one for the necklace, one for me . . . one for the necklace, one for me'. Make sure that the teacher and your child pay attention at craft time. See the nearby sidebar for a gluten-free recipe for play-dough.

- **Work with the catering team.** Teachers can help you to find contact information for the caterers. Having the opportunity to buy lunch from the school canteen even once a week may be a big deal to your child.

Most caterers are willing to work with you to find ways in which your child can eat at least one meal each week. Somehow, standing in that dinner queue is cool!

✔ **Packing it in.** On days when no lunch is provided, you need to pack your child off with a packed one. You can find lots of suggestions on Coeliac UK's website for making lunches that are both gluten-free and great. For cookery lessons, you'll probably need to supply the gluten-free ingredients.

✔ **Beware of the eating exchange.** Swapping food in school lunches is a very serious business. Kids get right down to it, swapping an egg sandwich for chocolate biscuits (not a fair trade). Talk to your child about the importance of not trading food – even if someone else's food looks okay, it may not be (not to mention the fact that your kid's just going to give away those £4 gluten-free biscuits you bought). Ask the lunchtime supervisors to be on the lookout, and make sure your child doesn't participate in the eating exchange.

✔ **Get a dietitian on the case if necessary.** If you feel there's still not enough support, contact a National Health Service dietitian, who should be able to liaise with the school on your behalf.

The key to success and to building confidence in managing the diet is letting your child take control. Your child will almost certainly not be the only one to need different foods sometimes. And remember: for kids, the diet is no big deal.

Child's play

Not many people know this, but play-dough is 40 per cent wheat flour. We know you're not supposed to eat play-dough, but it can easily find its way into a child's mouth. Here's a recipe for a gluten-free version:

340 grams gluten-free white flour mix

225 grams salt

30 millilitres vegetable oil

30 millilitres cream of tartar

360 millilitres water

Food colouring, as desired

1. Place all the dry ingredients in a non-stick pan and gradually mix in the oil, water and food colouring. Stir until smooth.

2. Place over a low heat for about five minutes, stirring well, until the mixture thickens.

3. Remove from the heat and knead the dough to get rid of any lumps, and then allow to cool. Store wrapped in clingfilm.

Guiding Your Gluten-Free Teenagers

You can't push a teenager any more than you can push a rope. By the time your kids are teenagers, the best you can do is hope that you've laid a good foundation and are still able to guide them in the direction you think they should go.

If your teenager is newly diagnosed, the teen years can be a scary time for everyone. It's a time when everything seems to be changing in life, and adopting a gluten-free lifestyle for the first time at that stage may be one change too many, making your teenager feel like a freak.

If your teenager has been diagnosed, even if that diagnosis happened years ago, you may see your child evolve from one who was very accepting and easy-going about the diet into one who fights it and may even cheat from time to time. All these responses are normal, if *any* definition of the word 'normal' applies to teenagers. You should handle these reactions with patience, understanding and communication on both sides.

Noticing changing symptoms

Now you see 'em, now you don't; sometimes children's symptoms seem to do a disappearing act during their teenage years – usually referred to as a *honeymoon period*. For some teenagers, the symptoms do go away – at least temporarily. At this point, they may be tempted to devour a pizza. They think that because they don't feel symptoms, they're going to be okay. Not true! In fact, the whole thing is just an illusion. Although kids may not *feel* the effects, the gluten still does damage.

For other teenagers, the symptoms don't really go away but evolve into those traits more characteristic in adults: headaches, fatigue and depression, for example. These teenagers, too, sometimes think that their symptoms have disappeared, because what they used to associate with eating gluten – diarrhoea, for instance – is no longer their typical reaction. They may not realise that the headaches they get, or other symptoms, are also signs of their gluten intolerance.

Understanding why teenagers may cheat on the diet

We cover the topic of cheating and being tempted to cheat on the gluten-free diet in Chapter 19. But teenagers are different animals, and they sometimes cheat or want to cheat for different reasons. Really, at this stage you can't stop them, but knowing why they want to cheat, so that you can be sympathetic and have an open discussion with them, may help.

No longer is their desire simply a matter of 'I want it, so I think I'll eat it.' Teenagers may want to eat gluten because of the following:

- **Peer pressure:** At no time in their lives is peer pressure greater than when kids are teenagers. Even if friends aren't applying pressure to conform with the rest of the group, your teenager may just *want* to be like everyone else and be tempted to cheat on the diet.

   Kids love to proclaim how they want to be unique, but they really don't want to be different, and this diet may make them feel different. Don't be surprised if your teenager orders a burger with a bun just to be like the rest of the gang.

- **Rebellion:** Your teenager may be tempted to eat gluten as a way of being rebellious. This may be a conscious decision or a subconscious one, but is probably more to do with exerting control – a type of 'I'll show you who's boss' behaviour – rather than wanting to eat gluten per se.

- **Curiosity and risk-seeking:** A child who's curious about what gluten tastes like or what effect it will have may actually have more restraint than a curious teenager. The teenage years are a time of spreading wings, becoming independent and taking risks. Youngsters who've been diligent about following the diet for years are most likely to succumb in the teenage years.

- **Experimenting with alcohol:** It's usually in the teens when people start drinking for the first time, and peer pressure comes into play here, not only to have a drink but to choose a cheaper one. It's possible your teenager is unaware that beer and lager contain gluten, so make sure you point this out well before you suspect that booze will come into the picture.

- **Weight control:** Many teenagers work out that if they eat gluten, they aren't absorbing all the available calories. Sadly, some intentionally cheat on the diet in an effort to lose weight.

Watch for signs of eating disorders in your kids. Sometimes they become obsessed with their restrictions and take them too far, or they use gluten as a means of losing weight or to become too ill to go to school or to take part in sports. Address this issue immediately – eating disorders are extremely serious issues.

So, what do you do about your cheating teenager? The best you can do is to have a two-way conversation. Try to find out why your teenager cheated and what the apparent consequences were, if any. Try to provide education about the harmful effects of eating gluten, even if these aren't immediately obvious, and point out that some effects aren't conducive to an active social life. Back it up with supporting resources from the media, particularly media that are popular with teenagers.

Helping teenagers after they move out

One of the hardest things for teenagers to handle, especially if they're new to the gluten-free lifestyle, is moving out. Being on their own and self-catering isn't quite so difficult as moving into college or university halls of residence, where lack of transport and a kitchen can limit them to the food in the dining halls. Whatever the case, make sure that your teenager fully understands the diet and can choose foods that are healthy and gluten-free.

If your teenager lives on campus and eats in dining halls, the catering manager may be able to help. Many of the available foods are already gluten-free – and many aren't. A supply of gluten-free condiments such as tamari would be useful to take along to the dining hall.

Many student residences offer self-catering facilities. If a fully equipped kitchen isn't available, having access to a fridge, microwave, toaster, food storage and a table-top oven is the next best thing, even if they're only used for breakfasts and occasional light meals. Coming up with snacks and menus that your teenager can make in the microwave (even gluten-free pasta!) is relatively easy. However, these facilities will almost certainly be shared, so your teenager may want to have a personal toaster and storage containers to avoid cross-contamination with other students' food.

Check the hall's policies before buying a mini refrigerator, a toaster or microwave. Even if these are allowed in students' rooms, some residences have size and power restrictions. Food parcels are sometimes the next-best thing to being there yourself, and can include long-lasting treats like fruit cakes. Think about sending some gluten-free goodies from time to time.

If your teenager gets gluten-free food on prescription, he or she needs to register with a new GP for prescriptions and for the annual health check. The foods permitted on prescription, and the procedure for getting repeat prescriptions, may be quite different in the new location than at home.

Coeliac UK has information targeted at this stage in life: have a look at the website, www.coeliac.org.uk.

Chapter 19

Beating the Gluten-Free Blues: Overcoming Emotional Obstacles

● ●

In This Chapter

▶ Coping when things don't feel so great

▶ Confronting and coming to terms with denial

▶ Dealing with dietary lapses

▶ Looking at the big picture

▶ Staying on track

● ●

Maybe we're just not looking hard enough, but we haven't seen many bestsellers in the bookshops with titles like *How to Cope When Things Are Going Really, Really Well for You*. No, you really need the most help when you're facing life's challenges. And some people feel that the gluten-free lifestyle is one big challenge. Some of that has to do with why they're going gluten-free in the first place.

People who embark on a gluten-free lifestyle usually do so for one of two reasons:

✔ **They've chosen to.** They haven't been diagnosed with any medical conditions, or if they have been tested, their tests came back negative. But they suspect that they're going to feel better on a gluten-free diet. Or maybe they just want to support a loved one who's going gluten-free.

✔ **They have to.** They've been diagnosed with a medical condition that requires a gluten-free diet.

Guess which group of people has the easiest time from a psychological perspective. Spot on! When you choose to do something, you're starting off with a huge emotional advantage. Not only are you mentally prepared for the challenge, but also you welcome the changes to come.

On the other hand, when someone tells you that you *have* to do something (those going gluten-free for the second reason), you're likely to have a harder time with it. (Think back to your childhood when you were just getting ready to clean your room voluntarily and then your mum yelled, 'Don't forget to clean your room!' Talk about a motivation drain.) Add in the unique social and practical challenges that arise when you're living a gluten-free lifestyle, and you may find yourself dealing with all sorts of complex emotional issues.

Looking at it from another perspective, people who have to go gluten-free, rather than who elect to do so, are less likely to backtrack later on. If you decided to do this for yourself, you're more at risk of changing your mind and deciding you don't want to be gluten-free after all, particularly if the going gets tough. Something about the binary, black-and-white, cold-turkey nature of eliminating every scrap of gluten from your diet is simple to grasp, and unarguable. When you look at it like that, you find that rather than being tempted to eat gluten-containing foods, you're repelled by them.

Whichever camp you're in, you face emotional challenges, and in this chapter we want to let you know what, in our experience, these may be and to help you overcome them. We discuss a range of different ways in which you can break out of negativity and see things in a more positive light. Yes, for some people this change is a difficult transition in life . . . but ultimately, you're going to be better for it.

The key thing to remember is this: deal with it; don't dwell on it. You can be mad, sad, uncomfortable, fed up or ready to stamp your foot and have a hissy fit. That's okay. All those reactions and emotions, and the others we talk about in this chapter, are perfectly normal when it seems as if someone has told you to change your entire life. But allowing yourself to get bogged down with the negativity and difficulty of the situation is easy, and these feelings may begin to consume you. Allow yourself the time to experience the difficult emotions, and then move on.

Recognising Common Emotional Struggles

The reasons that living gluten-free can be difficult from an emotional standpoint are vast:

- ✔ **Social activities revolve around food.** Now, because you don't eat gluten, you may feel isolated, or you may be afraid to participate in social functions because you think you can't eat anything. (If you're struggling with eating away from home, read Chapter 17.)

- ✔ **People you love don't understand.** In Chapter 17, we also talk about how to discuss the lifestyle with others. But sometimes, no matter how much you say or don't say, some people, many of whom are your closest friends or family, just don't get why you're doing this, particularly if your symptoms haven't been obvious or troublesome.

✔ **People may think you're picky.** When you try to explain the gluten-free diet to some people, or when they watch you stumble through one of your first experiences ordering at a restaurant, they may think that you have an eating disorder or are outlandishly high-maintenance or picky.

✔ **'Comfort food' is called that for a reason.** Many people find eating to be a stress-reliever. When your food options are limited, eating can be far from comforting, even disconcerting, adding to the stress you were hoping to alleviate.

✔ **Some people don't cope well with even the smallest of changes.** For them, changing their eating habits can be really disruptive.

✔ **You're losing control in your life.** You're hereby 'sentenced' to a life of dietary restrictions. Wow. How's that for taking control away? You've been eating since you were a baby and choosing your own foods not long after that, and now someone's telling you what you can and can't eat.

✔ **The problem seems so permanent.** Oh, wait. That's because it is. And that doesn't help someone who feels 'put upon' by the restrictions.

✔ **You don't like the idea of having a disease.** If you're coeliac – and there's a hint right there in our use of the word as an adjective, which you can use too – the word *disease* seems too strong, too extreme, to apply to you, especially if you don't feel ill.

✔ **You feel like you're on an island.** If you do, you'd better hope that the island's large, because millions of people are going gluten-free. But we digress. The gluten-free lifestyle seems isolating to some people; they even feel ostracised. If you're feeling like that, read on, because this chapter helps you to realise that you have control over those feelings and that you don't have to be isolated or feel like you're alone.

In this section, we talk about some of the common emotions that people experience when they hear they have to go gluten-free. You may notice that the issues people face look a lot like reactions you may see in people who've experienced trauma. It's not surprising, because for some people, discovering that they need to change their entire way of eating *can* be traumatic and stressful.

Total shock and panic

If you've ever seen a teenage girl who can't find her mobile phone, you've seen panic. For some people, changing to a gluten-free lifestyle is far worse than that.

It all seems so sudden. You're in the doctor's surgery talking about your bowel movements and blood tests, or maybe sitting up on the operating table getting over the endoscopy. The next thing you know, you're labelled with a disease or a condition you don't understand that changes the way you eat for the rest of your life. Wham, just like that. Yet in some ways, it's not sudden, is it? The chances are you've been having health problems for years. And now the issue has a name and also a treatment, and that's a start.

'You what?' That's about all you can think or say. You're numb – you're in shock. The good news (let's see, some good news has got to be here some-where – okay, here it is) is that, by definition, you get this shocked feeling only once. Next, the reality of the words 'diet for life' begins to sink in and you start to panic. What are you going to eat? How are you going to manage? Where can you find special foods?

Rest assured, these feelings are normal and they do pass. You'll soon work out what you can eat, and your panic subsides as you become more comfortable with the diet, which begins on day one. The learning curve is steeper for some than others, but you will adapt and the panic will wear off.

Anger and frustration

The shock and panic have subsided, and you're beginning to feel more com-fortable with what you can and can't eat. But something's eating away at you. You realise you're angry. Peeved. Fuming and frustrated!

Who or what you're angry with doesn't matter – some people in this situa-tion are angry at their parents for giving them a 'defective' gene; others are annoyed with themselves for passing the gene on to their kids. Some are furi-ous at their partner for not being more understanding. Most are irritated by the major food manufacturers who feel that a universal food law exists that means they must put wheat into everything nice. Then you have television with a stream of cookery shows using wheat flour in everything. And finally, a few are angry at the doctors for getting it all wrong.

The bottom line is, you're furious and that's making you stressed. Anger is a healthy emotion, and discovering how to deal with it is one of the most valu-able lessons you can learn in life. Taking your anger out on those closest to you is tempting, especially if they're adding to the frustration by being less than understanding about your new diet. If you need help dealing with your anger, ask for it. Whatever you do, don't lash out, especially at the people closest to you, because they're not to blame and they can be immensely supportive when you need it most.

Grief and despair

Are you grieving? Do you feel like you've lost your best friend? In a way, you may have. Food, your control over what you eat and even the simple act of putting food into your mouth can soothe you and bring you comfort. When you're forced to give up your favourite foods (if they weren't your favourites before, they're sure to be after you give them up!), the change can make you feel sad and nostalgic. Furthermore, some people feel that they're the only ones who have this problem, which can intensify feelings of isolation.

If your child is going gluten-free, those feelings of grief can magnify. You dreamed that your children's lives were going to be carefree and ideal; having to deal with dietary restrictions that prevent them from eating what seem to be staples in a child's diet isn't usually part of your plan.

Some people reach a point of desperation or despair. They find the diet to be cumbersome and difficult. They keep making mistakes. Then they decide that if they can't do this right, they may as well not do it at all, and they give up.

Grief and despair are normal emotions, but don't give in to them. You're going to get over your feelings of sadness and loneliness, and this lifestyle doesn't have to be in the least bit isolating or depriving. As for doing it right, give it your very best effort – truly 100 per cent – and you're sure to succeed. Dealing with a mistake from time to time is better than giving up and not trying at all.

Loss and deprivation

You may feel several of kinds of loss when someone tells you that you have to go gluten-free. You obviously lose some of your favourite foods – and what about the social situations that go hand in hand with them? You miss the takeaway pizza and beer during the football, or Granny's famous sponge cake. And what about the nibbles that you normally put out when the girls come around for the evening? (Okay, we'll stop the reminders now.)

Many of your favourite foods, in the form you currently know them, are a thing of the past. At first, social situations may not seem the same without them – and yes, they aren't totally the same. But these events aren't really about food – they're about socialising. And you can bring with you foods that you love; just follow the golden rules of going out gluten-free that we cover in Chapter 17.

Another sense of loss that people feel is that of convenience. These days food is prewashed, precut, prepeeled, precooked – practically pre-eaten, metabolised and stored as fat around your waist before you ever get it home from the shop. Ready meals and shop-bought cakes and biscuits are convenient, but many of them, for you, are a thing of the past. Your days of calling for a Chinese takeaway are behind you until the soy sauce makers drop the wheat flour (big pizza companies offer gluten-free pizza, so not all takeaways are out). No longer do you race through the supermarket mindlessly grabbing products off the shelves because they look good or they're on special offer.

Okay, so giving up gluten isn't as convenient – and you miss your old favourites. But look what you've gained: your health! The gluten-free diet is your key to better health, and that's priceless.

Sadness and depression

Occasionally, people get so overwhelmed with the whole concept of their medical condition and the gluten-free diet that they feel an impending doom and experience depression to a certain degree.

Be aware that depression is a symptom that you may experience if you eat gluten despite your intolerance. So ask yourself: is the depression due to accidental (or intentional) gluten ingestion, or is it a lingering emotional discomfort from the pre-diagnosis days? Some people, before they're diagnosed (and some even afterwards), are accused of making up their problems, or they're told that the symptoms are all in their head. These accusations can be so hurtful and frustrating that they cause the person to go into a state of depression.

People with coeliac disease have a higher incidence of depression and other neurological problems. We talk more about how gluten affects behaviour in Chapter 2.

Unfortunately, depression caused by illness can result in a vicious cycle. The physical symptoms lead to suffering and depression, and then the depression makes the physical symptoms worse. If you're feeling depressed, make sure that your diet is 100 per cent gluten-free, so you know that what you're feeling isn't a symptom of gluten ingestion. Also consider therapy of some type, whether that's confiding in friends or seeking professional help. Your GP is a good place to start, or try Mind, the charity for better mental health, which has a wealth of information online at www.mind.org.uk and a really helpful phone line: 0300 123 3393.

If you feel your case of the blues isn't serious and you want to try to work it out on your own, see whether these activities help:

- ✔ **Exercising:** When you exercise, your brain produces endorphins, and those chemicals create a natural high. Exercise also helps you get rid of stress hormones that build up in the body and wreak all sorts of physical and emotional havoc.

- ✔ **Eating well:** And that means, besides eating a healthy diet, staying strictly gluten-free. Eating gluten exacerbates the physical and mental symptoms you may experience, and if you're gluten-intolerant, gluten robs you of the important nutrients that are supposed to energise you and make you feel good. Stay away from the high-glycaemic-index foods we talk about in Chapter 6, because those mess up your blood-sugar levels and affect your moods.

✔ **Avoiding alcohol:** Booze is bad news for people suffering from depression. Alcohol is a depressant, and so, by definition, it brings you down – it also interrupts your sleep patterns, which are important for feeling your best.

✔ **Relaxing (whether you want to or not):** Chilling out is hard sometimes, we know! But relaxation (even if you force it) is important to maintaining your mental health. Sometimes you may forget to take care of yourself, but doing so is crucial – otherwise you aren't able to help anyone, least of all yourself.

✔ **Working out what to say to other people:** Have ready a few outline scripts and try them out on those closest to you, one at a time. See how they react and how the words sound to you, and develop your preferred way of talking about yourself and your new diet.

✔ **Doing something nice for others:** You've heard the expression, 'You only get back what you give.' Many people believe that the amount of happiness you feel is directly proportional to the happiness you bring to others. Have you ever been feeling down and done something nice for someone else? Not feeling better when you make someone's day is practically impossible.

Dealing with Denial

Denial comes in all sizes and shapes – some types affect you, other types affect those around you, but nearly everyone living gluten-free goes through denial to some extent.

When you're the one in denial

When you hear that you have to give up gluten for health reasons, deciding to run, not walk, to the nearest sand pit to start digging a hole for your head is quite common – this reaction is a form of denial. You go through several phases of denial.

Immediate denial

Denying what you've just heard from the doctor is common: 'I can't have that condition;' 'I'm not even sure what it is;' 'I'm too fat to have that;' 'I'm too old to have it;' 'I'm too [insert whatever adjective supports your denial] to have that.'

You can deny till the cows come home (where *were* they, anyway?), but that doesn't help your health much. What does help is getting on track as fast as you can, because you have improved health to look forward to.

Denial down the road

Another type of denial settles in after you've been gluten-free for a while and you're feeling great. In fact, you feel so good that you start to think that maybe nothing was really wrong with you. Or maybe you don't feel better, because you felt well and hadn't noticed any ill-effects before.

Of course, this moment is about the time that the reality starts to set in that you're following this diet for the rest of your life, and you're tempted to cheat – but surely it's not cheating if you don't really need to be gluten-free now, is it? So begins the battle in your brain, where good and evil don't see eye to eye.

The good half of your brain is telling you, 'Mmmmm, this is the most delicious gluten-free cracker I've ever had!' But the demon-in-denial side is saying, 'No way am I sitting through another football match eating rice cakes and sipping white wine while the other guys are ploughing through pizza and guzzling beer. Besides, I don't have an intolerance. Come on, just one slice of pizza won't hurt. . . . '

Get away from that pizza box! This phase is a period of ambivalence, in which you're hoping beyond hope that you don't really have to give up gluten and are 'proving' it to yourself by ignoring your conscience.

Acceptance

The biggest problem with denial is that it justifies eating gluten. When you have this fake epiphany – 'realising' that you don't need to be gluten-free – you're tempted to run, not walk, to the nearest bakery. Resist the temptation. If you've been gluten-free for a while, yes, you feel great, but that's *because* of the diet, not in spite of it. The danger in testing your little theory is that you may not have any reaction when you do, and then you're likely to jump to the obvious (by which we mean 'desired') conclusion that you never needed to eliminate gluten in the first place.

If you're still not sure that you really should be gluten-free, here are some steps that you can take to help clarify things for you:

- ✔ **Get properly tested.** Denial is one of the most compelling arguments in favour of proper testing. Flick to Chapter 2 for more information about testing.

- ✔ **Get another opinion.** If you're particularly stubborn, you may even want to get a third opinion. Getting tested or re-tested after you've been living without gluten for a while requires preparation and supervision by a doctor or dietitian. You'll have to eat gluten every day for a few weeks leading up to the test. It's a good opportunity to keep a food and symptom diary to record what foods you eat and how you react to them. If you have a bad reaction, you may decide that's all the proof you need and go back to your healing gluten-free diet.

✔ **Realise that 'negative' tests don't always mean you're free to become a glutton for gluten.** Wheat-allergy tests don't pick up coeliac disease; coeliac tests can be falsely negative. Testing techniques have changed over the years, and maybe your tests were done long ago. Problems with gluten can develop at any point, and so just because you were negative once doesn't mean you're going to be negative again. And finally, some people are negative on all the tests, yet their health improves dramatically on a gluten-free diet. That's gluten-sensitivity.

✔ **Talk to others who've been there, done it and got the gluten-free T-shirt.** Most people have gone through denial in one form or another. Talk to other people who've been diagnosed with coeliac disease; your local clinic or coeliac support group is a good place to start. They'll probably give you that smug smile with the yep-you've-got-a-classic-case-of-denial look on their faces, because they've been there before. You don't really need to hear much more.

When others are in denial

The most common type of denial that other members of your family can exhibit occurs when they themselves have all the symptoms but refuse to admit it. Why is it so hard for relatives to believe that they may have this? Problems with gluten, after all, run in the family, and family members often have classic symptoms.

Conditions that require you to be gluten-free, such as coeliac disease, have a unique common denominator: people don't always believe what you're telling them about your condition or the fact that a gluten-free diet may fully restore health. They also don't always understand how strict you really need to be in sticking to the diet.

On more than one occasion we've been accused of being neurotic about the need to avoid all sources of gluten, about making sure that food is gluten-free. Doctors have told Danna that she's going 'overboard' because she checks the ingredients of tiny pills. And she's heard more than her fair share of waiters muttering something about her being high-maintenance as they walk away from serving her.

It's particularly a problem when you're eating with people you don't know very well, maybe in workplace settings where you don't want to get into your personal health issues. This is where the script you've prepared – a way of simply saying you need your food to be gluten-free without having to justify or explain why – comes in handy. Talk about the food rather than your condition, and if people ask questions, you can just say it's a health matter and change the subject.

Getting Back on Track When You're Feeling Derailed

Even we admit that some difficult emotional challenges arise when you go gluten-free. But overcoming those challenges and getting back on track to enjoying life and all it has to offer – far beyond food – are important.

Regaining control

If you don't take control of this diet, the diet controls you. Part of the reason you sometimes feel out of control when you're told to go gluten-free, or you're thinking it might be beneficial, is because you're afraid. Afraid of making mistakes. Afraid that the gluten-free diet won't work. Afraid of letting go of your habits and favourite foods. Afraid you're going to feel deprived. Afraid of being different. Afraid of trying new foods.

The only way to get beyond the fear is to try new things. Be creative. Explore new foods. Tantalise your taste buds with all the gluten-free goodies you can think of. Arm yourself with accurate information. Be prepared when you're out and about. Taking control of the diet – and giving your kids control of theirs – is the key to living and loving the gluten-free lifestyle.

If you're finding that all your favourite comfort foods are now on the forbidden list, realise that those old comfort foods were probably *dis*comfort foods that actually made you feel bad because they contain gluten. Choose new favourites, but try to avoid the pitfall of undermining weight-management efforts by turning to food for comfort.

Getting beyond scary words with heavy implications

Many people embarking on a gluten-free lifestyle hear some rather scary words being bandied around. Words like *disease*, *chronic*, *restrictions*, *lifelong*, *malabsorption*, *intestinal damage* and *intolerance* are usually the catalysts for going gluten-free.

Although you can easily be somewhat stunned by the heavy implications of these words, looking beyond them is important. Thinking more about the fact that your health's going to improve and you're going to feel better and have more energy can help shift your perspective in a more optimistic direction.

Keeping a sense of perspective

Is going gluten-free really such a monumental change to your whole life? You'll still have the same job, same family, same personality, same hobbies, same home, same name, same clothes, same face, same friends as before. You'll still be you, just eating differently and feeling fit and well. And, as ubiquitous as gluten seems, it's not the be-all and end-all in your life, or even in your diet. If you think about what foods you like, most are gluten-free already, and, as we show you in Chapter 4, plenty of foods can replace the three cereals that contain gluten – well, four cereals if you count oats that have come into contact with gluten.

Also on the upside, the fix works fast and you can manage it yourself. The change in your eating habits is the only treatment you need. No complicated pharmaceuticals to deal with every day, no special apparatus, no frequent hospital visits for therapy, no bed rest, isolation or surgery. You're not contagious the way you'd be if you had an infectious condition, and not ill as you'd be with a debilitating condition.

Focusing on what you can eat

When the only food you can eat is gluten-free, every menu item begins to look like a croissant. Wanting what you can't have is human nature. Tell someone that he can't juggle flaming torches, and he's likely to have a sudden urge to do so.

Believe us, we know how depriving this lifestyle can be. After all, we've had to compromise, eating gluten-free dinners with nothing but lemon caper chicken, steak and peanut pepper pasta, and scallops with orange; boring side dishes, including sweet potato salad, lemon quinoa and Vietnamese rice wraps; and tedious desserts, such as luscious cheesecake and blueberry parfait. Depriving, indeed. For more deprivations, turn to the recipes in Part IV.

If you're feeling deprived, please don't let our sarcasm offend you. Imagining that your selections are limited (they're limited but not limit*ing*) and pining away for freshly baked baguettes is perfectly normal. Reading the menu and feeling like the only thing you can order is a salad is also normal – or staring into your cupboard and seeing only cream crackers.

We look to vegetarians as role models for how you can improve your perspective. They revel in their diets, usually celebrating their meat-free lifestyle without feeling compromised, because they adopt an innovative approach to keeping their diet healthy and well-balanced.

Feeling a bit grumpy? You may have dieter's depression

People who are on a diet of any kind usually feel a 'high' in the beginning, while they're still ultra-motivated and passionate about their commitment. But then, usually around the second or third week, something commonly called *dieter's depression* sets in, making the right food choices harder. Dieters in this stage aren't much fun to be around. Usually, they're feeling resentful and emotionally deprived, especially if food was a source of comfort for them.

Also, low levels of the hormone serotonin can lead to depression, and the brain needs carbohydrate to produce serotonin. Sometimes when people go gluten-free, they cut their carbohydrate intake significantly and become depressed as a result. If you think you may be falling into a dieter's depression, first make sure that you're getting good carbohydrates from fruits and vegetables as well as gluten-free cereals. If you find that cooking steamed garden favourites like broccoli and courgettes is too time-consuming, you may want to opt for grab-'n-go fruits and vegetables like apples, carrots and mangetout. All are an excellent source of slow-releasing carbohydrate, full of antioxidant vitamins and have other health benefits too. Then finish reading this chapter, which gives you lots of tips for lifting your spirits and focusing on the positives.

Focus on what you can eat, rather than what you can't. The list of things you can eat is much longer than the list of things you can't, and if you don't believe us, start writing. Make a list of all the things you can eat – that should keep you busy for a while!

One of the quickest ways to make a particular food take centre stage in your life is to ban it, because human nature is to want what you can't have. For many people, putting gluten on the banned list makes them want it even more. So if you're feeling deprived, indulge yourself! Not with gluten, of course, but with your favourite gluten-free treat. A splurge from time to time can remind you of lots of delicious things you can eat and help take your mind off the things you can't.

Deflecting the temptation to be annoyed or offended

When dealing with your dietary restrictions, you're likely to encounter people who appear unconcerned, uninterested, thoughtless and sometimes even downright rude. From time to time, you may feel hurt and even feel ostracised. Occasionally, you find that people do care but forget to make an allowance for you, or just miss the point and serve foods you can't eat.

Bear in mind that as you embark upon this new lifestyle, you're probably gaining an entirely new respect for food and a heightened awareness of what having dietary restrictions feels like. And you're probably much more aware of other people's restrictions and sensitivities.

Meanwhile, the rest of the world remains in the dark about the intricacies of the gluten-free lifestyle and may actually be insensitive enough to suggest you join them for dinner – at your (former) favourite Chinese restaurant.

Don't be annoyed or offended. People are busy and sometimes so focused on their own fast-paced lives that they can't possibly remember to accommodate yours. Most of the time they're not being rude or thoughtless; they're just unaware. Be glad that they asked you to dinner, call the restaurant to see if they have anything gluten-free to offer, or suggest a different restaurant. Save the negative energy for something that really matters – like your next-door neighbour who feels compelled to practise the drums at midnight.

Acting upbeat

Acting upbeat is when you pretend that you feel good about something that you really don't. Before you know it, you really do feel better about it. That's the amazing power of mind over matter! It's easier for some people than others, because everyone falls on different parts of the optimism spectrum to start with. Wherever you start, though, if you can act optimistic, you'll move towards the positive end of the spectrum.

Start by thinking of all the reasons the gluten-free lifestyle is a good thing (go to www.dummies.com/extras/livingglutenfreeuk if you need some help). Maybe you've improved your focus on nutrition; perhaps you're benefiting from spending more time with the family, eating home-cooked meals; maybe you're appreciating the improved health you're experiencing as a result of the diet; or perhaps you've helped someone else in the family discover the key to better health too.

Write out your list to convince (or remind) yourself that adopting this lifestyle is a wonderful thing in your life. Get excited about it: tell your friends and family how great you feel and why. Before you know it, you've convinced yourself and you aren't acting any more.

Spreading attitudes – they're contagious

Attitudes can spread like wildfire, but bad attitudes spread the quickest. If you're unhappy about having to adopt a gluten-free lifestyle and haven't found the tips in this chapter helpful for reducing your anxiety, at least don't spread your misery around to other unwitting victims. Most people aren't all that familiar with gluten, the gluten-free lifestyle and the medical conditions that benefit from such a lifestyle. You may well be the first person to tell them about gluten-free living, so try to be positive.

If you feel compelled to moan about the foods you miss or to express excessive feelings of deprivation and despair, people feel sad and sorry for your 'misfortune'. Do you really want their pity? Instead, when talking to others, try to portray living gluten-free as a great lifestyle and a healthy way to live, so that others can feel that way too.

You can grieve for the foods you can't eat any more, or you can rejoice in your new-found health and strength.

Redefining Who You Are

If your doctor has diagnosed you with a gluten-related disorder, you may feel different. You are different from other people – and that's okay. We're all different. Some have an interest in sports, others a head for numbers. We readily acknowledge and accept that we're different in those types of things, but sometimes we don't like to be different with the gluten-free diet. Yes, your diet is different – but in the big picture, your restrictions are no different from those of others, such as vegans or people with peanut allergies.

So you're on a diet. That makes you unique?

You can't eat certain things. If you do, you have to deal with physical consequences. Your selections on a menu may be limited, you have to be careful about what you eat when you're in social situations, and you can't always eat what everyone else is eating. Your diet is restricted, and it's a pain in the neck. So what's so different about you? You sound like you're on a diet. That makes you unique? We think not!

You can go on a diet for lots of reasons. People usually think of going on diets to lose weight, but some are on special diets to gain weight (much to the annoyance of those trying to lose it). Others are on special diets because they have high blood pressure, high cholesterol, heart disease, food allergies, diabetes or kidney failure. For health or religious reasons, some people choose to avoid meat or foods that contain certain additives. Athletes often have special diets, and pregnant or lactating women modify their diets to optimise their baby's health. Those of us on a gluten-free diet tend to think of it as being different from other diets – but in many ways, it's not.

Sometimes people let their condition define who they are. Try not to do this. Is having this condition a disappointment? Maybe; maybe not (we hope after you finish this book you don't think so!). What you're not is a victim, a martyr or an invalid. In fact, you're on the road to recovery and amazing health. Lots of people have some kind of adversity in their lives, and they deal with it. You can too.

If you're having trouble dealing with the gluten-free lifestyle from an emotional or psychological standpoint, step back and take a look at the bigger picture. Why are you giving up gluten in the first place? Probably because each and every scrap of gluten you've eaten has compromised your health.

Force yourself to remember that the gluten-free diet is key to improving your health, and focus on the great thing you're doing for your body by being gluten-free. Check out these extra tips to help you beat the blues:

- ✔ **Psych yourself up.** Change your perspective on why you eat, what you eat and how you eat. Remember, you're supposed to eat to live, not the other way around.

- ✔ **Think outside the box.** Getting stuck in *food ruts* – eating the same basic meals day after day, week after week – is easy. Explore new foods, find new favourites and be creative in tantalising your taste buds.

- ✔ **Remember: the diet gets easier with time.** If the gluten-free lifestyle seems difficult to you from an emotional or practical standpoint, realising that it gets easier with time can help.

- ✔ **Seek help.** Family members, support groups, friends or health professionals can help you make the transition easier. Coeliac UK has a great helpline that offers advice or an understanding ear – 0845 305 2060, or see www.coeliac.org.uk.

- ✔ **Avoid negative people and influences.** Basically, rid your life of the negative. If the gluten-free way of life is a struggle for you, the last thing you need is a malicious friend or relative sabotaging your efforts.

- ✔ **Recommit yourself.** Sometimes you need to reaffirm your commitment by remembering why you're living gluten-free.

Resisting the Temptation to Cheat

Sometimes we feel as if a million and one diets exist out there: low-fat, high-protein, low-carb, low-calorie, low-glycaemic and everything in between. The thing they all have in common is that people cheat on them, and that's a fact.

But you can't cheat on this diet. No, not even a little. Approaches such as 'everything in moderation' and 'a little isn't going to hurt you' don't apply if you have a gluten intolerance.

Realising why you want to cheat

You may want to eat forbidden glutenous goods for many reasons, and if you hope to resist the temptation, working out what's driving your desire is important. Some of the more common triggers that may tempt you to cheat on the gluten-free diet are as follows:

- ✔ **The food is just too good to resist.** We realise that this isn't a particularly profound insight as to why they do it, but most people who indulge in a food that's not in their diet do so because it's just too yummy to say no.

- ✔ **Just this once.** Not a good plan. 'Just this once' is the start of a slippery slope to a diet becoming long-forgotten.

- ✔ **You want to fit in.** If everyone else was jumping off a cliff, would you? (Bungee jumpers aren't allowed to answer that.) In reality, other people probably aren't paying much attention to what you're eating anyway. Social situations are about the company, the conversation and the ambience. Yes, they're about the food as well, but people aren't paying attention to what *you're* eating.

- ✔ **Comfort eating.** In difficult times, people sometimes turn to certain foods. If a gluten-containing food is your comfort food, a weak moment may send you straight to it, because you think it consoles you – even though you know it isn't going to make you feel better.

- ✔ **It's a special occasion.** Try again. This excuse may work for other diets, but not this one. Eating even a little bit of gluten may turn your social affair into a dreaded nightmare. No occasion is worth compromising your health for. Anyway, special occasions are about the *occasion*, not the food.

- ✔ **You're bored with the diet.** If all you're eating is rice cakes and celery, we don't blame you. Live it up, get creative, try new things. Use this book as a guide to work out exactly what you *can* eat, and then challenge yourself to try something new. If you need a little inspiration, check out Chapter 9, which offers ideas for getting creative in the kitchen and finding out how to make anything gluten-free.

- ✔ **A little gluten isn't going to hurt.** Yes, it is. If you plan to use this excuse, we urge you to read Chapters 2 and 3.

- ✔ **The diet's too hard.** Hey, this is a *For Dummies* book, remember? This book is supposed to make it really easy to work out what you can and can't eat, and how to live (and love!) the lifestyle. Sometimes changing your perspective isn't easy; we give you that. But you *can* do it, and between your friends, family, books like this and the helpful resources listed in Chapter 5, you've got plenty of support.

✔ **Someone's sabotaging your diet.** People really do this; in fact, it's common! Usually, they're not aware that they're doing it, and they all do it for different reasons. Sometimes people sabotage because they're jealous that you're getting healthier than they are. Sometimes they do it because they don't believe you need to be on the diet (see the earlier section 'When others are in denial'). Other people do it because they don't want to have to follow the clean-kitchen rules or have to put the effort into preparing gluten-free foods. Don't succumb to sabotage. Instead, try to find someone who seems particularly supportive of your gluten-free lifestyle and ask for help.

✔ **You're still thinking about it.** Procrastination pops by, stays over and moves in. This is a problem if you're not feeling any ill-effects from eating gluten, or maybe feeling them only now and again. You'll go gluten-free when you next have a bad reaction, tomorrow, in the new year, after that stag do, when you've had a chance to go shopping or when you've finished this book. If you've been advised to go gluten-free or if you've decided it for yourself, the sooner you start, the sooner you'll see the benefits. Have a look at the next section, 'Assessing the consequences' and then see Chapter 7 for a quick start.

✔ **You've already blown the diet, so you might as well do it again.** Not true. Any gluten is harmful; any more is destructive.

Although these are powerful factors in enticing you to go for the gluten, overcoming the temptation is important. Sometimes the key to saying no is taking a look at the consequences.

You choose to cheat – or not – because you have full control over what you put in your mouth. When you cheat on the gluten-free diet, you're cheating yourself out of better health.

Assessing the consequences

One of the most difficult parts about looking at the consequences of your actions is that if they're not immediate and drastic, you sometimes feel that they don't matter. People who are dieting to lose weight often don't notice any consequences from a setback or two, because they don't see the extra centimetres jump back onto their waistlines when they eat a bowl of ice cream – and, for that matter, they may never gain the weight back, because for them, a high-calorie indulgence from time to time may be okay.

If you can't tolerate gluten though, the consequences of eating it can seriously damage your health, and if you cheat repeatedly, the damage can be cumulative. In fact, you may be setting yourself up to develop conditions like osteoporosis, anaemia, thyroid disease, some cancers, plus other conditions that we bet aren't worth eating that chocolate digestive for. For a friendly reminder of how much damage you can do when you cheat, head to Chapters 2 and 3.

Overcoming temptation

After you discover why you want to cheat and you remind yourself of the consequences, you have to take the final step and just say no. Here are a few things you can do to make saying no a little easier:

- ✔ **Indulge in your favourite gluten-free goodie.** If you're craving a piece of shortbread, eat it – the gluten-free kind, of course. Just about anything that has gluten in it has a gluten-free counterpart these days. If you prefer to grab a (gluten-free) chocolate bar, that's fine too. If you're tempted to eat something with gluten, try to find something else that satisfies you just as much but still keeps you on track.

- ✔ **Reward yourself when you resist.** If you've been challenged by temptation and successfully overcome it, give yourself a treat. It doesn't have to be food – maybe buy yourself something special or do something nice for yourself.

- ✔ **Simplify what you need to do.** If the diet seems too much effort, perhaps you're trying to do too much and need to go back to the basics. When your menu plans are overwhelming, cut something out so that you don't have so much to think about. If you don't understand the diet, read parts of this book again, particularly Chapters 4 and 5. You may also want to seek out some of the resources in Chapter 5.

- ✔ **Make your lifestyle a priority.** This change is about you: your health and your future. If you find this lifestyle too difficult because of your work commitments, think about changing your work pattern. If you have negative people in your life who seem to sabotage your efforts, avoid them if you can. If something's not working in your life, change it. Being gluten-free is about more than a diet: it's about a lifestyle, and it should be a high priority.

Part VI

the
part of
tens

Go to www.dummies.com/extras/livingglutenfreeuk for online bonus content including an extra Part of Tens chapter: 'Ten Benefits of Being Gluten-Free'.

In this part . . .

- ✔ Read tips on taking control of your diet.

- ✔ Dip into the delights of international cuisine.

- ✔ Discover the support and benefits from joining Coeliac UK.

- ✔ Go to `www.dummies.com/extras/livingglutenfreeuk` for online bonus content including an extra Part of Tens chapter: 'Ten Good Things About Living Gluten-Free'.

Chapter 20

Ten Tips to Help You (Or Your Child) Love the Gluten-Free Lifestyle

*T*he transition from living on gluten to living gluten-free is harder for some people than for others. Discovering how to live gluten-free is one thing; finding out how to *love* living gluten-free is sometimes quite another. Here we give you our top ten tips for staying on track and really enjoying it too, whether you're the one going gluten-free or you're helping someone else to do it, especially a child.

Focus on What You Can Eat

Sometimes you may feel as if gluten is everywhere; yet the reality is that the list of things you can eat is a lot longer than the list of things you can't. You just have to shift your thinking a bit. Instead of thinking about the foods you can't have any more, focus on the foods you can eat, and put a special emphasis on those that you especially enjoy. Try to think outside the box and explore foods you may not have tried before, or work out how to turn your favourite gluten-loaded meal into a pleasurable gluten-free one (Chapter 9 helps you get creative in the kitchen). Before you know it, you'll realise that the gluten-free lifestyle may have its restrictions, but it's definitely not restrictive.

Expand Your Horizons

A big, bold, gluten-free world exists out there, filled with delicious and nourishing foods that many people miss out on: edamame beans, buttermilk, grilled polenta, chestnut flour, teff, buckwheat muesli and cornbread top the list of our new favourites. Living gluten-free encourages you to try new things and eat a much wider variety of foods than before, not only substitutes for wheat flour, but also the vast range of other naturally gluten-free foods on offer. And don't underestimate your children's willingness to try new foods with you. Even if they're reluctant at first, they usually give things a try if everyone else is enjoying them.

Enjoy Some International Flair

Lots of cultures don't have wheat as their main staple food, the way we do in the UK. These are the cultures to turn to for gluten-free inspiration. Many Asian cuisines, including Thai and Vietnamese, are largely gluten-free, as are many Mexican and Indian dishes. Go online to find out what ingredients a particular culture uses, or explore cookbooks and recipe websites that include dishes from around the world. The really great thing about cooking in Britain is that you can get your hands on little-known ingredients and cooking utensils from abroad. You can buy the books, go on cookery courses, explore ethnic shops and websites and probably find someone locally who knows all about any particular cuisine you fancy trying and is keen to show you. And keep the idea of fusion in mind. For example, it's okay to serve a Malaysian chicken curry with polenta and some plain steamed vegetables on the side. Just enjoy new gluten-free taste experiences – globally!

Gluten-Free Rocks; Don't Let It Rule

Whether you're 8 or 98, if you're going gluten-free, you need to take control of the diet. Otherwise, the diet controls you: what you eat, when, where, with whom and how much. For example, if you eat everything you're offered that's gluten-free and feel compelled to wipe the plate clean when someone's made you a special gluten-free meal, that's the diet taking control of you. On the gluten-free diet, you still need to watch what you eat. We show you how in Chapter 6.

Another way of taking control is to watch what you say. If you can't talk about anything but your diet and symptoms, you'll find your social invitations dry up. Your gluten-intolerance isn't a badge or part of your personality, and you don't need to advertise it.

Remember that you're the one in control, deciding everything about your food and what you say about your condition. Being prepared helps – we talk about menu planning and shopping in Chapter 8, eating out in Chapter 17, and overcoming emotional problems in Chapter 19.

If your child's on the gluten-free diet, hand over control from day one, no matter how young your child is. People vastly underestimate children's ability to understand the diet and why being strict about following it is so important.

Make the Diet Work in Your Life

For most people, food is a lot more than fuel. It's an important part of family, social, school and working life and a source of comfort, relaxation and enjoyment. Why else would we eat when we're not really hungry or enjoy some foods and dislike others? And why else would our homes be designed around cooking and dining? You probably spend a lot of time each day thinking about, acquiring, preparing and eating food, and it features in many social and business functions. To enjoy living gluten-free, you need to make the diet fit in with your life and you need to continue to take part in all the activities and events you've always enjoyed. And, of course, continue to enjoy your food. Doing so takes some forethought on your part and occasionally forewarning of others who are preparing food for you. But, with the request for gluten-free food becoming so common these days, most hosts and chefs can easily and discreetly accommodate your diet.

Realise That Everyone Is Different

People talk about wanting to be unique, and yet cringe when they're afraid they may stand out from the crowd. The bottom line is that everyone is different, even when people try to look the same. If you're on the gluten-free diet, your bread may look a little different, and you may sometimes appear to be a little demanding at a restaurant. So what? Many people ask to customise their meal from what's on the menu. Vegetarians avoid some dishes on the buffet table. Some people don't like fish, others can't tolerate milk, and some can even die if they eat foods to which they're severely allergic. Lots of people have different diets and lifestyles, so you don't need to apologise for yours. It just happens to be healthy, delicious and the key to your health.

Give Yourself a Break

If you put too many restrictions on yourself when trying to maintain a healthy, gluten-free lifestyle, you may just find yourself feeling deprived and sorry for yourself. Indulge from time to time in your favourite gluten-free treat. Or see these feelings as a sign that you're ready for a change and try something completely different in your diet, maybe a new recipe you've kept from a magazine and have been meaning to try. Have a go. Finding and maintaining a good balance is as important a part of a gluten-free lifestyle as of any other healthy diet.

Tune In to the Benefits

When you tune in and remind yourself of the benefits of being gluten-free (see www.dummies.com/extras/livingglutenfreeuk), it reinforces your thinking as to *why* you're living gluten-free. If you think that writing down all the good things about being gluten-free may be helpful, do it. Stick the list on the fridge, if you want a daily reminder, or keep it in a diary or on your computer. Maybe you want to challenge yourself to add an item to the list each day or week. When you focus on the reasons why being gluten-free is a good thing in your life, you can gain a new or renewed appreciation for the lifestyle itself.

Turn Away from Temptation

Avoid putting yourself in situations where you're tempted to eat any gluten-containing food. Save your strength for when you need to say 'Not for me, thanks.' You're not doing yourself any favours if you surround yourself with titbits of glutenous temptation, whether at work, at home or in social situations. Avoid the biscuit and cake aisle at the supermarket. You probably shouldn't take that job at the bakery, although we do know of one coeliac who was already working at one when she was diagnosed and persuaded them to launch a gluten-free range – she even got a promotion out of it! Enough gluten exists in this world without going out looking for it, setting yourself up for temptation – so when you can, make it easy for yourself.

Deal with It; Don't Dwell on It

If you're angry, sad, grief-stricken, confused, frustrated, agitated or just a bit put out about having to live without gluten, recognise that lots of people experience those feelings, deal with them and move on. Tell your friends, family and support groups, share with them how you're feeling and let them help you work through it. If you need professional help, get it. Not wallowing in the negativity of your circumstances is important, or your thoughts may intensify and even end up causing other physical and emotional problems. You'll find plenty of tips and techniques in self-help books and magazines and on TV and websites to turn your negative thoughts into positive ones. So make a start. Take a step into your new gluten-free lifestyle and you'll find that motivation soon shows up.

Chapter 21

Ten Reasons to Join Coeliac UK

Coeliac UK is the leading charity working for people with coeliac disease and dermatitis herpetiformis. It was founded in 1968 and today has more than 60,000 members. The charity provides information and support to people with coeliac disease, their friends and families, and anyone with an interest in the gluten-free diet. It provides membership for healthcare professionals, keeping GPs and dietitians up to date with the latest research on the condition and how to diagnose and treat it. And it provides membership for people in the food industry, which helps manufacturers, retailers and caterers to offer nutritious, appetising and convenient gluten-free foods.

Becoming a member of Coeliac UK is the best way to get the information and support you need to manage your gluten-free diet. If you haven't yet discovered Coeliac UK for yourself, this chapter contains the ten best reasons for doing so.

Coeliac UK receives no government funding and relies on the generosity of supporters through membership fees, donations, fundraising, sales of products and working with its commercial partners. To become a member and support the charity, you can contact Coeliac UK by visiting www.coeliac.org.uk, via the helpline on 0845 305 2060 or by post at 3rd Floor Apollo Centre, Desborough Road, High Wycombe, Buckinghamshire, HP11 2QW, UK.

Everyone's Welcome

If you are diagnosed with coeliac disease, struggling to get a diagnosis, interested in the gluten-free diet or simply want to support the charity, you can join for a small annual fee. Your fee helps the charity with its work to support people with coeliac disease, to campaign to improve awareness and services, and to research the causes, prevention and treatment of the disease.

What better reason to join? In fact, you've already helped by buying this book, which pays a royalty to the charity. So thank you.

Exploring Medical Matters

Coeliac UK is a source of expert medical information about the symptoms, diagnosis and ongoing health care you can expect if you have coeliac disease. This information is especially helpful if you're struggling to come to terms with being gluten-free or with managing your condition.

The website is a great place to start, packed full of information and helpful hints and tips to get you started on the gluten-free diet. The information is all written in an accessible, warm and calm tone that gets you to the key points fast. The 'Frequently Asked Questions' sections are full of useful facts, and if you can't find the answer to your question or if you want more detailed information, you can contact the helpline directly to talk to one of Coeliac UK's advisors.

Sourcing Dietary Advice You Can Trust

With so much information (and *mis*information) about the gluten-free diet available, you may have difficulty knowing where to turn for independent and reliable dietary information. We hope you find this book a good source, but we're also huge fans of the dietary support on offer from Coeliac UK:

- ✔ **Resources to order:** If you're new to the gluten-free diet, you may want to order resources from the online shop. Check out the *Food and Drink Directory*, listing thousands of products you can eat, and the *Getting Started* leaflet, which provides information on coeliac disease, the gluten-free diet, and hints and tips on shopping, cooking and eating out. Both of these resources come as part of the welcome pack, so joining the charity is definitely worthwhile.

- ✔ **Online guidance:** The website has pages of useful dietary advice on everything from food labelling and new products to recipes and suitable venues for eating out.

- ✔ **One-to-one guidance:** The helpline can link you to expert dietitians who are available to answer your food and health queries.

Seeking Support

Support is one of the most important things in helping you to follow a gluten-free diet long term. Coeliac UK can put you in touch with a network of over 90 local voluntary support groups around the UK, so that you can access the one nearest to you. The groups offer you a chance to meet and talk to other people in the same position, to share experiences, recipes and tips. Local groups run educational and social events as well as fundraising activities. Knowing that you're not alone is great.

Finding Safe Foods

Each year Coeliac UK produces a directory of safe foods. The *Food and Drink Directory* contains thousands of products you can eat and a handy list of all the products available on prescription in the UK. As a member of Coeliac UK, you receive a new directory each year; you can also buy the directory from the online shop.

The website has links to a whole range of manufacturers and retailers with online and telephone ordering of gluten-free products and services. Products range from beer, breads, mixes and muffins right through to a range of meals that can be delivered directly to your door.

Eating Out, Gluten-Free

When newly diagnosed with coeliac disease, you may feel as if eating out is off the menu or, at best, is never going to be the same again. Even if you've been managing okay for a while, you may feel you need more inspiration. Well, Coeliac UK is the place to find it. The website is packed with pages of information to help you cope with eating out, at home and abroad, including:

- ✔ A venue guide to restaurants and other eating establishments that can cater for you – all suggested and reviewed by other members.

- ✔ Coeliac UK trademarked symbols to look out for on food packaging and menus.

- ✔ Really useful translation sheets for nearly 40 countries, to take abroad and show to shopkeepers, waiters and hoteliers. The sheets also contain local information as about dining customs and gluten-free brands to look out for.

Finding Family-Friendly Facts

For parents with young children on a gluten-free diet, Coeliac UK can provide practical, family-friendly information. If you're having a particular problem, the chances are that someone else has found a solution to it. The website has a section dedicated entirely to child-friendly information and covers things such as pregnancy and weaning, children's party ideas, starting school, guidelines for school cookery classes, packed lunches, fun recipes, prescriptions for children, and even a template letter to give to the school to help the staff understand coeliac disease. Coeliac UK even produces a special children's storybook, *Me and My Tummy*, which can help you explain coeliac disease to a young child.

Keeping Up With The News

Getting stuck in a rut on any diet is all too easy – cooking the same old meals, buying the same old foods – and the gluten-free diet is no exception. Finding new recipes or products (including prescribable items) that are gluten-free is very useful. Coeliac UK has two publications to help you do just that:

- ✔ *Crossed Grain* magazine is sent out to all members three times a year and is a lively, vibrant magazine packed full of practical information, recipes and inspirational features.

- ✔ *eXG* is a monthly online newsletter containing news, details of medical updates and new food products, and the *Food and Drink Directory* updates.

Supporting Good Healthcare

Coeliac UK works with healthcare teams in hospitals and primary care, facilitating good management of coeliac disease and improving diagnosis and treatment. The charity also works closely with food manufacturers and the catering sector to raise awareness of coeliac disease and to influence food labelling and the availability of gluten-free food, in and out of the home. Finally, Coeliac UK works with the media to get coverage of coeliac disease and raise awareness among the general public and in the Government to get the issue high on the political agenda.

Even if you have your own condition sorted, you can improve things for others. By joining Coeliac UK you are adding your support to its campaigns.

Aiding Research

Coeliac UK not only raises money to support its members but also to support medical research into all aspects of coeliac disease, including diagnosis, prevention and treatment. One such project currently running that caught our eye aims to identify which fragments of gluten cause coeliac disease, with the ultimate hope of discovering a form of gluten that's non-toxic to people with coeliac disease.

Full details and updates on all ongoing research projects are covered in a consumer-friendly fashion on the website and in the online newsletter, *eXG*.

About the Authors

Hilary Du Cane graduated in nutrition with state registration in dietetics from the University of Surrey and has maintained her status as a registered dietitian ever since. Unusually for a dietitian, her career centred on the food industry, retailing and catering, starting out as a white-coated food technician in R&D and working her way up to become a suited director in marketing. Along the way, she got post-graduate qualifications including a masters degree, all gained the hard way by self-directed study with a full-time job.

She founded her company, Marketing Menu Ltd in 2002, and is busy blending her nutritional and business expertise as a freelance dietitian and marketer for commercial and public sector clients involved with food and health, including defence, manufacturing, catering, education and the media.

Hilary is a foodie and keen home-cook. She found out she was coeliac quite by chance following a routine cholesterol check, so she now has both a professional and a personal interest in living gluten-free. Since then, her big collection of cookbooks and equipment has been joined by a groaning store cupboard of intriguing gluten-free ingredients. She's eager to share her know-how, experience and enthusiasm for the gluten-free lifestyle with you.

Nigel Denby trained as a dietitian at Glasgow Caledonian University, following an established career in the catering industry. He is also a qualified chef and previously owned his own restaurant.

His dietetic career began as a Research Dietitian at the Human Nutrition Research Centre in Newcastle upon Tyne. After a period working as a Community Dietitian, Nigel left the NHS to join Boots Health and Beauty Experience where he led the delivery and training of Nutrition and Weight Management services.

In 2003 Nigel set up the food and nutrition consultancy www.grub4life.com. Nigel runs a private practice in Harley Street, specialising in Weight Management, PMS/Menopause and Irritable Bowel Syndrome. He also works extensively with the media, writing for the *Sunday Telegraph Magazine, Zest, Essentials,* and various other consumer magazines. His work in radio and television includes BBC and ITN news programmes, Channel 4's *Fit Farm,* BBC *Breakfast,* and BBC *Real Story.* He is the co-author, with Sue Baic, of *Nutrition For Dummies* and *The GL Diet For Dummies.*

Sue Baic is a Registered Dietitian (RD) and Registered Nutritionist (RNutr) with over 20 years' experience in the field of nutrition and health in the NHS. She now works as a nutrition consultant running Nutrition Basics (www.suebaic.org.uk). Sue worked for 10 years as a Senior Lecturer in Nutrition and Public Health at the University of Bristol and has a Master of Science degree in Human Nutrition from the University of London.

Sue feels strongly about providing the public with nutrition information that's evidence-based, up-to-date, unbiased and reliable. She acts as a media spokesperson for the British Dietetic Association, the Nutrition Society and the Science Media Centre and provides advice and training in nutrition for a variety of groups and organisations. She has written for both the health and consumer press on a variety of nutrition-related health issues and is the co-author of *Nutrition For Dummies* and *The GL Diet For Dummies*.

Sue lives in Bristol and spends her spare time running up and down hills in the Cotswolds in an attempt to keep fit.

Danna Korn is the author of *Wheat-Free, Worry-Free: The Art of Happy, Healthy, Gluten-Free Living* and *Kids with Celiac Disease: A Family Guide to Raising Happy, Healthy Gluten-Free Children*. She is respected as one of the leading authorities on the gluten-free diet and the medical conditions that benefit from it.

Dedication

This book is dedicated to everyone who has generously cooked gluten-free food for me, including my lovely husband, family and friends.

— Hilary

This book is dedicated to the people who have patiently supported my some-times-over-zealous-and-usually-over-the-top efforts as The Glutenator, singing the praises of a gluten-free lifestyle. Most importantly, to my family and friends, who encourage, inspire and energise me. Your support means more to me than you could ever know, and I couldn't have written a word without you. And to those of you who embrace or are planning to embrace the gluten-free lifestyle, I hope I can make a difference, if only a small one, in your lives by inspiring you to love the gluten-free way of life.

— Danna

Authors' Acknowledgements

Special thanks to Sue for proposing me to revise this edition of the book and to Nigel for supporting the idea. Who would have thought a gluten-free salad could lead to such an opportunity? A big, big thank you too to everyone on the teams at Coeliac UK and Wiley for getting us to the finishing line so expertly, and finally to Mark for never failing to taste and comment insightfully on my recipe developments and tests.

— Hilary

Thanks to John and Rosie and close friends for their interest and encouragement whilst I've been writing this book, and it's been a pleasure, as ever, to work with my co-author Nigel.

— Sue

Thanks as always to my writing partner Sue, for keeping me focused and to our schedule. My part in writing this book is dedicated to a dear friend Denise Helmn who was always so encouraging and supportive in everything I did. Denise passed away whilst I was working on this book, and I miss her very much.

We would both like to thank the excellent team at Wiley for their part in bringing this book to fruition. Thank you too to Lynne Garton and Claire Loades for their valuable contributions.

— Nigel

A huge thank-you to the hard-working team at Wiley. I'm extremely grateful to my friends and colleagues, Michelle Pietzak, M.D. and Cynthia Kupper, R.D., for their careful technical review of the book. Both of you go far and above the 'call of duty' in helping the gluten-free community each and every day.

To the entire gluten-free community, thank you for your steadfast encouragement. You motivate me to be passionate.

And last, but by no means least, I'm incredibly grateful to my family and friends. After I finished the book before this one, I asked you to slip cyanide in my coffee if I ever thought about writing another book. Thanks for not doing that. Seriously, without your patience, encouragement, support, optimism, love and inspiration, I couldn't have written a word.

— Danna

Publisher's Acknowledgments

We're proud of this book; please send us your comments at http://dummies.custhelp.com. For other comments, please contact our Customer Care Department within the U.S. at 877-762-2974, outside the U.S. at (001) 317-572-3993, or fax 317-572-4002.

Some of the people who helped bring this book to market include the following:

Acquisitions, Editorial, and Vertical Websites

Commissioning Editors: Kerry Laundon and Sarah Blankfield

Project Editor: Rachael Chilvers

Assistant Editor: Ben Kemble

Development Editor: Charlie Wilson

Technical Editor: Kathryn Miller, Coeliac UK

Proofreader: Mary White

Recipe Tester and Nutritional Analysis: Hilary Du Cane

Production Manager: Daniel Mersey

Publisher: Miles Kendall

Cover Photo: © David Cannings-Bushell / iStockphoto

Composition Services

Sr. Project Coordinator: Kristie Rees

Layout and Graphics: Erin Zeltner

Proofreaders: John Greenough

Indexer: Estalita Slivoskey

Index

FOR DUMMIES®

Making Everything Easier! ™

UK editions

BUSINESS

978-1-118-34689-1

978-1-118-44349-1

978-1-119-97527-4

MUSIC

978-1-119-94276-4

978-0-470-97799-6

978-0-470-66372-1

HOBBIES

978-1-118-41156-8

978-1-119-99417-6

978-1-119-97250-1

Asperger's Syndrome For Dummies
978-0-470-66087-4

Basic Maths For Dummies
978-1-119-97452-9

Body Language For Dummies, 2nd Edition
978-1-119-95351-7

Boosting Self-Esteem For Dummies
978-0-470-74193-1

Business Continuity For Dummies
978-1-118-32683-1

Cricket For Dummies
978-0-470-03454-5

Diabetes For Dummies, 3rd Edition
978-0-470-97711-8

eBay For Dummies, 3rd Edition
978-1-119-94122-4

English Grammar For Dummies
978-0-470-05752-0

Flirting For Dummies
978-0-470-74259-4

IBS For Dummies
978-0-470-51737-6

ITIL For Dummies
978-1-119-95013-4

Management For Dummies, 2nd Edition
978-0-470-97769-9

Managing Anxiety with CBT For Dummies
978-1-118-36606-6

Neuro-linguistic Programming For Dummies, 2nd Edition
978-0-470-66543-5

Nutrition For Dummies, 2nd Edition
978-0-470-97276-2

Organic Gardening For Dummies
978-1-119-97706-3

FOR DUMMIES®

Making Everything Easier! ™

UK editions

SELF-HELP

Cognitive Behavioural Therapy For Dummies
978-0-470-66541-1

Creative Visualization For Dummies
978-1-119-99264-6

Mindfulness For Dummies
978-0-470-66086-7

LANGUAGES

Spanish For Dummies
978-0-470-68815-1

Polish For Dummies
978-1-119-97959-3

British Sign Language For Dummies
978-0-470-69477-0

HISTORY

The Tudors For Dummies
978-0-470-68792-5

Medieval History For Dummies
978-0-470-74783-4

British History For Dummies
978-0-470-97819-1

Origami Kit For Dummies
978-0-470-75857-1

Overcoming Depression For Dummies
978-0-470-69430-5

Positive Psychology For Dummies
978-0-470-72136-0

PRINCE2 For Dummies, 2009 Edition
978-0-470-71025-8

Project Management For Dummies
978-0-470-71119-4

Psychology Statistics For Dummies
978-1-119-95287-9

Psychometric Tests For Dummies
978-0-470-75366-8

Renting Out Your Property For Dummies, 3rd Edition
978-1-119-97640-0

Rugby Union For Dummies, 3rd Edition
978-1-119-99092-5

Sage One For Dummies
978-1-119-95236-7

Self-Hypnosis For Dummies
978-0-470-66073-7

Storing and Preserving Garden Produce For Dummies
978-1-119-95156-8

Teaching English as a Foreign Language For Dummies
978-0-470-74576-2

Time Management For Dummies
978-0-470-77765-7

Training Your Brain For Dummies
978-0-470-97449-0

Voice and Speaking Skills For Dummies
978-1-119-94512-3

Work-Life Balance For Dummies
978-0-470-71380-8

12-47776-187x234mm

FOR DUMMIES®

Making Everything Easier! ™

COMPUTER BASICS

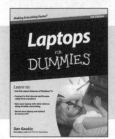

978-1-118-11533-6

978-0-470-61454-9

978-0-470-49743-2

DIGITAL PHOTOGRAPHY

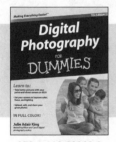

978-1-118-09203-3

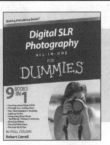

978-0-470-76878-5

978-1-118-00472-2

SCIENCE AND MATHS

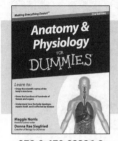

978-0-470-92326-9

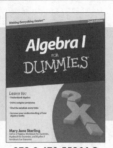

978-0-470-55964-2

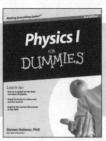

978-0-470-90324-7

Art For Dummies
978-0-7645-5104-8

Computers For Seniors For Dummies,
3rd Edition
978-1-118-11553-4

Criminology For Dummies
978-0-470-39696-4

Currency Trading For Dummies,
2nd Edition
978-0-470-01851-4

Drawing For Dummies, 2nd Edition
978-0-470-61842-4

Forensics For Dummies
978-0-7645-5580-0

French For Dummies, 2nd Edition
978-1-118-00464-7

Guitar For Dummies, 2nd Edition
978-0-7645-9904-0

Hinduism For Dummies
978-0-470-87858-3

Index Investing For Dummies
978-0-470-29406-2

Islamic Finance For Dummies
978-0-470-43069-9

Knitting For Dummies, 2nd Edition
978-0-470-28747-7

Music Theory For Dummies, 2nd Edition
978-1-118-09550-8

Office 2010 For Dummies
978-0-470-48998-7

Piano For Dummies, 2nd Edition
978-0-470-49644-2

Photoshop CS6 For Dummies
978-1-118-17457-9

Schizophrenia For Dummies
978-0-470-25927-6

WordPress For Dummies, 5th Edition
978-1-118-38318-6

12-47776-187x234mm

Think you can't learn it in a day? Think again!

The *In a Day* e-book series from *For Dummies* gives you quick and e
access to learn a new skill, brush up on a hobby, or enhance your
personal or professional life — all in a day. Easy!